GENERAL AVERAGE:
LAW AND PRACTICE

OTHER TITLES IN THIS SERIES:

Shipbuilding Contracts
SECOND EDITION
by Malcolm A. Clarke
1992

Time-Barred Actions
SECOND EDITION
Edited by Francesco Berlingieri
1993

*Liability for Damage to the
Marine Environment*
Edited by Colin de la Rue
1993

The York-Antwerp Rules
SECOND EDITION
by N. Geoffrey Hudson
1996

*The Modern Law of
Marine Insurance*
Edited by D. Rhidian Thomas
1996

The Bill of Lading: A Document of Title to Goods
by Michael Bools
1997

Shipbrokers and the Law
by Andrew Jamieson
1997

Ship Arrest Handbook
Edited by Paul Smith
1997

*Douglas and Geen on the Law
of Harbours, Coasts and Pilotage*
FIFTH EDITION
by Richard Douglas, Peter Lane and Monica Peto
1997

GENERAL AVERAGE: LAW AND PRACTICE

BY

F. D. ROSE

FOREWORD BY
LORD JUSTICE STEYN

LONDON   HONG KONG
1997

LLP Reference Publishing
69–77 Paul Street
London EC2A 4LQ
Great Britain

SOUTH EAST ASIA
LLP Asia Limited
Room 1101, Hollywood Centre
233 Hollywood Road
Hong Kong

© F. D. Rose, 1997

British Library Cataloguing in Publication Data
A catalogue record for this book
is available from the
British Library

ISBN 1 85978 158 6

All rights reserved. No part of this publication may be reproduced,
stored in a retrieval system, or transmitted, in any form or by any
means, electronic, mechanical, photocopying, recording or
otherwise, without the prior permission of
LLP Limited.

Whilst every effort has been made to ensure that the information
contained in this book is correct, neither the author nor
LLP Limited can accept any responsibility for any
errors or omissions or for any consequences
resulting therefrom.

Are you satisfied with our customer service?

These telephone numbers are your service hot lines for questions and queries:
Delivery: +44 (0) 1206 772866
Payment/invoices/renewals: +44 (0) 1206 772114
LLP Products & Services: +44 (0) 1206 772113
e-mail: Publications@LLPLimited.com or fax us on +44 (0) 1206 772771
We welcome your views and comments in order to ease any problems
and answer any queries you may have.
LLP Limited, Colchester CO3 3LP, U.K.

Typeset in 10/12 Plantin
by Mendip Communications Ltd
Printed in Great Britain by
WBC Limited
Bridgend, Mid-Glamorgan

To Lynda

FOREWORD

The misfortunes attendant upon maritime adventures are many. Sometimes a master of a stricken vessel can avoid disaster by jettisoning part of the cargo, thereby perhaps saving lives, the vessel and most of the cargo. That in such a case those whose property survives should make restitution proportionately to the persons whose goods have been sacrificed has made sense to trading communities for many centuries. The idea germinated in maritime equity. General average requires no other justification.

Such equitable principles were established and observed under the laws of trading nations generally. But in the course of time the differences between national systems became irksome to mercantile interests. The great breakthrough was the publication of the York-Antwerp Rules. Admittedly these rules do not have independent binding force, but the widespread incorporation of the York-Antwerp Rules, as amended, into charterparties, bills of lading and marine insurance policies demonstrates the important role of general average in international trade.

Like much of international trade law, general average is not a wholly coherent and rational system. It has largely been shaped by experience rather than logic. Not surprisingly, general average is an intractable subject. Indeed to uninitiated lawyers it is more baffling than voodoo. For the cognoscenti it remains a complex subject. Even they need a systematic analysis of the subject.

Professor Rose has made a valuable contribution to the legal literature on general average. He has rigorously re-examined its structure and principles. His observation that the law evolves within an historical and practical framework, interweaving principle, policy, precedent and experience is important. This approach is noticeable throughout his authoritative account of the modern law and practice of general average. This book will be an indispensable guide to general average far beyond the shores of the United Kingdom.

JOHAN STEYN

House of Lords
September 1997

PREFACE

The practice and law of general average stretch back into antiquity, beyond Justinian's *Digest* to the laws of Rhodes and beyond them, it seems, to the Phoenicians. To most, its workings are no doubt as obscure as its origins. Yet it is not an insignificant part of shipping practice and it continues to evolve. Its precise place within the framework of the law appears uncertain. Discussion of General Average features both in books on the Law of Carriage of Goods by Sea and the Law of Marine Insurance, and in books on the Law on Restitution of Unjust Enrichment, besides attracting a limited number of specialised monographs. In that respect, it exemplifies the common law (though its influences are in fact from both admiralty law and common law), which has traditionally striven to provide practical, yet rational, solutions to real problems, which themselves rarely fit neatly into legal categories.

In modern times, it is an area of law which is particularly dominated by practice, for the adjustment of General Average is largely determined by an internationally agreed set of rules, the York-Antwerp Rules. They are an amalgam of attempts at codifying, declaring and changing the rules governing the rights and liabilities of parties engaged in a maritime adventure during which extraordinary losses are incurred for the common safety. They are made applicable by most charterparties, bill of lading contracts and marine insurance policies. It is therefore not surprising that the principal monographs in this area focus on the Rules. This contrasts with the position in books of which discussion of General Average forms but a part, where the account of the law can appear unrealistic if too far removed from discussion of what actually applies in practice.

The object of this book is to take a fresh look at the structure and principles of both the law and practice of General Average, to show how the different parts of the subject co-exist and, it is hoped, to provide an account of the modern law and practice in a reasonably accessible form.

Anyone researching this area of law and practice must acknowledge a debt to those who have gone before. Many lawyers are no doubt unaware of the existence of this specialised area of law, let alone its history, rules and principles. Yet, as has recently been pointed out, there is a rich tradition of scholarly and practical literature in the broad field of marine insurance, with which General

Average is traditionally most closely associated. The current account does not attempt to reproduce the full content of that literature, which remains essential reading, but to present a different perspective within a more compact framework.

I have benefited greatly from comments made by John Macdonald, a member of the Richards Hogg Group and a past Chairman of the Association of Average Adjusters. Of course, he bears no responsibility for remaining errors or infelicities, but he must be thanked for observations which were careful, practical, and indeed learned. Having consulted him for the current practitioner's point of view, I was slightly surprised that he should also draw support from Justinian's *Digest*.

Yet this, of course, is how it should be. The law evolves within an historical and practical framework, interweaving principle, policy, precedent and experience. Though there is controversy over the future of general average, it cannot be forgotten that it has survived and developed over a long period of time, and that there are reasons why it has developed as it has. It is a familiar observation that an account of any area of law is like a picture of a moving vehicle. No matter how familiar one is with the vehicle's history and traffic patterns, one can never be quite sure how, if at all, that vehicle will continue on its way. What should be clear is that its progress should be better plotted the better its current workings are understood.

FRANCIS ROSE

ABOUT THE AUTHOR

FRANCIS ROSE is Professor of Commercial and Common Law at the University of Buckingham and was previously a University Lecturer in Law and Fellow of St John's College, Cambridge. He has published numerous articles and books on shipping, commercial and common law. He is the author of *The Modern Law of Pilotage*, co-author of *Kennedy's Law of Salvage* (both published by Sweet & Maxwell) and editor of *Restitution and the Conflict of Laws* (published by the Mansfield Press), *Consensus ad Idem: Essays on the Law of Contract in Honour of Guenter Treitel* (published by Sweet & Maxwell) and *Failure of Contracts: Contractual, Restitutionary and Proprietary Consequences* (published by Hart Publishing). He is also General Editor of both *Lloyd's Maritime and Commercial Law Quarterly* and the *Restitution Law Review* and Editor-in-Chief of the *Company, Financial and Insolvency Law Review*.

TABLE OF CONTENTS

Foreword	vii
Preface	ix
About the author	xi
Table of Cases	xix
Table of Legislation, Conventions and Rules	xxvii
Abbreviations	xxix

CHAPTER 1—THE NATURE OF GENERAL AVERAGE	1
Definition	1
Partial losses	3
Examples of general average	5
Justification of the doctrine	6
The governing rules	8
The "common safety" of and "common benefit" to the common adventure	8
Salvage and necessity generally	9
Variation by contract	10
The York-Antwerp Rules	10
Claims procedure	12
CHAPTER 2—THE CONDITIONS FOR GENERAL AVERAGE	13
Burden of proof	13
Subject matter	13
Cargo	13
Freight	14
Human lives	15
Maritime adventure in the nature of a voyage	16
There must be a real danger	17
Danger must be to a common adventure	19
There must be a common adventure	19
Duration of the common adventure	20
Port of refuge expenses	21
Interests in same ownership	23
Danger not threatening all interests	23

Effect of the danger on different interests	24
Loss exceeding benefit	25
The intended beneficiary	25
Effect of general average act on different interests	26
Authority to act	26
The proper actor	26
Whether authority exercisable	30
Sacrifice or expenditure of an extraordinary nature	31
Differences in kind and in degree	34
The sacrifice or expenditure must be real	35
General average act must be intentionally incurred for the benefit of the common adventure	36
Intention	36
Intention to benefit the common adventure	37
The action taken must be reasonable	38
Success: contribution may be claimed from an interest of value at place of termination of the adventure	39
Contributory interest must be of value at the end of the voyage	39
Sacrifices	41
Expenditure	41
Conclusion: common law rule on sacrifice and expenditure	42
Preservation of ship	43
Excluding the requirement of success	44
Failure	45
General average loss must be a direct consequence of the general average act	45

CHAPTER 3—QUALIFYING LOSSES 47

Causation and remoteness	47
York-Antwerp Rules	49
Contractual liability	50
Negligence and third party liability	50
Salvage, lightening and the environment	51
Port of refuge expenses	55
The common law	55
Current practice	56
Substituted expenses	59
Temporary repairs	61
Mitigation of loss	63

CHAPTER 4—EXCEPTIONS TO LIABILITY TO CONTRIBUTE 65

Deck cargo	65

Claimant's fault	66
Basis of the rule	66
Content of the rule	68
Actionable fault	69
Danger arising from condition of cargo	69
Joint tortfeasors	70
Limitation of action	71
Limitation of liability	71
Exclusion of liability	71
The New Jason Clause	75
Fault does not prejudice third parties	76
Contractual qualification of liability to general average	76
Illegality	78

CHAPTER 5—EFFECTS OF A GENERAL AVERAGE ACT — 79

A defence	79
Contribution	79
Security: liens, average bonds, average guarantees and cash deposits	81
Basis of liability; whose liability? Average bonds	82
The time, place and law governing adjustment	84
A tort claim for economic loss	84
Limitation of action	84
Limitation of liability	85
Interest	85
Insurer's liability	86

CHAPTER 6—ADJUSTMENT — 87

General principles	87
The parties' interests are generally valued at the end of the voyage	88
The end of the voyage	88
Valuation of sacrifices, expenditures and contributory interests	89
Determining the place at which contributory values are assessed	89
Average adjusters	92
Jurisdiction	93
Governing law and practice	94
Valuation	97
General rule	97
Ship: the general rule	98
Ship—deductions from cost of repairs	99
Cargo: the general rule	100

Sale of cargo	101
Where cargo forwarded from port of refuge to destination by other means	102
Freight	102
Hire	102
Other interests	103
General average disbursements	103

CHAPTER 7—INSURANCE CONTRACTS 105

Liability to contribute determined independently of insurance	106
Assured with more than one interest	106
Insurer's liability	107
Subject-matter and peril insured	107
Value insured	109
Loss suffered	110
Insured's rights to indemnity and contribution	111
General average sacrifice	111
General average expenditure	111
Institute clauses	113
Salvage and the environment	113
Measure of indemnity: insurer's liability proportionate to insured amount	114
Adjustment regime; place of adjustment; foreign adjustment	116
Protection and Indemnity Association cover	118

APPENDICES

1	STATUTES	119
	Marine Insurance Act 1906	119
	Supreme Court Act 1981, ss.20–24	139
2	YORK-ANTWERP RULES	145
	York-Antwerp Rules 1974	145
	York-Antwerp Rules 1994	152
3	RULES OF PRACTICE OF THE ASSOCIATION OF AVERAGE ADJUSTERS	160
4	INSTITUTE CLAUSES	173
	Institute Time Clauses (Hulls) 1/11/95	173
	Institute Voyage Clauses (Hulls) 1/11/95	184
	Institute Time Clauses (Freight) 1/11/95	191
	Institute Voyage Clauses (Freight) 1/11/95	197
	Institute Cargo Clauses (A)	202
	Institute Cargo Clauses (B)	206
	Institute Cargo Clauses (C)	211
	Institute Time Clauses—Hulls: Excess Liabilities 1/11/95	216
	Institute Time Clauses—Hulls: Disbursements and Increased Value (Total Loss only, including Excess Liabilities)— 1/11/95	218
	Institute Average Disbursement Clauses (A) 14/5/87	224
	Institute Average Disbursement Clauses (B) 14/5/87	226

5	LLOYD'S STANDARD FORMS	228
	Average Bond (LAB 77)	228
	Guarantee	229
	General Average Bond and Guarantee (Form Y)	230
	General Average Deposit Receipt	232
	Valuation Form	233
	Lloyd's Standard Form of Salvage Agreement (No Cure—No Pay) (LOF 95)	234
	LOF 1995 Procedural Rules	240
Index		243

TABLE OF CASES

Achard v. Ring (1874) 2 Asp MLC 422; 31 LT (NS) 647 .... 5, 16, 20, 49, 94
African Steamship Co v. Swanzy (1856) 2 K & J 660 98
Aga, The [1968] 1 Lloyd's Rep 431 66
Aktieselkabet Ocean v. B Harding & Sons Ltd [1928] 2 KB 371 67
Alma Shipping Corp v. Union of India (*The Astrea*) [1971] 2 Lloyd's Rep 494 .... 7, 74
Alpha, The [1991] 2 Lloyd's Rep 515 .... 39, 48, 79
Alppi, The [1989] Nordiske Domme i Sjofartsannliggender 397 20
Al Taha, The [1990] 2 Lloyd's Rep 117 74
Amerada Hess Corp v. S/T Mobil Apex [1979] AMC 2406 4
Anderson Tritton & Co v. Ocean SS Co (1884) 10 App Cas 107 .... 38, 39, 52, 53, 81,
82, 106, 109
Andree-Moran, The [1930] AMC 631 29
Anglo-Argentine Livestock Agency v. Temperley [1899] 2 QB 403 49
Anglo-Grecian Steam Trading Co Ltd v. T Beynon & Co (1926) 24 Ll L Rep 122 .... 30, 37,
38, 44, 48, 50, 51, 89
Antigoni, The [1990] 1 Lloyd's Rep 45 74
Apollinaris Co v. Nord Deutsche Insurance Co [1904] 1 KB 252 .... 17, 65
Arenson v. Casson Beckman Rutley & Co [1977] AC 405 93
Armar Shippng Co Ltd v. Caisse Algérienne d'Assurance et de Reassurance (*The Armar*)
[1981] 1 WLR 207 .... 95, 96
Aspinwall v. Merchant Shipping Co (1862) Unreported, 45 LJQB 648n 49
Assicurazioni Generali v. SS Bessie Morris Co Ltd [1892] 2 QB 652 59
Athel Line Ltd v. Liverpool & London War Risks Ins Assn Ltd [1944] KB 87 ..... 26, 30, 36,
37, 38
Atkinson v. Stephens (1852) 7 Ex 567 .... 41, 45, 101
Attaleia Marine Co Ltd v. Bimeh Iran (Iran Insurance Co) (*The Zeus*) [1993] 2 Lloyd's Rep
497 93
Atwood v. Sellar & Co (1879) 4 QBD 342; (1880) 5 QBD 286 ..... 10, 12, 21, 22, 47, 55, 56
Austin Friars SS Co Ltd v. Spillers & Bakers Ltd [1915] 1 KB 833; affd [1915] 3 KB 586   1, 5,
7, 44, 47, 70
Australian Coastal Shipping Commission v. Green [1971] 1 QB 456 ...... 2, 4, 5, 30, 38, 39,
48, 50

Barge *J Whitney*, The [1968] AMC 995 18
Barnard v. Adams (1850) 10 How 270 91
Beatrice, The [1924] AMC 914 29
Beatrice, The [1975] 1 Lloyd's Rep 220 42
Bell v. Smith (1806) 2 Johnson R 98 98
Berry, Barclay v. Louis Dreyfus (1929) 35 Ll L Rep 183 96
Bijela, The [1992] 1 Lloyd's Rep 636; affd [1993] 1 Lloyd's Rep 411; rvrsd [1994] 1 WLR
615 .... 62, 63
Birkley v. Presgrave (1801) 1 East 220 .... 1, 5, 27, 34, 47, 79
Blackett v. Royal Exchange Assurance Co (1832) C & J 244 33
Blenheim, The (1886) 10 PD 167 91

TABLE OF CASES

Bona, The [1895] P 125 .... 6, 32, 34
Bowring *v.* Thebaud (1890) 42 Fed Rep 796 60
Boyd *v.* Dubois (1811) 3 Camp 133 69
Brabant, The [1967] 1 QB 588 73
Bradley *v.* Cargo of Lumber (1886) 29 Fed Rep 648 91
Brandeis Goldschmidt & Co *v.* Economic Insurance Co Ltd (1922) 11 Ll L Rep 42 .. 82, 108, 117
Brigella, The [1893] P 189 .... 19, 106, 116
Briggs *v.* Merchant Traders Association (1849) 13 QB 167 52
Brown *v.* Stapyleton (1827) 4 Bing 119; 12 JB Moore 334 14
Burton & Co *v.* English & Co (1883) 10 QBD 426; (1883) 12 QBD 218 .... 7, 65, 74, 96
Butler *v.* Wildman (1820) 3 B & Ald 398 25

Carisbrook Steamship Co *v.* London & Provincial Marine & General Insurance Co [1901] 2 KB 861 .... 15, 106, 107
Carron Park, The (1890) 15 PD 203 .... 72, 73, 76
Castle Ins Co Ltd *v.* Hong Kong Islands Shipping Co Ltd (*The Potoi Chau*) [1984] AC 226 .. 83
Castor, The [1932] P 142 100
Chandris *v.* Argo Insurance Co [1963] 2 Lloyd's Rep 65 .... 42, 84, 85, 92
Charter SS Co Ltd *v.* Bowring Jones & Tidy Ltd (1930) 36 Ll L Rep 272 .... 17, 18
Chellew *v.* Royal Commission on the Sugar Supply [1921] 2 KB 627; affd [1922] 1 KB 12 .... 40, 41, 42, 88, 89
China Pacific SA *v.* Food Corp of India (*The Winson*) [1982] AC 939 21
Choko Star, The [1990] 1 Lloyd's Rep 216 30
Clarke *v.* Earl of Dunraven (*The Satanita*) [1897] AC 59 96
Coastal Wrecking Co *v.* Phoenix Assurance Co (1881) 7 Fed Rep 236 54
Columbian Insurance Co *v.* Ashby (1839) 13 Peters 331 44
Constancia, The (1846) 2 W Rob 487 9
Copenhagen, The (1799) 1 Chr Rob 289 1
Corfu Navigation Co *v.* Mobil Shipping Co Ltd (*The Alpha*) [1991] 2 Lloyd's Rep 515 .... 11, 13, 35, 39, 50, 74, 85
Corrie *v.* Coulthard (1877) 3 Asp MLC 546 .... 19, 24, 35
Covington *v.* Roberts (1806) 2 B & P NR 378 .... 31, 32, 34
Cox *v.* May (1815) 4 M & S 152 15
Crockett *v.* Dodge (1835) 3 Fairf 190 24
Crofts *v.* Marshall (1836) 7 C & P 597 92
Crooks & Co *v.* Allan & Co (1879) 5 QBD 38 .... 16, 74, 81, 92
Cunard Steamship Co *v.* Marten [1902] 2 KB 624 109
C Czarnikow Ltd *v.* Koufos (*The Heron II*) [1969] 1 AC 350 49

Dabney *v.* New England Co (1867) 14 Allen 300 .... 15, 20
Da Costa *v.* Newnham (1788) 2 TR 407 56
Dalglish *v.* Davidson (1824) 5 Dowl & Ry KB 6 .... 81, 94
Danae Shipping Corp *v.* TPAO (*The Daffodil B*) [1983] 1 Lloyd's Rep 498 74
Danica Brown, The [1995] 2 Lloyd's Rep 264 74
Daniolos *v.* Bunge & Co (1937) 59 Ll L Rep 175, affd (1938) 62 Ll L Rep 65 ..... 18, 19, 36
Deering *v.* Earl of Winchelsea (1787) 2 Bos & Pul 270 (Ex) 6, 7, 67
De Hart *v.* Compania Anonima Aurora [1903] 1 KB 109 117
Dickenson *v.* Jardine (1868) LR 3 CP 639 111
Dobell & Co *v.* SS Rossmore Co [1895] 2 QB 408 76
Dobson *v.* Wilson (1813) 3 Camp 480 101
Dollar *v.* La Fonciere (1908) 162 Fed Rep 563 23
Dominic de Larrinaga, The [1928] AMC 64 91
Drew Brown Ltd *v.* The Orient Trader and her Owners (*The Orient Trader*) [1974] SCR 1286; (1973) 34 DLR (3d) 339; [1973] 2 Lloyd's Rep 174 (Can SC) 67, 96
Duncan *v.* Benson (1847) 1 Exch 537 5

EB Aaby's Rederi A/S *v.* Union of India (*The Evje*) (No 2) [1976] 2 Lloyd's Rep 714 .... 66, 76

TABLE OF CASES

Eisernz GmbH v. Federal Commerce & Navigation Co Ltd (*The Oak Hill*) [1970] 2 Lloyd's Rep 332 (Can Ex Ct) 92
Eliza Lines, The (1902) 114 Fed Rep 307 100
Ellerman Lines v. Gibbs (Canada) (*The City of Colombo*) (1986) 26 DLR (4th) 161; [1986] AMC 2217 91
Ernestina, The (1919) 259 Fed Rep 772 75
Ettrick, The (1881) 6 PD 127 .... 67, 71

Falcke v. Scottish Imperial Ins Co Ltd (1886) 34 Ch D 234 .... 9, 16, 17
Federal Commerce & Navigation Co Ltd v. Eisernz GmbH (*The Oak Hill*) [1975] 1 Lloyd's Rep 105 (Can SC) 79
Fletcher v. Alexander (1868) LR 3 CP 375 .... 14, 41, 43, 87, 88, 89, 90, 94, 100
Food Corporation of India v. Carras [1980] 2 Lloyd's Rep 577 89
Frayes (or Trayes) v. Worms (1865) 19 CB(NS) 159 14

Garrels v. S Behr & Mathew Ltd (1933) 47 Ll L Rep 319 49
Glaucus, The (1948) 81 Ll L Rep 262 21
Goeben, The (1912) (Hamburg CA), affd (1913) (Imperial Court at Leipzig) 14
Goulandris Bros Ltd v. B Goldman & Sons Ltd [1958] 1 QB 74 ... 10, 11, 67, 68, 69, 71, 74, 76, 84
Gould v. Oliver (1837) 4 Bing (NC) 134 65
Grainger v. Martin (1863) 4 B & S 9 98
Grange & Co v. Taylor (1904) 9 Com Cas 223 96
Gratitudine, The (1801) 3 C Rob 240 .... 15, 30, 31, 38, 39, 40, 79, 101
Greenshields, Cowie & Co v. Stephens & Sons [1908] 1 KB 51; affd [1908] AC 431 .... 49, 66, 70, 73, 74
Green Star Shipping Co Ltd v. The London Assurance (*The Andree*) [1933] 1 KB 378 .... 42, 88, 92, 112
Gulf Refining Co v. Atlantic Mutual Insurance Co (1929) 279 US 708; 35 Ll L Rep 21 116

Hahlo v. Benedict (1914) 216 Fed Rep 303 23
Hain SS Co Ltd v. Tate & Lyle Ltd (1936) 41 Com Cas 350 .... 66, 67, 80, 83
Hall v. Janson (1855) 4 E & B 500 .... 55, 56
Hallett v. Wigram (1845) 9 CB 580 .... 5, 48, 56, 101
Hamel v. Peninsular & Oriental Steam Navigation Co [1908] 2 KB 298 .... 48, 55
Hansen v. Dunn (1906) 11 Com Cas 100 31
Harmonides, The [1903] P 1 100
Harris v. Scaramanga (1872) LR 7 CP 481 .... 107, 117
Harrison v. Bank of Australasia (1872) LR 7 Ex 39 33
Harrison v. Bank of Australia [1894] AC 687 .... 31, 34
Hartford v. Jones (1698) 1 Ld Raym 393 9
Henderson v. Merrett Syndicates Ltd [1995] 2 AC 145 93
Henderson v. Shankland [1896] 1 QB 525 .... 5, 98
Hendricks v. Australian Insurance Co (1874) LR 9 CP 460 117
Heye v. North German Lloyd (1887) 36 Fed Rep 705 14
Hick v. London Assurance (1895) 1 Com Cas 244 107
Hill v. Wilson (1879) 4 CPD 329 .... 92, 96
Hingston v. Wendt (1876) 1 QBD 367 .... 43, 81
Hohenzollern, The [1906] P 339 100
Holman & Sons Ltd, for Owners of the SS Nefeli v. Merchants' Marine Insurance Co Ltd [1919] 1 KB 383 109
Hopper v. Burness (1876) 1 CPD 137 101
Humber Conservancy Board v. Federated Coal and Shipping Co [1928] 1 KB 492 57
Hunter v. Northern Marine Insurance Co Ltd (1888) 13 App Cas 717 57
Huth v. Lamport (1886) 16 QBD 735 82

Interior Freighting Co Inc v Universal Ins Co (*The Mohican*) [1934] AMC 112 20

TABLE OF CASES

International Navigation Co v. Atlantic Mutual Insurance Co (1900) 100 Fed Rep 304, affd
(1901) 108 Fed Rep 988 116
International Navigation Co v. Sea Insurance Co (1904) 129 Fed Rep 13 116
Iredale v. China Traders Insurance Co [1899] 2 QB 356; [1900] 2 QB 515 .... 35, 36, 44
Irrawaddy, The (1898) 171 US 187 75
Isis, The [1933] AMC 1565; (1933) 48 Ll L Rep 35 76

Jason, The (1908) 162 Fed Rep 56; (1910) 175 Fed Rep 414; 225 US 32 .... 54, 75
JH Wetherall & Co Ltd v. London Assurance [1931] 2 KB 448 49
Job v. Langton (1856) 6 E & B 779 .... 31, 53, 56
John Perkins, The (1822) Ware (US) 87; 3 Kent Comm 243n 19
Johnson v. Chapman (1865) 19 CB(NS) 563 .... 24, 35, 37, 65, 70
Joseph Watson & Son Ltd v. Firemen's Fund Insurance Co of San Francisco [1922] 2 KB
355 .... 18, 28
Joyce v. Kennard (1871) LR 7 QB 78 109
JP Donaldson, The (1897) 167 US 599 (US SC) 19
Julia Blake, The (1882) 107 US 418 91

Kacianoff v. China Traders Insurance Co Ltd [1914] 3 KB 1121 18
Kafiristan, The [1937] P 63; [1938] AC 136 67
Kemp v. Halliday (1865) 34 LJQB 233, affd (1866) LR 1 QB 520 .... 19, 53, 54
Kulukundis v. Norwich Union Fire Insurance Society [1937] 1 KB 1 .... 31, 59

L'Amerique, The (1888) 35 Fed Rep 835 48
Lawrence v. Minturn (1854) 17 How 100 18
Lee v. Southern Insurance Co (1870) LR 5 CP 397 .... 60, 61
Leitrim, The [1902] P 256 .... 49, 56
Lenox v. United Insurance Co (1802) 3 Johns NY Cas 178 (NY SC) 33
Lindsay v. Klein [1911] AC 194 66
Lloyd v. Guibert (1865) LR 1 QB 115 94
Logan, The [1936] AMC 993 42
Louis Dreyfus & Co v. Tempus SS Co [1931] AC 726 .... 71, 73
Lubovsky v. Snelling [1944] 1 KB 44 84
LW & P Armstrong Inc v. SS Mormacmar [1947] AMC 1611; affd *The Mormacmar* [1956]
AMC 1028 59
Lyric Shipping Inc v. Intermetals Inc (*The Al Taha*) [1990] 2 Lloyd's Rep 117 74

Makedonia, The [1962] 1 Lloyd's Rep 316 73
Maldonado v. British & Foreign Marine Insurance Co (1910) 182 Fed Rep 744 ...... 14, 116
Marida v. Oswal Steel (*The Bijela*) [1992] 1 Lloyd's Rep 636; affd [1993] 1 Lloyd's Rep 411;
rvrsd [1994] 1 WLR 615; 2 Lloyd's Rep 1 .... 1, 10, 11, 12, 26, 31, 32, 57, 58,
59, 62, 94
Maritime Insurance Co Ltd v. Alianza Insurance Co of Santander [1907] 1 KB 660 57
Marpessa, The [1891] P 403 84
Marvigor CN SA v. Romanoexport State Co for Foreign Trade (*The Corinthian Glory*)
[1977] 2 Lloyd's Rep 280 .... 10, 77, 80
Mavro v. Ocean Marine Insurance Co (1875) 2 Asp MLC 590; (1875) LR 10 CP
414 .... 88, 90, 117
Mary Thomas, The [1894] P 108 .... 41, 66, 112, 117
M'Call & Co Ltd v. Houlder Bros (1897) 2 Com Cas 129 .... 5, 19, 48, 50, 56
McAndrews v. Thatcher (1865) 3 Wall 347 (US SC) 54
McLoon v. Cummings (1873) 73 Penn St Rep 98 91
Merryweather v. Nixan (1799) 8 TR 186 70
Milburn & Co v. Jamaica Fruit Transporting and Trading Co of London [1900] 2 QB
540 .... 7, 72, 73, 76
Miller v. Titherington (1862) 7 H & N 954 65
Milward v. Hibbert (1842) 3 QB 120 65
Minneapolis SS Co v. Manistee Co (1907) 156 Fed Rep 424 29
Minnetonka, The (1905) 10 Asp MLC 142 .... 60, 101

TABLE OF CASES

Montgomery & Co *v.* Indemnity Mutual Marine Insurance Co [1902] 1 KB 734 ...... 15, 23, 38, 106, 107, 116
Moran *v.* Jones (1857) 7 E & B 523 .... 15, 54
Morrison Steamship Co Ltd *v.* Greystoke Castle (Cargo Owners) (*The Cheldale*) [1947] AC 265 .... 20, 27, 30, 42, 84, 106
Mouse's Case (1609) 12 Co Rep 63 29
MR Currie & Co *v.* Bombay Native Ins Co (1869) LR 3 PC 72 30

Nesbitt *v.* Lushington (1792) 4 TR 783 24
New Zealand Shipping Co Ltd *v.* AM Satterthwaite & Co Ltd (*The Eurymedon*) [1975] AC 154 96
Nimick *v.* Holmes (1855) 25 Penn Rep 366 49
Noreuro Traders Ltd *v.* E Hardy & Co (1923) 16 Ll L Rep 319 84
Northland Navigation Co *v.* Paterson Boiler Works (*The Sea Comet*) (1983) 2 CF 59 ... 20
Norway, The (1864) Br & L 377 82

Oak Hill, The [1975] 1 Lloyd's Rep 105 (Can SC) 39
Ocean SS Co *v.* Anderson, Tritton & Co (1883) 13 QBD 651; (1885) 1 TLR 615 ..... 39, 43
Oppenheim *v.* Fry (1863) 3 B & S 874; affd (1864) 5 B & S 348 .... 19, 106

Pacific Mail SS Co *v.* NYH & R Min Co (1896) 74 Fed Rep 564 49
Papayanni *v.* Grampian SS Co Ltd (1896) 1 Com Cas 448 .... 5, 27, 28, 29, 30
Pappa *v.* Rose (1872) LR 7 CP 525 93
Parsons *v.* Scott (1810) 2 Taunt 362 .... 5, 78, 81
Peters *v.* Milligan (1787) 1 Park 296 14
Phelps, James & Co *v.* Hill [1891] 1 QB 605 .... 31, 38
Pirie & Co *v.* Middle Dock Co (1881) 44 LT 426; 4 Asp MLC 388 .... 7, 15, 19, 36, 41, 49, 68, 70
Pirie *v.* Steele (1837) 8 C & P 200 92
Place *v.* Potts (1855) 5 HLC 383 9
Plummer *v.* Wildman (1815) 3 M & S 482 .... 55, 62
Port of Caledonia and the Anna, The [1903] P 184 50
Potoi Chau, The [1984] AC 226 .... 81, 83, 84, 92
Potter *v.* Ocean Assurance Co (1837) 3 Sumner 27 23
Powell *v.* Gudgeon (1816) 5 M & S 431 101
Power *v.* Whitmore (1815) 4 M & S 141 .... 34, 56, 62
Price *v.* Middle Dock Co (1881) 44 LT 426 7
Price *v.* Noble (1811) 4 Taunt 123 .... 5, 28, 29
Prinz Heinrich, The (1888) 13 PD 31 52
Progress, The (1810) Edw 210 15

Raisby, The (1885) 10 PD 114 52
Ralli *v.* Troop (1894) 157 US 386 29
Reardon Smith Line *v.* Black Sea & Baltic General Insurance Co Ltd (1938) 60 Ll L Rep 353 66
Reliance Marine Insurance Co *v.* New York & Cuba Mail Steamship Co (1895) 70 Fed Rep 262; (1896) 77 Fed Rep 317; 165 US 720 .... 50, 54, 77
Republic of India *v.* India Steamship Co Ltd (No 2) (*The Indian Endurance*) [1997] 2 WLR 538 97
Richardson *v.* Nourse (1819) 3 B & Ald 237 101
Risley *v.* Insurance Co of North America (1910) 189 Fed Rep 529 23
Roanoke, The (1894) 46 Fed Rep 297 29
Robinson *v.* Price (1876) 2 QBD 91 .... 33, 66
Rosamond, The [1960] AMC 195 (US CA) 63
Rose *v.* Bank of Australasia [1894] AC 687 .... 5, 16, 21, 27, 37, 55
Rowson *v.* Atlantic Transport Co [1903] 2 KB 666 76
Royal Exchange Shipping Co Ltd *v.* Dixon (1886) 12 App Cas 11 65
Royal Mail Steam Packet Co *v.* English Bank of Rio de Janeiro Ltd (1887) 19 QBD 362 .... 8, 14, 25, 37, 38, 43, 48, 53, 54

TABLE OF CASES

Ruabon Steamship Co Ltd v. London Assurance [1900] AC 6	31
Salvage Association v. Suzuki & Co Ltd (1929) 35 Ll L Rep 45	82
Sameon Co SA v. NV Petrofina (*The World Hitachi Zosen*) [1996] 5 CL 114; affd (May 1997) Unreported (CA)	93, 94
San Onofre, The [1917] P 96	100
Sarquy v. Hobson (1827) 4 Bing 131	101
Scaife v. Tobin (1832) 3 B & Ad 523	79, 80, 81, 83
Schade v. National Surety Corp [1961] AMC 1225	76
Schloss v. Heriot (1863) 14 CB(NS) 59	66, 67, 68
Schmidt v. Royal Mail Steamship Co (1862) 45 LJQB 646	49, 74
Schothorst & Schuitema v. Franz Dauter GmbH (*The Nimrod*) [1973] 2 Lloyd's Rep 91	95, 96
Schuster v. Fletcher (1878) 3 QBD 418	5, 27
SC Loveland Co v. USA [1963] AMC 260 (US DC)	20
Sea-Land Services Inc v. Aetna Insurance Co (*The Beauregard*) [1976] AMC 2164; [1977] 2 Lloyd's Rep 84 (US CA)	13, 47
Seapool, The [1934] P 53	2, 12, 19, 37, 38, 44, 60, 79
Shepherd v. Kottgen (1877) 2 CPD 578	5, 35, 36
Shoe v. Low Moor Iron Co (1891) 46 Fed Rep 125; 49 Fed Rep 252	15
Simonds v. White (1824) 2 B & C 805	10, 81, 94
Simpson v. Thomson (1877) 3 App Cas 279	106
Slater v. Hayward Rubber Co (1857) 26 Conn 128	24
Société Nouvelle d'Armement v. Spillers & Bakers Ltd [1917] 1 KB 865	8, 18, 32, 33, 34
Spring v. Guardian Assurance plc [1995] 2 AC 296	93
Star Shipping AS v. China National Foreign Trade Transportation Corp (*The Star Texas*) [1993] 2 Lloyd's Rep 445	95
State Trading Corp of India v. Doyle Carriers Inc (*The Jute Express*) [1991] 2 Lloyd's Rep 55	67, 85
Steamship Balmoral Co Ltd v. Marten [1902] AC 511; 1 Magens 245, Case XIX	115, 116
Stewart v. West India and Pacific Steamship Co (1873) LR 8 QB 88	10, 49, 94
Strang, Steel & Co v. A Scott & Co (1889) 14 App Cas 601	6, 65, 66, 72, 76, 79, 81
Strathdon, The (1899) 94 Fed Rep 206	75
Sucarseco, The (1935) 51 Ll L Rep 238 (US SC)	84
Susan V Luckenbach, The [1951] P 197	67
Sutcliffe v. Thackrah [1974] AC 727	93
Svendsen v. Wallace Bros (1884) 13 QBD 69; affd (1885) 10 App Cas 404	9, 10, 12, 21, 22, 47, 52, 54, 55, 56, 81, 170
Swiss Bank Corp v. Novorossiysk Shipping Co (*The Petr Schmidt*) [1995] 1 Lloyd's Rep 202	94
Tate & Lyle Ltd v. Hain SS Co (1934) 39 Com Cas 259; 151 LT 249	7, 42
Taylor v. Curtis (1816) 6 Taunt 608, affg (1815) 4 Camp 337	31, 32, 34
Tempus Shipping v. Louis Dreyfus & Co [1930] 1 KB 699; [1931] 1 KB 195; [1931] AC 726	49, 68
Texas, The [1970] 1 Lloyd's Rep 175	66
Tharsis Sulphur & Copper Co Ltd v. Jones (1872) LR 8 CP 1	93
Tojo Maru (Owners) v. NV Bureau Wijsmuller (*The Tojo Maru*) [1972] AC 242	4, 9
Trafalgar Steamship Co v. British and Foreign Marine Insurance Co [1904] *Shipping Gazette*, Nov 18	18
Transamerican Ocean Contractors Inc v. Transchemical Rotterdam BV (*The Ioanna*) [1978] 1 Lloyd's Rep 238	94
Transpacific Steamship Co v. Marine Office of America [1957] AMC 1070	42
Troilus, The [1951] AC 820	21
Tudor v. Macomber (1833) 14 Pickering 34	90
Union of India v. EB Aaby's Rederi A/S (*The Evje*) [1975] AC 797	7, 10, 12, 74, 84, 94
Union of India v. EB Aaby's Rederi A/S (*The Evje*) (No 2) [1976] 2 Lloyd's Rep 714, affd [1978] 1 Lloyd's Rep 351	74
Unique Mariner, The (No 2) [1979] 1 Lloyd's Rep 37	4

TABLE OF CASES

US v. Wilder, re Schooner *Jasper* (1838) 3 Sumner 308 13
US Shipping Board v. R Durell & Co Ltd [1923] 23 KB 739 96

Vlassopoulos v. British and Foreign Marine Insurance Co (*The Makis*) [1929] 1 KB 187 .... 11, 18, 19, 58

Walford de Baerdemaecker & Co v. Galindez Bros (1897) 2 Com Cas 137 .... 77, 79, 80
Walthew v. Mavrojanni (1870) LR 5 Ex 116 .... 31, 53, 54, 56
Wamsutta Mills v. Old Colony Steamboat Co (1884) 137 Mass 471 29
Wavertree SS Co Ltd v. Love [1897] AC 373 .... 88, 92, 93, 94
Western Canada Steamship Co Ltd v. Canadian Commercial Corporation [1960] SCR 632; [1960] 2 Lloyd's Rep 313 (Can SC) 60
Westfal-Larsen A/S v. Colonial Sugar Co Ltd [1960] 2 Lloyd's Rep 206 (NSW SC) 73
West Imboden, The [1936] AMC 696 18
Westoll v. Carter (1898) 3 Com Cas 112 .... 23, 57, 66
White v. Jones [1995] 2 AC 207 93
Whitecross Wire Co v. Savill (1882) 8 QBD 653 .... 16, 18, 20, 24, 27, 36, 38, 49
Willcox, Peck & Hughes v. American Smelting and Refining Co (*The Trojan*) (1913) 210 Fed Rep 89 24
William J Quillan, The (1909) 168 Fed Rep 407; (1910) 175 Fed Rep 207; 180 Fed Rep 681 70
Williams v. London Assurance Co (1813) 1 M & S 318 15
Wilson v. Bank of Victoria (1867) LR 2 QB 203 .... 5, 32, 34, 59, 60, 62
Winson, The [1982] AC 939 30
Woods v. Olsen (1900) 99 Fed Rep 451 5
Wordsworth, The (1898) 88 Fed Rep 313 18
World Hitachi Zosen, The [1996] 5 CL 114 93
Wright v. Marwood (1886) 7 QBD 62 .... 6, 65

TABLE OF LEGISLATION, CONVENTIONS AND RULES

Bratislava Convention 17
Brussels Convention on Jurisdiction and the Enforcement of Judgments in Civil and Commercial Matters 1968 93
   Art. 5(1) 93
   17 93

Carriage of Goods by Sea Act 1971—
   Sched. 118
   Art. III(6) 71, 84
       IV(2)(a) 39, 74
       (6) 74
Carriage of Goods by Sea Act 1992 .. 83
   s.3 80
Civil Aviation Act 1982—
   s.87 141
Civil Jurisdiction and Judgments Act 1982 93
   s.2(2), Sched. 1, Art. 2 93
Civil Liability (Contribution) Act 1978 70
CMI International Convention on Salvage 1989 .... 140, 141, 235
   Art. 1 238
       6 238
       (2) 30
       8 239
       13 .... 53, 77, 235, 239
       (1) 239
       (b) .. 53, 147, 154, 176, 194, 199
       (h) 239
       (i) 239
       (j) 239
       14 .... 53, 77, 97, 113, 147, 154, 157, 177, 194, 199, 239
       (4) 147, 154
Companies Act 1862 136
Contracts (Applicable Law) Act 1990—
   Sched. 1 96
Convention on Limitation of Liability for Maritime Claims 1976 85
   Art. 3(a) 85

County Courts Act 1984—
   ss.26–31 94
Crown Proceedings Act 1947—
   s.38(2) 144

Danube Rules 17

EEC Convention on the Law Applicable to Contractual Obligations 1980 (Rome Convention) 96

Hague Rules 74, 76
   Art. III(6) 71, 84
Hague-Visby Rules 74, 84, 118
   Art. IV(2)(a) 39
       (6) 74
Harbour Docks and Piers Clauses Act 1847—
   s.74 79
Harter Act (USA) 75, 76
Hovercraft Act 1968—
   s.2(3) 143, 144

I.V.R. Rhine Rules 17

Law Reform (Married Women and Tortfeasors) Act 1935 70
Limitation Act 1980—
   s.5 84
Limitation Convention 1976—
   Art. 6.1(b) 193, 198

Marine Insurance Act 1906 .... 3, 4, 17, 98, 108, 115, 119–139
   s.2(1) 17
      6 1
      16 115
      (1) 115
   30, Sched. 1 .... 124, 137–139
      56(1) 3
      60 98
   s.64–66 3
   s.64(2) 3
   65(1) 3

TABLE OF LEGISLATION

Marine Insurance Act 1906—*cont.*
s.65(2)	3, 4, 52
66	11, 26
(1)	19, 47
(1)–(2)	2
(2)	16, 38
(4)	111, 112
(5)	110
(6)	108
(7)	23, 106
69	98
73	110, 114, 115, 163
(1)	115, 116
78	105
(1)	4
(2)	4
(3)	4
(4)	4
87	1, 11, 108
Sched., r.15	98

Merchant Shipping Act 1862—
s.54	67

Merchant Shipping Act 1894—
s.502	74
(i)	73
503	71
742	57

Merchant Shipping Act 1995
	140, 141, 143
Part VI, Chap III	140
Chap. VI	140
s.85	143
185, Sched. 7, Part I	67, 71
186	73
217, Sched. 4	85
224	141

Merchant Shipppng Act 1995—*cont.*
s.224(2)	17
224, Sched. 11—	
Part I	30, 53, 77
Art. 16	15
Part II, para. 2	17
226	153
313(1)	57

Merchant Shipping (Salvage and Pollution) Act 1994 235
s.1	30

Rhine Navigation Convention 1868 .. 143
Rome Convention 10, 96

Salvage Convention 1989 53
Stamp Act 1891 136
Supreme Court Act 1981—
ss.20–24	94, 139–144
s.20(2)(j)	9
(q)	9, 82, 94
21(4)	82
35(a)	85

United States Carriage of Goods by Sea Act 1936 76

York Rules 1864 11
York-Antwerp Rules 1877 11
York-Antwerp Rules 1890 11
York-Antwerp Rules 1924 .... 11, 164, 172
York-Antwerp Rules 1950 .... 11, 164, 165
York-Antwerp Rules 1974 .. 11, 83, 145–152, 165, 172
York-Antwerp Rules 1994 .... 152–159, 165, 177, 187

ABBREVIATIONS

[*The following materials are cited in the abbreviated form given here. Citations are to the editions stated unless otherwise specified.*]

Arnould	Sir MJ Mustill and JCB Gilman (eds), *Arnould's Law of Marine Insurance and Average*, 16th ed. (vols 1–2, 1981; vol. 3, 1997)
Carver	R Colinvaux (ed.), *Carver's Carriage by Sea*, 13th ed. (1982)
Goff & Jones	GH Jones (ed.), Lord Goff of Chieveley and GH Jones, *The Law of Restitution*, 4th ed. (1993)
Hudson	NG Hudson, *The York-Antwerp Rules*, 2nd ed. (1996)
Kennedy	DW Steel QC and FD Rose, *Kennedy's Law of Salvage*, 5th ed. (1985)
Lowndes & Rudolf	DJ Wilson and JHS Cooke, *Lowndes & Rudolf: The Law of General Average and the York-Antwerp Rules*, 12th ed. (1997)
Macdonald	JA Macdonald, "General Average Ancient and Modern" [1995] LMCLQ 480
Rose	FD Rose, "Restitution for the Rescuer" (1989) 9 OJLS 167

CHAPTER 1

THE NATURE OF GENERAL AVERAGE[1]

Definition

"The Rhodian law decrees that if in order to lighten a ship merchandise is thrown overboard, that which has been given for all shall be replaced by the contribution of all."[2]

This statement in Justinian's *Digest* is one of the earliest definitions of a principle that has existed in relation to the carriage of goods by sea from time immemorial.[3] The classic definition of general average given by an English judge is that of Lawrence J in *Birkley* v. *Presgrave*[4]:

"All loss which arises in consequence of extraordinary sacrifices made or expenses incurred for the preservation of the ship and cargo come within general average and must be borne proportionately by all those who are interested."

General average is now statutorily defined by the Marine Insurance Act 1906, s.6[5]:

---

1. See generally DJ Wilson and JHS Cooke, *Lowndes & Rudolf: The Law of General Average and the York-Antwerp Rules*, 12th ed. (1997); NG Hudson, *The York-Antwerp Rules*, 2nd ed. (1996); Lord Goff of Chieveley and GH Jones, *The Law of Restitution*, 4th ed. (1993), Chap. 13(E); Sir MJ Mustill and JCB Gilman (eds), *Arnould's Law of Marine Insurance and Average*, 16th ed. (1981), Chap. 26; SC Boyd QC, AS Burrows and D Foxton (eds), *Scrutton on Charterparties and Bills of Lading*, 20th ed. (1996), 272–284; R Colinvaux (ed.), *Carver's Carriage by Sea*, 13th ed. (1982), Chap. 14; RJ Lambeth (ed.), *Templeman on Marine Insurance*, 6th ed. (1986), Chaps 9–10; D O'May & J Hill, *Marine Insurance Law and Policy* (1993), Chap. 12; *From The Chair* (1978); J Crump, "General Average, Salvage and the Contract of Affreightment" [1985] LMCLQ 19; J Macdonald, "General Average Ancient and Modern" [1995] LMCLQ 480.
2. Dig. lib. xiv, tit. 2, fol. 1. On the Rhodian Law (the relevant principles in which seem to have derived from the Phoenicians), see generally W Ashburner, *The Rhodian Sea Law* (1909).
3. At least 1000 BC. The ancient origin of general average is a fact that continues to be emphasised: see, e.g., *Marida Ltd* v. *Oswal Steel (The Bijela)* [1993] 1 Lloyd's Rep 411, 420, per Hoffmann LJ.
4. (1801) 1 East 220, 228. See also *The Copenhagen* (1799) 1 Chr Rob 289, per Lord Stowell: "General average is for a loss incurred, towards which the whole concern is bound to contribute *pro rata*, because it was undergone for the general benefit and preservation of the whole."
5. In *Austin Friars SS Co Ltd* v. *Spillers & Bakers Ltd* [1915] 1 KB 833, 835, Bailhache J said that the statutory definition must now prevail, a view doubted by *Goff & Jones*, 334 n. 23, on the ground that "the Act is only concerned with marine insurance". However, the marine insurance aspects of general average are linked with its other aspects; and the Act mainly codified the common law, states the principle in broad terms and need not be interpreted restrictively. Moreover, according to the Marine Insurance Act 1906, s.87, the provisions of the Act may generally be overridden by

"(1) General average loss is a loss caused by or directly consequential on a general average act. It includes a general average expenditure as well as a general average sacrifice.

(2) There is a general average act where any extraordinary sacrifice or expenditure is voluntarily and reasonably made or incurred in time of peril for the purpose of preserving the property imperilled in the common adventure."

Rule A of the York-Antwerp Rules 1994, which in practice apply to the adjustment of general average,[6] provides[7]:

"There is a general average act when, and only when, any extraordinary sacrifice or expenditure is intentionally and reasonably made or incurred for the common safety for the purpose of preserving from peril the property involved in a common maritime adventure."

The word "average" means loss.[8] As a general rule, any loss or damage suffered by a particular interest, whether resulting from a danger which is peculiar to itself or to other interests as well, must be borne by that interest alone[9]: in marine insurance parlance, it is *particular average*. A *general average* situation occurs where a danger threatening a common adventure justifies action taken for the benefit of the interests imperilled—"a general average act". General average acts are of two types: extraordinary sacrifices and extraordinary expenditures. An extraordinary expenditure may be either expenditure actually made or the incurring of liability to make payment.[10] The result of a general average act is a general average loss. General average losses include: the loss suffered by virtue of a general average sacrifice; the loss or liability incurred by virtue of a general average expenditure; or any other loss directly consequent upon a general average act.[11] The person who suffers a general average loss is entitled to claim a contribution from those who benefit from it (hereafter "contributors") in proportion to the values of the interests which have been sacrificed and those which have been saved. The liability of such contributors may in turn be a loss for which they can claim against their own insurers and is also described as a general average loss.

---

agreement or usage, and in practice general average is in most cases governed by the York-Antwerp Rules. Any variation in nuance between the statutory and other definitions seems therefore to be of minimal, if any, practical importance.

6. See *infra*, 10–12. In *Australian Coastal Shipping Commission* v. *Green* [1971] 1 QB 456, 478, Lord Denning MR observed that the definitions in the York-Antwerp Rules supplement those in the Marine Insurance Act 1906, s.66(1)–(2).

7. See, e.g., *The Seapool* [1934] P 53.

8. So, strictly speaking, it is tautologous to speak of a general average loss or a particular average loss.

9. E.g., routine ship repairs or damage to cargo by overheating or insects. Of course, the fact that a person suffering a loss cannot claim a general average contribution does not mean that he may not have a claim against someone liable for his loss.

10. Thus, where "general average expenditure" is a consequence of incurring contractual liability, e.g. entering a towage contract, the general average act is the making of the contract and any payment falling due under the contract is a direct consequence of it: *Australian Coastal Shipping Commission* v. *Green* [1971] 1 QB 456.

11. See further *infra*, Chap. 3.

Partial losses[12]

Losses arising during maritime adventures are almost invariably the subject of marine insurance contracts. The treatment of general average under the law of marine insurance is dealt with specifically below.[13] It is, however, convenient at this stage to outline the classifications of loss employed. For purposes of marine insurance, a loss may be either total or partial.[14] A loss occurring for the purpose of general average may be total—for instance, where the whole of a single consignment of cargo is sacrificed by jettison, or where the vessel becomes a total loss as a result of, for example, a voluntary stranding but cargo is saved—though general average losses are generally grouped by the Marine Insurance Act 1906 under the heading of "Partial losses (including salvage and general average and particular charges)".[15] There are three types of partial loss, namely particular average losses, general average losses, and particular charges.

A "particular average" loss is a partial loss of the subject-matter insured, caused by a peril insured against, and which is not a general average loss or a particular charge.[16] The charges recoverable under maritime law by a salvor independently of contract are called "salvage charges" by the Marine Insurance Act 1906.[17] Subject to any express provision in the policy, salvage charges incurred in preventing a loss by perils insured against may be recovered as a loss by those perils.[18]

"General average" was defined in the previous section. General average losses include the expenses of services in the nature of salvage rendered by any person employed for hire by the assured or his agents for the purpose of averting a peril insured against[19]—i.e., they include salvage services provided under contract and not classifiable as "salvage charges" payable under the maritime law.

"Particular charges" are expenses incurred by or on behalf of the assured for the safety or preservation of the subject-matter insured, other than particular average or general average.[20] They include[21] the expenses of services "in the nature of salvage"[22] rendered by the assured or his agents.[23] Under the Marine

---

12. See generally, FD Rose, "Aversion and Minimisation of Loss", Chap. 7 of DR Thomas (ed.), *The Modern Law of Marine Insurance* (1996), 215–219.
13. Infra, Chap. 7.
14. Marine Insurance Act 1906, s.56(1).
15. Marine Insurance Act 1906, ss.64–66.
16. Marine Insurance Act 1906, s.64.
17. *Ibid.*, s.65(2).
18. *Ibid.*, s.65(1).
19. *Ibid.*, s.65(2).
20. *Ibid.*, s.64(2).
21. "Particular charges" seem to include steps taken to avert or minimise a loss (i) before the property is in the grip of a peril, the expense of which should be borne by the assured, and (ii) when the insured interest is in the grip of a peril, which is generally indemnifiable under suing and labouring provisions.
22. Though "in the nature of salvage", they cannot normally be salvage unless rendered by someone external to the adventure—a so-called "volunteer": see *Kennedy*, Chap. 6.
23. Marine Insurance Act 1906, s.65(2).

Insurance Act 1906[24] or by a contractual "sue and labour clause"[25] it is generally the duty of the assured to take such measures as may be reasonable for the purpose of averting or minimising an insured loss. Expenses thereby incurred— other than general average losses and contributions and salvage charges[26]—are generally subject to a separate indemnity under the policy.[27] Particular charges are expenses incurred for the benefit of the assured's own interest, rather than for the common adventure.

The legal status of services in the nature of salvage which are rendered under contract is not obvious.[28] The Marine Insurance Act 1906, s.65(2) states that "salvage charges" means the charges recoverable under maritime law by a salvor independently of contract and do not include the expenses of services rendered by any person employed for hire by the assured or his agents, which may be recovered as particular charges or as a general average loss according to the circumstances. In practice services in the nature of salvage rendered under a contract are unlikely to fall within the definition of general average since salvage contracts generally provide that each interest is separately liable for the service rendered in respect of his interest,[29] rather than, say, that the shipowner is liable for a service rendered to the common adventure (for which he may claim a general average contribution from the other interests).[30] One view is that "salvage charges" includes services in the nature of salvage obtained under contract so long as the relationship between the parties remains basically to be determined by the principles and rules of admiralty law, rather than by contract or the common law.[31] But the Marine Insurance Act 1906, s.65(2) specifically excludes "the expenses of... any person employed for hire", which would seem to exclude all contractual services from "salvage charges", so that, if contractual salvage also falls outside general average, it would constitute particular charges.

Though marine insurance contracts usually indemnify against all the losses under discussion, the distinctions between the types of claim are not solely academic. An insurer's liability for sue and labour charges is in addition to his overall liability under the rest of the policy[32]; salved values (at the place of safety at which salvage services terminate) and contributory values (at the place of

---

24. *Ibid.*, s.78(4).
25. See, e.g., Institute Time Clauses (Hulls) 1/11/95, cl.11; Institute Voyage Clauses (Hulls) 1/11/95, cl.9; Institute Cargo Clauses (A), (B) and (C), cl.16.
26. Marine Insurance Act 1906, s.78(2).
27. *Ibid.*, s.78(1), (3). See further *infra*, 105–106.
28. Salvage is discussed further *infra*, 51–54.
29. See *infra*, 52.
30. The suggestion in *Australian Coastal Shipping Commission* v. *Green* [1971] 1 QB 456, 480, per Lord Denning MR, that "If the tug had rendered salvage services on the usual terms of 'no cure, no pay', the contract would undoubtedly have been a 'general average act' " seems therefore to be wrong. Cf *Amerada Hess Corp* v. *S/T Mobil Apex* [1979] AMC 2406.
31. *Lowndes & Rudolf*, paras 6.05–6.07. But cf the speech of Lord Diplock in *Tojo Maru (Owners)* v. *NV Bureau Wijsmuller (The Tojo Maru)* [1972] AC 242 and *The Unique Mariner (No 2)* [1979] 1 Lloyd's Rep 37.
32. See the Marine Insurance Act 1906, s.78(1); Institute Time Clauses (Hulls) 1/11/95, cl.11.6; Institute Voyage Clauses (Hulls) 1/11/95, cl.9.6; Institute Cargo Clauses (A), (B) and (C), cl.16.

termination of the adventure) may differ; and salvees might make settlements with salvors on different bases from those on which general average is adjusted. However, the practical importance of these distinctions has been reduced by Rule VI of the York-Antwerp Rules 1994, which provides that "Expenditure incurred by the parties to the adventure in the nature of salvage, whether under contract or otherwise, shall be allowed in general average provided that the salvage operations were carried out for the purpose of preserving from peril the property involved in the common maritime adventure."[33]

Examples of general average

Examples of general average acts include jettisoning part of the cargo or ship's stores,[34] cutting away masts[35] or cables,[36] extinguishing a fire by pouring water into the hold,[37] scuttling the ship,[38] a voluntary stranding,[39] putting the cargo into lighters to lighten the vessel,[40] employing an agent to act on behalf of the adventure,[41] engaging salvage services,[42] paying money to secure the vessel's release from detention,[43] hypothecation of the ship[44] or sale of part of the cargo,[45] additional fuel consumption,[46] employment of towage services,[47] tipping the vessel to repair the propeller,[48] incurring damage to property belonging to third parties and consequent tortious liability.[49] General average losses include the expense of ship repairs and of reconditioning cargo, and general average disbursements[50]; and the cost of insuring general average disbursements.[51]

The classic example of a general average act is jettison of cargo, to which it has been said other situations should be analogous to qualify for a general average contribution.[52] In modern times, the act in question is much more likely to be a

---

33. See also the problem of differential salvage awards, *infra*, 54.
34. *Price* v. *Noble* (1811) 4 Taunt 123.
35. *Henderson* v. *Shankland* [1896] 1 QB 525. Cf *Shepherd* v. *Kottgen* (1872) 2 CPD 578.
36. *Birkley* v. *Presgrave* (1891) 1 East 220.
37. See *infra*, 49.
38. *Achard* v. *Ring* (1874) 2 Asp MLC 422; *Papayanni* v. *Grampian SS Co Ltd* (1896) 1 Com Cas 448.
39. Possibly: see *infra*, 44.
40. *Hallett* v. *Wigram* (1845) 9 CB 580, 608, per Cresswell J; *M'Call* v. *Houlder Bros* (1897) 2 Com Cas 129, 132, per Mathew J.
41. *Rose* v. *Bank of Australasia* [1894] AC 687, disapproving *Schuster* v. *Fletcher* (1878) 3 QBD 418.
42. But see *infra*, 53–54.
43. See *Woods* v. *Olsen* (1900) 99 Fed Rep 451. However, payment of a ransom might be illegal, thereby precluding a general average contribution: *Parsons* v. *Scott* (1810) 2 Taunt 362.
44. Cf *Duncan* v. *Benson* (1847) 1 Exch. 537.
45. York-Antwerp Rules 1994, Rule XX. See *infra*, 101 n. 81.
46. E.g., *Wilson* v. *Bank of Victoria* (1867) LR 2 QB 203.
47. *Australian Coastal Shipping Commission* v. *Green* [1971] 1 QB 456.
48. *M'Call* v. *Houlder Bros* (1897) 2 Com Cas 129.
49. *Austin Friars Steamship Co Ltd* v. *Spillers & Bakers Ltd* [1915] 3 KB 586.
50. See *infra*, 103.
51. York-Antwerp Rules 1994, Rule XX.
52. This is the classic case of general average.

loss incurred by the shipowner. In any case, however, it is not the nature of the act which is done which decides whether a general average contribution is due, but the purpose and effect of the act.

Justification of the doctrine

There is no single, authoritative explanation of the basis of the doctrine of general average. It has been justified in general terms on the grounds of mercantile custom, equity, convenience, utility and natural justice. Delivering the opinion of the Privy Council in *Strang, Steel & Co* v. *A Scott & Co*,[53] Lord Watson said:

"The principle upon which contribution becomes due does not appear to [their Lordships] to differ from that upon which claims of recompense for salvage services are founded. But, in any aspect, the rule of contribution has its foundation in the plainest equity."

In *Deering* v. *Earl of Winchelsea*,[54] the leading case on contribution generally, Eyre CB said,

"In the case of average there is no contract express or implied, nor any privity in any ordinary sense. This shews that contribution is founded on equality, and established by the law of all nations."

It is also supportable on public policy grounds:

"The rule of a general contribution, by rendering it immaterial whose property is taken in the first instant and material only that that should be taken which will most surely and effectually, and at least cost, save the whole, does away with this conflict in the captain's mind between interest and duty, leaves him alone with purely nautical considerations, and thus, no doubt, does more than any statesman or philanthropist can effect for the preservation of life and property at sea."[55]

When delivering the judgment of the Court of Appeal in *Wright* v. *Marwood*,[56] Bramwell LJ ventured the opinion, understandably attractive to a Victorian judge, that the rule arose "from an implied contract inter se to contribute 'by those interested' ". Counsel in one case, no doubt conscious of the presumed practice in the very early days of maritime trade, asserted that "this principle ... is based on a supposed bargain, between the master and the owners of the cargo, at the moment of danger ...".[57] In modern circumstances, however, it appears decidedly artificial. Indeed, as the basis of the claim for general average, this

---

53. (1889) 14 App Cas 601, 608.
54. (1787) 2 Bos & Pul 270 (Ex), 274.
55. *Lowndes & Rudolf*, 9th ed. (1964), para 11. See now *Australian Coastal Shipping Commission* v. *Green* [1971] 1 QB 456, 464–465, per Mocatta J; *Lowndes & Rudolf*, 12th ed. (1997), para 00.11.
56. (1881) 7 QBD 62, 67.
57. *The Bona* [1895] P 125, 136.

theory has been decisively rejected.[58] The basic rules derive from the maritime common law, not from contract,[59] albeit the common law rules may now be regarded as implied contractual terms and are commonly subject to express contractual provision.[60]

Given the fact that, rather than conclude a supposed bargain at the moment of danger, co-adventurers contemplate, indeed generally expressly provide for, general average, it can loosely be regarded as a form of mutual insurance. If so, the insurance of general average events would operate at two levels, since the parties commonly insure expressly against the consequences of such events. But the analogy should not be taken too far. Subject to contract, rights and obligations in general average are determined independently of insurance.[61]

The rejection of the implied contract theory of general average is in line with the more recent, general supersession of the theory in the law governing restitution of unjust enrichment,[62] of which general average seems to form a part.[63] The currently conventional theory of restitution is that it is available where (1) there has been an enrichment of the defendant (2) at the expense of the plaintiff (3) for which justice requires the defendant to make restitution to the plaintiff, though (4) subject to defences, (5) the normal measure of restitution being either the value received by the defendant or the value surviving.[64] General average appears to be a part of the law of restitution, albeit with its own specialised rules. In particular, it should be noted that the measure of a contributor's liability is not the amount of benefit he has received from the plaintiff but a proportion of the plaintiff's loss.[65]

The principle of requiring those benefiting from a loss incurred on their behalves to contribute towards payment to whomsoever incurs such a loss seems sound,[66] general average has a venerable (pre-)history and it is sensible to permit shipmasters the freedom to do what is best for all interests in time of peril. But the practice has been criticised as cumbersome, time-consuming and costly, as well as for tending to prejudice cargo interests, by the gradual extension of losses and expenses allowable under the York-Antwerp Rules and

---

58. *Burton* v. *English* (1883) 12 QBD 218, 220–221, per Brett MR (followed in *Austin Friars SS Co Ltd* v. *Spillers & Bakers Ltd* [1915] 1 QB 833, 837, per Bailhache J, and in *Tate & Lyle Ltd* v. *Hain SS Co* (1934) 39 Com Cas 259, 280, per Greer LJ); *Price* v. *Middle Dock Co* (1881) 44 LT 426, 428, per Williams J; *Milburn & Co* v. *Jamaica Fruit Transporting and Trading Co of London* [1900] 2 QB 540, 546 (AL Smith LJ), 550 (Vaughan Williams LJ). See also *Pirie Co* v. *Middle Dock Co* (1881) 44 LT 426, 428–429.

59. As was previously stated in *Deering* v. *Earl of Winchelsea* (1787) 2 Bos & Pul 270, 274, per Eyre CB (see *supra*, text to n. 54).

60. See, e.g., *Alma Shipping Corp* v. *Union of India (The Astrea)* [1971] 2 Lloyd's Rep 494; *Union of India* v. *EB Aaby's Rederi A/S (The Evje)* [1975] AC 797.

61. See *infra*, 106.

62. See, e.g., PBH Birks, *An Introduction to the Law of Restitution* (rev. ed., 1989), 29–39.

63. See further FD Rose, "General Average as Restitution" (1997) 113 LQR 569.

64. See Birks (*supra*, n. 62) 21.

65. See *infra*, 79. It may also be noted that a person claiming contribution for a benefit conferred may be entitled not to set off incidental benefits which he acquires: see, e.g., York-Antwerp Rules 1994, Rules F and XIV ("without regard to the saving, if any, to other interests").

66. See *supra*, 6.

carriers' growing ability to impose on cargo interests costs which they ought to bear themselves.[67] However, given the difficulty of finding consensus on which of a number of suggestions should be adopted to replace the current system, it seems likely to remain for the foreseeable future.[68]

The governing rules

The "common safety" of and "common benefit" to the common adventure[69]

The ancient doctrine of general average has, not surprisingly, been incorporated into the municipal law of different states. Perhaps less expectedly, however, no uniform international "common law" has emerged, and different states have different legal rules.[70] In particular, the tradition of English law is that general average is concerned with the "common safety", i.e., preservation of the property involved in the "common adventure"[71] (which is achievable without continuing the adventure).[72] However, Continental legal systems have focused on a commercial concern—the safe prosecution of the adventure,[73] which has been and may therefore, if somewhat vaguely, be referred to as "the common benefit". The Continental conception of the common adventure favours the shipowner by bringing within general average expenses for continuing the adventure which he would normally have to bear himself under English law, though it is not inherently defective for that reason.

There is an obvious overlap between the expressions "common safety" and "common benefit", especially since English law has always treated as a general average loss an expenditure incurred as a direct consequence of a general average act, even when incurred after the ship and cargo have been brought to a place of safety.[74] The essence of the distinction is that English law treats within general average those acts necessary to bring the common adventure to a place of safety (together with directly consequential losses)[75] but not further acts

---

67. It is, however, not necessarily the case that general average prejudices cargo owners. A shipowner who could not recover contributions for what is currently regarded as a general average loss might be justified in abandoning the voyage altogether where the circumstances were sufficiently serious.
68. See generally *Lowndes & Rudolf*, Appx 5; K Selmer, *The Survival of General Average* (1958); CS Hebditch, JA Macdonald and PA Stacey, *General Average Briefing Notes* (Association of Average Adjusters, 1996).
69. It is convenient to use different expressions to distinguish between the English and Continental ideas of the purpose(s) of general average. The distinction has long been recognised, though the two terms used cannot be said to be terms of art or as clearly distinct as might be desirable.
70. A notable difference is that between English and American rules.
71. The term "common adventure" is used to refer to the interests at risk, i.e. (primarily), ship, cargo and freight.
72. See, e.g., *Royal Mail Steam Packet Co* v. *English Bank of Rio* (1887) 19 QBD 362, 370–371.
73. See, e.g., *Société Nouvelle d'Armement* v. *Spillers & Bakers Ltd* [1917] 1 KB 865, 869.
74. See further *infra*, Chap. 3.
75. See *infra*, Chap. 3.

necessary to complete the safe prosecution of the adventure, which are strictly speaking a cost to be borne by freight.[76] The extended idea of "common benefit" is a factor which has become a concern of English practice by its influence on the internationally based York-Antwerp Rules.[77] However, the difference between the common law and the York-Antwerp Rules 1994 should not be exaggerated: repairs to enable further prosecution of the adventure have traditionally been included within general average by English law so long as they are properly treated as losses consequent upon a general average act; and most port of refuge allowances under Rule XI(b)[78] of the Rules only arise after a ship has entered a port of refuge for the common safety under Rule X(a).[79]

Salvage and necessity generally

Dealing as it does with claims for benefits conferred in situations of necessity, general average has an affinity with the law of salvage[80] and with the general law on necessity.[81] However, the three areas have tended to develop separately.[82] In particular, whereas salvage has always been a subject of admiralty law and jurisdiction,[83] general average was largely taken over and developed by the common law courts,[84] albeit it has more recently reverted to admiralty jurisdiction.[85] Lord Wright once said that, "general average, like salvage, is still essentially a matter of maritime equity and should be kept apart from common law or equitable ideas of equity or quasi-contract"[86] (or, in modern terminology, the general law of restitution for unjust enrichment). Nonetheless, the three areas do share common characteristics,[87] which it is important to recognise while paying proper respect to their idiosyncrasies.

---

76. See in particular the decision of the majority of the Court of Appeal in *Svendsen* v. *Wallace Bros* (1884) 13 QBD 69 (a decision which is discussed *infra*, 22). Brett MR was clearly in no doubt that English law should retain its purity: "I should doubt the expediency of making the law of the greatest commercial and maritime country in the world bend to the law of other countries where commercial operations are far less extensive, and where commercial adventure is far more timid": *ibid.*, 73.
77. Cf Rule A of the York-Antwerp Rules 1994, which defines a general average act as one done to preserve "... *only* ... for the *common safety* for the purpose of preserving ... the *property* involved in a common maritime *adventure*" (emphasis added).
78. See *infra*, 58.
79. See *infra*, 57.
80. See DW Steel and FD Rose, *Kennedy's Law of Salvage*, 5th ed. (1985); G Brice, *Maritime Law of Salvage*, 2nd ed. (1993) with Supp (1995). See further *supra*, 4, *infra*, 51–54.
81. See *Goff & Jones*, Chap. 15.
82. *Falcke* v. *Scottish Imperial Ins. Co* (1886) 34 Ch D 234, 248–249, per Bowen LJ. See also *The Tojo Maru* [1972] AC 242, 268, per Lord Reid.
83. Though see *Hartfort* v. *Jones* (1698) 1 Ld Raym 393.
84. See *The Constancia* (1846) 2 W Rob 487. Cf *Place* v. *Potts* (1855) 5 HLC 383.
85. See Supreme Court Act 1981, s.20(2)(j) (salvage), (q) (general average). See further *infra*, 94.
86. *Legal Essays and Addresses* (1939), 55.
87. See e.g. FD Rose, "Restitution for the Rescuer" (1989) 9 OJLS 167.

Variation by contract

It is essential in practice to recognise that the "common law" rules on general average apply only to the extent that no, or incomplete, provision is made by contract.[88] General average may be, and commonly is, regulated (whether extended, limited, or even excluded) by contract.[89] Moreover, whether the parties' rights and liabilities regarding general average are initially governed by the common law or by a contract of carriage or charterparty, it is in practice common for them to be superseded by a new contract at the time of discharge.[90]

However, whereas freedom of contract is prone to facilitate divergence, it has been the principal means of achieving uniformity in this area. Though uniformity in international trade is commonly achieved by the municipal implementation of an international convention, in the case of general average confusion has in practice been avoided by universal practical adherence to an internationally agreed set of rules, the York-Antwerp Rules.[91]

The York-Antwerp Rules

The York-Antwerp Rules do not have inherent binding force[92] but their wide acceptance is shown by their frequent incorporation into charterparties, bills of lading and marine insurance policies in standard form clauses. The Rules have been developed since the mid-nineteenth century for the purpose of removing differences between municipal laws, and for reaching general agreement on

---

88. *Svendsen* v. *Wallace* (1885) 10 App Cas 404, 415, per Lord Blackburn; *Goulandris Bros Ltd* v. *Goldman & Sons Ltd* [1958] 1 QB 74, 91, per Pearson J (common law applies where no provision in the York-Antwerp Rules). See also *infra*, 76–77, and the discussion of the foreign adjustment clause (*infra*, 116–118) and of the governing law and practice (*infra*, 94–97). No doubt it is only a matter of time before the courts have to decide that there are legal (in particular statutory) limits on the parties' freedom to contract in respect of general average, e.g., under the Rome Convention: see *infra*, 96.

89. *Simonds* v. *White* (1824) 2 B & C 805, 811, per Abbott CJ; *Stewart* v. *West India and Pacific Steamship Co* (1873) LR 8 QB 88, affd *ibid.*, 362 (though cf *Atwood* v. *Sellar* (1879) 4 QBD 342); *Union of India* v. *EB Aaby's Rederi A/S (The Evje)* [1975] AC 797; *Marida Ltd* v. *Oswal Steel (The Bijela)* [1993] 1 Lloyd's Rep 411, 420, per Hoffmann LJ ("there seems to be no rigid principle that sacrifice or expenditure cannot qualify for general average because the owner was under a contractual duty to make it"). See also *infra*, 105.

Though the parties are in a contractual relationship in which there is normally liability to contribute in general average, the liability may arise at common law: see, e.g., *Marvigor C.N. SA* v. *Romanoexport State Co for Foreign Trade (The Corinthian Glory)* [1977] 2 Lloyd's Rep 280, 287, per Donaldson J (charterers whose liability under the charterparty had ceased and who had become owners of the cargo by the time of the general average act could be liable under the maritime law rather than under the York-Antwerp Rules).

90. See *infra*, 83.

91. They are by far the most important rules dealing with general average, though not the only ones: see, e.g., *infra*, Chap. 2 n. 37.

92. The ubiquity of the Rules does not require their enforcement as a kind of customary law, particularly since the content of the rules is subject to revision. Cf EP Ellinger [1984] LMCLQ 578, 583–586.

matters of detail and principle.[93] As Hoffmann LJ has commented, "It is ... not surprising that those concerned with international shipping sought to devise general conditions which, even if to some extent arbitrary and not necessarily reflecting a single consistent principle, were at least clear in their practical application."[94] The Rules have been regularly revised, most recently in 1994.[95]

A Rule of Interpretation provides that, in those circumstances where they apply, the Rules override inconsistent law and practice.[96] Thereafter, the Rules are divided into seven lettered rules stating general principles and twenty-two, more specific Rules. General average should be adjusted according to the lettered Rules, but subject to an overriding requirement of reasonableness[97] and in particular to the numbered Rules, even if the numbered Rules result in qualification of the general principles.[98] In respect of the numbered Rules at least, it seems that each Rule should be interpreted so as to be given practical effect according to its terms.[99] If a situation fails to qualify for a general average

---

93. The York Rules of 1864 and the York-Antwerp Rules of 1877 and 1890 dealt with matters of detail. Subsequent York-Antwerp Rules (1924, 1950, 1974 and 1994) have dealt specifically with matters of both detail and principle.

94. *Marida Ltd* v. *Oswal Steel (The Bijela)* [1993] 1 Lloyd's Rep 411, 421.

95. The York Rules 1864 and the York-Antwerp Rules 1877, 1890, 1924, 1950 and 1974 are set out in *Lowndes & Rudolf*, Appx 2. They are set out together with the 1994 Rules in *Hudson*, Appxs 1–2. Note that the contractual incorporation of a specific set of Rules may include an interim revision of existing rules (e.g., the 1974 Rules were amended in 1990) but not a different version of the Rules (albeit many of the provisions of new versions of the Rules repeat earlier provisions). Unless otherwise provided, references to the Rules here are to the York-Antwerp Rules 1994.

96. Though, in cases where the Rules make no provision, the general law continues to apply: *Goulandris Bros Ltd* v. *Goldman & Sons Ltd* [1958] 1 QB 74, 91, per Pearson J. It is possible to override the (limited) provision for general average in the Marine Insurance Act 1906, s.66, since the obligations implied by the Act may be varied by agreement or usage: *ibid.*, s.87.

97. In the Rule Paramount: see *infra*, 39.

98. *Corfu Navigation Co* v. *Mobil Shipping Co Ltd (The Alpha)* [1991] 2 Lloyd's Rep 515, 518. The Rule of Interpretation, giving precedence to the numbered Rules, overrides the decision in *Vlassopoulos* v. *British and Foreign Marine Insurance Co (The Makis)* [1929] 1 KB 187 (that the numbered Rules were subservient to the lettered Rules) and implements "the Makis agreement" of January 1929, which was made to disapply the decision in practice.

99. *Marida Ltd* v. *Oswal Steel (The Bijela)* [1992] 1 Lloyd's Rep 636; aff'd [1993] 1 Lloyd's Rep 411; rvrsd [1994] 1 WLR 615 involved the interpretation and the interrelationship of several of the Rules. (The case is discussed *infra*, 62–63.) Hobhouse J, whose judgment was affirmed by Neill and Mann LJJ, found that, on a literal construction, Rule XIV was ineffective to support the claim for general average and should be redrafted. Hoffmann LJ (dissenting in the Court of Appeal) was reluctant "to accept such a construction of a standard condition intended to be contained in a commercial document and which in fact has been in use for nearly seventy years" and adopted certain assumptions "to give business efficacy to the rule and as a matter of principle and common sense": [1993] 1 Lloyd's Rep 411, 423. The House of Lords agreed with the result achieved by Hoffmann LJ but not with his method of interpretation, indicating that the Rules should be interpreted literally ("even if the paragraph is wholly devoid of effect, the rules must be given their plain meaning": [1994] 1 WLR 615, 618), thereby returning to the approach of Hobhouse J and the Court of Appeal majority but with a different result. Given the appallingly obscure drafting of Rule XIV, the real effect of *The Bijela* seems to be that each of the numbered York-Antwerp Rules must be interpreted to be given effect individually according to its terms—i.e., a combination of literal and purposive construction, best exemplified by the approach of Hoffmann LJ.

claim under the numbered Rules, it may still do so under the lettered Rules.[100] In effect the Rules are "a series of exceptions to the wider principles of general average".[101]

In practice the rules governing average adjustment are supplemented by the Rules of Practice of the Association of Average Adjusters.[102] Though not legally binding, such rules are of persuasive force.[103] However, neither these Rules nor the general usage of average adjusters can override inconsistent legal or contractual provision.[104]

Claims procedure[105]

In general, a plaintiff claiming a general average contribution can assert a lien.[106] In most cases this is easily achieved since most claims are brought by shipowners. The lien is normally released in return for the defendant's providing an average bond, whereby he undertakes to pay the contribution due and to provide particulars of the value of his property, and security in the form of either or both of a cash deposit or (more commonly) a "guarantee"[107] from his insurers.[108] The claimant then generally appoints an average adjuster, who in turn carries out a detailed and often lengthy assessment of the rights and liabilities of all interested parties, though, unless otherwise agreed, his adjustment is not binding on them.[109]

---

100. *The Seapool* [1934] P 53.
101. J Macdonald [1995] LMCLQ 480, 480.
102. The Association was formed in 1869, its objects being "The promotion of correct principles in the adjustment of averages, uniformity of practice amongst Average Adjusters and the maintenance of good professional conduct". Its Rules, of which *general* average adjustment forms two sections, were originally drawn up to codify the Customs of Lloyd's and to introduce uniformity of practice. They are periodically revised. Section B contains general rules affecting the adjustment of general average or the duties of adjusters, whatever the basis of adjustment. Section F is of restricted significance in practice, dealing with adjustment of general average under general English law and practice (i.e., where the York-Antwerp Rules do not apply). For the text of the Rules of Practice of the Association of Average Adjusters, see *infra*, Appx 3.
103. See *Svendsen* v. *Wallace* (1885) 10 App Cas 404, 416, per Lord Blackburn: "a general practice, long continued amongst English average adjusters, affords strong ground for thinking that the practice is one which is not in general inconvenient, and that it throws a considerable onus on those who impugn it to shew that the particular circumstances are such as to render an adherence to the practice in that case against principle." See also *Atwood* v. *Sellar & Co* (1879) 4 QBD 342, 352, per Manisty J. Cf *Union of India* v. *EB Aaby's Rederi A/S (The Evje)* [1975] AC 797.
104. *Marida Ltd* v. *Oswal Steel (The Bijela)* [1992] 1 Lloyd's Rep 636, 641–642, per Hobhouse J; [1993] 1 Lloyd's Rep 411, 419, per Mann LJ. This, of course, remains true even if the precise ambit of the legal or contractual provision requires resolution.
105. See further *infra*, 81–83.
106. See *infra*, 81–82.
107. See *infra*, 82–83.
108. For Lloyd's standard forms for general average security, see *infra*, Appx 5.
109. See further *infra*, 92–93.

CHAPTER 2

THE CONDITIONS FOR GENERAL AVERAGE

Burden of proof

Rule E of the York-Antwerp Rules 1994 generally states the common law rule that the onus of proof is upon the party claiming a general average contribution to show that the loss claimed is properly allowable in general average.[1] Specific stipulation may also be made, albeit without necessarily enlarging the general requirement. Thus, Rule VII provides that:

"Damage caused to any machinery and boilers of a ship which is ashore and in a position of common peril, in endeavouring to refloat, shall be allowed in general average when shown to have arisen from an actual intention to float the ship for the common safety at the risk of such damage . . ."[2]

In general, however, it is necessary for the following conditions to be satisfied.[3]

1. Subject-matter

In English law, general average is traditionally understood to concern preservation of property[4] which is involved in, and at risk during, a maritime adventure in accordance with the customs of the trade,[5] principally ship, cargo and freight.

Cargo

In general, contribution is payable by the owners[6] of goods[7] carried for commercial purposes and attracting liability to pay freight, and not by the

---

1. See *Corfu Navigation Co* v. *Mobil Shipping Co Ltd (The Alpha)* [1991] 2 Lloyd's Rep 515; *Sea-Land Services Inc* v. *Aetna Insurance Co (The Beauregard)* [1976] AMC 2164; [1977] 2 Lloyd's Rep 84. Rule E also provides for timely collection of evidence: see *infra*, 85.
2. York-Antwerp Rules 1994, Rule VII.
3. There is no requirement that the property be insured or that it be uninsured. See *infra*, 106.
4. See *supra*, 8.
5. See *infra*, 65–66.
6. The liability also applies to Government property: *US* v. *Wilder, re Schooner Jasper* (1838) 3 Sumner 308 (Story J).
7. Including containers: see further *Lowndes & Rudolf*, para 17.66. It also includes specie, a cargo which attracts special difficulties: e.g., whether, being less susceptible to destruction, it is as subject

13

owners of personal effects unless carried under a bill of lading for freight.[8] Items of a personal nature which might be carried as merchandise or used on the voyage (e.g. jewellery) are in principle excepted if they are on board in the latter capacity. Rule XVII of the York-Antwerp Rules 1994 provides that "Mails,[9] passengers' luggage and personal effects and accompanied private motor cars[10] shall not contribute in general average." Owners of items exempted from liability to contribute are nevertheless entitled to claim a contribution if they incur a loss as a result of a general average act.[11]

Freight

There are different bases for classifying and calculating freight, so it is important to ascertain how the freight in question is calculated and at whose risk it is in order to discover whether and to what extent it has been sacrificed or saved as a result of a general average act.[12] Pre-paid freight at the risk of a charterer has been held liable to contribute[13]; but freight at the risk of the charterer or cargo owner has generally been treated as forming part of the value of the cargo, and therefore as not requiring independent treatment.[14] However, if it is at the risk

---

to the common danger as other interests; whether a service to this valuable cargo is incurred solely for its benefit rather than for the common adventure; whether, because of its value, the master should prefer saving this cargo to other, or all, interests; and whether early removal of this cargo from the common danger unfairly relieves its owner from liability to contribute for subsequent general average services. See *Royal Mail Steam Packet Co Ltd* v. *English Bank of Rio de Janeiro Ltd* (1887) 19 QBD 362, esp 375–376, per Wills J.

8. This applies to the personal effects of both passengers and the master and crew. See *Brown* v. *Stapyleton* (1827) 4 Bing 119; 12 JB Moore 334. See also *Peters* v. *Milligan* (1787) 1 Park 296. Cf *Heye* v. *North German Lloyd* (1887) 36 Fed Rep 705.

9. Mails are also traditionally regarded as excepted at common law. The exception for mails may be justified on the grounds that they have no definite pecuniary value (*Lowndes & Rudolf*, para 17.59) or on the grounds of maintaining the secrecy of the post and the difficulty of enforcing a lien (see *The Goeben* (1912) (Hamburg CA), aff'd (1913) (Imperial Court at Leipzig), noted *Lowndes & Rudolf*, para 17.58 n. 62. It has been argued that bank notes should be excepted on the ground that they are not property but merely evidence of property (2 Phillips, para 1397); *Lowndes & Rudolf*, para 17.69, argues that securities should only be excepted to the extent that their loss puts an end to the obligation which it creates.

10. The value of passengers' motor cars is outweighed by the delay, inconvenience and ill-will which would result from having to complete general average formalities: *Lowndes & Rudolf*, para 17.60.

11. See, e.g., *Lowndes & Rudolf*, para 17.58.

12. Freight will be at the risk of the carrier if it is ordinary freight collect (payable at destination on so much of the cargo as is delivered, whether or not in a damaged condition—therefore not earned on those parts of the cargo which are not delivered in merchantable condition), pro rata freight (which is payable by agreement and not for mere partial performance of the contract) or lump sum freight (payable in full if part of the cargo is delivered—therefore lost if none is delivered). It is at the cargo owner's risk if it is non-returnable advance freight or freight deemed earned "ship and/or cargo lost or not lost".

13. *Frayes (or Trayes)* v. *Worms* (1865) 19 CB(NS) 159.

14. See *Fletcher* v. *Alexander* (1868) LR 3 CP 375; *Maldonado* v. *British & Foreign Marine Insurance Co* (1910) 182 Fed Rep 744; York-Antwerp Rules 1994, Rule XVII ("The value of the cargo shall include the cost of insurance and freight unless and insofar as such freight is at the risk of interests other than cargo").

of the carrier, it constitutes a separate interest for purposes of general average.[15] Thus, Rule XV of the York-Antwerp Rules 1994 provides that:

"Loss of freight arising from damage to or loss of cargo shall be made good as general average, either when caused by a general average act, or when the damage to or loss of cargo is so made good."

Human lives

Danger may imperil both property and lives, so a claim for salvage or general average contribution may successfully be brought by a plaintiff who has benefited both. However, whereas admiralty judges were in practice content to inflate salvage awards to reflect the benefit to human life, as admiralty jurisdiction was originally based on a proceeding against property, the jurisdiction to award salvage simply for preserving human life was not recognised at common law but was conferred by statute.[16] Not having developed in admiralty, general average is not subject to this inhibition and, in the only known judicial utterance on the point in English law, a dictum of the Court of Appeal[17] supports the view that (at least where the life or lives to be preserved form part of the original adventure[18]) a general average claim should succeed where the sacrifice or expenditure is incurred for the preservation of life. However, whereas the dictum correctly reflects the view that a sacrifice may be made to save life[19] and that the act in question may justify a general average claim, it does not go so far as to support the view that the claim should succeed in the unlikely[20] event that there is no danger to either ship, freight or cargo, and that such interests should bear the cost of benefiting a different interest or collection of interests,[21] none of whom are themselves ever liable as contributors.[22] The issue is accommodated by the assumption that general average is

---

15. *Pirie* v. *Middle Dock Co* (1881) 4 Asp MLC 388; *Cox* v. *May* (1815) 4 M & S 152, 159, citing *Williams* v. *London Assurance Co* (1813) 1 M & S 318 (freight payable on arrival home for voyage out and home liable to contribute in full for general average loss incurred on outward voyage), which was applied in *Carisbrook Steamship Co* v. *London and Provincial Marine and General Insurance Co* [1902] 2 KB 681, citing also *The Progress* (1810) Edw 210 and *Moran* v. *Jones* (1857) 7 E & B 523. However, freight on a subsequent voyage should not be taken into account if not at risk at the time of the general average act. See *infra*, 102.

16. See *Kennedy*, Chap. 3(2) and now Merchant Shipping Act 1995, s.224, Sched. 11, Part I, art. 16.

17. *Montgomery & Co* v. *Indemnity Mutual Marine Insurance Co* [1902] 1 KB 734, 740 (CA: per Vaughan Williams LJ). *"Pour Sauver leurs corps la neef, et les darrées"*, Jugemens d'Oleron, art. 8. See the other sources cited by *Arnould*, para 918 n. 22. Contra *Shoe* v. *Low Moor Iron Co* (1891) 46 Fed Rep 125; 49 Fed Rep 252.

18. See *Dabney* v. *New England Co* (1867) 14 Allen 300, discussed *infra*, 20 n.54.

19. *The Gratitudine* (1801) 3 C Rob 240.

20. But not unimaginable: e.g. if cargo were ejected from a sealed compartment into which persons retreated to avoid noxious gases.

21. This in any event raises the objection that, whether the threat is to one life or more, there is basically no danger to the common adventure.

22. Cf *infra*, 82–83.

concerned with either property or commerce[23] (although admittedly it casts doubt on the validity of that debate). Certainly, action to save lives is outside the definition of a general average act in marine insurance law[24] and in the York-Antwerp Rules.[25] It is probably a matter for the general law of restitution, if anything.[26]

2. The right only arises from a maritime adventure in the nature of a voyage

General average services may be performed at sea or on land.[27] However, no matter how closely sacrifice or expenditure is connected with a maritime adventure, general average contribution may not be claimed unless the danger giving rise to the loss or damage arises during a maritime adventure in the nature of a voyage.[28] The doctrine only applies, at least so far as English law has been concerned, to ships or goods in peril at sea.[29] Thus, nothing in the nature of general average contribution may be claimed by the owner of goods stored in another's warehouse (even a floating warehouse) which are damaged during the extinction of a fire in that warehouse. Similarly, goods which are transferred from a ship to a railway for carriage to their final destination cannot, after transfer, be the subject of a general average claim[30] and it would seem to make no difference that they were being carried under a through bill of lading. The situation would be no different where goods have been unloaded from one ship and are about to be loaded on to another.

Although it is clear that the law of general average in general does not extend to goods on land or, it seems, to goods being carried in an aircraft,[31] there are no precise guidelines as to the meaning of a "maritime adventure in the nature of a voyage". Definitions of "marine" and "maritime" commonly indicate that the adventure must be connected with the sea but that is of little help since it would seem to apply to goods which have been transferred to land but which have at

---

23. See *supra*, 8. See also Dig. 14.2.2.2, quoting the opinion of Paulus, which has been translated to the effect that "The amount of loss must be divided in proportion to the value of goods. No valuation can be made of free persons" and/or "The total amount of the loss should be apportioned in relation to the market value of the property, freemen not being valued."
24. Marine Insurance Act 1906, s.66(2).
25. York-Antwerp Rules 1994, Rule A.
26. See Rose (1989) 9 OJLS 167; NJ Gaskell, *Current Law Statutes 1995*, 21–248.
27. See, e.g., *Rose* v. *Bank of Australia* [1894] AC 687 (cargo landed in wet condition and stored in a field taken by land to Boulogne, where steps taken to protect from deterioration and destruction before forwarding to destination in London).
28. The definition covers events on a ship which has not completed unloading for, although the voyage may be over, the maritime adventure is not necessarily so: *Whitecross Wire Co* v. *Savill* (1882) 8 QBD 653, 661, per Lord Coleridge CJ; *Achard* v. *Ring* (1874) 31 LT (NS) 647.
29. *Falcke* v. *Scottish Imperial Ins Co* (1886) 34 Ch D 234, 248–249, per Bowen LJ.
30. *Crooks* v. *Allan* (1879) 5 QBD 38, 40. Cf *Whitecross Wire Co* v. *Savill* (1882) 8 QBD 653.
31. Cf Macdonald [1995] LMCLQ 480, 482.

some time been on the sea. Similarly, the definitions of "marine insurance", "marine adventure" and "maritime perils" in the first three sections of the Marine Insurance Act 1906 take us no further since not only are they basically concerned with the particular field of marine insurance but, although contracts of marine insurance are *prima facie* limited to perils consequent on or incidental to the navigation of the sea, it is recognised that a contract of marine insurance may be extended so as to protect the assured against losses on inland waters or on any land risk which may be incidental to any sea voyage.[32]

Thus, general average appears to arise only in respect of ships and cargoes which are afloat. There appears to be the further qualification that the vessel must be used in navigation, so that there is an adventure in the nature of a voyage: thus, floating warehouses would not be involved in general average claims.[33]

It is an open question whether the principle applies to voyages on inland waters, such as rivers or canals or lakes, or to voyages solely within the confines of a port, or whether the vessel must be on the high seas, on sea water or on tidal water.[34] Therefore, it will be for the courts to decide whether they are going to apply the particular maritime rules instead of the general common law rules,[35] in recognition of the fact that voyages by water may attract the operation of particular rules whether the water is tidal or non-tidal. Possibly, there will be more inclination to treat within general average the case of goods carried under through bills of lading which are transhipped from ocean-going to river-going vessels,[36] though in some localities the matter is dealt with by specific provision.[37]

3. There must be a real danger

There must be a real danger to the property involved in the common adventure. Traditionally this has meant a threat to the physical integrity of the property involved. This conforms to the common law notion that general average is concerned with the preservation of property. Despite the practical influence, through the York-Antwerp Rules, of the Continental concern for the safe prosecution of the adventure for the common benefit,[38] it nonetheless remains

---

32. Marine Insurance Act 1906, s.2(1).
33. See also *Lowndes & Rudolf*, para A.50. A ship which had been loaded but which had not yet begun to sail would seem, however, to come within the principle: *Apollinaris Co* v. *Nord Deutsche Insurance Co* [1904] 1 KB 252.
34. Cf the position of claims for maritime salvage on inland waters and harbours in *The Goring* [1988] AC 831. See now the Merchant Shipping Act 1995, s.224(2), Sched. 11, Part II, para. 2.
35. An approach which would probably have found little favour with Bowen LJ: see *Falcke* v. *Scottish Imperial Insurance Co* (1886) 34 Ch D 234, 248–249.
36. See *Apollinaris Co* v. *Nord Deutsche Ins Co* [1904] 1 KB 252. Cf *Charter SS Co Ltd* v. *Bowring Jones & Tidy Ltd* (1930) 36 Ll L Rep 272.
37. Thus, the I.V.R. Rhine Rules, the Danube Rules and the Bratislava Convention make provision for general average on the Rhine and Danube rivers.
38. See *supra*, 8–9.

the case that the mere risk of loss of economic value or commercial utility is insufficient[39]; there must still be a danger to the safe prosecution of the adventure.

The master of a vessel must conduct himself as a person of ordinary firmness and sound judgement. He is expected to cope with ordinary perils of the sea (even when they are rendered more plentiful, as in wartime) and it is only when a danger becomes a reality that he is entitled to incur general average losses where they are the only means of averting the peril. Thus, in *Société Nouvelle d'Armement* v. *Spillers & Bakers*[40] a claim for contribution was disallowed on failure to prove real and imminent danger of submarine attack, even though no one would have been surprised if such an attack had occurred. However, if a danger really does exist, it is not necessary that the peril be immediate or that disaster be imminent, and the law recognises the necessity of taking precautionary measures in order to avert disaster in good time.[41]

Nevertheless, the mere potential of danger to the common adventure is insufficient. Thus the mere fact that a vessel is aground does not mean there is a danger for general average purposes,[42] a point emphasised by the requirement in Rule VII of the York-Antwerp Rules 1994 that, for damage caused to machinery and boilers in endeavouring to refloat to be allowed as general average, the ship must be both "ashore *and in a position of peril*".[43]

Similarly, the fact that the master's reasonable and bona fide belief that there is an imminent peril may not give rise to any claim in general average unless a peril actually exists. Thus, in *Joseph Watson & Son Ltd* v. *Firemen's Fund Insurance Co of San Francisco*,[44] Rowlatt J thought there was no general average loss in respect of cargo damaged by steam turned into the hold to extinguish a fire which the master had mistakenly assumed to be burning.[45] The better course would seem to be to judge the case according to the master's reasonable belief at the time. The approach in *Joseph Watson* is mitigated to some extent in that, once a peril has been found to exist, it is immaterial that it differs from the one which the master suspected.[46] Furthermore, if a peril does exist, it seems

---

39. *The Barge J Whitney* [1968] AMC 995 (arbitration at San Francisco): asphalt which had solidified on a barge and was not removable except at enormous expense because of the non-functioning of heating coils, so then of no economic value but capable of having value restored, was not in peril for general average purposes.

40. [1917] 1 KB 865.

41. *Vlassopoulos* v. *British and Foreign Marine Insurance Co (The Makis)* [1929] 1 KB 187, 199, per Roche J; *Lawrence* v. *Minturn* (1854) 17 How 100. Cf *Charter SS Co Ltd* v. *Bowring, Jones & Tidy Ltd* (1930) 36 Ll L Rep 272.

42. *Trafalgar Steamship Co* v. *British and Foreign Marine Insurance Co* [1904] *Shipping Gazette*, November 18; *Daniolos* v. *Bunge & Co* (1937) 59 Ll L Rep 175.

43. Emphasis added.

44. [1922] 2 KB 355.

45. This is a dictum, the case turning on the decision that the loss was not one which had been insured against. See also *Whitecross Wire Co* v. *Savill* (1882) 8 QBD 653, 662, per Brett LJ. Cf *Kacianoff* v. *China Traders Insurance Co Ltd* [1914] 3 KB 1121.

46. *The Wordsworth* (1898) 88 Fed Rep 313; *The West Imboden* [1936] AMC 696. Rowlatt J distinguished *The Wordsworth* without disapproving it in *Joseph Watson* and it seems English and

THE DANGER MUST BE TO A COMMON ADVENTURE   19

that the court is likely to accept the view of the master formed at the time the peril existed as to what would be the outcome of that peril.[47] The York-Antwerp Rules do not seem to affect the position.[48]

4. The danger must be to a common adventure and the action taken must be necessary[49] for the safety of the common adventure or a direct consequence of such action

This section embraces four related conditions: (a) there must be a common adventure (and not a single interest at risk); (b) the danger must be to the common adventure; (c) the action taken must be necessary to avert or minimise the threat, or a direct consequence of such earlier action; and (d) the action must be taken for the safety of the common adventure.

There must be a common adventure

It is a distinguishing feature of general average that there should be a common adventure, with at least two interests actually exposed to the danger of damage.[50] The presence of a single interest should in principle give rise only to a particular average loss or a particular charge.[51] However, a single interest which is divisible into separate parts (e.g., hull and machinery) may by agreement be treated as separate interests so that action taken for the benefit of such an interest as a whole may be adjusted as general average[52] and parties may agree that, even where only one interest is at risk, their relationship is to be governed by rules of general average.[53]

There is no English authority on whether it is a general average situation when the interests involved are not at risk on a single vessel.[54] The issue may

---

American law agree on this point. The reasonableness of measures taken to avoid disaster is presumably measured against the peril which actually existed.

47. "The question . . . is, not whether the event shews the wisdom of what was done, but whether, under all the circumstances, it was the exercise of a reasonable, prudent, sound judgment": *Corrie* v. *Coulthard* (1877) 3 Asp MLC 546n, 547n, per Cockburn CJ. See also *M'Call & Co* v. *Houlder Bros* (1897) 2 Com Cas 129.

48. See *Vlassopoulos* v. *British and Foreign Marine Insurance Co (The Makis)* [1929] 1 KB 187; *The Seapool* [1934] P 53; *Daniolos* v. *Bunge & Co Ltd* (1937) 59 Ll L Rep 175.

49. In *Pirie & Co* v. *Middle Dock Co* (1881) 44 LT 426, 430, Watkin Williams J states as a separate condition that "There must be a necessity for the sacrifice."

50. *The Brigella* [1893] P 189; *Kemp* v. *Halliday* (1865) 34 LJQB 533, 542, per Blackburn J; by implication from the Marine Insurance Act 1906, s.66(1).

51. See *supra*, 3.

52. *Oppenheim* v. *Fry* (1863) 3 B & S 874; aff'd (1864) 5 B & S 348 (insurance policy on steamer, hull and machinery separately valued, "average payable on the whole or on each as if separately insured").

53. See the Institute Time Clause (Hulls) 1/11/95, cl. 10.3, which provides that the York-Antwerp Rules 1994—but excluding Rules XI(d) (*infra*, 53), XX (*infra*, 101, 103) and XXI (*infra*, 85)—shall apply to ships in ballast and not under charter.

54. Foreign authority is inconclusive. In *The JP Donaldson* (1897) 167 US 599 (US SC) (cf *The John Perkins* (1822) Ware (US) 87; 3 Kent Comm 243n), there was held to be no common adventure between sailing barges and a tug towing them on the terms of receiving part of the freight

arise where a tug is towing a (laden or unladen) barge or an oil rig.[55] In principle, the case may fall within general average so far as two conditions are satisfied (which will not inevitably be the case): the danger is common to all the relevant interests; and the general average act is for the benefit of all such interests. Rule B of the York-Antwerp Rules 1994 now provides that there is a common adventure when one or more vessels are towing or pushing another vessel or vessels, provided that they are all involved in commercial activities and not in a salvage operation. The York-Antwerp Rules are stated to apply when measures are taken to preserve the vessels and their cargoes, if any, from a common peril; but a vessel is not in common peril with another vessel or vessels if by simply disconnecting from the other vessel or vessels she is in safety, though if the disconnection is itself a general average act the common adventure continues.

Duration of the common adventure

Where there has been a common adventure, liability to a general average contribution continues while an interest continues to be involved in that common adventure. Thus, where part of the cargo has been discharged and a danger afterwards arises which threatens the ship and all that remains on board, only the interests imperilled may be called on to contribute to general average. Thus the owners of cargo remaining on board a vessel on which a fire breaks out can claim contribution for damage caused to their property during the extinction of the fire.[56] The maritime adventure does not end until all the cargo is delivered as contemplated by the contracts of carriage.[57] However, once an interest has ceased to be part of the adventure (e.g. cargo is delivered as intended at a port other than the final port of call) or has been brought to a place of safety, in principle it is not entitled to or liable for a general average contribution for acts done after that time, unless such cargo has been discharged as part of a "complex salvage operation".[58]

---

which they would have earned. The decision turned on the tug captain's authority over the barges and their cargoes, so it is arguable that the decision would have gone the other way if he had been in command of the adventure. But this is doubtful in view of the decision in *Dabney* v. *New England Co* (1867) 14 Allen 300, where the Supreme Court of Massachusetts held there to be no general average loss when cargo was thrown overboard in order to receive the passengers and crew of another vessel in distress. See also *Interior Freighting Co Inc* v. *Universal Ins Co (The Mohican)* [1934] AMC 112. A different result was reached in *SC Loveland Co* v. *USA* [1963] AMC 260 (US DC), where a barge run aground after a casualty to prevent its sinking recovered general average contributions. See also *Northland Navigation Co* v. *Paterson Boiler Works (The Sea Comet)* (1983) 2 CF 59; *The Alppi* [1989] Nordiske Domme i Sjofartsannliggender 397 (Eidsiating Appeal Court); noted RA Hewett [1990] LMCLQ 173. Cf *Morrison SS Co Ltd* v. *Greystoke Castle (Cargo Owners) (The Cheldale)* [1947] AC 265: the owners of a colliding ship are liable to contribute to general average losses sustained by the interests involved with the other ship.

55. See Macdonald [1995] LMCLQ 480, 481–482.
56. *Whitecross Wire Co* v. *Savill* (1882) 8 QBD 653.
57. *Achard* v. *Ring* (1874) 2 Asp MLC 422; *Whitecross Wire Co* v. *Savill* (1882) 8 QBD 653.
58. See *infra*, 53–54.

English law has traditionally been concerned with preservation of the property rather than the commercial adventure imperilled.[59] Strictly speaking, therefore, once property is in a place of safety, general average services are no longer necessary. However, though property has been brought to a safer place than it was when the initial danger arose, further necessary services to bring it to a place of complete safety may come within general average.[60] Furthermore, direct consequences of general average acts come within general average: e.g. repairs at a port of refuge which are necessitated by an earlier general average sacrifice and which enable the voyage to be completed.[61] Indeed, the general common law principle must be considered in the light of the different circumstances which may occur in relation to calling at a port of refuge and the responses of English law and the now prevailing practice in the York-Antwerp Rules to those circumstances. The Rules include "non-separation" terms, whereby, in circumstances where cargo is separated from the voyage before the vessel reaches the originally intended destination, the rights to general average contribution which the carrier would have had, if the common adventure had remained intact until termination in the normal course of events, are preserved.[62]

Port of refuge expenses

Though English law treats as a general average act that which is done for the physical safety of the property imperilled rather than the safe prosecution of the commercial adventure, when the ship has been brought to a place of safety subsequent acts may still qualify for general average contribution provided they are a direct consequence of earlier general average acts and are not done solely for the benefit of individual interests.[63]

These principles were generally accepted in *Atwood* v. *Sellar & Co*[64] and *Svendsen* v. *Wallace Bros*[65] on similar facts, though with different results. In both cases the vessel put into a port of refuge for repairs, during which the cargo was unloaded and warehoused. In *Atwood* v. *Sellar* the Court of Appeal (Bramwell, Baggallay and Thesiger LJJ) held that the expenses of unloading, warehousing and reloading the cargo and the expenses of pilotage and other charges in

---

59. See *supra*, 8.
60. For salvage purposes, the mere fact that a vessel is in a place of comparative safety does not mean that she may not need to be taken to a final place of safety. See *The Troilus* [1951] AC 820; *The Glaucus* (1948) 81 Ll L Rep 262; *China Pacific SA* v. *Food Corp of India (The Winson)* [1982] AC 939, 956–957; and generally *Kennedy*, paras 331–341. See also *Rose* v. *Bank of Australia* [1894] AC 687 (cargo landed in wet condition and stored in a field taken by land to Boulogne, where steps taken to protect from deterioration and destruction before forwarding to destination in London).
61. See *infra*, Chap. 3.
62. See *infra*, 91–92.
63. The common law is summarised *infra*, 55–56.
64. (1880) 5 QBD 286.
65. (1884) 13 QBD 69; affd (1885) 10 App Cas 404.

leaving the port were general average expenses. The governing principle was expressed by Thesiger LJ as follows[66]:

"the going into port, the unloading, warehousing, and reloading of the cargo and the coming out of port, are at all events part of one act or operation contemplated, resolved upon, and carried through, for the common safety and benefit, and properly to be regarded as continuous."

In *Svendsen* v. *Wallace* the cargo owners admitted liability for a contribution to the expenses of unloading and for the entire cost of warehousing. Following *Atwood* v. *Sellar*, Lopes J (with whom Baggallay LJ, dissenting, in the Court of Appeal agreed) held they were also liable to contribute to the expenses of reloading and to port and pilotage charges etc. in leaving the port; but his decision was reversed by the majority of the Court of Appeal (Brett MR and Bowen LJ), the judgment of which, on appeal in relation to the reloading expenses, was upheld by the House of Lords. Distinguishing *Atwood* v. *Sellar*, the Court of Appeal majority: (1) declared that the English law of general average was concerned with the common safety, and not with benefiting the common commercial enterprise, except where the two were inseparable[67]; (2) acknowledged that expenses incurred after the property had been brought to safety could be allowed in general average if necessarily consequent upon a prior general average sacrifice[68]; and asserted (3) that point (2) was a ground for distinguishing *Atwood* v. *Sellar*[69] (where the reason for putting in to port was the general average act of cutting away a mast, rather than perils of the sea, as in *Svendsen*); but (4) indicated that there would generally not be a general average contribution due for subsequent acts from property which was in physical safety (such as cargo which had been unloaded), though Bowen LJ suggested that contribution might be due from cargo if the ship had not simply availed herself of temporary shelter at the port of refuge but had obtained repairs without which the adventure could not have been safely continued.[70] The House of Lords[71] agreed with Bowen LJ that "whether extraordinary expenditure after the entry into a port of refuge is rightly chargeable to general average *necessarily* depends on the circumstances of each case".[72]

Atwood v. *Sellar* and *Svendsen* v. *Wallace* are reconcilable, but with difficulty. Their net result is that *at common law* it is a (difficult) question of fact whether expenses incurred in putting into, while at, and on leaving a port of refuge come within general average, though the latter case indicates that, once ship or cargo

66. (1880) 5 QBD 286, 290.
67. See *supra*, 8.
68. *Svendsen* v. *Wallace* (1884) 13 QBD 69, 85, per Bowen LJ.
69. *Supra*, 21–22.
70. (1884) 13 QBD 69, 90, per Bowen LJ.
71. In a reasoned speech given by Lord Blackburn, with whom Lords Watson and Fitzgerald agreed.
72. (1884) 15 QBD 69, 85, per Bowen LJ; (1885) 10 App Cas 404, 414, per Lord Blackburn. The italics were added by Lord Blackburn. See also *ibid.*, 420, where Lord Blackburn referred to Thesiger LJ's principle of continuous operation in *Atwood* v. *Sellar* (1880) 5 QBD 286, 290, quoted *supra*, text to n. 66, and vaguely to the question whether the expense of reloading "ought" to be borne by all or freight alone.

has been brought to a place of safety, services rendered to it (e.g. warehousing cargo or repairing the ship, and expenses of recommencing the voyage) are likely to be treated as particular charges. So far as the factual circumstances at issue in the cases are concerned, however, their authority is today of little, if any, practical importance, as expenses of entry to, remaining at, and leaving ports of refuge are now provided for in detail by the York-Antwerp Rules.[73]

Interests in same ownership: no legally enforceable right to contribution necessary
Provided there are at least two interests at risk in the adventure, it is not necessary that they be owned by different parties: the ability to enforce a right of contribution by legal action is not a condition for general average. In *Montgomery* v. *Indemnity Mutual Insurance Co*,[74] Vaughan Williams LJ,[75] who delivered the judgment of the Court of Appeal, declared that general average can occur independently of contribution, for

"The object of this maritime law seems to be to give the master of the ship absolute freedom to make whatever sacrifice he thinks best to avert the perils of the sea, without any regard whatsoever to the ownership of the property sacrificed."

This widely stated opinion he sustained partly by his view that general average loss may be sustained for the purpose of preserving life.[76] Further support he derived from the American case of *Potter* v. *Ocean Assurance Co*,[77] which would seem to give weight to the view that only one interest need be at stake, if it were not for the fact that in the USA the liability of underwriters appears to count as a separate interest.[78] It was held in the *Montgomery* case that an indemnity could be recovered from insurers of the cargo in respect of a notional general average contribution due to the shipowners although the two interests—the ship and the cargo—were owned by the same party, so that there would be no contribution between them. Joint ownership does not affect the position of insurers of one of the interests[79] or the owner's personal allocation of the losses between the respective interests.[80]

Danger not threatening all interests
It is a case of general average if a danger threatens the common adventure, even though the threat to individual interests is capable of being eliminated,[81] but not

---

73. See *infra*, 56–59.
74. [1902] 1 KB 734.
75. *Ibid.*, 740.
76. But see *supra*, 15–16.
77. (1837) 3 Sumner 27.
78. *Ibid.*, 41; *Dollar* v. *La Fonciere* (1908) 162 Fed Rep 563. See also *Risley* v. *Insurance Co of North America* (1910) 189 Fed Rep 529; *Hahlo* v. *Benedict* (1914) 216 Fed Rep 303.
79. See the Marine Insurance Act 1906, s.66(7).
80. See per Mathew J at first instance in *Montgomery* v. *Indemnity Mutual Insurance Co* [1901] 1 QB 147, 152.
81. Cf *Westoll* v. *Carter* (1898) 3 Com Cas 112, 114, where Bigham J said, of cargo on board an unseaworthy ship which had to return to her port of loading, which then became ice-bound, so

where the danger threatens only a separate part of the common adventure. Thus, there was no general average loss where a mob forced the master to sell a cargo of wheat for less than its invoice value, since the only threat that existed was with regard to the corn, which the mob wanted to prevent suffering at a time of scarcity; there was no threat to the ship or to other parts of the cargo.[82]

Effect of the danger on different interests

Provided there is a danger to the common adventure, there is no necessity for danger of an immediate total loss of the whole adventure.[83] Nor is it necessary for the interests to be imperilled to an equal extent.[84]

Where the danger is only to one interest, this will give rise to a particular average loss or the incurring of particular charges to prevent it; and the master would appear to have a duty to cut away worthless wreckage which is imperilling the safety of the common adventure—albeit that in itself will not prevent its being a general average act.[85] However, it seems right that, where the danger which renders the position of the thing sacrificed hopeless is that which is common to the whole adventure, the sacrifice is a general average act, even though the common danger may be such that it can be averted by the sacrifice of that particular thing only.[86] It has been settled that, where the property sacrificed was in a peculiarly perilous position, or even was itself endangering the rest of the adventure, this will not prevent the loss from being a general average sacrifice, so long as its position is not hopeless and the sacrifice is for the preservation of the imperilled interests.[87] Thus, where deck cargo (which had been lawfully loaded) had broken loose in a storm and was drifting about the deck so as to impede the working of the pumps and become a common source of danger, its jettison was held to be a general average sacrifice.[88] So long as there is a possibility of saving the thing sacrificed, there is a general average loss; if not, there is no real sacrifice and the dangerous thing must be jettisoned to safeguard the remaining interests.[89]

It is generally recognised that English law prefers the view that general average is concerned with a physical threat to property, while Continental law

---

necessitating the services of an ice-breaker, that "there was no danger threatening the safety of ship and cargo, which could easily have been discharged if there had been such danger."

82. *Nesbitt* v. *Lushington* (1792) 4 TR 783.

83. *Whitecross Wire & Iron Co Ltd* v. *Savill* (1882) 8 QBD 653, 662, per Brett LJ.

84. *Willcox, Peck & Hughes* v. *American Smelting and Refining Co (The Trojan)* (1913) 210 Fed Rep 89.

85. This seems to be suggested in the note of the judgments in *Corrie* v. *Coulthard* (1877) 3 Asp MLC 546. Lowndes suggested that a mast *in situ* is presumed not to be in a state of wreck unless there is no reasonable possibility of saving it: *Lowndes & Rudolf*, 9th ed. (1964), para 206.

86. *Carver*, 13th ed., para 1360.

87. See further *infra*, 37–38.

88. *Johnson* v. *Chapman* (1865) 19 CB(NS) 563.

89. *Crockett* v. *Dodge* (1835) 3 Fairf 190 (scuttled ship not bound to contribute to owners of lime which was on fire and necessitated the scuttling which caused its loss); *Slater* v. *Hayward Rubber Co* (1857) 26 Conn 128 (no general average sacrifice of goods on fire).

admits its extension to the commercial threat to the completion of the adventure. Not surprisingly, though mainly consistent with the English view, the York-Antwerp Rules embrace both positions, accommodating repairs "necessary for the safe prosecution of the voyage", expenses incurred "during the prolongation of the voyage",[90] and "temporary repairs of accidental damage ... effected in order to enable the adventure to be completed".[91]

Loss exceeding benefit

It is possible that the amount of a general average loss exceeds the combined value of the interests preserved. Under the law of salvage, the tribunal's overriding discretion in assessing a salvage award accommodates such difficulty by enabling it to reduce the amount of the notional award, thereby attempting to ensure that, however unfortunate that may be for the salvor, the salvee does in fact benefit from the service rendered.[92] However, no such flexibility has been recognised in the law of general average, although a common practical solution seems to be to restrict the amount of contribution to the value of the property preserved, with any excess being divided between the party incurring it and his insurers.[93] If the object of general average is simply to achieve physical safety, the contributors' liabilities should not be reduced or negatived by financial considerations. Alternatively, if the object is commercial, at least three possibilities exist: that any action to be taken is financially pointless, therefore outside general average by virtue of unreasonableness[94]; that such action is not commercially beneficial, and for that reason outside general average; or that such action is within general average only insofar as it is beneficial (i.e. in accordance with the practice just mentioned).

The intended beneficiary

Though there is a danger to the common adventure, if action is taken only for the benefit of a single interest, it will not be a general average act.[95] So far as there is a wide principle in English law entitling the provider of services in an emergency to restitution, it limits recovery to action taken to benefit the defendant.[96] Awards under the maritime law of salvage are also dependent upon benefit to the salvee but balance this against a policy of encouraging

---

90. York-Antwerp Rules 1994, Rules X, XI.
91. York-Antwerp Rules 1994, Rule XIV.
92. See *Kennedy*, Chap. 12.
93. See Macdonald [1995] LMCLQ 480, 488. For discussion of methods of dealing with this problem in different jurisdictions, see the Reports of the A.I.D.E. working group chaired by DJ Wilson and delivered at Bruges in 1987 and York in 1989.
94. See *infra*, 38–39.
95. *Butler* v. *Wildman* (1820) 3 B & Ald 398, 404, per Holroyd J. See also *Royal Mail Steam Packet Co Ltd* v. *English Bank of Rio de Janeiro* (1887) 19 QBD 362 and the other cases on "complex salvage operations", *infra*, 53–54.
96. See, e.g., Rose (1989) 9 OJLS 167, 194–198.

intervention by the incentive of an attractive level of reward.[97] The very nature of common adventure underlying the law of general average is such that a general average act is designed to benefit both the shipowner with whose authority the act will normally be done and one or more other interests in the adventure. Thus, Hoffmann LJ has commented that "A policy of giving the owner or master a financial incentive in an emergency to give priority to the safety of the vessel or delivery of its cargo seems also to play a part."[98] The relevant policy, however, is directed to furthering the interests involved in the *common* adventure, and it is as a consequence of that that the shipowner is justified in looking after his own interests. Hoffmann LJ's dictum should not be interpreted as justifying the type of self-interest which is encouraged by the law of salvage and which provides a common source of criticism of shipowners' claims for general average contributions.

Effect of general average act on different interests

So long as action is undertaken for the purpose of the common adventure, even though it benefits only some of the interests involved, a general average contribution can be claimed, but only from such interests.[99]

5. Authority to act

It is a curious feature of accounts of the law of general average that they focus on liability for acts done in the interests of contributors without scrutiny of the plaintiff's entitlement to generate that liability. This section considers three issues: (i) who is the proper person to sanction a general average act, and therefore to impose liability for a general average contribution; (ii) whether another person may be entitled to override the authority of the person generally entitled to sanction a general average act (namely the ship's master) and also to create liability to a general average contribution; and (iii) to what extent the owners of interests involved in the common adventure can exclude their liability to a general average contribution and/or restrict the freedom of the master (or his substitute) in dealing with a danger.

(a) The proper actor

There is very little authority on who is the proper person to sanction a general average act.[100] As a matter of general principle, it seems correct to say that the

---

97. See *Kennedy*, Chap. 1.
98. *Marida Ltd* v. *Oswal Steel (The Bijela)* [1993] 1 Lloyd's Rep 411, 420.
99. See *infra*, 37–38, 82–83.
100. *Athel Line Ltd* v. *Liverpool & London War Risks Ins Assn Ltd* [1944] KB 87, 96, per Tucker J ("... there is no clear authority ... "). Rule A of the York-Antwerp Rules 1994 and the Marine Insurance Act 1906, s.66 are also silent on the matter.

act must have been sanctioned by a proper person.[101] More cautiously, it can be said that the act must have been exercised by or under the authority of the master. Since it is the master who is entrusted with the conduct of the adventure and the care of the ship and cargo, and since in extraordinary circumstances he becomes the agent for all parties,[102] then it is he who should order or authorise a general average act; and he must decide what steps are reasonable in the circumstances.[103] This may include the appointment of an agent to act on behalf of the imperilled community of interests.[104]

Should the master be unable to act during an emergency due to absence or any other reason, there seems little reason to doubt that general average sacrifices and expenditures made or incurred under the direction of the officer or member of the crew discharging the master's duties would be treated as general average acts if they could have been so treated if performed by the master.[105]

In *Papayanni* v. *Grampian SS Co Ltd*,[106] the master put into port for the purpose of extinguishing a fire on board his ship. On intimation of the existing state of affairs, the captain of the port came aboard and directed operations which led to the scuttling of the ship. The master of the ship retained possession of the vessel throughout and considered scuttling to be the best thing for ship and cargo, although he had nothing to do with it since he was only obeying the orders of the captain of the port acting under his official powers. Mathew J, in a reported judgment of only sixty-six words, held that this was a general average act:

"This evidence shows that what was done was in the interest of ship and cargo. There is no evidence that there was any other motive for scuttling the ship. The captain, who had not parted with the possession of his ship, did not object. There seems to be clear

---

101. Cf Rose (1989) 9 OJLS 167, 188–193.
102. *Whitecross Wire Co* v. *Savill* (1882) 8 QBD 653, 663, per Brett LJ. In *Morrison SS Co* v. *Greystoke Castle (Cargo Owners) (The Cheldale)* [1947] AC 265, the *Greystoke Castle* collided with the *Cheldale* and the former incurred port of refuge expenditure. Owners of cargo on board were bound to contribute. They could claim part of this sum from the *Cheldale*, for the master of the *Greystoke Castle* had incurred liability on their behalf as well as on behalf of the owners of the *Greystoke Castle*; they were not just bound to indemnify the owners for an expenditure incurred on their behalf only.
103. The view was formerly held that the master should, before resorting to a general average sacrifice, consult principal members of the crew and representatives of the cargo owners if they happened to be on board (see *Arnould*, 15th ed. (1961), para 919, *Carver*, 13th ed., para 1379 and references cited therein). Unless there is an express provision that this should be done (as in many modern commercial codes), the master is not bound to comply with any particular procedures before he acts. Whether or not he has consulted other parties may be relevant in deciding the prudence of his actions, although of course the danger may well be too urgent to admit of such deliberation and he must proceed quickly as he thinks best: *Birkley* v. *Presgrave* (1801) 1 East 220, 228, per Lord Kenyon CJ.
104. *Rose* v. *Bank of Australasia* [1894] AC 687, disapproving *Schuster* v. *Fletcher* (1878) 3 QBD 418.
105. *Lowndes & Rudolf*, para A.10.
106. (1896) 1 Com Cas 448.

evidence that he sanctioned what was done. The loss must be adjusted as a general average sacrifice."

This leaves many questions to be answered. Is it sufficient, in order to constitute a general average act, that the master hands over the reins to a third party and acquiesces in all the measures taken? This surely cannot be right, even if the master remains in possession of the ship, for he has a duty to act on behalf of the interests involved in the adventure and cannot escape his responsibilities by delegating them to another party. However, the *Papayanni* case was not a simple case of delegation. In the interests of the ship and the cargo, the master put into port in order to fulfil his duty. By doing so, he came under the authority of the captain of the port, who had powers enabling him to step into the master's shoes. Thus, indirectly, the master can be taken to have authorised the scuttling.

Mathew J's judgment, however, allows of a wider principle. Is the only requirement of a general average act that it be done in the interest of ship and cargo? If so, it is consistent with *Papayanni* and with the principle of "natural justice" on which the law of general average is supposedly based[107] that, provided the steps taken are necessary, they may be taken not only by someone acting on behalf of the master but even by a stranger to the adventure. A similar situation to that in *Papayanni* occurred in *Price* v. *Noble*.[108] A captured vessel was put under the command of a prize-master and a prize crew was put on board. Of the original ship's complement, only the mate and two members of the crew remained; the captain and the rest of the crew were taken off. During an ensuing storm ship's stores were jettisoned at the individual direction of the mate, who had been entrusted with the navigation by his captors.[109] This, it was held, enabled the shipowners to claim contribution from the cargo owners. However, the case is of little assistance in that it seems to have turned on the necessity of what was done and not on the status of the person ordering the jettison. On the one hand, it can be said that the jettison was directed by the mate standing in the master's shoes. On the other, it is possible to say that he was merely advising the prize-master, who was a stranger to the adventure: but even in that case it can be said that the prize-master, like the captain of the port in *Papayanni*, was standing in the master's shoes, albeit the latter was powerless to remove him.[110]

Neither *Papayanni* nor *Price* v. *Noble* settle the question whether or not a general average act must be carried out under the master's authority. They only go so far as to require that the master in some way "sanctions" the act, either

---

107. See *supra*, 6.
108. (1811) 4 Taunt 123.
109. See *ibid.*, 126, per Mansfield CJ.
110. Cf *Joseph Watson & Son Ltd* v. *Firemen's Fund Insurance Co of San Francisco* [1922] 2 KB 355, 358, where, in relation to the existence of a peril, Rowlatt J said that "much depends upon the view taken at the time by the captain *or person in authority*". These words are not wide enough to include a stranger who is not the person in authority.

because he has ordered it, or because it is performed by someone acting in his place carrying out his duties.[111] *Mouse's Case*[112] shows that jettison by a passenger in order to save lives in a case of great and imminent danger is lawful and supports the view that general average acts may be performed by a stranger. If this is so, then it supports the view that there is a lawful general average sacrifice where it is made by the crew without the master's assent and even against his wishes.[113] However, it is submitted that a stranger's ability to incur general average losses for the common good should be confined to cases in which the master can be said to sanction his acts, either because the "stranger" has acted in his place or because the master has ratified his acts. The latter would be unlikely to ratify acts done against his wishes[114] and the absence of the master's sanction would detract from the finding that the general average act was necessary or reasonable.[115]

In the American case of *Ralli v. Troop*[116] contribution was disallowed where harbour authorities, acting independently but with the master's consent, scuttled a ship. The United States Supreme Court decided (by a majority) that the person entrusted with the command and safety of the adventure and of the interests therein (or the person who acts under him or succeeds to his authority) should decide what, how and when to sacrifice, and it should not be done by the compulsory act of others.[117] The case was distinguished in *The Beatrice*,[118] in which damage done in putting out a fire by strangers was held recoverable as general average, the strangers being firemen acting at the request of the owners and with the approval of the officers and crew, although for the safety of a particular ship and cargo. In this respect, English and American law may differ but it is submitted there is room in both for a common principle to the effect that, since the emergency gives the master authority to act as agent for the

---

111. Arguably without his tacit consent. This would be the situation if it were the prize-master in *Price* v. *Noble* who is held to be the one authorising the jettison.

112. (1609) 12 Co Rep 63.

113. See, e.g., *Lowndes & Rudolf*, para A.13; *Carver*, para 1379. Possibly, the stranger can be regarded as coming within the common law rules on necessitous intervention: see *Goff & Jones*, 339. If so, it is unlikely that strangers can act contrary to the master's wishes but can only act where he is unable to do so. For it is a requirement of the doctrine of necessitous intervention that it be impracticable for the intervenor to communicate with the owner. The master is generally authorised to act on behalf of the shipowners and the cargo owners, so he should be the one to be consulted.

114. He is more likely to do so where this would give his owners a claim against the cargo owners. It is contrary to principle to allow such inconsistency to creep into the law.

115. The judgments of Mansfield CJ in *Price* v. *Noble* (1811) 4 Taunt 123 and Mathew J in *Papayanni* v. *Grampian* (1896) 1 Com Cas 448 revolved around the necessity of the acts done.

116. (1894) 157 US 386. See also *Wamsutta Mills* v. *Old Colony Steamboat Co* (1884) 137 Mass 471; *Minneapolis SS Co* v. *Manistee Co* (1907) 156 Fed Rep 424; *The Andree-Moran* [1930] AMC 631. But cf *The Roanoke* (1894) 46 Fed Rep 297; *The Beatrice* [1924] AMC 914.

117. It seems that the court was to some extent influenced by the fact that the sacrifice was not made for the benefit of the common adventure alone but also in the interests of the port.

118. [1924] AMC 914.

shipowners and the cargo owners,[119] then he alone must sanction whatsoever steps are taken (and by whomsoever they are taken) in order to preserve the interests imperilled in the common adventure; when he is absent or otherwise incapable of acting, or when he has lawfully delegated the carrying out of his duties, a stranger may take steps to act in his place for the preservation of those interests. *Papayanni* would also suggest that, at least in English law, a stranger is not required to act for the purpose alone of preserving the common adventure.

Finally, it should be noted that, where a loss is the result of superior orders, a general average contribution may be disallowed simply for the reason that it was not intentionally incurred for the benefit of the common adventure.[120]

(b) Whether authority exercisable

Where the master's principal intervenes to arrange general average services, this is justifiable on the basis that the master may assent to his employer's acts.[121] An alternative explanation is that a person liable to incur a general average loss is personally entitled to decide what action is appropriate, even if his agent disagreed with him. It is a principle of the general law of restitution that a necessitous intervener can only recover if he was unable to obtain proper instructions from the defendant.[122] Where interests are at risk on a common adventure, it is reasonable to assume that the person encharged with the safe prosecution of that adventure should have authority on behalf of all parties, and arguably irrevocable authority, to do what is best in times of peril.[123] However, there was held to be no common law rule nor implied term in *The Choko Star*[124] that a ship master could bind cargo owners to salvors by contract. This particular rule has been reversed by statute.[125] But it remains an open question whether the statutory rule can be overridden by contract[126] and whether the general common law rule is that a potential contributor can exclude his liability to make a general average contribution. Though most charterparties and bill of

---

119. *The Gratitudine* (1801) 3 C Rob 240; *Morrison SS Co* v. *Greystoke Castle (Cargo Owners) (The Cheldale)* [1947] AC 265. "But neither the owners of the ship nor their master have authority to bind the goods, or the owners of the goods, by any contract": *Anderson* v. *Ocean SS Co* (1884) 10 App Cas 107, 117, per Lord Blackburn.
120. See *Athel Line Ltd* v. *Liverpool & London War Risks Ins Assn Ltd* [1944] KB 87; *infra*, §8.
121. See *Lowndes & Rudolf*, para A.15, discussing *Australian Coastal Shipping Commission* v. *Green* [1971] 1 QB 456, where tugs were hired by the shipowners' shore officers, their entitlement to incur general average expenditure not being disputed. Cf *Anglo-Grecian Steam Trading Co Ltd* v. *T Beynon & Co* (1926) 24 Ll L Rep 122, 125, where the master's acquiescence in the advice of the pilot was ultimately superseded by the similar decision of the owners' superintendent.
122. See *The Winson* [1982] AC 939; Rose (1989) 9 OJLS 167, 186–188.
123. *The Gratitudine* (1801) 3 C Rob 240; *MR Currie & Co* v. *Bombay Native Ins Co* (1869) LR 3 PC 72, 83; *Kennedy*, paras 720–722.
124. [1990] 1 Lloyd's Rep 216; noted Munday [1991] LMCLQ 1; Reynolds [1990] JBL 505.
125. Merchant Shipping Act 1995, s.224, Sched. 11, Part 1; consolidating Merchant Shipping (Salvage and Pollution) Act 1994, s.1; and giving effect to the International Convention on Salvage 1989, esp art. 6(2). See also Lloyd's Standard Form of Salvage Agreement (LOF 1995).
126. See Gaskell, *Current Law Statutes 1995*, 21–383 to 21–386.

lading contracts make positive provision for general average, this may be interpreted as providing for the method of adjusting accrued liability and therefore leave open the possibility, even once performance of the contract has begun, of a potential contributor's precluding his own liability to general average by forbidding action on his behalf, especially with respect to shipowner's expenses. It is arguable, even perhaps in the case of an express agreement between all interested parties, that as a matter of public policy the master's general authority to act in the best interests of a community of interests in time of danger should not be restricted by the selfishness of one particular interest.[127] However, the common law of general average may normally be overridden by agreement,[128] so (at least where there is a pre-existing contract) a party may at common law exclude liability for a general average contribution.

Of course, notification to the carrier of an attempt to exclude general average liability is unlikely to be effective against third parties; and no attempt to exclude such liability will have effect where statutory provisions otherwise provide.[129]

Moreover, even if a potential contributor could withdraw the master's authority to act on his behalf, only the shipowner is likely[130] to be able to insist on positive action differing from what the master would otherwise do.

6. There must be a sacrifice or expenditure of an extraordinary nature

As a general rule, a person cannot claim a payment from another merely because the latter has derived a benefit from the actions of the former; *a fortiori* where the former is contractually bound to provide the benefit.[131] In particular, under the contract of affreightment, the shipowner is bound to do all that is requisite, in the ordinary course of the voyage, for the safe transport of the goods to their port of delivery[132] and for this he is entitled to be remunerated by the agreed freight but no more.[133] Even where a general average situation has arisen,

---

127. This is the clear effect of Sir William Scott's judgment in *The Gratitudine* (1801) 3 C Rob 240.
128. See *supra*, 10.
129. See *supra*, 17 n. 34.
130. Subject to the above discussion on intervention by someone other than the master: *supra*, 27–30.
131. *Ruabon Steamship Co Ltd* v. *London Assurance* [1900] AC 6; *Goff & Jones*, 55–58.
132. *Phelp James* v. *Hill* [1891] 1 QB 605, 610, per Lindley LJ; *Hansen* v. *Dunn* (1906) 11 Com Cas 100; *Kulukundis* v. *Norwich Union Fire Insurance Society* [1937] 1 KB 1, 16, per Greene LJ; *Marida Ltd* v. *Oswal Steel (The Bijela)* [1992] 1 Lloyd's Rep 636, 642–643, per Hobhouse J. See also the cases discussed *infra* Chap. 3, n. 51, on whether salvage services to a vessel from which cargo has been removed qualify for a general average contribution: e.g., *Job* v. *Langton* (1856) 6 E & B 779; *Walthew* v. *Mavrojani* (1870) LR 5 Ex 116. And, where cargo has been removed from the vessel, see *Harrison* v. *Bank of Australia* [1894] AC 687.
133. This principle seems to explain the fact that steps taken to avoid enemy capture, whether by carrying an unusual spread of canvas (*Covington* v. *Roberts* (1806) 2 B & P NR 378) or by fighting (*Taylor* v. *Curtis* (1816) 6 Taunt 608, affg (1815) 4 Camp 337), have been held not to be general average acts. In *Taylor* v. *Curtis*, *ibid.*, Gibbs CJ acknowledged the advantage in underwriters' making gratuitous payments to encourage such action but seemed to think that such acts by their

this obligation continues, thereby restricting the options available to the shipowner as to how to respond to the danger and the possibility of claiming a contribution for expenditure incurred.[134] Contributions for general average sacrifices and expenditures can only be claimed if made or incurred for something over and beyond the ordinary duties and expenses of the navigation.[135]

In *Wilson* v. *Bank of Victoria*,[136] a clipper sailing ship with an auxiliary steam screw and 550 tons of coal was sailing from Australia to England when she was damaged in a collision with an iceberg. She lost all power of sailing and used most of her supply of coal to reach Rio de Janeiro by steam. The high cost of repairs there (as against the lower cost in London) and the necessity for unloading and warehousing the cargo and the delay that this would have caused decided the master to have temporary repairs carried out and to complete the voyage under steam. He purchased two more loads of coal for this purpose. The shipowners claimed a contribution for the cost of the coal from the cargo owners either as an expenditure incurred in substitution, beneficial to all parties, for a greater expenditure which the captain was entitled to incur by repairing at Rio de Janeiro, or as an extraordinary expenditure incurred for the general advantage. The Court of Queen's Bench rejected both of these arguments. (The case thus constitutes the leading authority of the common law on substituted expenses, which are discussed below.)[137] As to the argument on extraordinary expenditure, according to Blackburn J, who delivered the court's judgment[138]:

"the disaster . . ., no doubt, caused the engine to be used to a much greater extent than would generally occur on such a voyage, and so caused the disbursement for coals to be extraordinarily heavy; but it did not render it an extraordinary disbursement."

If the vessel had sailed without any auxiliary means of propulsion but was in other respects seaworthy, the master would have had to incur expenditure for repairs at Rio de Janeiro and this would have come under general average. But,

---

very nature could not qualify for general average, even though requiring extreme measures. The cases should now be read in the light of the discussion below in this section of *The Bona* [1895] P 125 (where, at 134, Lord Esher MR stated that the Court of Appeal would not be disposed to extend *Covington* v. *Roberts*) and *Société Nouvelle d'Armement* v. *Spillers & Bakers Ltd* [1917] 1 KB 865 (in which Sankey J relied on *Taylor* v. *Curtis*).

134. This tension underlies the debate about what may be claimed as substituted expenses under Rules F and XIV of the York-Antwerp Rules 1994: see *infra*, 59–61.

135. *The Bona* [1895] P 125. Cf *Marida Ltd* v. *Oswal Steel (The Bijela)* [1993] 1 Lloyd's Rep 411, 420, per Hoffmann LJ: "The theory of common benefit . . . cannot logically be divorced from the contractual rights of the parties. The cargo owners certainly benefit from the temporary repairs which enable the voyage to be completed, but if the owner was under a duty under the contract of affreightment to make such repairs, the benefit may be said to be one for which the cargo owners have already paid. On the other hand, there seems to be no rigid principle that sacrifice or expenditure cannot qualify for general average because the owner was under a contractual duty to make it."

136. (1867) LR 2 QB 203.

137. *Infra*, 59–61.

138. (1867) LR 2 QB 203, 212. Cf *The Bona* [1895] P 125 (see, *supra*, n. 135, *infra*, 34).

so long as a ship is fitted up with auxiliary means of power, it is the owner's duty to make some provision for supplying the engine with fuel. He is not bound to have on board enough for every possible emergency but is bound to have a reasonable supply, having regard to the nature of the voyage, the season of the year, the quality of the cargo, the condition of the ship, and what experience has shown to be prudent to provide under those conditions. If he fails to do so,[139] he cannot call upon the owners of the cargo to contribute towards that reasonable supply and if, under such circumstances, the opportunity occurs during a time of peril of buying fuel from a passing ship, he could not charge its cost as an extraordinary expenditure entitling him to general average contribution.[140]

However, if the ship has a reasonable supply of fuel and that is exhausted by the particular circumstances of the occasion, then general average contribution may be claimed in respect of cargo and ship's materials[141] used as fuel in order to save the common adventure.[142] Thus, in relation to "cargo, ship's materials and stores for fuel", Rule IX of the York-Antwerp Rules 1994 provides:

"Cargo, ship's materials and stores, or any of them, necessarily used for fuel for the common safety at a time of peril shall be admitted as general average, but when such an allowance is made for the ship's materials and stores the general average shall be credited with the estimated cost of the fuel which would otherwise have been consumed in prosecuting the intended voyage."

In *Société Nouvelle d'Armement* v. *Spillers & Bakers Ltd*,[143] a captain had hired a tug to tow his sailing ship quickly between two ports during wartime in order to avoid submarine attacks which were likely to occur and from which he wished to take measures to preserve the ship and cargo.[144] It was usual to hire a tug to take the vessel in and out of a port, but the general average was claimed in respect of the intervening voyage. The claim was disallowed. The case has been regarded as specific authority for Sankey J's statement that the expenditure "must have been incurred on an abnormal occasion".[145] However, that assertion adds nothing to the real justification for the decision: that general average only arises in respect of imminent perils (whether perpetual or temporary) and that the danger from submarine attack was not imminent, merely apprehended.[146] As to the nature of the peril, Sankey J remarked that a

---

139. See *infra*, 66–76.
140. *Robinson* v. *Price* (1876) 2 QBD 91, 295.
141. The view that ship's boats might be excluded from general average if slung outside the ship at the stern is now discredited. See *Blackett* v. *Royal Exchange Assurance Co* (1832) C & J 244; *Lenox* v. *United Insurance Co* (1802) 3 Johns NY Cas 178 (NY SC).
142. *Robinson* v. *Price* (1876) 2 QBD 91, 295. Cf *Harrison* v. *Bank of Australasia* (1872) LR 7 Ex 39.
143. [1917] 1 KB 865.
144. His crew had just seen the dead bodies from the torpedoed *Lusitania* being brought ashore and they insisted on his engaging a tug before proceeding on the voyage.
145. *Ibid.*, 871.
146. See above, §3. The judge noted that no submarine was sighted on this trip and that three-quarters of the vessels alleged to have been sunk or damaged by submarines in the area were steamships. One may wonder whether an ordinary and reasonable sailing ship captain would have been comforted by the second fact.

general average expenditure must be incurred to avoid extraordinary and abnormal perils as distinguished from the ordinary and normal perils of the sea, and the risk of being attacked or destroyed by the King's enemies was not an extraordinary and abnormal peril upon a voyage of the kind during the war[147]; it is insufficient that a master may minimise the risk and so confer a benefit on the property involved by taking extra precautions.[148] This is true, though it is nevertheless the case that any peril will justify a general average act if it is real and the sacrifice is of an extraordinary nature.

Differences in kind and in degree

Must expenditure be extraordinary in kind as well as in degree? It is tempting to conclude from *Wilson* v. *Bank of Victoria*[149] and *Harrison* v. *Bank of Australasia*,[150] that expenditure of a greater degree than usual is insufficient, but it is questionable whether this is realistic in a mercantile sense.[151] It is debatable whether there is an adequate distinction between the extraordinary consumption of fuel and taking on extra fuel or between the enhancement of the crew's wages and taking on extra crew to justify the imposition of a qualification that expenditure must be different in kind as well as in degree.

In *The Bona*[152] the Court of Appeal and Jeune P decided that coal consumed in straining ship's engines (which became damaged) to refloat a stranded ship was the subject of general average contribution since the engines were unusually strained. The defendants submitted that the screw was in the water and was used for the purpose for which it was intended but, said Lindley LJ,[153] "The screw was not used to navigate the ship afloat, but to get her afloat, which was an extraordinary purpose" and he distinguished two cases in which ships had been subjected to unusual strain while afloat.[154] However, it is submitted that there is no conclusive authority to the effect that extraordinary expenditure must be different in kind as well as in degree and that the cases in which extraordinary expenditure has been disallowed as general average as being only different in degree are merely illustrations of the stringent requirements which the law exacts from a master in fulfilling the contract of carriage. In *Société Nouvelle d'Armement* v. *Spillers & Bakers Ltd*,[155] Sankey J stated that: "There must be

---

147. [1917] 1 KB 865, 872.
148. *Ibid.*, 870–872; *Taylor* v. *Curtis* (1816) 6 Taunt 608. In view of the fate of the *Lusitania*, it seems that, if a general average situation should arise, it might be more useful to take note of the particular waters in which a vessel is sailing than to ask whether the vessel's national state is belligerent.
149. (1867) LR 2 QB 203: see *supra*, 32.
150. [1894] AC 687.
151. It is also an unnecessary elaboration of the principle expressed in the Rhodian Law and in the definition of Lawrence J in *Birkley* v. *Presgrave* (1801) 1 East 220, 228. See *supra*, 1.
152. [1895] P 125.
153. *Ibid.*, 141.
154. *Covington* v. *Roberts* (1806) 2 B & P (NR) 378 and *Power* v. *Whitmore* (1815) 4 M & S 141.
155. [1917] 1 KB 865, 871.

expenditure abnormal in kind or degree." In practice, the issue may be resolved by specific provision. Thus, under Rule VII of the York-Antwerp Rules 1994, where a ship is afloat, no loss or damage caused by working the propelling machinery and boilers shall in any circumstances be treated as general average; but, where the ship is ashore and in a position of peril, damage to any machinery and boilers in endeavouring to refloat her for the common safety at the risk of such damage shall be allowed in general average.[156]

Finally, it should be noted that Rule II of the York-Antwerp Rules 1994 provides in general terms that:

"Loss of or damage to the property involved in the common maritime adventure by or in consequence of a sacrifice made for the common safety, and by water which goes down a ship's hatches opened or other opening made for the purpose of making a jettison for the common safety, shall be made good as general average."

7. The sacrifice or expenditure must be real

There is no general average loss if there is a sacrifice of something which has no value.[157] Thus, where coal had imperilled the voyage by overheating and was discharged, and was incapable of being carried on to destination, there was no abandonment of freight in deciding not to complete the voyage.[158]

Similarly, if part of the ship's superstructure is in a state of wreck, there is no sacrifice in abandoning it, even where this is done before it is completely lost.[159] In *Shepherd* v. *Kottgen*[160] rigging (which in all probability, said Bramwell LJ, had been imperfectly fitted) gave way and fouled the mainmast, which began lurching violently and probably would have torn up the ship's deck. After vainly attempting to secure the mast, the master cut it away. The owners later claimed contribution for it. In such circumstances the question to be asked is whether, having regard to all the circumstances, the mast was virtually a wreck and valueless; and there is no necessity to consider whether, if the storm had moderated, the mast might possibly have been saved or whether it was cut away to save the adventure, or, as being wreck, as a mere encumbrance or lumber. It is now specifically provided, in Rule IV of the York-Antwerp Rules 1994, that:

"Loss or damage sustained by cutting away wreck or parts of the ship which have been previously carried away or are effectively lost by accident shall not be made good as general average."

The opinion has been expressed[161] that the question whether or not something is absolutely lost has to be answered by reference to the circum-

---

156. See *Corfu Navigation Co* v. *Mobil Shipping Co Ltd (The Alpha)* [1991] 2 Lloyd's Rep 515.
157. *Shepherd* v. *Kottgen* (1877) 2 CPD 578, 585 approving (*sub nom Corry* v. *Coulthard*) *Corrie* v. *Coulthard* (1877) 3 Asp MLC 546n; (1877) 2 CPD at 583n; *Iredale* v. *China Traders Insurance Co* [1900] 2 QB 515.
158. *Iredale* v. *China Traders Insurance Co* [1900] 2 QB 515.
159. Carver, para 1360; *Johnson* v. *Chapman* (1865) 19 CB (NS) 563, 582; York-Antwerp Rules 1994, Rule IV.
160. (1877) 2 CPD 578, 585.
161. *Iredale* v. *China Traders Insurance Co* [1899] 2 QB 356, 360, per Bigham J.

stances as they appeared at the time of the act, and not by reference to subsequent events, so that the master may be properly said to have substituted a certain loss of part for a probable loss of the whole of the adventure. This seems sensible. But the contrary view, that the test depends on the true facts (so that the decision is to be taken objectively in the light of all the facts known at the time of adjustment[162]) is consistent with the test whether there is a sufficient danger.[163]

The exact limits of the requirement that the sacrifice should be real are not clear from *Shepherd* v. *Kottgen* for that case (as is clear from Brett LJ's judgment[164]) was only concerned with a situation in which there was no common danger, so that general average would have been inapplicable anyway. Certainly, where the danger is only to one interest, this will be a particular charge. But, if the danger rendering the position of the thing sacrificed hopeless is one which is common to the whole adventure, the sacrifice is a general average act, even though the common danger can be averted by the sacrifice of that particular thing only.[165]

It is arguable that if the only possibility of safety lies in the sacrifice of a particular thing, then, since that thing must be lost anyway, it is valueless, so there is no real sacrifice.[166] This view has not found acceptance[167]; there is no encouragement for a master further to imperil the adventure by, for example, hanging on to parts of the ship's tackle in order to reduce the owner's loss to as little as possible.

8. The general average act must be intentionally incurred for the benefit of the common adventure

To qualify for general average, the act done must be done intentionally, and there must be an intention to benefit the common adventure.

Intention

A general average act must be intentional[168]: it must be both made or incurred with the sole object of preserving from peril the interests involved[169] and a result of the master's free choice, i.e. he must not be acting under superior orders.[170]

---

162. *Lowndes & Rudolf*, para 4.08, n. 11.
163. See *supra*, 17–19.
164. (1877) 2 CPD 578, 590.
165. See *supra*, 24.
166. See *Carver*, para 863 and *Lowndes & Rudolf*, paras 4.01–4.02 and the other writers cited therein.
167. The point was taken but not approved of in *Pirie* v. *Middle Dock Co* (1881) 44 LT 426; *Whitecross Wire Co* v. *Savill* (1882) 8 QBD 653; *Iredale* v. *China Traders' Insurance Co* [1899] 2 QB 356; [1900] 2 QB 515.
168. York-Antwerp Rules 1994, Rule A.
169. *Daniolos* v. *Bunge & Co Ltd* (1937) 59 Ll L Rep 175, 180, affd (1938) 62 Ll L Rep 65; *Athel Line* case, *infra*.
170. *Athel Line Ltd* v. *Liverpool & London War Risks Assn Ltd* [1944] KB 87.

ACT MUST BE INTENTIONALLY INCURRED

Yet, although an act is one out of a range of options available to the master,[171] it can still be deemed intentional if it is the only reasonable course that a master could take, e.g. if the particular jettison made is the only one which would save the common adventure.[172] An act is intentional for these purposes though the exact result intended is not achieved; e.g. where a vessel intended to be beached takes the ground in an unintended place.[173]

In *Athel Line Ltd* v. *Liverpool & London War Risks Insurance Assn Ltd*,[174] Tucker J said that the York-Antwerp Rules clearly envisage

"the exercise by someone of his reasoning powers and discretion applied to a particular problem with freedom of choice to decide to act in one out of two or more possible ways, and the language is quite inappropriate to describe the blind and unreasoning obedience of a subordinate to the lawful orders of a superior authority."

It is submitted that the common law rule is to the same effect and the effect of his Lordship's statement is that the master must be able to make up his own mind as to what he is to do. Beyond that, it is only necessary that he be able to decide whether to do or not to do something. Willes J must surely have been right in *Johnson* v. *Chapman*,[175] when he said that it is a general average sacrifice to jettison the one piece of cargo which it is especially necessary to jettison in order to save the common adventure.[176] However, if the master had pursued this course under superior orders, then, albeit he would have done so anyway, there is no general average loss.

Intention to benefit the common adventure[177]

As Wills J has said,[178] "the purpose for which an act causing loss is done may determine whether it constitutes general average or not". Thus, where the master removes cargo from a stranded vessel for the purposes of the common adventure and while he is still considering whether to continue the adventure, the expenses incurred may be chargeable to general average, even though the voyage is subsequently abandoned.[179] But, whatever the master ought to do for the purposes of the common adventure, if he acts solely to remove a particular

---

171. *The Seapool* [1934] P 53, 64, per Langton J, following the requirement of the sacrifice or expenditure being intentional in Rule A of the York-Antwerp Rules 1924.
172. Such as that of the deck cargo in *Johnson* v. *Chapman* (1865) 19 CB(NS) 563.
173. *Anglo-Grecian Steam Trading Co Ltd* v. *T Beynon & Co* (1926) 24 Ll L Rep 122.
174. [1944] KB 87, 94.
175. (1865) 19 CB(NS) 563, 584.
176. Cf York-Antwerp Rules 1994, Rule V: when a ship is intentionally run on shore for the common safety, whether or not she might have been driven on shore, the consequent loss or damage to the property involved in the common maritime adventure shall be allowed in general average.
177. See also *supra*, 24–26.
178. *Royal Mail Steam Packet Co* v. *English Bank of Rio* (1887) 19 QBD 362, 373, per Wills J (distinguishing cases where removal of goods is for lightening the ship, for the purposes of the common adventure, or of saving the goods).
179. *Rose* v. *Bank of Australasia* [1894] AC 687. The House of Lords did not decide whether those expenses were in fact general average. See *infra*, 55.

cargo (e.g. specie) to safety, the expense of so doing may be treated as solely on account of that cargo, which may also be freed from liability to contribute for general average services subsequently provided to the remaining interests.[180] Similarly, Rule VII of the York-Antwerp Rules 1994 provides:

"Damage caused to any machinery and boilers of a ship which is ashore and in a position of common peril, in endeavouring to refloat, shall be allowed in general average when shown to have arisen from an actual intention to float the ship for the common safety at the risk of such damage . . ."

9. The action taken must be reasonable

A general average contribution cannot be recovered for an act which was unreasonably done.[181] Thus, if a master chooses to jettison an item other than that which would most benefit the common adventure, this should not qualify as a general average sacrifice and the owner of the item lost should be able to claim compensation for the whole loss from the shipowners.[182]

In situations where the master has a choice, he has absolute freedom to make whatever sacrifice he thinks best to avert the perils of the sea.[183] The criterion of reasonableness applies equally to extraordinary sacrifice and expenditure[184] and is decided according to what the master deems judicious with reference to the state of things at the time the act is performed.[185] Similarly, in selecting a place of refuge, a master may have to weigh comparative proximity, expense and convenience, and may justifiably select a port which is more suitable than the one which is simply nearest.[186] It will generally be reasonable to enter into a well known and widely used contract, e.g. on the United Kingdom Standard Conditions for Towage.[187] Entry into an onerous contract when the master has no reasonable alternative will constitute a general average act.[188]

---

180. See *Royal Mail Steam Packet Co* v. *English Bank of Rio* (1887) 19 QBD 362, esp 375–376, per Wills J, and the other cases on "complex salvage operations", *infra*, 53–54.
181. The requirement of reasonableness is contained in the Marine Insurance Act 1906, s.66(2) and in the York-Antwerp Rules 1994, Rule A and the new Rule Paramount, on which see *infra*, 39.
182. *Whitecross Wire Co* v. *Savill* (1882) 8 QBD 653, 663, per Brett LJ.
183. *Montgomery & Co* v. *Indemnity Mutual Insurance Co* [1902] 1 KB 734, 740.
184. *Athel Line Ltd* v. *Liverpool & London War Risks Insurance Assn Ltd* [1944] KB 87, 93. Cf *The Seapool* [1934] P 53, 64–65. Not only must the decision to incur expenditure be reasonable but so must the amount of the expenditure: *Anderson Tritton & Co* v. *Ocean SS Co* (1884) 10 App Cas 107, 117, per Lord Blackburn; (1883) 13 QBD 651, 662, per Brett MR.
185. See *Anglo-Grecian Steam Trading Co Ltd* v. *T Beynon & Co* (1926) 24 Ll L Rep 122. Though the presence of danger (*supra*, § 3) and possibly the question whether property has already been lost (*supra*, 24) may be judged objectively with hindsight, the reasonableness of the necessary action must be judged in the light of the circumstances at the time of danger.
186. *Phelps, James & Co* v. *Hill* [1891] 1 QB 605.
187. See *Australian Coastal Shipping Commission* v. *Green* [1971] 1 QB 456, 485, 486, per Phillimore LJ.
188. *The Gratitudine* (1801) 3 C Rob 240; *Australian Coastal Shipping Commission* v. *Green* [1971] 1 QB 456, 483, per Lord Denning MR.

SUCCESS

The danger necessitating a general average act may, of course, justify action which would, but for the danger, normally entitle the person suffering it to compensation for the resulting loss. However, it will not excuse conduct not required for purposes of general average, such as negligence in carrying out a general average operation,[189] albeit such fault may not be actionable for some other reason.[190] Nevertheless, it was held in *The Alpha*[191] that, where such conduct is not actionable, the actor may still claim a general average contribution if the loss is nonetheless a direct consequence[192] of the general average act. Since then, a Rule Paramount has been introduced into the York-Antwerp Rules, providing that "In no case shall there be any allowance for sacrifice or expenditure unless reasonably made or incurred"—an apparently benign requirement but one which may prove to be unpredictable and, for good or ill, disruptive of existing practical wisdom.[193]

A plaintiff who has acted unreasonably is nevertheless entitled to a contribution so far as his action was reasonable.[194]

10. Success: contribution may be claimed from, and only from, an interest which is of value at the place of termination of the adventure

As seen above, to qualify for general average, an act must be done with the intention of benefiting the common adventure.[195] But the mere fact that an act is done with the requisite intention will not entitle the actor to a general average contribution. It is also, as a general rule, necessary that the property in respect of which contribution is claimed be brought safely to the place where the adventure is intended to terminate ("the end of the voyage"). It is not, however, necessary that the preservation of the contributor's property be a consequence of the general average act.

Contributory interest must be of value at the end of the voyage

It is clear, both at common law and under the York-Antwerp Rules, that, regardless of any indulgence shown by the shipowner to any particular interest

---

189. Losses which would not have arisen but for the general average act but which are not direct consequences of that act, e.g. arising from stevedores' negligence at a port of refuge, may be recompensable for breach of contract or tort: see *The Oak Hill* [1975] 1 Lloyd's Rep 105 (Can SC); *The Alpha* [1991] 2 Lloyd's Rep 515, 522–523.
190. Such as under the Hague-Visby Rules, art. IV(2)(a): Carriage of Goods by Sea Act 1971, Sched., art. IV(2)(a).
191. *Corfu Navigation Co* v. *Mobil Shipping Co Ltd (The Alpha)* [1991] 2 Lloyd's Rep 515.
192. See *infra*, 47–48 n. 4.
193. See Macdonald [1995] LMCLQ 480, 489–493.
194. A plaintiff who has unreasonably incurred an unreasonable amount of liability under contract with a third party can claim a general average contribution to the extent of a reasonable amount: *Anderson Tritton & Co* v. *Ocean SS Co* (1884) 10 App Cas 107; *Ocean SS Co* v. *Anderson, Tritton & Co* (1885) 1 TLR 615; *Australian Coastal Shipping Commission* v. *Green* [1971] 1 QB 456, 483, per Lord Denning MR. See also *The Gratitudine* (1801) 3 C Rob 240, 277.
195. *Supra*, 37–38.

(e.g. where goods are carried free of liability to freight), each interest which is preserved after a general average act and which is of value at the end of the voyage is liable to make a general average contribution.[196]

In *Chellew* v. *Royal Commission on the Sugar Supply*,[197] a ship sustained damage to her hull and engines, so the master put into a port of refuge, thereby incurring expenditure. After leaving the port of refuge, fire broke out and the ship and its cargo were lost. The shipowner claimed a contribution for the port of refuge expenses from the cargo consignees as general average expenditure. The dispute was referred to arbitration, the arbitrator (later Mackinnon LJ) deciding that the claimant was not entitled to recover contribution. Sankey J and the Court of Appeal agreed. The York-Antwerp Rules had been incorporated into the bill of lading and Rule XVII provides that contribution is to be assessed according to the values of the property at the port of destination, so if property is then valueless (either because it fails to arrive or because it arrives worthless) the owner cannot be called upon to contribute. The arbitrator and Sankey J believed this to be the position at common law[198] and their view is sustained by the practice of adjusters in determining the question as if the usual situation applies, that the York-Antwerp Rules have been incorporated into the contract of affreightment.[199]

So, where the York-Antwerp Rules apply, a general average contribution is only recoverable in respect of an interest which has successfully been brought to the end of the voyage. Given the dominance of the Rules in practice, it has been unnecessary to consider the wider question (which might have to be answered if the Rules did not apply) whether successful preservation of the interests intended to be benefited is necessary for general average, or whether it is sufficient that a loss has been incurred with the mere intention to benefit. Certainly (albeit with different rules on assessment), the successful enrichment of the defendant is a prerequisite of liability under the general law of restitution,[200] the law of salvage[201] and the law governing necessitous intervention.[202] Mere similarity between general average and these areas of law does not dictate an identical rule. However, it is submitted that principle and the

---

196. *The Gratitudine* (1801) 3 C Rob 240, 278.
197. [1921] 2 KB 627; aff'd [1922] 1 KB 12.
198. Unfortunately, the commercially expert Court of Appeal (Bankes, Scrutton and Atkin LJJ) did not avail itself of the opportunity to consider the merits of the claim and the position at common law.
199. *Arnould*, para 976 n. 86.
200. See *Goff & Jones*, Chap. 1(3)(a).
201. See *Kennedy*, Chap. 7.
202. See Rose (1989) 9 OJLS 167, 198–199.

consensus of opinion[203] is that success is a requirement of a general average contribution.[204]

Sacrifices

The situation is straightforward as regards an extraordinary sacrifice for there seems to be universal agreement that contribution should only be claimed from an interest which has a value at the place of adjustment (which will be the port of destination if the voyage has not been abandoned earlier[205]); the principle of compensation rests on the loss sustained on the one hand and the ultimate benefit derived on the other.[206] The sacrifice is not made in relation to the values of the property saved but for the safety of the adventure as a whole.

Expenditure

There has been support for the view that a different rule applies in the case of extraordinary expenditure.[207] It is certainly arguable that a sacrifice is justifiable for the common interest and subject to a contribution on success, but that a shipowner at least is authorised to create liability for expenses regardless of success. One view is that, since the shipowner obtains the money for the expenditure from his own funds or from a loan, he should have a personal and absolute claim against the parties on whose behalf the money is laid out; otherwise, if all the property then perishes, the person laying out the money would be worse off than the other parties. This view is fallacious insofar as it is based on an analogy with salvage cases, for in those cases salvors have a direct claim against the cargo and its owners (in relation to the value of the cargo at the place to which it is brought), so that the shipowner's payment of salvage on their behalf is reclaimable from the cargo owners as an indemnity and not as contribution; general average expenditure is not incurred by the master on behalf of the cargo and its owners for he incurs liability on behalf of the shipowner when he pays port of refuge charges, wages of the crew, etc.[208] It is

---

203. See the discussion and references cited in *Chellew* v. *Royal Commission on the Sugar Supply* [1921] 2 KB 627 (Sankey J); *Arnould*, paras 919, 976–978; *Carver*, paras 1454–1459; *Lowndes & Rudolf*, 9th ed. (1964), paras 78, 341–356; 12th ed., paras G.03–G.05.
204. *Pirie & Co* v. *Middle Dock Co* (1881) 44 LT 426, 430, per Watkin Williams J. This seems also to have been the view of the court in *Atkinson* v. *Stephens* (1852) 7 Ex 567.
205. *Fletcher* v. *Alexander* (1868) LR 3 CP 375.
206. *Ibid.*, 382, per Bovill CJ. The actual point decided by that case was that jettisoned goods are to be valued according to what they would have been worth at the port of actual destination. Logically, if they had remained on board the adventure would have failed entirely, so that all interests would be valueless at the intended port of destination, and this would obviate the need for general average contributions altogether in cases of jettison!
207. See *The Mary Thomas* [1894] P 108 (Gorrell Barnes J); judgment affd *ibid.* (CA).
208. See *Carver*, para 1457.

also inconsistent with the general principle regarding extraordinary sacrifices to value the interests saved at the time at which they are saved instead of at the end of the voyage; and it is to pursue an uncertain course to suggest that, where ultimate values are insufficient, assessment should be made upon what values would have been but for the subsequent disaster. Moreover, there is no need for the shipowner to incur a double loss in the case of supervening disaster since he is free to insure the risk of becoming unable to recover a general average contribution and to add the premium to the general average expenditure.[209] To recognise this obviates the need for the sort of compromise suggested by Carver[210]: that, if the ship and cargo are lost (or if what is saved is insufficient to meet the expenditure), all the interests existing at the time of the expenditure remain under an obligation to contribute in relation to their interests at that time; while if the ship alone survives, the shipowner alone should be liable as the only party to reap the benefit of the expenditure.

So long as it is open to the party incurring the expenditure to insure against the loss of his right to contribution then we can obtain justice as well as certainty and convenience by having one adjustment at the port of destination, where the values of the contributing interests can be ascertained with precision. This is consistent with the principle that general average sacrifice or expenditure is made or incurred for the benefit of the common adventure and is dependent on the ultimate benefit derived. The fact that assessment is to be made at a later date is independent of the rule that the liability to contribute arises at the time of the expenditure,[211] so that time begins to run from then for questions of limitation.[212]

Conclusion: common law rule on sacrifice and expenditure

In principle, the common law rule should be the same as the practice embodied in Rule XVII of the York-Antwerp Rules and there is judicial support for the view that, in the cases of both sacrifice and expenditure, the liability for contribution and the shipowner's lien come into existence on the doing of the act, though the liability and the lien are subject to being defeated if the property saved has no value at the port of adjustment.[213]

---

209. *Chellew* v. *Royal Commission on the Sugar Supply* [1921] 2 KB 627, 631–632, per Mr FD Mackinnon KC, the legal arbitrator.
210. *Carver*, paras 1455–1456.
211. Roche J seems to have confused the two in *Green Star SS Co* v. *The London Assurance (The Andree)* [1933] 1 KB 378, 390. See *Arnould*, 15th ed. (1961), para 976 n. 82.
212. *Chandris* v. *Argo Insurance Co* [1963] 2 Lloyd's Rep 65, 79. Under US law, the cause of action accrues from the termination of the adventure and is subject to the defence of laches: *The Logan* [1936] AMC 993; *Transpacific Steamship Co* v. *Marine Office of America* [1957] AMC 1070; *The Beatrice* [1975] 1 Lloyd's Rep 220.
213. *Tate & Lyle* v. *Hain SS Co* (1934) 39 Com Cas 259, 278; 151 LT 249, 256, per Greer LJ; cited with approval by Lord Roche in *Morrison SS Co* v. *Greystoke Castle (Cargo Owners) (The Cheldale)* [1947] AC 265, 283. See also *ibid.*, 285 (Lord Roche), 312 (Lord Uthwatt); *Chellew's* case [1921] 2 KB 627, 633–634 (per FD Mackinnon KC), 639 (per Sankey J); *Green Star Shipping Co Ltd* v. *London Assurance (The Andree)* [1933] 1 KB 378, 390 (Roche J). In *Chellew*, Mackinnon LJ

Success not resulting from general average act

So long as action is undertaken for the purpose of the common adventure, even though it benefits only some of the interests involved,[214] a general average contribution can be claimed, though only from those interests which benefit from it.[215] The same is true, we have seen, where property is saved by a general average act done in order to preserve the common adventure from a danger which was different from that which the master supposed to exist.[216] It has been argued that, provided property has a value at the end of the voyage, contribution may be claimed from its owners in respect of a general average sacrifice made even though the property was not saved as a result of the general average sacrifice itself.[217] However, the law of unjust enrichment appears to make liability for restitution generally dependent on the defendant's being enriched "at the expense of" the plaintiff.[218] Thus, if this principle extends to general average, contribution should not be due if the safety of the defendant's property is not a consequence of the plaintiff's act.

The values of both the property which is ultimately preserved and the property which is sacrificed are assessed according to what they are or would have been at the port of destination.[219] Thus, if some cargo is jettisoned for general average purposes but the ship is subsequently lost, and then the remaining cargo is raised in a damaged condition (and the jettisoned cargo would also have been raised in a damaged condition if it had remained on board), the surviving cargo must contribute to the loss suffered by the sacrificed cargo, both cargoes being valued according to their damaged value at the end of the voyage.

Preservation of ship

Though there is copious literature, there is no decision in English law answering the question whether it is necessary for the ship to survive the general average danger[220] in order for an interest suffering a general average loss (e.g. jettisoned cargo) to claim from interests ultimately brought to a place of safety (e.g. the

---

(as he later became) thought that the opinion of Brett MR tended the same way in *Ocean SS Co v. Anderson* (1883) 13 QBD 651, 662; the case concerned a general average expenditure incurred on terms that it was to be payable whether the services hired were successful or not.

214. "Property ... is liable to contribution, provided that in consequence of that operation the whole adventure be preserved from destruction.": *Royal Mail Steam Packet Co Ltd v. English Bank of Rio de Janeiro Ltd* (1887) 19 QBD 362, 372, per Wills J.

215. *Hingston v. Wendt* (1876) 1 QBD 367, 371–372.

216. *Supra*, 46.

217. *Carver*, para 1361; and see the references cited therein.

218. See *supra*, 7.

219. *Fletcher v. Alexander* (1868) LR 3 CP 375; *Carver*, paras 1361, 1441, 1442. Thus, a mast which has suffered particular average damage on the voyage before it is sacrificed will be valued as if it arrives at the port of destination as a damaged mast.

220. The position where the vessel survives the general average danger but is subsequently lost before reaching destination is considered *supra*, 40.

remaining cargo).[221] A particular, nowadays uncommon, aspect of the question, voluntary stranding, is answered by Rule V of the York-Antwerp Rules 1994. Rule V provides[222]:

"When a ship is intentionally[223] run on shore[224] for the common safety, whether or not she might have been driven on shore, the consequent loss or damage to the property involved in the common maritime adventure shall be allowed in general average."

This accords with the prevailing view that survival of the vessel is not necessary.[225]

The question is what would have been the values of the sacrificed and surviving cargoes at the end of the voyage if the sacrifice had not been made, contribution only being due if the effect of the sacrifice was that the plaintiff's interest was worth less than if it had continued on the adventure. Thus, if for the sake of the common adventure some cargo is put into lighters and lost, then the ship is wrecked and the cargo remaining on board is raised and forwarded to destination in a damaged condition, and this would also have been the fate of the lightered cargo if it had remained on board, the lightered cargo can in principle claim a contribution from the other cargo, but not if the effect of lightering was that it did not suffer a loss and in fact benefited.[226]

Excluding the requirement of success

So far as there is a requirement of success, it may be limited or extinguished by contract.[227]

---

221. See *Arnould*, paras 977–978.
222. See also *Columbian Insurance Co* v. *Ashby* (1839) 13 Peters 331 (Story J). See also the Rules of Practice of the Association of Average Adjusters, Rule F4. Though there is no decision on the point, there seems no reason why a voluntary stranding should not be *capable* of being a general average act at common law.
223. Provided there is intention to run on shore for the common safety, it is unnecessary that the consequences are not precisely as intended, e.g. where the vessel grounds sooner or in a different place: *Anglo-Grecian Steam Trading Co Ltd* v. *T Beynon & Co* (1926) 24 Ll L Rep 122.
224. Rule V only applies to a voluntary stranding or running on shore, not to action taken to avoid such an event, e.g., putting the vessel broadside against a pier to avoid damage that would be incurred by running ashore: *The Seapool* [1934] P 53. Cf *Austin Friars Steamship Co Ltd* v. *Spillers & Bakers Ltd* [1915] 1 KB 833; affd [1915] 3 KB 586.
225. This was decided in the US in *Columbia Insurance Co* v. *Ashby* (1839) 13 Peters 331 (Story J), which was cited with approval in *Iredale* v. *China Traders Insurance Co* [1899] 2 QB 356 (Bigham J).
226. See *Carver*, para 1361. *Contra* Benecke, 212, who considered that the ship should be saved before contribution should be allowed to goods placed in lighters.
227. Cf the Institute hulls clause Duty of Assured (Sue and Labour) clause [Institute Time Clauses (Hulls) 1/11/95, cl.11.5; Institute Voyage Clauses (Hulls) 1/11/95, cl.9.5.], which provides: "When a claim for total loss of the Vessel is admitted under this insurance and expenses have been reasonably incurred in saving or attempting to save the Vessel and other property and there are no proceeds, or the expenses exceed the proceeds, then this insurance shall bear its pro rata share of such proportion of the expenses, or of the expenses in excess of the proceeds, as the case may be, as may reasonably be regarded as having been incurred in respect of the Vessel, excluding all special compensation and expenses as referred to in [sub-clause 5 of the General Average and Salvage clause: Institute Time Clauses (Hulls) 1/11/95, cl.10.5; Institute Voyage Clauses (Hulls) 1/11/95, cl.8.5. See *infra*, 113–114]; but if the Vessel be insured for less than its sound value at the

Failure

The loss flowing from an act which, because it is unsuccessful, fails to give rise to a claim for general average contribution must be treated as a particular average loss or a particular charge for the account of the interest on behalf of which it was incurred.[228]

11. The general average loss must be a direct consequence of the general average act

This requirement is considered in the next chapter.

---

time of the occurrence giving rise to the expenditure, the amount recoverable under this clause shall be reduced in proportion to the under-insurance."
228. *Atkinson* v. *Stephens* (1852) 7 Ex 567.

CHAPTER 3

QUALIFYING LOSSES

The party claiming a general average contribution must prove that the relevant loss was a general average loss and that it was caused by a general average act. General average losses include, obviously, general average sacrifices and general average expenditures. In addition, they include other losses resulting from general average acts.

Causation and remoteness

Despite its traditional exclusion from general average of acts done after the property has been brought to a place of safety, English law has always included within general average both losses caused by the initial general average act and expenses necessarily incurred in consequence of it.[1] Thus, the Marine Insurance Act 1906, s.66(1) provides that: "A general average loss is a loss caused by or directly consequential on a general average act." Therefore, a claimant can recover a contribution for such loss as he can show was the direct[2] consequence of a general average act,[3] and if there has been no breach in the chain of causation.[4]

---

1. See in particular the famous definition by Lawrence J in *Birkley* v. *Presgrave* (1801) 1 East 220, 228 (quoted *supra*, 1) and the judgments of the majority (Brett MR and Bowen LJ) in *Svendsen* v. *Wallace Bros* (1884) 13 QBD 69; though cf the discussion of the decisions of *Atwood* v. *Sellar & Co* (1880) 5 QBD 286 and *Svendsen* v. *Wallace*, *supra*, 21–23.
2. The word "direct" is commonly incorporated in stating the causation rule but is not insisted on by the definition in the Marine Insurance Act 1906, s.66(1).
3. There cannot be contribution for a loss occurring after a general average act if the loss would have occurred anyway, and so was not consequent upon the act. See, e.g., *Sea-Land Service Inc* v. *Aetna Insurance Co (The Beauregard)* [1977] 2 Lloyd's Rep 84 (US CA); *infra*, n. 4.
4. Marine Insurance Act 1906, s.66(1); *Svendsen* v. *Wallace* (1884) 13 QBD 69, 84, per Bowen LJ ("as to the object of general average contribution. It is to indemnify the person making the general average sacrifice against so much of the loss caused directly thereby as does not fall to his proportionate share"); *Austin Friars Steamship Co Ltd* v. *Spillers & Bakers Ltd* [1915] 1 KB 833; affd [1915] 3 KB 586 (damage to pier in attempting entry to dock); *Sea-Land Service Inc* v. *Aetna Insurance Co (The Beauregard)* [1977] 2 Lloyd's Rep 84 (US CA) (failure to prove that bottom damage after tow rope parted would not have occurred if tow not engaged).
   Stating the common law (though also making more detailed provision), Rule C of the York-Antwerp Rules 1994 provides that: "Only such losses, damages or expenses which are the direct consequence of the general average act shall be allowed as general average." By virtue of the Rule of Interpretation, the lettered Rules must give way to the numbered Rules. It is therefore

In particular, loss of freight is a common consequence of jettison of cargo.[5] The cost of ensuing legal proceedings[6] and, in practice, the costs of employing an average adjuster are also treated as general average losses.

Mathew J has said that "it is not necessary that a particular loss should have been contemplated, if it be incidental to the general average act."[7] Thus, where the vessel is tipped to repair the propeller and cargo is damaged by seawater, the damage gives rise to a general average contribution.[8] Similarly, if, to facilitate the carrying ship's refloating or reaching a port of refuge, cargo is put into lighters which sink before reaching shore, contribution is due for the loss suffered[9]; but, if lightered cargo is saved and the ship is lost, the cargo owners are not bound to contribute to the loss suffered by the ship owners, because the ship's loss resulted from the danger, not from a general average act.[10] However, if cargo was never in peril, and was damaged during unloading to facilitate particular average repairs to the ship, the cargo owner is not entitled to a general average contribution from the ship.[11]

Mathew J's comment raises the perennial difficulty of the distinction and relationship between requirements of causation and remoteness. Both requirements exist in general average, though they have not been clearly distinguished in the cases and, in particular, there has not been close scrutiny of the test of remoteness.[12] The two requirements are generally subsumed in the requirements that, to qualify for a right to contribution, the loss must have been *caused by* the action taken, and that action must have been *a general average act*. Although they do not totally eliminate the need to consider, for example, whether an "incidental" loss was reasonably foreseeable or within the master's reasonable contemplation, the criteria for a general average act (e.g., that the

---

possible for the numbered Rules to provide a different rule of causation. Thus, *Lowndes & Rudolf*, para 5.22 argues that "consequent loss or damage" recoverable under Rule V (voluntary stranding) (see *supra*, 44) may include indirect loss or damage. However, it is submitted, where the numbered Rule fails to make clear provision, its interpretation should be in accordance with the general principles in the lettered Rules.

" 'Direct consequences' are those which flow in an unbroken sequence from the act; whereas 'indirect consequences' are those in which the sequence is broken by an intervening or extraneous cause": *Australian Coastal Shipping Commission* v. *Green* [1971] 1 QB 456, 481H, per Lord Denning MR. See also *Anglo-Grecian Steam Trading Co Ltd* v. *T Beynon & Co* (1926) 24 Ll L Rep 122, esp 127; *The Alpha* [1991] 2 Lloyd's Rep 515, 521. Cf Ulrich, *Grosse-Haverei*, 5 (discussed in *Australian Coastal Shipping Commission* v. *Green* [1971] 1 QB 456 and *The Alpha*), where liability for general average (sacrifice, at least) is said to depend on what is reasonably foreseeable at the time of the general average act.

5. See *supra*, 14–15.
6. *Australian Coastal Shipping Commission* v. *Green* [1971] 1 QB 456.
7. *M'Call* v. *Houlder Bros* (1897) 2 Com Cas 129, 132, per Mathew J.
8. *M'Call* v. *Houlder Bros* (1897) 2 Com Cas 129.
9. *Hallett* v. *Wigram* (1845) 9 CB 580, 608–609, per Cresswell J; *M'Call* v. *Houlder Bros* (1897) 2 Com Cas 129, 132, per Mathew J; *Royal Mail Steam Packet Co* v. *English Bank of Rio de Janeiro* (1887) 19 QBD 362, 372, per Wills J. Cf *L'Amerique* (1888) 35 Fed Rep 835.
10. *Arnould*, para 929. See also Dig. 14.2.4.
11. *Hamel* v. *Peninsular & Oriental Steam Navigation Co* [1908] 2 KB 298. But see the York-Antwerp Rules 1994, Rules X(b) *infra*, 57–58 and XII *infra*, 50.
12. Cf *Australian Coastal Shipping Commission* v. *Green* [1971] 1 QB 456.

action be taken *reasonably* and *intentionally* for the *benefit* of the imperilled property) generally fulfil the functions of remoteness tests in other areas of the law for controlling the extent of liability.[13]

York-Antwerp Rules

Not surprisingly, many of the York-Antwerp Rules 1994 are not only framed to make specific provision for losses which shall or shall not be treated as general average losses, but also define, enlarge or restrict the qualifying losses.[14]

Thus, Rule C provides generally that "Demurrage, loss of market,[15] and any loss or damage sustained or expense incurred by reason of delay,[16] whether on the voyage or subsequently, and any indirect loss whatsoever, shall not be admitted as general average."

Rule II provides that "Loss of or damage to the property involved in the common maritime adventure *by or in consequence of* a sacrifice made for the common safety, and by water which goes down a ship's hatches opened or other opening made *for the purpose of making a jettison for the common safety*, shall be made good as general average."[17]

Rule III of the York-Antwerp Rules 1994 ("extinguishing fire on shipboard") provides that:

"Damage done to a ship and cargo, or either of them, by water[18] or otherwise, including damage by beaching or scuttling a burning ship, in extinguishing a fire[19] on board the ship, shall be made good as general average; except that no compensation shall be made for damage by smoke however caused[20] or by heat of the fire."[21]

---

13. Cf *Lowndes & Rudolf*, paras C.04–C.11.

14. The immediately following discussion does not refer to all the relevant Rules.

15. In practice "reversing" *Anglo-Argentine Livestock Agency* v. *Temperley* [1899] 2 QB 403. Cf *C Czarnikow Ltd* v. *Koufos (The Heron II)* [1969] 1 AC 350.

16. See also *The Leitrim* [1902] P 256; *JH Wetherall & Co Ltd* v. *London Assurance* [1931] 2 KB 448.

17. Italics added. See further *supra*, 18–19.

18. The practice of disallowing water damage (presumed to be based on the theory that property on fire was already lost) was disapproved in *Stewart* v. *West India and Pacific Steamship Co* (1873) LR 8 QB 88, affd *ibid.*, 362, and denied in *Achard* v. *Ring* (1874) 2 Asp MLC 422, whereafter it was discontinued. See also *Nimick* v. *Holmes* (1855) 25 Penn Rep 366; *Aspinwall* v. *Merchant Shipping Co* (1862) Unreported, 45 LJQB 648n; *Schmidt* v. *Royal Mail Steamship Co* (1862) 45 LJQB 646; *Pirie* v. *Middle Dock Co* (1881) 4 Asp MLC 388; *Whitecross Wire Co* v. *Savill* (1882) 8 QBD 653; *Greenshields, Cowie & Co* v. *Stephens & Sons* [1908] 1 KB 51; affd [1908] AC 431; *Pacific Mail SS Co* v. *NYH & R Min Co* (1896) 74 Fed Rep 564. Where seawater entered oil-carrying tank due to heavy weather and for the purpose of extinguishing fire, cargo owners could only claim contribution for the estimated loss due to flooding to extinguish the fire: *Garrels* v. *S Behr & Mathew Ltd* (1933) 47 Ll L Rep 319.

19. "Mere heating which has not arrived at the state of incandescence or ignition is not within the specific word 'fire' ": *Tempus Shipping Co* v. *Louis Dreyfus & Co* [1930] 1 KB 699, 708, per Wright J.

20. The Rule disallows smoke damage whether the smoke arises from the original fire alone or is encouraged by measures taken to control the fire, e.g., carbon dioxide used instead of water: see *Lowndes & Rudolf*, para 3.11.

21. Although the Rule allows, into general average, losses not otherwise qualifying, or easily provable, as such (because caused by the danger rather than by steps taken to avert its consequences), it has the advantage of obviating the practical difficulty of deciding to what extent

In respect of voluntary stranding, Rule V restricts contribution to "the *consequent* loss or damage to the property involved in the common adventure".[22]

In relation to claims respecting damage to machinery and boilers, Rule VII requires that damage to ship's engines be done while the vessel was aground and in a position of peril, while trying to refloat the vessel, and from an actual intention to float the ship at the risk of such damage.[23]

Rule VIII provides that: "When a ship is ashore and cargo and ship's fuels and stores or any of them are discharged as a general average act, the extra cost of lightening, lighter hire and reshipping (if incurred), and any loss or damage to the property involved in the common maritime adventure in consequence thereof, shall be admitted as general average."

Under Rule XII, damage to or loss of cargo, fuel or stores sustained in direct consequence of their handling, discharging, storing, reloading and stowing shall be made good as general average when and only when the cost of those measures is admitted in general average, but not losses arising from collateral events such as fire or theft.

Contractual liability

Where the general average act is entry into a contract, a liability under that contract to the contractor is a direct consequence of the general average act.[24] A plaintiff who has unreasonably incurred an unreasonable amount of liability under contract with a third party can claim a general average contribution to the extent of a reasonable amount.[25] Presumably, if as a result of illegitimate pressure the plaintiff entered into a contract which was not enforced but the contractor was awarded reasonable remuneration,[26] the liability for the reasonable remuneration would constitute a general average loss.

Negligence and third party liability

Although action taken to avert the consequences of the danger must be reasonable[27] and the persons taking such action must exercise care not to cause loss negligently, a resultant loss may count as a general average loss though it

---

the losses can be attributed to the two different causes. Cf *Reliance Marine Insurance Co* v. *New York & Cuba Mail Steamship Co* (1895) 70 Fed Rep 262, (1896) 77 Fed Rep 317, 165 US 720.

22. Emphasis added.

23. *Corfu Navigation Co* v. *Mobil Shipping Co Ltd (The Alpha)* [1991] 2 Lloyd's Rep 515. See also *McCall* v. *Houlder Bros* (1897) 2 Com Cas 129 (tipping ship to repair propeller, whereby water damaged cargo); *Anglo-Grecian Steam Trading Co* v. *T Beynon & Co* (1926) 24 Ll L Rep 122.

24. *Australian Coastal Shipping Commission* v. *Green* [1971] 1 QB 456 (shipowner's claim for costs of successfully defending tug's claim for total loss; and for indemnity to tug for salvage payable after tow-rope parted and tug itself required salvage).

25. See *supra*, 39.

26. See, e.g., *The Port Caledonia and the Anna* [1903] P 184.

27. See *supra*, 38–39.

could have been avoided if the circumstances had enabled more care to be taken in considering and executing the action taken, for example, if there is reasonably foreseeable but unavoidable incompetence and inefficiency.[28] However, the mere fact that a loss caused by negligence during general average operations would not have occurred but for the operation does not justify its treatment as a general average loss.[29] A loss is not recoverable if it results from "some intervening or supervening act of negligence or some accident which was not something unexpected not connected with the original" action taken.[30]

However, provided it is reasonable *vis-à-vis* the contributors,[31] a liability incurred to third parties as a direct consequence of a general average act (e.g. environmental pollution resulting from lightening a stranded tanker as a general average act) may give rise to a general average claim at common law. Thus, in order to disassociate general average acts from environmental pollution, to avoid property insurers' perceived exposure to liability insurers' risks and to avoid delay in adjustment, Rule C of the York-Antwerp Rules 1994 now provides that:

"In no case shall there be any allowance in general average for losses, damages or expenses incurred in respect of damage to the environment or in consequence of the escape or release of pollutant substances from the property involved in the common maritime adventure."

The same opinion may be regarded as applying to Rule VI of the York-Antwerp Rules 1994, which deals with salvage.[32]

Salvage,[33] lightening and the environment

The significance of contractual and non-contractual salvage in relation to general average and particular charges was discussed above,[34] as was the place of salvage within the general law on necessity.[35]

"A salvage service [is] a service which confers a benefit by saving or helping to save a recognised subject of salvage when in danger from which it cannot be extricated unaided, if and so far as the rendering of such service is voluntary in the sense of being attributable neither to a pre-existing obligation nor solely for the interests of the salvor,[36] ... the cause of action for which accrues and is complete at the date of the termination of the services."[37]

---

28. See *Hudson*, 192.
29. See *supra*, 39 n. 189.
30. *Anglo-Grecian Steam Trading Co Ltd* v. *T Beynon & Co* (1926) 24 Ll L Rep 122, esp 127.
31. See *supra*, 38–39.
32. See *infra*, 52–54.
33. See generally DW Steel and FD Rose, *Kennedy's Law of Salvage*, 5th ed. (1985); G Brice, *Maritime Law of Salvage*, 2nd ed. (1993), with 1st Supp. (1995).
34. *Supra*, 3–5.
35. *Supra*, 9.
36. This means that persons interested in the adventure cannot be salvors.
37. *Kennedy*, para 11.

A successful salvor is entitled to a maritime lien and to a reward for "salvage charges" under admiralty law.[38] Since, under English law, each party who incurs liability to pay a salvage reward only does so in respect of his own property,[39] a shipowner does not incur liability on behalf of other persons interested in the adventure and therefore, on one view at least,[40] no consequent entitlement to claim a general average contribution from such persons.[41]

In modern times salvage services are more commonly provided after conclusion of a salvage contract rather than under the general law. And, if a shipowner contracts for salvage services on behalf of himself and of the other interests involved in the adventure, and with their authority, his liability under the salvage contract may entitle him to a general average contribution[42] for so much of the liability as was in fact incurred for purposes of general average.[43] In fact, Lloyd's Standard Form of Salvage Agreement,[44] which is the commonest salvage contract in use, provides that the master contracts with salvors separately on behalf of each party requiring services,[45] so that each salvee neither incurs liability on behalf of other interests for salvage services nor, it would seem therefore, a right to a general average contribution from them. However, the position has been reversed in practice by the York-Antwerp Rules. Rule VI(a) of the York-Antwerp Rules 1994 provides:

"Expenditure incurred by the parties to the adventure in the nature of salvage, whether under contract or otherwise, shall be allowed in general average provided that the salvage operations were carried out for the purpose of preserving from peril the property involved in the common maritime adventure."

Rule C of the York-Antwerp Rules 1994 generally excludes from general average any allowance for losses, damages and expenses incurred in respect of damage to the environment or in consequence of the escape or release of pollutant substances from the property involved in the common maritime adventure. Nonetheless, Rule VI(a) provides that expenditure allowed in general average shall include any salvage remuneration in which the skill and efforts of the salvors in preventing or minimising damage to the environment

---

38. See Marine Insurance Act 1906, s.65(2).
39. *The Raisby* (1885) 10 PD 114. This case drew a distinction between English law and the laws of other countries, where salvage expenditure was generally treated as general average.
40. See *Carver*, paras 1401–1403.
41. See, e.g., *Svendsen* v. *Wallace* (1884) 13 QBD 69, per Brett MR. But cf *Anderson Tritton & Co* v. *Ocean Steamship Co* (1884) 10 App Cas 107, 114, per Lord Blackburn. Payment on behalf of such persons may be recovered from the salvor in restitution.
42. Marine Insurance Act 1906, s.65(2). See *The Prinz Heinrich* (1888) 13 PD 31; *Briggs* v. *Merchant Traders Association* (1849) 13 QB 167.
43. *Anderson Tritton & Co* v. *Ocean Steamship Co* (1884) 10 App Cas 107. Cf Rules of Practice of the Association of Average Adjusters, Rule C1.
44. See *infra*, Appx 5.
45. See LOF 1995, cl.16: "The Master or other person signing this Agreement on behalf of the property to be salved enters into this Agreement as agent for the vessel her cargo freight bunker stores and any other property thereon and the respective Owners thereof and binds each (but not the one for the other or himself personally) to the due performance thereof."

SALVAGE, LIGHTENING AND THE ENVIRONMENT

such as is referred to in Article 13(1)(b) of the CMI International Convention on Salvage 1989[46] have been taken into account. Furthermore, Rule XI(d) of the York-Antwerp Rules 1994 provides:

"The cost of measures taken to prevent or minimise damage to the environment shall be allowed in general average when incurred in any or all of the following circumstances:
  (i) as part of an operation performed for the common safety which, had it been undertaken by a party outside the common maritime adventure, would have entitled such party to a salvage reward;
  (ii) as a condition of entry into or departure from any port or place in the circumstances prescribed in Rule X(a)[47];
  (iii) as a condition of remaining at any port or place in the circumstances prescribed in Rule XI(b),[48] provided that when there is an actual escape or release of pollutant substances the cost of any additional measures required on that account to prevent or minimise pollution or environmental damage shall not be allowed as general average;
  (iv) necessarily in connection with the discharging, storing or reloading of cargo whenever the cost of those operations is admissible as general average."

However, under Rule VI(b) of the York-Antwerp Rules 1994, "special compensation" payable to a salvor by the shipowner, with respect to services rendered in a case of threatened environmental damage, under Article 14 of the Salvage Convention, to the extent that such special compensation is greater than any award recoverable by the salvor under Article 13 of the Convention or under any other substantially similar provision, shall not be allowed in general average.[48a]

In practice, in respect of what are commonly called "complex salvage operations"[49] (e.g., where cargo is removed to safety before operations can continue on the carrying vessel) it may be easier to state the general principle—that contribution is due in respect of an operation carried out for the benefit of the whole adventure but not if the operation or part of it is solely for the benefit of a single interest[50]—than to apply it to the facts. The tendency in nineteenth-century cases to disallow claims for contribution in respect of subsequent services to the vessel rather than to treat them as part of one continuous operation[51] reflected the tradition of English law that general

---

46. Reproduced in [1990] LMCLQ 54 and enacted in English law in the Merchant Shipping Act 1995, s.224, Sched. 11.
47. See *infra*, 57.
48. See *infra*, 58.
48a. The Salvage Convention 1989 (*supra*, n. 46), Attachment 2 specifically authorises this exclusion.
49. It is not necessarily the salvage operations nor the legal principles or rules which are difficult, so much as the application of the law to the facts. See, e.g., *Kemp* v. *Halliday* (1865) 34 LJQB 233, 243; *Royal Mail Steam Packet Co* v. *English Bank of Rio* (1887) 19 QBD 362, 371, per Wills J.
50. In *Kemp* v. *Halliday* (1865) 34 LJQB 233, 243, Blackburn J suggested that, "if the cargo could be easily and cheaply taken out of the [sunken] ship, and saved by itself, it would not be proper to charge it with any portion of the joint operation, which, in that case, would not be incurred for the preservation of the cargo." *Sed quaere.* Cf *Anderson Tritton & Co* v. *Ocean Steamship Co* (1884) 10 App Cas 107, 114, per Lord Blackburn.
51. General average contribution from unloaded cargo in respect of subsequent services to the vessel was held to be *not due* in *Job* v. *Langton* (1856) 6 E & B 779 (expense of refloating unladen

average was only due while a community of interest remained[52] and property had not been brought to safety.[53] However, the decisions on the facts in those cases would not necessarily be the same today and there has been a tendency in practice to treat the situation in question as one continuous operation for the sake of the whole adventure. The position has been clarified in practice in respect of "expenses lightening a ship when ashore, and consequent damage", by Rule VIII of the York-Antwerp Rules 1994, which provides:

"When a ship is ashore and cargo and ship's fuels and stores or any of them are discharged as a general average act, the extra cost of lightening, lighter hire and reshipping (if incurred), and any loss or damage to the property involved in the common maritime adventure in consequence thereof, shall be admitted as general average."

A consequence of the fact that individual interests receiving salvage services are only liable to the salvor for services rendered in respect of their own property is that there may not be uniformity of treatment in respect of release of property and determination of liability. Rightly or wrongly, differential salvage awards may advantage or disadvantage individual salvees; yet the difference between the systems for assessing general average and salvage[54] would be further exacerbated if general average adjustment were to deal with salvage awards other than as actually made. Accordingly, in practice the actual amounts of the relevant sums are generally brought into the adjustment and reapportioned, in accordance with the Advisory Committee of the Association of Average Adjusters'

"opinion that Rule VI is mandatory as between the parties to a contract of affreightment providing for adjustment according to the York-Antwerp Rules 1974. The Committee accordingly takes the view that subject to the overall requirement of reasonableness in the amounts claimed by parties to the adventure, differential expenditure, including costs, on account of the salvage should be allowed in general average and apportioned as such."[55]

---

vessel and taking her to Liverpool for repair; cargo carried to destination by another vessel but treated as carried on by original ship after repairs), *Walthew* v. *Mavrojani* (1870) LR 5 Ex 116, *Royal Mail Steam Packet Co* v. *English Bank of Rio* (1887) 19 QBD 362 or *Kemp* v. *Halliday* (1865) 34 LJQB 233, affd (1866) LR 1 QB 520 but *due* in *Moran* v. *Jones* (1857) 7 E & B 523 (in which "it appears that the only goods which were removed were, not the general cargo, but a small portion only of goods belonging to the shipowner himself ": *Walthew* v. *Mavrojani* (1870) LR 5 Ex 116, 122, per Bovill CJ) (the decision in *Moran* v. *Jones* was disapproved in *Svendsen* v. *Wallace* (1884) 13 QBD 80).

See also *McAndrews* v. *Thatcher* (1865) 3 Wall. 347 (US SC); *Coastal Wrecking Co* v. *Phoenix Assurance Co* (1881) 7 Fed Rep 236; *Reliance Marine Insurance Co* v. *New York & Cuba Steamship Co* (1896) 77 Fed Rep 317; 165 US 720.

52. Though, of course, the fact that a voyage is interrupted does not mean that the shipowner ceases to be entitled to complete it. See *infra*, 90.

53. See *Walthew* v. *Mavrojani* (1870) LR 5 Ex 116, 126, per Brett J; *Royal Mail Steam Packet Co* v. *English Bank of Rio* (1887) 19 QBD 362.

54. See *supra*, 3–5.

55. (1 July 1983) Association of Average Adjusters Advisory Opinion No. 40. See also *The Jason* (1908) 162 Fed Rep 56; (1910) 175 Fed Rep 414; 225 US 32.

Port of refuge expenses

The term "port of refuge expenses" is used here to encompass a number of different expenses incurred on entry to, at, and on leaving a port of refuge, some of which have been treated as general average losses and some as particular charges. It is especially important here to distinguish clearly the common law on port of refuge expenses from the rules applied in practice. The somewhat complicated and illogical common law rules are now principally of historical interest, having made minimal contribution to the rules which now apply in practice.[56]

(a) The common law

It is easier to summarise the principles which have been addressed in the cases than to justify all of the actual decisions. In general, contribution is due for a loss caused by a general average act or its direct consequences, and it should be this principle, rather than the results on the facts of individual cases, that determines at common law when expenses are the subject of a general average contribution.

Port of refuge expenses may be regarded as constituting part of a continuous operation qualifying for general average.[57] Otherwise, services rendered as a result of a particular average loss, or after property has been brought to physical safety, are for the account of the person normally responsible for them. Thus, where entry to a port is, or is the result of, a general average act, the expenses of entry to the port (e.g. towage, pilotage and harbour dues) are in principle the subject of contribution.[58] Where a general average operation necessitates the unloading and warehousing of cargo, the expense may be attributed to general average, especially if entry to a port of refuge was necessitated by a general average sacrifice.[59] Similarly, the House of Lords decided *obiter* in *Rose* v. *Bank of Australasia*[60] that, where the master removes cargo from a stranded vessel for the purposes of the common adventure and while he is still considering whether to continue the adventure, the expenses incurred, and commission to merchants[61] engaged to sell unidentified bales of cargo, may, depending on the circumstances, be chargeable to general average, even though the voyage is

---

56. See TG Carver, "Expenses at a Port of Refuge" (1892) 8 LQR 229.
57. *Atwood* v. *Sellar & Co* (1880) 5 QBD 286. See also *Hall* v. *Janson* (1855) 4 E & B 500.
58. *Plummer* v. *Wildman* (1815) 3 M & S 482; *Atwood* v. *Sellar & Co* (1880) 5 QBD 286; *Svendsen* v. *Wallace Bros* (1884) 13 QBD 69, 87–88, per Bowen LJ (cf *ibid.*, 76–77, per Brett MR); *Hamel* v. *Peninsular & Oriental Steam Navigation Co* [1908] 2 KB 298.
59. *Atwood* v. *Sellar & Co* (1880) 5 QBD 286.
60. [1894] AC 687. The first instance judgment of Lawrance J (1891) and an account of his contribution to the foundation of the Commercial Court appear in VV Veeder, "Mr Justice Lawrance: The 'True Begetter' of the English Commercial Court" (1994) 110 LQR 292.
61. And *possibly* even charges made by the master himself: *Rose* v. *Bank of Australia* [1894] AC 687, 697.

subsequently abandoned.[62] However, expenses incurred after entry into the port and after the relevant property is in a place of safety may normally be regarded as properly to be borne by the particular interest (e.g. where unloaded cargo needs to be warehoused or wetted cargo to be dried), especially if entry to the port of refuge was necessitated by perils of the sea, which normally causes the ship a particular average loss.[63] In principle, additional wages for master and crew incurred as a consequence of a general average act should be the subject of contribution; but they have at common law generally been treated as an ordinary expense of the shipowner.[64] If the cargo and ship are in safety, the expenses of recommencing the voyage (e.g. reloading the cargo and the pilotage expenses of leaving port) are arguably part of one continuous operation,[65] but at common law are more likely to be treated as ordinary expenses at the risk of freight.[66]

(b) Current practice

Port of refuge expenses are principally dealt with in the York-Antwerp Rules 1994 in Rule X (expenses at port of refuge etc.) and Rule XI (wages[67] and maintenance of crew and other expenses, such as fuel, stores and port charges, bearing up for and in a port of refuge). As numbered Rules, these Rules must, of course, be interpreted according to their terms and not limited by general principles, whether arising from the lettered Rules or from the common law.[68] Subject to that important proviso, their general aim is that such expenses shall attract a general average contribution insofar as they constitute expenditure which was "caused by" a general average act.[69]

---

62. In fact it was held that those charges were not chargeable to freight alone but might be chargeable to general average, or to cargo, or to cargo and freight, depending on the circumstances.

63. *Svendsen* v. *Wallace Bros* (1884) 13 QBD 69, affd (1885) 10 App Cas 404; *Power* v. *Whitmore* (1815) 4 M & S 141; *Hallett* v *Wigram* (1850) 9 CB 580; *Walthew* v. *Mavrojani* (1870) LR 5 Ex 116. Cf *Hall* v. *Janson* (1855) 4 E & B 500; *Job* v. *Langton* (1856) 6 E & B 779; *M'Call & Co Ltd* v. *Houlder Bros* (1897) 2 Com Cas 129. It is not necessarily the case that warehousing of cargo is purely for cargo's benefit, since freight is in principle dependent on cargo's arrival at destination in merchantable condition.

64. *Power* v. *Whitmore* (1815) 4 M & S 141. Cf *Da Costa* v. *Newnham* (1788) 2 TR 407 (disapproved in *Svendsen* v. *Wallace Bros* (1884) 13 QBD 69, affd (1885) 10 App Cas 404); *Atwood* v. *Sellar & Co* (1880) 5 QBD 286, 291, per curiam (CA); *The Leitrim* [1902] P 256, 268, per Gorell Barnes J.

65. *Atwood* v. *Sellar & Co* (1880) 5 QBD 286. See also *Hall* v. *Janson* (1855) 4 E & B 500.

66. *Svendsen* v. *Wallace Bros* (1884) 13 QBD 69, aff'd (1885) 10 App Cas 404.

67. York-Antwerp Rules 1994, Rule XI(c): "For the purpose of this [Rule XI] and the other Rules wages shall include all payments made to or for the benefit of the master, officers and crew, whether such payments be imposed by law upon the shipowners or made under the terms or articles of employment."

68. See *supra*, 11–12.

69. Of course, whether or not there is a situation of general average, wages are in fact likely to be paid because there is a continuing contract of employment, rather than because there has been a general average act. The general object is to attribute to general average the additional expense required by the general average act.

PORT OF REFUGE EXPENSES

Rule X(a) provides for expenses on entry to a place of refuge, removal to a different place of refuge, and departure therefrom to be allowed in general average:

"When a ship shall have entered a port or place of refuge[70] or shall have returned to her port or place of loading in consequence of accident,[71] sacrifice or other extraordinary circumstances which render that necessary for the common safety, the expenses of entering such port or place shall be admitted as general average; and when she shall have sailed thence with her original cargo, or a part of it, the corresponding expenses of leaving[72] such port or place consequent upon such entry or return shall likewise be admitted as general average.

When a ship is at any port or place of refuge and is necessarily removed to another port or place because repairs cannot be carried out[73] in the first port or place, the provisions of this Rule shall be applied to the second port or place as if it were a port or place of refuge and the cost of such removal including temporary repairs and towage shall be admitted as general average. The provisions of Rule XI shall be applied to the prolongation of the voyage occasioned by such removal."

Rule XI(a) provides that:

"Wages and maintenance of master, officers and crew reasonably incurred and fuel and stores consumed during the prolongation of the voyage occasioned by a ship entering a port or place of refuge or returning to her port or place of loading shall be admitted as general average when the expenses of entering such port or place are allowable in general average in accordance with Rule X(a)."

Rule X(b) provides that costs of handling and discharging cargo, fuel or stores shall be treated as general average when incurred for that purpose:

---

70. A place of refuge need not necessarily exhibit the characteristics of a port. See *Hunter* v. *Northern Marine Insurance Co Ltd* (1888) 13 App Cas 717; *Maritime Insurance Co Ltd* v. *Alianza Insurance Co of Santander* [1907] 1 KB 660; and *Humber Conservancy Board* v. *Federated Coal and Shipping Co* [1928] 1 KB 492, 495, in which Scrutton LJ said of the Merchant Shipping Act 1894, s.742 (now Merchant Shipping Act 1995, s.313(1)) (" 'Port' includes 'place' ") that " 'place' following 'port' must be interpreted as *ejusdem generis* with 'port', as a locality having some or many of the characteristics of a port."

71. See *infra*, n. 74.

72. In *Westoll* v. *Carter* (1898) 3 Com Cas 112, the vessel had to return to her port of loading (in fact, due to initial unseaworthiness, so no general average contribution was due: see *infra*, 66–76). While there, ice formed and an ice-breaker had to be employed to enable her to leave. Bigham J opined (at 114) that "this expenditure was not ... an 'expense of leaving' her berth within the meaning of [the York-Antwerp Rules]. The expenses meant by the rules are, in my opinion, the ordinary expenses of leaving the place of loading, 'corresponding' to the expenses of entering such place. This expenditure was part of the cost of prosecuting the voyage, which must be borne by the shipowner." *Sed quaere*.

73. In *Marida Ltd* v. *Oswal Steel (The Bijela)* [1992] 1 Lloyd's Rep 636 (discussed *infra*, 62–63), Hobhouse J at first instance held that, where a vessel was at a port at which temporary repairs could be effected, there was no necessity to remove her to another place to carry out permanent repairs, so the expense incurred in such removal would not count for general average under Rule X(a). His decision was affirmed by the Court of Appeal [1993] 1 Lloyd's Rep 411, the decision of which was reversed by the House of Lords [1994] 1 WLR 615. Neither superior court had to deal with this point (see *ibid.*, 620), though it may be regarded as implicit in the decision of the House of Lords that removal to the port at which the (alternative) permanent repairs were to be effected at least forms part of the putative cost of such permanent repairs against which to measure the extent to which the cost of temporary repairs effected can be allowed as a substituted expense. It seems that

"The cost of handling on board or discharging cargo, fuel or stores whether at a port or place of loading, call or refuge, shall be admitted as general average, when the handling or discharge was necessary for the common safety or to enable damage to the ship caused by sacrifice or accident[74] to be repaired, if the repairs were necessary for the safe prosecution of the voyage,[75] except in cases where the damage to the ship is discovered at a port or place of loading or call without any accident or other extraordinary circumstance connected with such damage having taken place during the voyage.

The cost of handling on board or discharging cargo, fuel or stores shall not be admissible as general average when incurred solely for the purpose of restowage due to shifting during the voyage, unless such restowage is necessary for the common safety."

Rule XI(b) provides generally for expenses incurred during detention in a port of refuge for purposes of general average:

"When a ship shall have entered or been detained in any port or place in consequence of accident, sacrifice or other extraordinary circumstances which render that necessary for the common safety, or to enable damage to the ship caused by sacrifice or accident to be repaired, if the repairs were necessary for the safe prosecution of the voyage, the wages and maintenance of the master, officers and crew reasonably incurred during the extra period of detention in such port or place until the ship shall or should have been made ready to proceed upon her voyage, shall be admitted in general average.

Fuel and stores consumed during the extra period of detention shall be admitted as general average, except such fuel and stores as are consumed in effecting repairs not allowable in general average.

Port charges incurred during the extra period of detention shall likewise be admitted as general average except such charges as are incurred solely by reason of repairs not allowable in general average.

Provided that when damage to the ship is discovered at a port or place of loading or call without any accident or other extraordinary circumstance connected with such damage having taken place during the voyage, then the wages and maintenance of master, officers and crew and fuel and stores consumed and port charges incurred during the extra detention for repairs to damages so discovered shall not be admissible as general average, even if the repairs are necessary for the safe prosecution of the voyage."

---

the Rule was originally intended to apply to permanent repairs but may now be regarded as applying to any necessary repairs: see *Hudson*, 156.

74. In *Vlassopoulos v. British and Foreign Marine Insurance Co (The Makis)* [1929] 1 KB 187 Roche J held that the numbered Rules were subservient to the lettered Rules and that, consistently with Rule A (see *supra*, 2), the word "accident" was confined to accidents threatening the common safety. The Rule of Interpretation (see *supra*, 11) now makes the lettered rules subservient to the numbered Rules, and the word "accident" does not need to be interpreted subject to this qualification. On "accident" generally, see MA Clarke, *The Law of Insurance Contracts*, 2nd ed. (1994, with Supp. 1996), Chap. 17–5.

75. In *Marida Ltd v. Oswal Steel (The Bijela)* [1992] 1 Lloyd's Rep 636, affd [1993] 1 Lloyd's Rep 411, rvrsd [1994] 1 WLR 615, [1994] 2 Lloyd's Rep 1 (discussed *infra*, 62–63), if permanent repairs had been carried out to the vessel at New York, they would have been attended by the cost of discharging, storing and reloading the cargo, and both types of expenditure would *prima facie* have been allowable as general average. However, the shipowners effected temporary repairs at Jamestown, claiming them as substituted expenses under Rule XIV (on which, see *infra*, 61). The House of Lords upheld their claim, rejecting the cargo owners' argument that, since temporary repairs were in fact carried out, permanent repairs at New York were not "necessary for the safe prosecution of the voyage" under Rule X(b).

Expenses of storage, reloading and stowage may be included in general average under the terms of Rule X(c)[76]:

"Whenever the cost of handling or discharging cargo, fuel or stores is admissible as general average, the costs of storage, including insurance if reasonably incurred,[77] reloading and stowage of such cargo, fuel or stores shall likewise be admitted as general average. The provisions of Rule XI shall be applied to the extra period of detention occasioned by such reloading or restowing."

However, when the ship is condemned[78] or does not proceed on her original voyage, storage expenses, wages and maintenance of master, officers and crew, fuel and stores consumed and port charges shall be admitted as general average only up to the date of the ship's condemnation or of the abandonment of the voyage or up to the date of completion of discharge of cargo if the condemnation or abandonment takes place before that date.[79]

Substituted expenses

The general rule at common law is that a contribution can only be claimed in respect of a loss directly caused by a general average act, not one incurred instead of such a loss. In *Wilson* v. *Bank of Victoria*[80] the master of a disabled sailing vessel with auxiliary steam power declined to carry out expensive repairs at a port of refuge. He effected temporary repairs and purchased additional coal to complete the voyage home. The shipowner's claim for a general average contribution in respect of the additional coals was disallowed. A number of observations can be made with respect to such a claim. First, it is clear that no expenditure is allowable in general average if it represents merely a more onerous method of performing the voyage, as opposed to an extraordinary expenditure.[81] Secondly, if a loss is incurred as a substitute for a clear general average loss, it is at least arguable that no general average loss has occurred. But, thirdly, whether in performing the voyage or effecting a general average act, the master must act reasonably.[82] This may require the master to take inexpensive rather than expensive action; and, so long as the inexpensive action is a general average act, it will give rise to a claim for a general average contribution. Under the law of marine insurance, action taken to avert or minimise an insured loss

---

76. Rule X(c) enlarges Rule X(b) and should be interpreted similarly: see *The Bijela*, *supra* n. 75, where Rule X(c) was mentioned by the Court of Appeal alongside Rule X(b), though not specifically mentioned by Hobhouse J or the House of Lords.
77. In *LW & P Armstrong Inc* v. *SS Mormacmar* [1947] AMC 1611; affd *The Mormacmar* [1956] AMC 1028, it was held to be the duty of the carrier to insure goods placed ashore against risks such as fire.
78. See *Assicurazioni Generali* v. *SS Bessie Morris Co Ltd* [1892] 2 QB 652; *Kulukundis* v. *Norwich Union Fire Insurance Soc* [1937] 1 KB 1.
79. York-Antwerp Rules 1994, Rules X(c), XI(b).
80. (1867) LR 2 QB 203.
81. See *supra*, 31–32.
82. See *supra*, 38–39.

may give rise to a claim under the insurance contract.[83] It is, therefore, not unreasonable that action taken alternatively to action which would qualify as a general average act should give rise to a claim for general average contribution.

However, *Wilson* v. *Bank of Victoria* has traditionally been regarded as a disapproval of this possibility in English law[84] unless there is a custom to that effect tacitly constituting part of the contract.[85] Moreover, action taken to avoid action qualifying as a general average act under a lettered Rule of the York-Antwerp Rules 1994 will not justify a claim under that Rule.[86] The difficulty has been overcome in practice by Rule F of the York-Antwerp Rules 1994. Rule F embraces substituted expenses not allowable in general average at common law and those which are allowable at common law by custom. It provides:

"Any additional expense incurred in place of another expense which would have been allowable as general average shall be deemed to be general average and so allowed without regard to the saving, if any, to other interests, but only up to the amount of the general average expense avoided."

The Rule does not apply to expenses which the shipowner would normally incur in his own interest, those for which the shipowner is liable under the contract of carriage or those which qualify as general average expenditure in their own right; it concerns *additional* expenses incurred in substitution for possible (and not merely hypothetical) allowable general average expenses.[87] Examples (the first and second of which were formerly the subject of a separate Rule of the York-Antwerp Rules[88] and remain the subject of separate Rules of the Rules of Practice of the Association of Average Adjusters[89]) are: towage of the vessel from a port of refuge at which it is practicable to repair her; forwarding cargo from such a port; temporary repairs (normally dealt with under Rule XIV of the York-Antwerp Rules 1994)[90]; the extra expense of drydocking with cargo on board[91]; additional overtime; and air freighting spare parts.[92]

Where the relevant expenses are attributable partly to substitution for general average expenditure (in practice often because they save time) and partly to other purposes, only the former proportion is allowable in general average

---

83. *Lee* v. *Southern Insurance Co* (1870) LR 5 CP 397. See *infra*, 105.
84. Cf *The Minnetonka* (1905) 10 Asp MLC 142.
85. *Wilson* v. *Bank of Victoria* (1867) LR 2 QB 203, 212.
86. *The Seapool* [1934] P 53.
87. Thus, the following examples are only allowable as substitute expenses so far as (1) the shipowner is not liable to bear the cost personally and (2) a genuine general average expenditure is a legitimate course of action.
88. Rule X(d), instituted in 1890 and deleted in 1974.
89. Rules of Practice of the Association of Average Adjusters, Rules F14 (towage from a port of refuge) and F15 (cargo forwarded from a port of refuge). As it is customary to allow these substituted expenses, they would qualify for contribution at common law: see *supra*, n. 85.
90. See *infra*, 61.
91. See *Bowring* v. *Thebaud* (1890) 42 Fed Rep 796.
92. *Western Canada Steamship Co Ltd* v. *Canadian Commercial Corporation* [1960] SCR 632; [1960] 2 Lloyd's Rep 313 (Can SC).

under Rule F, and only up to the amount otherwise allowable in general average.[93] However, no deduction is made for savings to other interests: for example, where cargo storage charges during repairs at a port of refuge are avoided by towing the vessel to destination, a shipowner who benefits from lower repair charges at destination does not have to bring this saving into account.

Rule F does not authorise claims for *losses* incurred in substitution for allowable general average expenditure (e.g., where handling charges are avoided by selling the cargo at the port of refuge at a lower price than at destination, or by having to shut out additional cargo) or, indeed, expenses which are incurred in substitution for putative losses which would have been incurred, and allowed in general average. In practice special agreements are made to cover such losses and/or expenses.[94]

Temporary repairs

Temporary repairs are normally part of the responsibilities of the carrier in performing the contract of affreightment. Where effected in substitution for allowable general average expenditure, temporary[95] repairs generally fall within Rule F of the York-Antwerp Rules 1994. However, when such repairs are carried out in port, they are accorded specific treatment in Rule XIV of the Rules (which, by virtue of being a numbered Rule, overrides the general position in the lettered Rule F).[96] Rule XIV provides:

"Where temporary repairs are effected to a ship at a port of loading, call or refuge, for the common safety, or of damage caused by general average sacrifice, the cost of such repairs shall be admitted as general average.

Where temporary repairs of accidental damage are effected in order to enable the adventure to be completed, the cost of such repairs shall be admitted as general average without regard to the saving, if any, to other interests, but only up to the saving in expense which would have been incurred and allowed in general average if such repairs had not been effected there.

No deductions 'new for old' shall be made from the cost of temporary repairs allowable as general average."[97]

The first paragraph of the Rule merely expresses general principle in specific terms in declaring that expenditures incurred, first, on temporary repairs

---

93. See also *Lee* v. *Southern Insurance Co* (1870) LR 5 CP 397.
94. On sale of cargo, see *infra*, 101.
95. The rules on *temporary* repairs will not apply to repairs which, although of a temporary nature, are intended to have effect as permanent repairs; but they probably do apply to repairs which are *intended* to be temporary (at least, if carried out for the purpose of concluding the voyage in question) yet turn out to be of a more enduring nature.
96. See above, *supra*, 11.
97. No allowance is made "new for old" on the principle that *ex hypothesi temporary* repairs confer no enduring benefit. On deductions from cost of repairs generally, see York-Antwerp Rules 1994, Rule XIII: *infra*, 99–100.

incurred for the common safety or, secondly, to make good damage caused by a general average sacrifice are allowable in general average.

The third set of circumstances dealt with by the Rule, in its second paragraph, concerns temporary repairs in a port of refuge to *accidental* damage so as to enable safe continuation and completion of the adventure. An early justification for contribution in this situation is the rather simplistic one that a temporary repair is strictly speaking of no enduring benefit to the shipowner.[98] Including this third situation within the Rules enables the shipowner to claim a contribution even though the property involved in the adventure has been brought to a place of safety. It also overcomes the possibility that the common law rule against substitute expenses[99] might dictate that the avoidance of a permanent repair allowable in general average means that no general average loss has in fact been incurred.[100] However, whatever the possible arguments behind individual Rules, their effect is ultimately a matter of construction.

In *The Bijela*,[101] a vessel bound for India ran aground shortly after leaving Providence, Rhode Island. She therefore put into the nearest port, Jamestown. Two courses of action appeared to be open. First, she could discharge part of the cargo at Jamestown and the rest at Providence, then have permanent repairs effected at New York. The cost of unloading, storing and reloading the cargo would have been $535,000. Secondly, she could carry out temporary repairs at Jamestown, complete the voyage to India, and carry out permanent repairs at Singapore, at lower cost than at New York; so the cargo owners would receive the cargo more quickly and the owners would benefit from cheaper permanent repairs. The second course was taken, the temporary repairs costing $282,606, for which the shipowners ultimately recovered contribution under Rule XIV as a substitute for general average expenses which they would have been entitled to incur for unloading, storing and reloading the cargo under Rule X(b)–(c).[102] Hobhouse J, with whom the majority of the Court of Appeal agreed, accepted the cargo owners' argument that the cost of temporary repairs was not allowable as the facts that temporary repairs had been carried out and the voyage had been safely completed demonstrated that

---

98. One interpretation of Lord Ellenborough's judgment in *Plummer* v. *Wildman* (1815) 3 M & S 482 was that temporary repairs, incurred simply to enable completion of the voyage in hand, inevitably justified a general average contribution. But the true principle is that temporary repairs only give rise to a claim for a general average contribution if constituting or consequent upon a general average loss: see *Power* v. *Whitmore* (1815) 4 M & S 482.

99. In *Wilson* v. *Bank of Victoria* (1867) LR 2 QB 203, discussed *supra*, 32.

100. This argument would depend on permanent repairs and temporary repairs not being each capable of qualifying as general average losses.

101. *Marida Ltd* v. *Oswal Steel (The Bijela)* [1992] 1 Lloyd's Rep 636; noted NG Hudson [1992] LMCLQ 322; DJ Wilson [1993] LMCLQ 13; affd [1993] 1 Lloyd's Rep 411; noted N Meeson [1993] LMCLQ 476; rvrsd [1994] 1 WLR 615; [1994] 2 Lloyd's Rep 1; noted NJJ Gaskell [1994] LMCLQ 342.

102. See *supra*, 57–59.

neither the cargo handling costs nor permanent repairs involving such costs were necessary for the safe prosecution of the voyage. Hoffmann LJ, dissenting in the Court of Appeal, accepted the shipowners' secondary argument that, to give business efficacy to the Rule, it had to be assumed that (though they were in fact carried out) temporary repairs *could not* be carried out at Jamestown. The House of Lords, however, disapproved this approach and accepted the shipowners' primary argument, that Rule XIV be construed literally, requiring the assumption that temporary repairs *had not* been carried out. The result was that permanent repairs in New York would have been necessary, so that a contribution could be claimed in respect of substitute temporary repairs.

Rule XIV therefore requires an enquiry as to what would have happened if temporary repairs had not been effected. If allowable general average expenditure had been incurred, then contribution could be claimed in respect of temporary repairs effected in substitute for such expenditure. Unfortunately, it remains unclear from *The Bijela* exactly when expenditure on temporary repairs is allowable under Rule XIV. First, it is possible that contribution for substitute temporary repairs under Rule XIV is only due where permanent repairs are possible at the port of refuge (i.e. in Jamestown—where permanent repairs were *not* possible). Secondly, Hobhouse J thought that the situation in *The Bijela* was covered by Rule X(a) of the York-Antwerp Rules,[103] so that temporary repairs at Jamestown were a substitute for handling expenses at Providence incurred because repairs could not be carried out at Jamestown—which was obviously not the case. Unfortunately, both points were conceded by the cargo owners.

Mitigation of loss

Just as an allowance can be made for "substituted expenses", so should an allowance be made for "substituted gains". Thus, where as a result of a general average act a shipowner loses freight and then earns freight on a substitute cargo, the net proceeds of the substitute cargo should be set off from the value of the freight lost.[104] However, though there is merit in requiring the plaintiff to minimise his loss, no rule has been established that he cannot recover for such losses as he could have avoided.[105] Perhaps the new Rule Paramount[106] may effect a change here, by demanding reasonableness in the allowance.

---

103. See *supra*, 5–7.
104. See *The Rosamond* [1960] AMC 195 (US CA). *Lowndes & Rudolf*, para 15.11 argues that it is more correct to state that the new net freight should go in diminution of the *total general average*.
105. Cf AS Burrows, *The Law of Restitution* (1993), 475; FD Rose, "Passing On", Chap. 10 of PBH Birks (ed.), *Laundering and Tracing* (1995), 275–276.
106. See *supra*, 39.

CHAPTER 4

EXCEPTIONS TO LIABILITY TO CONTRIBUTE

1. Deck cargo

Stowage of cargo on deck has traditionally been regarded as improper. It has been treated as a danger to safe navigation[1]; "liable to be unduly jettisoned owing to the facility of doing it when cargo under hatches would not be"[2]; such jettison being "a justifiable riddance of encumbrances which ought never to have been there, and not as a sacrifice for the common safety".[3] Accordingly, though the owner of deck cargo is liable to contribute if jettisoned deck cargo is preserved by a general average act, he is generally unable to recover a contribution for such jettison.[4] In general, it makes no difference that the shipper has consented to deck carriage; though, if the cargo is stowed on deck without the owner's consent, he is entitled to an indemnity from the carrier.[5] However, contribution is recoverable where *all* those interested in the adventure consent to such carriage[6] or where deck carriage is customary,[7] which is of course in modern times often the case.[8] Rule I of the York-Antwerp Rules 1994 now states that: "No jettison of cargo shall be made good as general

---

1. *Strang, Steel & Co* v. *A Scott & Co* (1889) 14 App Cas 601, 609 (PC: per Lord Watson). In *Apollinaris Co* v. *Nord Deutsche Ins Co* [1904] 1 KB 252, 259, Walton J supposed that the exception for coastal trade was on the ground that it was less dangerous.
2. *Wright* v. *Marwood* (1881) 7 QBD 62, 67, per Bramwell LJ.
3. *Strang, Steel & Co* v. *A Scott & Co* (1889) 14 App Cas 601 (PC), 608–609 (per Lord Watson).
4. *Wright* v. *Marwood* (1881) 7 QBD 62; *Strang, Steel & Co* v. *A Scott & Co* (1889) 14 App Cas 601 (PC); *Miller* v. *Titherington* (1862) 7 H & N 954 (custom of Liverpool that underwriters not liable for general average jettison of deck cargo).
5. *Wright* v. *Marwood* (1881) 7 QBD 62, 67–68 (CA: per Bramwell LJ); *Royal Exchange Shipping Co Ltd* v. *Dixon* (1886) 12 App Cas 11.
6. *Johnson* v. *Chapman* (1865) 19 CB(NS) 563 (single shipper loading full cargo).
7. *Gould* v. *Oliver* (1837) 4 Bing (NC) 134; *Milward* v. *Hibbert* (1842) 3 QB 120; *Wright* v. *Marwood* (1881) 7 QBD 62, 67; *Strang, Steel & Co* v. *A Scott & Co* (1889) 14 App Cas 601, 609 (PC); *Apollinaris Co* v. *Nord Deutsche Ins Co* [1904] 1 KB 252, 259. See also *Burton* v. *English* (1883) 10 QBD 426 (clause providing that cargo carried on deck by custom of the trade was carried "at merchant's risk" excluded shipowner's liability as carrier but not for general average contribution).
8. Similarly, the view that ship's boats (properly) slung outside the ship at the stern might by virtue of their location be excluded from general average is now rightly discredited: see *supra*, Chap. 2 n. 141.

average, unless such cargo is carried in accordance with the recognised custom of the trade."

2. Claimant's fault

Rights and liabilities to contribution are adjusted independently of the fault of the parties to the common adventure; but, where the necessity for general average arises from the fault of one of the parties and that fault is actionable at the suit of another party, the rights, remedies and defences between the two parties are preserved; in particular, the party not at fault is *prima facie* not obliged to pay contribution to the party at fault.

If the danger resulted from the fault of the plaintiff or of those for whom he is legally responsible and that would give the party from whom contribution is claimed a cause of action against the plaintiff, then the plaintiff loses his right to contribution from that defendant.[9] Thus, in the leading case of *Schloss* v. *Heriot*,[10] a shipowner was unable to claim contribution from cargo owners where his ship was unseaworthy at the beginning of the voyage and it was this unseaworthiness which occasioned the general average act. The position is similar where the loss arises from negligent navigation,[11] where goods are jettisoned which have been wrongfully shipped in a dangerous condition and have occasioned the peril,[12] or after an unjustifiable deviation which has not been excepted or waived.[13] Provided the fault is actionable, the contributor is relieved from liability though he has suffered no loss other than his notional liability to contribute.

(a) Basis of the rule

It was once thought that, where fault necessitated the taking of steps to avert a peril, this took the situation out of general average, that it was not a case for

---

9. *Strang, Steel & Co* v. *A Scott & Co* (1889) 14 App Cas 601, 608 (PC: per Lord Watson: "He cannot be permitted to claim either recompense for services rendered, or indemnity for losses sustained by him, in the endeavour to rescue property which was imperilled by his own tortious act, and which it was his duty to save"); *EB Aaby's Rederi A/S* v. *Union of India (The Evje) (No 2)* [1976] 2 Lloyd's Rep 714, 716.

10. (1863) 14 CB(NS) 59. See also *Westoll* v. *Carter* (1898) 3 Com Cas 112. Cf *The Texas* [1970] 1 Lloyd's Rep 175 (no contribution for general average loss caused by fire where vessel sailed with smoke in hold owing to neglect or fault of shipowners' agents); *The Aga* [1968] 1 Lloyd's Rep 431 (no contribution where ship beached due to heavy list, she having left port with insufficient reserve stability, due diligence not having been exercised to make her seaworthy); *Robinson* v. *Price* (1877) 2 QBD 91 [affd *ibid.*, 295], 95, per Lush J: (shipowner cannot claim general average unless he sails with a reasonable supply of fuel); *Lindsay* v. *Klein* [1911] AC 194.

11. *Strang, Steel & Co* v. *A Scott & Co* (1889) 14 App Cas 601, 608, per Lord Watson. Cf *The Mary Thomas* [1894] P 108.

12. *Greenshields, Cowie & Co* v. *Stephens & Sons* [1908] AC 431; see *infra*, 70.

13. *Reardon Smith Line Ltd* v. *Black Sea & Baltic General Insurance Co Ltd* (1938) 60 Ll L Rep 353; *Hain SS Co Ltd* v. *Tate & Lyle Ltd* (1936) 41 Com Cas 350, 361, per Lord Wright MR ("the casualty and consequent general average loss must be deemed to have been caused by the deviation since it is

contribution and innocent parties should seek redress from the party at fault.[14] This view has been rejected. General average losses are to be adjusted in the normal way, with allowance for contributions, but subject to the rule that the party at fault cannot claim what would otherwise be due to him.[15]

Speaking of the general law on contribution in *Deering v. Earl of Winchelsea*,[16] Eyre CB said:

"If these were circumstances which could work a disability in the Plaintiff to support his demand, it must be on the maxim, 'that a man must come into a court of Equity with clean hands;' but general depravity is not sufficient. It must be pointed to the act upon which the loss arises, and must be in a legal sense the cause of the loss ... There might indeed be a case in which a person might be in a legal sense the author of the loss, and therefore not entitled to contribution; as if a person on board a ship was to bore a hole in the ship, and in consequence of the distress occasioned by this act it became necessary to throw overboard his goods to save the ship."

In *Schloss v. Heriot*,[17] Erle CJ gave two reasons for disallowing the claim of the guilty party. One of these was that the defendant would be entitled in a cross-action to recover back the whole sum originally claimed by the plaintiff; so, in order to avoid circuity of action, judgment should be entered for the defendant. That signifies that the plaintiff does have a claim but that he cannot obtain a favourable judgment. This view, however, does not provide for situations where the rule against circuity of action is inapplicable. For example, in *The Ettrick*,[18] a shipowner paid into court the amount of his statutory liability for damages in respect of the loss to ships or goods and contended that he should thereafter be treated as an innocent party and be permitted to claim contribution from the cargo owners for general average expenditure in raising his sunken ship. The relevant statutory provision,[19] it was held, did not have this effect: although it had the effect of limiting his liability to the cargo owners, it did not give him the right to claim full (or any) contribution from them for general average losses.[20] The rule against recovery in cases of fault,

---

impossible to say that the casualty would have occurred if there had been no deviation"). Cf *Drew Brown Ltd v. The Orient Trader and her Owners (The Orient Trader)* [1974] SCR 1286; (1973) 34 DLR (3d) 339; [1973] 2 Lloyd's Rep 174 (Can SC).

14. See *Carver*, para 1363, referring to Beawes (1813), 244; Malynes, 113; Molloy, 4th ed. (1688), 249.

15. See, e.g., *State Trading Corp of India v. Doyle Carriers Inc (The Jute Express)* [1991] 2 Lloyd's Rep 55.

16. (1787) 2 Bos & Pul 270, 271 (Ex).

17. (1863) 14 CB(NS) 59. See also *Hain SS Co Ltd v. Tate & Lyle Ltd* (1936) 41 Com Cas 350, 361, per Lord Wright MR.

18. (1881) 6 PD 127.

19. Merchant Shipping Act 1862, s.54. See now Merchant Shipping Act 1995, s.185, Sched. 7 Part I.

20. For other situations in which the rule against circuity of actions is inapplicable, see *Goulandris Bros Ltd v. B Goldman & Sons Ltd* [1958] QB 74; *Aktieselskabet Ocean v. B Harding & Sons Ltd* [1928] 2 KB 371 (the defence of avoiding circuity of action is "strictly limited to cases where, if the plaintiff recovered against the defendant, the defendant could recover exactly the same sum": *ibid.*, 385, per Scrutton LJ). See also *The Susan V Luckenbach* [1951] P 197; *The Kafiristan* [1937] P 63, 69; [1938] AC 136, 148.

sometimes called "the equitable defence", is a matter of defence and not of cross-claim.[21]

It is perhaps best explained on the other ground put forward by Erle CJ: that the claimant should not be able to recover for the consequences of his own wrong.[22] In other words, it is not merely a question of procedure but that the plaintiff's cause of action is actually taken away. It is possible to go further and to say that, since the guilty party would, but for the general average act, have been wholly or partly liable to the innocent party as regards the loss averted by the general average act, then any sacrifice is made wholly or partly for the benefit of the guilty party alone and not for the adventure as a whole.[23] The difficulty with this approach is that it suggests that there is not a general average situation; yet there clearly is, for adjustment of losses is to be made in the ordinary way but subject to the exclusion of recovery on the part of the guilty party. The steps taken to avert the peril may not be part of the master's ordinary obligations; but, even though those steps are taken for the benefit of all, that does not give a guilty party a right to contribution.

(b) Content of the rule

Rule D of the York-Antwerp Rules 1994 states the rule thus:

"Rights to contribution in general average shall not be affected, though the event which gave rise to the sacrifice or expenditure may have been due to the fault of one of the parties to the adventure; but this shall not prejudice any remedies or defences which may be open against or to that party in respect of that fault."

The Rule is infelicitously drafted, though its intention is reasonably clear. First, the values of the general average loss and of the benefited interests, and the *prima facie* rights and liabilities to contribution, are adjusted in the normal way. Then it must be determined to what extent a loss was caused by fault of the claimant (of a general average contribution) which is actionable at the suit of the person from whom the contribution is claimed ("the contributor"). This includes determining rights and remedies. The Rules preserve the contributor's rights of action, defences and cross-claims.[24] To the extent that the contributor has an action against the claimant, he may pursue that action and defend the claim to a general average contribution.

---

21. *Goulandris Bros Ltd* v. *B Goldman & Sons Ltd* [1958] 1 QB 74, 95, per Pearson J.
22. *Schloss* v. *Heriot* (1863) 14 CB(NS) 59, 64; *Pirie & Co* v. *Middle Dock Co* (1881) 44 LT 426, 429, per Watkin Williams J; *Goulandris Bros Ltd* v. *B Goldman & Sons Ltd* [1958] QB 74, 95.
23. *Tempus SS Co* v. *Dreyfus* [1931] 1 KB 195, 211–212, per Greer LJ; approved by Lord Warrington of Clyde [1931] AC 726, 742.
24. *Goulandris Bros Ltd* v. *B Goldman & Sons Ltd* [1958] 1 QB 74.

(c) Actionable fault

Whatever its rationale, the rule itself seems clear—contribution cannot be claimed by a party whose actionable fault caused the sacrifice or expenditure. The test of an actionable wrong is stated by Carver as "whether, had the general average sacrifice or expenditure not been made, the person making it would have been liable in damages, to the person against whom he is claiming contribution, for the loss or damage to that person's interest in the adventure which the sacrifice or expenditure was intended to avert".[25] In *Goulandris Bros Ltd* v. *B Goldman & Sons Ltd*,[26] Pearson J added a rider to the definition by defining "fault" as a legal wrong which is actionable as between the parties at the time when the general average sacrifice or expenditure is made. Since at that time no loss or damage may have arisen, and in fact may not arise thanks to preventive measures taken, the innocent party may be protected by asking whether, but for the general average act, the fault would have been actionable when loss or damage otherwise might have occurred. Thus, it can be said that no contribution may be claimed where the danger arose through the claimant's fault. There may be wider repercussions. If, for example, the claimant commits a tort, then this may cause no harm to a particular defendant and so not bar the claim for contribution. But the fault may consist of a breach of contract which, although it causes (and would cause) no harm to a particular defendant, may give that defendant a defence to the claim: for example, if the shipowner is in breach of his warranty of seaworthiness but this causes no loss or damage to the defendant, the latter can still escape by pleading his right to sue for nominal damages—the claimant's fault is still actionable.

(d) Danger arising from condition of cargo

The view was once held that there can be no contribution in respect of the sacrifice of an article which caused the danger rendering the sacrifice necessary. Thus, it was said, if cargo were jettisoned because it was in a state of wreck, no contribution could be claimed, since the cargo was the cause of the danger.[27] Similarly, if hemp heated and caused a fire, or was likely to occasion a fire, and was jettisoned for that reason, contribution could not be claimed, for, again, the cargo would have been the cause of the danger.[28] However, in the latter

---

25. *Carver*, para 1374.
26. [1958] QB 74, 104. Pearson J's judgment can be limited to situations in which Rule D of the York-Antwerp Rules applies; but no useful purpose would be achieved by doing this.
27. *Lowndes & Rudolf*, 9th ed., para 124, citing Baily, *General Average*, 56–58. However, if goods are in a state of wreck, contribution will generally be barred by their condition anyway: see *supra*, 24.
28. *Lowndes & Rudolf*, 9th ed., para 124, citing *Boyd* v. *Dubois* (1811) 3 Camp 133, 133–134, per Lord Ellenborough. The case was in fact one where the assured failed to recover from his insurer on the ground of inherent vice.

situation, said Willes J in *Johnson* v. *Chapman*,[29] a distinction should be drawn between heating which arose due to a peril of the voyage and heating caused by an inherent defect of the cargo: the latter situation would not be a case of a maritime peril common to the whole adventure but, he said, of a peculiar danger from the fault of the person putting it on board, in which case contribution was not permissible. The wisdom of taking these words too far was shown in *Pirie* v. *Middle Dock Co*,[30] in which the distinction was pointed out between danger arising from cargo because of its owner's fault (as where he knowingly ships goods in a dangerous condition) and danger of which the shipper was, without fault, ignorant. In the former situation, the cargo owner could not recover contribution in respect of a loss resulting from, or from the discovery of, its inherent vice. But where, for example, coal is taken on board ship in the Tropics and the shipper and shipowner are familiar with its liability to spontaneous combustion and the surrounding circumstances, then the shipper will be able to claim contribution for a sacrifice made as a result of a fire arising from the coal's spontaneous combustion. Thus, it has been decided by the House of Lords in *Greenshields, Cowie & Co* v. *Stephens & Sons*[31] that a cargo owner is only precluded from claiming a contribution for general average loss where his conduct in shipping cargo has been wrongful or negligent.[32] In respect of "undeclared or wrongfully declared cargo", Rule XIX of the York-Antwerp Rules 1994 both excludes certain losses from general average and preserves liability to contribute.[33]

(e) Joint tortfeasors

In *Austin Friars Steamship Co Ltd* v. *Spillers & Bakers Ltd*[34] a vessel attempting to enter a dock collided with a pier, causing damage to the pier and the dock. The ship recovered a general average contribution in respect of both types of damage. Without accepting the cargo owners' argument that the ship and cargo were joint tortfeasors, it was held that the (now reversed)[35] common law rule[36]

---

29. (1865) 19 CB(NS) 563, 581.
30. (1881) 44 LT 426, 429.
31. [1908] AC 431. In that case the claim was in respect of coal damaged in putting out the fire and did not include the coal damaged by the fire. "Apart from any question of inherent vice, there [was] a practice not to allow the damage done to bales or packages which have been on fire" (*Lowndes & Rudolf*, 9th ed., para 127, n. 63). This is understandable, for to jettison burning coal could be compared with the jettison of cargo in a state of wreck: see *supra*, 24. However, the practice was reversed in 1974. See now York-Antwerp Rules 1994, Rule III: damage done in extinguishing a fire on board ship shall be made good in general average, though "no compensation shall be made for damage by smoke however caused or by heat of the fire".
32. Cf *The William J Quillan* (1909) 168 Fed Rep 407; (1910) 175 Fed 207; 180 Fed Rep 681.
33. See *infra*, 77.
34. [1915] 1 KB 833; affd [1915] 3 KB 586.
35. See Law Reform (Married Women and Tortfeasors) Act 1935. See also Civil Liability (Contribution) Act 1978.
36. *Merryweather* v. *Nixan* (1799) 8 TR 186.

that there cannot be contribution between joint tortfeasors should not be extended and does not apply to contribution in general average.

(f) Limitation of action

Where a contributor has a right of action against the claimant but it is subsequently discharged, the contributor's defence to the claim for contribution may nevertheless remain. Thus, in *Goulandris Bros Ltd* v. *B Goldman & Sons Ltd*[37] the fact that the Hague Rules, Article III(6)[38] discharged the carrier's liability after twelve months did not bar the cargo owner's "equitable defence" to his claim for a general average contribution. Moreover, the limitation (for loss or damage related to the cargo owner's goods) was held not to apply to matters related to general average contributions.[39]

(g) Limitation of liability

When delivering his speech in *Louis Dreyfus & Co* v. *Tempus SS Co*,[40] Lord Atkin was careful not to disapprove the decision in *The Ettrick*,[41] the effect of which is that a fault remains actionable despite a statutory limitation of the amount recoverable for that fault. All the members of the House of Lords in *Dreyfus* v. *Tempus* agreed that the effect of the statutory limitation of liability they were considering was the same as if it had been inserted into the contract by the parties; so it can be concluded that fault remains actionable for the purposes of barring a claim to contribution whenever the parties limit their liability by contract.

(h) Exclusion of liability

A contractual or statutory provision may: override fault which would otherwise bar a party's claim to a general average contribution[42]; and/or exclude his own liability to contribute.[43]

---

37. [1958] 1 QB 74.
38. See now Carriage of Goods by Sea Act 1971, Sched., art. III(6).
39. So, the cargo owner could set up his cross-claim against the shipowner's claim for a general average contribution; to avoid circuity of action, judgment was given for the cargo owner. Pearson J stated that the general average claim was related not to the contributor's goods but to the interest incurring the loss; moreover, whereas the running of time from the date of delivery was appropriate in connection with losses to goods (of which the cargo owner would normally be aware from that time), it was not obviously relevant to claims to general average contributions (of which the cargo owner might then be unaware).
40. [1931] AC 726, 747. The case is discussed *infra*, 73.
41. (1881) 6 PD 127. The provision in question was the forerunner of the Merchant Shipping Act 1894, s.503. See now the Merchant Shipping Act 1995, s.185, Sched. 7, Part I.
42. See *supra*, 70.
43. See further *infra*, 76–77.

(1) CONTRACTUAL EXCLUSIONS

The relationship of the parties regarding fault might be varied by contract.[44] In *The Carron Park*,[45] a servant of shipowners negligently left open a valve through which water seeped, damaging the plaintiffs' cargo. Nevertheless, the shipowners were entitled to a general average contribution from the cargo owners, for the charterparty contained an exception of "any neglect or default whatsoever of the ... servants of the shipowners". Thus, where a party exempts himself from liability to another party, the latter's "equitable defence" falls. *The Carron Park* was approved by a majority of the Court of Appeal in *Milburn & Co v. Jamaica Fruit Co*.[46] In that case, shipowners were unable to claim contribution for general average expenditure resulting from their master's negligence because, under the instructions of charterers, bills of lading had been issued without a clause excepting liability for negligence. By the terms of the charterparty, negligence of the servants of the shipowners and the charterers was to be always mutually excepted and the charterers were to indemnify the owners from any consequences that might arise from the master following the charterers' instructions and signing bills of lading. The shipowners were held to be entitled to an indemnity from the charterers to cover the loss sustained as a result of their loss of contribution rights.

Vaughan Williams LJ in *Milburn v. Jamaica* dissented vigorously from the majority opinion and from the decision in *The Carron Park*. As he put it, since the right to contribution arose from the maritime law and not from contract, the shipowner can only recover a contribution for a general average act arising from the fault of his master and crew where they, by the terms of a charterparty or otherwise, have ceased to be his agents. It is open, he continued, to two co-adventurers to agree to waive rights to general average between themselves or to contract to allow a claim to contribution though one of them be at fault: but those rights would arise from contract and not from the maritime law. His Lordship noted, quite reasonably, that the effect of the mutual exceptions clause was to throw on each party the responsibility of insuring against his own losses, to relieve him from a liability that would otherwise fall upon him. "I cannot see how the exception from these liabilities can give the party excepted a claim which he would not otherwise have had, or render the party who has the benefit of the exception liable to a claim to which but for the exception he would not have been liable."[47]

The other members of the Court of Appeal in *Milburn v. Jamaica* took a much broader view and found the effect of the exceptions clause to be not only to exclude the liability of the shipowner but to give him a cause of action. AL Smith LJ noted that a party could not claim contribution for general average if he were

---

44. *Strang, Steel & Co v. A Scott & Co* (1889) 14 App Cas 601, 609 (PC: per Lord Watson).
45. (1890) 15 PD 203.
46. [1900] 2 QB 540.
47. *Ibid.*, 553.

a wrongdoer but that to "create the shipowner a wrongdoer as regards the cargo owner there must be the breach of some duty, and, if by agreement between the two it has been agreed that it shall be no breach of duty for the master to be guilty of negligence",[48] then the master's negligence does not operate as fault so as to disallow the shipowner's claim to contribution. In the words of Romer LJ, "the position of equality is the very essence of the right to contribution".[49] Thus, the effect of the exception clause was to wipe out fault completely.

This result has since been approved by the House of Lords in *Louis Dreyfus & Co* v. *Tempus SS Co*,[50] which was discussed by Hewson J in *The Makedonia*.[51] In *The Makedonia*, shipowners were protected by a clause in a bill of lading from liability to cargo owners for loss or damage to cargo caused by the neglect or default of the carrier or its servants, the cargo being carried at the sole risk of the owner. Although the shipowners were not liable for the cargo and were not bound to take steps to save it from physical loss (resulting from unseaworthiness), once general average expenditure had been incurred for the benefit of the common adventure, the cargo owners were liable to contribute. The clause operated as a sword as well as a shield.[52]

(II) STATUTORY EXCLUSION OF LIABILITY

In *Louis Dreyfus & Co* v. *Tempus SS Co*,[53] the defendants were indorsees of bills of lading which contained no exception clause in respect of unseaworthiness. However, by statute, the shipowner was not liable for loss or damage caused by fire without his actual fault or privity.[54] There was a fire due to unseaworthiness without the fault or privity of the owners. This damaged the cargo and the master incurred general average expenditure. It was held by the House of Lords,[55] applying the statute, that the plaintiffs were not liable to the defendants for loss or damage to the cargo and, moreover, that the latter were bound to contribute to general average. The effect of the statutory exception was held to be the same as that of contractual exceptions which was settled in *The Carron Park*[56] and *Milburn* v. *Jamaica*.[57] Lord Atkin said:

---

48. *Ibid.*, 546. As Kennedy LJ pointed out in *Greenshields, Cowie & Co* v. *Stephens & Sons* [1908] 1 KB 51, 61, "the default must be something which is wrongful in the eyes of the law, that is to say, something which constitutes an actionable wrong". Once the wrong ceases to be actionable, there is no justification for distinguishing between the results of non-actionable fault, for fault in the abstract does not ground the exception to the right to contribution.
49. [1900] 2 QB 540, 554.
50. [1931] AC 726.
51. [1962] 1 Lloyd's Rep 316.
52. Cf *Westfal-Larsen, A/S* v. *Colonial Sugar Co Ltd* [1960] 2 Lloyd's Rep 206 (NSW SC) (approved in *The Brabant* [1967] 1 QB 588).
53. [1931] AC 726.
54. Merchant Shipping Act 1894, s.502(i). See now Merchant Shipping Act 1995, s.186.
55. Affirming the decision of the Court of Appeal [1931] 1 KB 195, which reversed by a majority (Greer and Slesser LJJ; Scrutton LJ dissenting) part of the judgment of Wright J [1930] 1 KB 699.
56. (1890) 15 PD 203.
57. [1900] 2 QB 540.

"I myself find it difficult to conceive of a fault in this relation which, though not actionable, is yet in some manner so blameworthy as to deprive the party of his right to contribution ... The object of the exception is to protect the person committing the act in question from liability for any consequences of it; and this is effectively secured whether it is said that there shall be no duty to avoid doing the act or no obligation to pay any compensation if it is done."[58]

Thus, there was no substance in the argument that there was still an actionable wrong and all the statute did was to deny the right to payment for it.

(III) SCOPE OF EXCLUSION

Of course, the effect of an exception is a matter of construction, one principle of which is to confine the effect of exculpatory provisions. First, the protective provision may be generally unavailable. Thus, the operation of the actionable fault bar is considerably reduced in practice by the Hague(-Visby) Rules' exemption of negligence in navigation and management in bill of lading contracts[59]; but the carrier cannot rely on this if the cargo owner proves that the vessel was unseaworthy and that this was the cause of his loss, and the shipowner then fails to prove that he had exercised due diligence to make the vessel seaworthy.[60] Secondly, an otherwise effective provision may not apply to the matter in issue. Thus, a provision excluding liability for non-performance of the contract of carriage will not per se exclude liability to contribute in general average (which historically does not arise because of the contract but because of the general maritime law).[61] In particular, an exculpatory provision may specifically preserve the rules of general average. Thus, the Hague-Visby Rules, Article IV(6) entitle the carrier to deal with dangerous goods "without liability on the part of the carrier except to general average, if any".[62]

---

58. [1931] AC 726, 747 and 750.
59. Carriage of Goods by Sea Act 1971, Sched., art. IV(2)(a). See *Corfu Navigation Co* v. *Mobil Shipping Co (The Alpha)* [1991] 2 Lloyd's Rep 515, 517.
60. *Union of India* v. *EB Aaby's Rederi A/S (The Evje) (No 2)* [1976] 2 Lloyd's Rep 714, affd [1978] 1 Lloyd's Rep 351. See also *Union of India* v. *EB Aaby's Rederi A/S (The Evje)* [1975] AC 797, 816, per Lord Salmon; *Danae Shipping Corp* v. *TPAO (The Daffodil B)* [1983] 1 Lloyd's Rep 498 (reasonable deviation); *The Antigoni* [1990] 1 Lloyd's Rep 45; *Lyric Shipping Inc* v. *Intermetals Inc (The Al Taha)* [1990] 2 Lloyd's Rep 117 (reasonable deviation); *The Danica Brown* [1995] 2 Lloyd's Rep 264; Hudson, 59. Cf *Goulandris Bros Ltd* v. *B Goldman & Sons Ltd* [1958] 1 QB 74, 106.
61. A shipowner's liability to contribute will not be excluded by a contractual or statutory exception to liability under a bill of lading contract for "fire on board" (*Schmidt* v. *Royal Mail SS Co* (1876) 45 LJQB 646), a clause that jettisoned deck cargo was carried "at merchant's risk" (*Burton & Co* v. *English & Co* (1883) 12 QBD 218) or an exclusion of liability "for any damage ... capable of being covered by insurance" (*Crooks* v. *Allan* (1879) 5 QBD 38). It was held in *Greenshields, Cowie & Co v Stephens & Sons Ltd* [1908] AC 431 that the Merchant Shipping Act 1894, s.502 did not protect the shipowner from a claim for contribution, for "The Statute is not dealing with average at all": *ibid.*, 436, per Lord Halsbury. Cf *Alma Shipping Corp* v. *Union of India (The Astrea)* [1971] 2 Lloyd's Rep 494; *Union of India* v. *EB Aaby's Rederi A/S (The Evje)* [1975] AC 797 (charterparty arbitration clause applicable to general average).
62. See Carriage of Goods Act 1971, Sched., art. IV(6) for the precise circumstances.

(i) The New Jason Clause

In the USA, a bill of lading clause exempting the liability of the shipowner and his servants for negligence was void at common law as being contrary to public policy. The first two sections of the Harter Act[63] declared that clauses purporting to relieve the shipowner from his duty to take care of the cargo and to provide a seaworthy ship should be null and void, but it was enacted by section 3 that, if a shipowner exercises due care to make the vessel seaworthy, neither he, the vessel, her agent, nor her charterers should be liable for damage or loss arising from (*inter alia*) faults or errors in navigation, or in the management of the vessel. Not unreasonably, this led to the view that a shipowner could recover contribution for general average sacrifices or expenditure made or incurred for the sake of minimising the greater loss which would naturally result from the negligence of his servants but from which he was relieved from liability. Arguably it is sound policy to allow this result and to discourage the master from risking the adventure by hesitating to make a general average sacrifice.

Nonetheless, it was held by a majority of the Supreme Court of the United States in *The Irrawaddy*[64] that a shipowner was not entitled to recover contributions for general average acts necessitated by his servants' negligence: i.e., whether or not it was actionable, fault for which the shipowner was responsible barred a claim to contribution. The law had not been changed with regard to general average. It was later held in *The Jason*[65] that a shipowner is not exonerated from liability to contribute in general average to the loss of the cargo (for this would put the shipowner in a better position if his servants had been negligent) and in *The Strathdon*[66] that the shipowner's sacrifices and expenditure must be brought into account in the average adjustment and so perhaps operate to reduce or to extinguish the claim of the cargo owners for contribution to their losses (otherwise the shipowner might be paying for losses for which he was not liable).

However, the United States Supreme Court held in *The Jason*[67] that a shipowner could validly insert a clause into a contract to safeguard his right to contribution in a situation where his servants' negligence might otherwise deprive him of that right. It is common to insert a New Jason Clause (an amended version of the clause in *The Jason*) into bills of lading where general average adjustment is likely to be made according to American law or any similar law which adopts *The Irrawaddy*. Provided due diligence has been

---

63. The Act now only applies before loading and after discharge of goods.
64. (1898) 171 US 187.
65. (1910) 225 US 32. See also *The Ernestina* (1919) 259 Fed Rep 772.
66. (1899) 94 Fed Rep 206; (1900) 101 Fed Rep 600.
67. (1910) 225 US 32.

exercised to make the ship seaworthy and properly manned, equipped and supplied,[68] the shipowner will be able to take advantage of it.[69]

The argument that the incorporation into an English contract of the provisions of the Harter Act should take effect according to American law and so deprive the shipowner of the benefit of the decisions in *The Carron Park*[70] and *Milburn* v. *Jamaica*[71] is untenable in view of the decision in *Dobell & Co* v. *SS Rossmore Co*[72] to construe the words of the Act as if they are written into the contract as ordinary negligence clauses: thus, they will be interpreted according to English law. In any case, the importance of the decisions under the Harter Act has diminished with the passing of the United States Carriage of Goods by Sea Act 1936, which gives effect to the Hague Rules as regards contracts of carriage to and from American ports and restricts the application of the Harter Act to before loading and after discharge.

(j) Fault does not prejudice third parties

It was held by the Privy Council in *Strang, Steel & Co* v. *Scott & Co*[73] that, where cargo is jettisoned to avert a common danger occasioned by the shipowner's fault, the owners of the jettisoned goods can claim a contribution in general average from the other cargo owners; they are not bound to make good the fault of the shipowners' servants.

3. Contractual qualification of liability to general average

It was seen in the previous section that a clause excluding liability for fault can restore a *prima facie* right to claim a general average contribution.[74] Exemption and similar such clauses can also define the range of losses which fall within general average and/or exclude losses which would or might otherwise give rise to a claim for contribution.

---

68. *The Isis* [1933] AMC 1565; 48 Ll L Rep 35. It was held in *Schade* v. *National Surety Corp* [1961] AMC 1225 that the clause determined the shipowner's duties under the contract in relation to general average.
69. In *Goulandris Bros Ltd* v. *B Goldman & Sons Ltd* [1958] 1 QB 74, 106, Pearson J refrained from commenting on whether the New Jason Clause affects the interpretation of Rule D of the York-Antwerp Rules (*supra*, 68). However, if the Harter Act does not apply, because it has been struck out of the contract or does not apply as a matter of law, and the shipowner fails to prove the exercise of due diligence as required by the clause, he may recover a contribution if he can show either that his fault was not actionable or that it had no causal connection with the general average act: *EB Aaby's Rederi A/S* v. *Union of India (The Evje) (No 2)* [1976] 2 Lloyd's Rep 714, 716, per Donaldson J.
70. (1890) 15 PD 203.
71. [1900] 2 QB 540.
72. [1895] 2 QB 408. Cf *Rowson* v. *Atlantic Transport Co* [1903] 2 KB 666.
73. (1889) 14 App Cas 601.
74. See *supra*, 72–74. The above discussion is also relevant to the remainder of this section but will not be repeated here. See generally *supra*, 10.

CONTRACTUAL QUALIFICATION OF LIABILITY 77

Of course, the effect of an exemption clause is a matter of construction. Thus, a bill of lading may provide that consignees of cargo shall not be liable for a general average contribution but that shippers will remain liable.[75] Moreover, an exclusion of liability may not be total. Thus, if a charterer has become the owner of cargo by the time of a general average act, he may be liable to contribute under the rules of the maritime law, despite a clause providing for the cesser of his liability under the charterparty.[76]

The York-Antwerp Rules 1994 contain a number of qualifications on liability to contribute in general average.

The contract may define what is capable of being a general average loss. Thus, Rule III provides that damage done in extinguishing a fire shall be made good as general average[77] but that "no compensation shall be made for damage by smoke however caused or by heat of the fire."[78] Similarly, Rule VII allows in general average damage to machinery and boilers in endeavouring to refloat a ship but specifically provides that "where a ship is afloat no loss or damage caused by working the propelling machinery and boilers shall in any circumstances be made good as general average."[79]

Under Rule VI ("salvage remuneration"), special compensation payable to a salvor by the shipowner, with respect to services rendered in a case of threatened environmental damage, under Article 14 of the CMI International Convention on Salvage 1989[80] shall not be allowed in general average to the extent the compensation exceeds the salvor's reward fixed by the general criteria in Article 13 of the Convention.[81]

In respect of "undeclared or wrongfully declared cargo",[82] Rule XIX of the York-Antwerp Rules 1994 both excludes certain losses from general average and preserves liability to contribute. It provides:

"Damage or loss caused to goods loaded without the knowledge of the shipowner or his agent or to goods wilfully misdescribed at time of shipment shall not be allowed as general average, but such goods shall remain liable to contribute, if saved.
Damage or loss caused to goods which have been wrongfully declared on shipment at a value which is lower than their real value shall be contributed for at the declared value, but such goods shall contribute upon their actual value."

---

75. *Walford de Baerdemaecker & Co* v. *Galindez Bros* (1897) 2 Com Cas 137.
76. *Marvigor C.N. SA* v. *Romanoexport State Co for Foreign Trade (The Corinthian Glory)* [1977] 2 Lloyd's Rep 280.
77. See *supra*, 49.
78. Although this exception allows, into general average, losses not otherwise qualifying, or easily provable, as such (because caused by the danger rather than by steps taken to avert its consequences), it has the advantage of obviating the practical difficulty of deciding to what extent the losses can be attributed to the two different causes. Cf *Reliance Marine Insurance Co* v. *New York & Cuba Mail Steamship Co* (1896) 70 Fed Rep 262, 77 Fed Rep 317, 165 US 720.
79. See further *supra*, 35.
80. Reproduced in [1990] LMCLQ 54 and enacted in English law in the Merchant Shipping Act 1995, s.224, Sched. 11.
81. York-Antwerp Rules 1994, Rule VI(b). See further *supra*, 53.
82. Upon which there is no English authority.

4. Illegality

Though contribution may be claimed in respect of acts giving rise to liability to third parties (e.g. by tortiously damaging property of a third party[83] in order to avoid a greater loss),[84] it cannot be claimed in respect of acts which are prohibited by law.[85]

---

83. *Ex hypothesi*, conduct which might normally constitute a tort or breach of contract with respect to the property of a party interested in the adventure is excused by the circumstances: see *infra*, 79. Cf the discussion of general average acts necessitated by the claimant's actionable fault: *supra*, 66–76.

84. See *infra*, 79.

85. *Parsons* v. *Scott* (1810) 2 Taunt 362 (payment of ransom to an enemy).

CHAPTER 5

EFFECTS OF A GENERAL AVERAGE ACT

1. A defence

Action which, *vis-à-vis* the other parties interested in the adventure, would normally be actionable as a tort or breach of contract is excused to the extent that it is done for purposes of general average.[1] Necessity may also be a defence to a claim brought by third parties to the adventure for a loss suffered by them as a result of a general average act.[2]

2. Contribution

The owner of each interest which benefits from a general average act must contribute to the loss suffered as a result of that act in proportion to the net value of the property preserved at the end of the voyage. A right to a general average contribution is enforceable by action.[3]

"Each owner of jettisoned goods becomes a creditor of ship and cargo saved, and has a direct claim against each of the owners of ship and cargo, for a pro rata contribution towards his indemnity, which he can enforce by a direct action."[4]

A consignee of goods is not liable for a general average contribution merely because he receives goods with notice that they are the subject of a claim for contribution.[5] For a person to bring an action for general average contribution, it is incumbent on him to show: that the defendant was the owner of the property to be charged at the time of the loss or that there was an express or

---

1. *The Gratitudine* (1801) 3 C Rob 240, 258; *Federal Commerce & Navigation Co Ltd* v. *Eisernz GmbH (The Oak Hill)* [1975] 1 Lloyd's Rep 105 (Can SC). And see *The Alpha* [1991] 2 Lloyd's Rep 515, 522–523.
2. The extent of the defence of necessity is not entirely clear. See *Clerk & Lindsell on Torts*, 17th ed. (1995), paras 3–57 to 3–63. It seems to be assumed that third party claims will not be defeated by the defence. See *The Seapool* [1934] P 53, in which liability for damage to a pier was probably strict: see Harbour Docks and Piers Clauses Act 1847, s.74.
3. *Birkley* v. *Presgrave* (1801) 1 East 220.
4. *Strang, Steel & Co* v. *A Scott & Co* (1889) 14 App Cas 601, 606 (PC: per Lord Watson). In an appropriate case, the claim may be brought by a demise charterer, either alone or jointly with the shipowner: *Walford de Baerdemaecker & Co* v. *Galindez Bros* (1897) 2 Com Cas 137.
5. *Scaife* v. *Tobin* (1832) 3 B & Ad 523.

79

implied contract that he would pay general average, e.g. an average bond signed by him.[6]

In *The Corinthian Glory*[7] a charterparty provided that disputes should be settled according to an arbitration clause, and liability for general average was to be settled according to the York-Antwerp Rules, but that the charterer's liability should cease as soon as cargo was shipped, the owners having a lien on the cargo for average. Cargo was shipped under a bill of lading which was subject to the terms of the charterparty and therefore incorporated the charterparty general average clause. By the time of the general average act the charterers had become the owners of the cargo but, since their relationship with the shipowners was governed by the charterparty and not by the bill of lading, and since their liability for general average according to the terms of the charterparty had ceased, Donaldson J concluded[8] that the charterers were, as cargo owners, liable for general average under the general maritime law, and not according to the York-Antwerp Rules; though the claim could not be enforced according to the arbitration clause. The charterers argued that, although after presentation of the bill of lading they had obtained possession of the cargo, the shipowners' claim to a contribution was only enforceable against them so far as they enforced their lien over cargo. However, Donaldson J held[9]:

"the tender by cargo owners of a document which, by incorporation, records an obligation to pay general average contribution thereby obtaining possession of cargo on which a lien had previously been asserted, seems to me to involve, by necessary implication, either a variation of the charterparty to incorporate an undertaking to pay general average contribution notwithstanding the terms of the cesser clause or a waiver of the protection of that clause. Alternatively, although this was not argued, it amounts to a representation that the cesser clause will not be relied upon, this representation being acted upon to their detriment by the owners releasing the cargo. Accordingly, the charterers are now estopped from relying upon the cesser clause."

Since an underlying principle of general average is equality of treatment of the common adventurers,[10] the owner of the interest sacrificed must also bear a proportion of the general average loss, assessed on the value of his interest remaining (if any) plus the amount nominally to be made good to him by the other interests—i.e. on the value which his interest would have had at the place of destination if it had been a beneficiary of the general average act.[11]

---

6. *Scaife* v. *Tobin* (1832) 3 B & Ad 523 (as interpreted in *Marvigor C.N. SA* v. *Romanoexport State Co for Foreign Trade (The Corinthian Glory)* [1977] 2 Lloyd's Rep 280); *Walford de Baerdemaecker & Co* v. *Galindez Bros* (1897) 2 Com Cas 137; *Hain Steamship Co Ltd* v. *Tate & Lyle Ltd* (1936) 41 Com Cas 350. See now Carriage of Goods by Sea Act 1992, s.3.
7. *Marvigor C.N. SA* v. *Romanoexport State Co for Foreign Trade (The Corinthian Glory)* [1977] 2 Lloyd's Rep 280.
8. [1977] 2 Lloyd's Rep 280, 287.
9. [1977] 2 Lloyd's Rep 280, 288.
10. See *infra*, 87–88.
11. See *infra*, 89.

3. Security: liens, average bonds, average guarantees and cash deposits[12]

There attaches to all property which has been preserved in consequence of a general average act, "till the contributions are paid or secured,"[13] a possessory lien in favour of those who have suffered legal[14] general average losses, regardless of whether the person exercising the lien has a right to sue the person against whom the lien is exercised.[15] The lien attaches at the time of the general average act. The "right of lien can only be enforced through the ship-master, whom the law of England, following the principles of the Lex Rhodia, regards as [the claimant's] agent for that purpose."[16] The master is answerable to all those entitled to contribution to exercise the lien at the time of discharge of preserved cargo in such a way as will provide equivalent security for all general average claimants (i.e., both shipowner and cargo owners).[17] Being a possessory and not a maritime lien, it is exercisable only against the consignee of cargo; but it is exercisable whether or not the consignee was owner of the consignment at the time of the general average act giving rise to it, a fact of which the shipowner may well be unaware.

At the time of discharge, the sum for which the lien is security is normally unquantifiable until after there has been an average adjustment. Indeed, in the case of some consignees of cargo that has been preserved in part only or damaged in consequence of a general average loss, they may turn out to be entitled, rather than liable, to a contribution. It may therefore be difficult for a master to know whether or not he can lawfully withhold delivery.

Shipowners are entitled to refuse to deliver goods until paid the amount of general average contribution due, and are not bound to accept security for that amount in lieu of immediate payment. They are, however, bound to supply sufficient information to enable the cargo owner to ascertain how much is due. If the shipowners refuse to deliver cargo to a consignee who offers to pay a

---

12. See *The Potoi Chau* [1984] AC 226, 234 (PC: per Lord Diplock); *Svendsen* v. *Wallace* (1885) 10 App Cas 404, 410, per Lord Blackburn; *Strang, Steel & Co* v. *A Scott & Co* (1889) 14 App Cas (PC: per Lord Watson).
13. *Anderson Tritton & Co* v. *Ocean Steamship Co* (1884) 10 App Cas 107, 115, per Lord Blackburn.
14. *Parsons* v. *Scott* (1810) 2 Taunt 362 (payment of ransom prohibited by law). See further *supra*, 78.
15. *Simonds* v. *White* (1824) 2 B & C 805, 811; *Dalglish* v. *Davidson* (1824) 5 Dowl & Ry KB 6; *Scaife* v. *Tobin* (1832) 3 B & Ad 523; *Hingston* v. *Wendt* (1876) 1 QBD 367.
16. *Strang, Steel & Co* v. *A Scott & Co* (1889) 14 App Cas 601, 606 (PC: per Lord Watson). See Dig.14.2.2 (opinion of Paulus).
17. *Crooks & Co* v. *Allan* (1879) 5 QBD 38 (carrier liable to cargo owner for not preserving his rights to general average). See also Rules of Practice of the Association of Average Adjusters, Rule B32 ("where general damage to ship is claimed direct from underwriters, average adjusters shall ascertain whether shipowners have taken necessary steps to enforce their lien").

reasonable sum or to put up a reasonable security, they may be liable in conversion.[18]

Possessory liens rank below previously arising maritime liens, which arise in a limited number of situations, two of which are general average and salvage claims. Plaintiffs in such claims (whether or not in possession of property) are effectively secured by maritime lien and the action *in rem* by virtue of the Supreme Court Act 1981, ss.20(2)(j), (q) and 21(4).[19]

In practice, acting on behalf of those entitled to a contribution, the master normally releases the preserved cargo to the consignees in return for security,[20] commonly the execution by each consignee of an average bond[21] in one or other of Lloyd's standard forms, accompanied, in the comparatively rare cases of cargo that is uninsured or where the cargo insurer is not acceptable to the shipowner as a guarantor, by a deposit in a bank in joint names of money as security or, more usually, by a letter of guarantee from the insurer of the cargo.

In relation to cash deposits, Rule XXII of the York-Antwerp Rules 1994[22] provides:

"Where cash deposits have been collected in respect of cargo's liability for general average, salvage or special charges, such deposits shall be paid without any delay into a special account in the joint names of a representative nominated on behalf of the shipowner and a representative nominated on behalf of the depositors in a bank to be approved by both. The sum so deposited, together with accrued interest,[23] if any, shall be held as security for payment to the parties entitled thereto of the general average, salvage or special charges payable by cargo in respect to which the deposits have been collected. Payments on account of refunds of deposits may be made if certified to in writing by the average adjuster. Such deposits and payments or refunds shall be without prejudice to the ultimate liability of the parties."

4. Basis of liability; whose liability? Average bonds

At common law, the personal liability to pay the general average contribution due in respect of any interest preserved in consequence of a general average act

---

18. *The Norway* (1864) Br & L 377, 396–398 (judgment varied *ibid.*, 424); *Anderson Tritton & Co* v. *Ocean Steamship Co* (1884) 10 App Cas 107, 115, per Lord Blackburn; *Huth* v. *Lamport* (1886) 16 QBD 735.

19. See *infra*, 94.

20. He must not demand an unreasonable security, which, if given, will not be upheld, e.g., if it makes the shipowner's adjuster an arbitrator, favours the shipowner in an appeal from an arbitrator, requires cash deposits to be in the joint names of shipowner and arbitrator, or entitles the shipowner to draw on such deposits without the depositor's consent, possibly in full and so beyond the amount for which the depositor is ultimately found to be liable: *Huth* v. *Lamport* (1886) 16 QBD 735. See also *Brandeis, Goldschmidt & Co* v. *Economic Insurance Co Ltd* (1922) 11 Ll L Rep 42 (in which insurers refused an indemnity for a cash deposit paid to a representative of the shipowner without security); *Salvage Association* v. *Suzuki & Co Ltd* (1929) 35 Ll L Rep 45.

21. Average bonds are discussed in the next section.

22. See also Rules of Practice of the Association of Average Adjusters, Rules B34–B35 (refunds of cash deposits to be noted).

23. See also Rules of Practice of the Association of Average Adjusters, Rule B36 (interest on deposits generally to be credited to depositor or his successor).

lies in theory upon the person who was owner of the interest at the time of the act. In modern practice, however, liability for a general average contribution is based on a charterparty or bill of lading contract, or on a substitute agreement (entered into to secure release of the general average lien[24]) contained in, for example, "one or other of the forms that are usually, though inaccurately, referred to as Lloyd's average bonds".[25] Indeed, "so far as claims in general average between parties to the maritime adventure are concerned, the almost invariable use of average bonds eliminates the need to rely directly on the general average clause in the contract of affreightment."[26] Such bonds may provide for security in the form of a cash deposit on joint account in a bank or may be used in conjunction with what are inaccurately described as underwriters' guarantees, though in fact the insurers assume a primary liability.[27]

Obviously the effect of a contractual provision for general average depends on the construction of the contract. Thus, the incorporation of the York-Antwerp Rules 1974 would include those Rules but not the York-Antwerp Rules 1994. Nevertheless, general average clauses are not construed narrowly, and their normal effect will be that general average liability is based on the common law rules as amended by the stated version of the York-Antwerp Rules.[28] Endorsement of a bill of lading "creates a contractual liability on the part of the consignee as indorsee of the bill of lading to pay general average contribution, if there be any on the cargo shipped, whether it was he, the shipper or some immediate indorsee of the bill of lading, who happened to be the owner of the goods at the time when a general average [act occurred]".[29]

Agreement to an average bond constitutes a fresh contract independently of a bill of lading contract and is for fresh consideration on either side: the release by the shipowner of his claim to any possessory lien for a general average contribution he may have; and the assumption by the consignee of a personal liability, secured by a cash deposit or an insurer's guarantee, to pay at the time when the general average statement has been completed by an average adjuster appointed by the shipowners a liquidated sum, representing the general average contribution which may have been payable, at common law, by the owner of the consignment at the time of the general average act or by the shipper.[30]

---

24. See *supra*, 81. *Scaife* v. *Tobin* (1832) 3 B & Ad 523; *Hain Steamship Co Ltd* v. *Tate & Lyle Ltd* (1936) 41 Com Cas 350.
25. *Castle Ins Co Ltd* v. *Hong Kong Islands Shipping Co Ltd (The Potoi Chau)* [1984] AC 226, 232 (PC: per Lord Diplock): see also *ibid.*, 238.
26. *The Potoi Chau* [1984] AC 226, 238.
27. *The Potoi Chau* [1984] AC 226, 232, 238–239, 241–242. For the form of Lloyd's average bonds and guarantees, see *infra*, Appx 5.
28. See *The Potoi Chau* [1984] AC 226, 238.
29. *The Potoi Chau* [1984] AC 226, 235. See now the Carriage of Goods by Sea Act 1992.
30. *Hain SS Co Ltd* v. *Tate & Lyle Ltd* (1936) 41 Com Cas 350; *The Potoi Chau* [1984] AC 226, 239–240.

5. The time, place and law governing adjustment

General average contributions are generally assessed according to values fixed at the time and place of the termination of the adventure and according to the law prevailing there. However, there are a number of detailed circumstances to consider in this respect, which are considered more fully below.[31]

6. A tort claim for economic loss

Despite the law's general opposition to claims in tort for damages for pure economic loss, exceptionally, a person who has become liable to make a general average contribution as a result of a third party's tort (e.g. where the defendant's ship negligently collides with the carrying vessel) may recover damages for his loss in having to pay contribution.[32]

7. Limitation of action

At common law or under contract, liability to contribute to general average accrues at the time of the general average act.[33] This position is unaffected by the publication of a general average statement, which, in the absence of contrary agreement, is intended to quantify liability, but does not affect rights or limitation periods.[34] However, in practice, liability is determined by a contract on the terms of an average bond[35] and accrues at the time when the general average statement is issued.[36] Since in practice general average is governed by contract, time runs for the limitation period governing the contract[37] and it is unnecessary to determine the common law limitation period.[38]

In practice, a shipowner gives notice of a claim to general average by appointing an average adjuster and by a declaration of general average and/or by

---

31. Chap. 6.
32. *Morrison SS Co* v. *Greystoke Castle (Cargo Owners) (The Cheldale)* [1947] AC 265, overruling *The Marpessa* [1891] P 403. See also *The Sucarseco* (1935) 51 Ll L Rep 238 (US SC).
33. *The Potoi Chau* [1984] AC 226, 235–236; *Chandris* v. *Argos Ins Co Ltd* [1963] 2 Lloyd's Rep 65.
34. *Noreuro Traders Ltd* v. *E Hardy & Co* (1923) 16 Ll L Rep 319; *The Potoi Chau* [1984] AC 226, 237: the adjustment is an expression of a professional opinion and is not capable of giving rise to any fresh cause of action or of postponing the accrual of an existing cause of action for a liquidated sum.
35. See *supra*, 83.
36. *The Potoi Chau* [1984] AC 226.
37. The normal contractual limitation period is six years: Limitation Act 1980, s.5. A claim governed by the Hague-Visby Rules must be brought within twelve months of discharge: Carriage of Goods by Sea Act 1971, Sched., art. III(6). It seems that different limitation periods from those laid down by statute can be imposed by contract: *Union of India* v. *EB Aaby's Rederi (The Evje)* [1975] AC 797 (arbitration clause required claim to be made within twelve months of discharge); and see generally *Lubovsky* v. *Snelling* [1944] 1 KB 44. The Hague-Visby Rules, art. III(6) limitation on a cargo owner's right to sue the carrier will not override the cargo owner's "equitable defence" arising from the carrier's actionable fault (see *supra*, 66–76) nor will it limit his claim for a general average contribution: *Goulandris Bros Ltd* v. *B Goldman & Sons* [1958] 1 QB 74.
38. This could be unlimited or subject to laches.

a declaration of general average accompanied by the appropriate forms, e.g. an average bond and/or an underwriters' guarantee. Where the York-Antwerp Rules 1994 apply, once one party has appointed an average adjuster, all claims must be asserted under the procedure in Rule E. At common law, though highly persuasive, an average adjustment is not conclusive in the absence of express agreement.[39] Under Rule E of the York-Antwerp Rules 1994, all parties claiming in general average must give written notice of their claims to the average adjuster within twelve months of the date of termination of the common maritime adventure. If this is not done, or if any parties fail within twelve months to comply with his request for evidence of a notified claim or particulars of value in respect of a contributory interest, the average adjuster may estimate the extent of the allowance or the contributory value on the basis of information available to him, which estimate may be challenged only on the ground that it is manifestly incorrect.

8. Limitation of liability

Many maritime claims are subject to limits on the amount of liability under the provisions of the Convention on Limitation of Liability for Maritime Claims 1976.[40] However, the rules of the Convention do not apply to claims for contribution in general average.[41]

9. Interest

Under Rule XXI of the York-Antwerp Rules 1994:

"Interest shall be allowed on expenditure, sacrifices and allowances in general average at the rate of 7 per cent per annum, until three months after the date of issue of the general average adjustment, due allowance being made for any payment on account."

After publication of the adjustment, interest is calculable according to the general law.[42]

In practice, subject to contrary agreement, interest allowed on amounts made good shall be apportioned between assured and underwriters, taking into account the sums paid by underwriters and the dates when such payments were made, notwithstanding that by the addition of interest the underwriter may receive a larger sum than he has paid.[43]

---

39. *Chandris* v. *Argo Ins Co Ltd* [1991] 2 Lloyd's Rep 65, 76; *State Trading Corp of India* v. *Doyle Carriers Inc (The Jute Express)* [1991] 2 Lloyd's Rep 55.
40. See Merchant Shipping Act 1995, s.217, Sched. 4.
41. Art. 3(a).
42. In the Supreme Court Act 1981, s.35A; *Corfu Navigation Co* v. *Mobil Shipping Co Ltd (The Alpha) (No 2)* [1991] 2 Lloyd's Rep 515.
43. Rules of Practice of the Association of Average Adjusters, Rule B37.

10. Insurer's liability

A general average loss will, subject to the terms of the policy, entitle the person suffering the loss to claim under any applicable insurance policy.[44]

---

44. This is discussed *infra*, Chap. 7.

CHAPTER 6

ADJUSTMENT

1. General principles

Adjustment of general average is founded on "the principle that the loss to the individual whose goods are sacrificed for the benefit of the rest is to be compensated according to the loss sustained on the one hand and the benefit derived on the other."[1] This principle must be applied to real, not hypothetical, circumstances. A comparison must be made between what would have happened if there had been no general average act and what has in fact happened. For example, if goods would in any event have arrived damaged, they are not to be valued as if they would have arrived undamaged. "The owner of goods jettisoned is to be indemnified against loss; but he is not to be a gainer by the sacrifice of his goods for the general benefit. He is not to be put in a better position than those whose goods have not been jettisoned."[2] "The rules as to contribution and adjustment ... depend upon the probable state of things at, and to have reference to, the time and place [at which the voyage ends]."[3]

To ensure equality of treatment between the parties (to endeavour to ensure that it makes no difference whose property is sacrificed, and that the claimant does not end up better off than the contributors), contributions are assessed on both the property preserved and the property sacrificed. It is generally said that the contributory value of the claimant's interest is the value remaining at the end of the voyage (if any) plus "the amount made good in general average" (by contribution from the interests benefited). This means that the value of the claimant's property is taken as the value which it would have had at the end of the voyage if, like the contributors' property, it had been subjected to the effects of both the danger and the general average act. Any expense incurred in realising the value at destination but which would have been avoided if the general average act had not been made (e.g. freight payable at destination on cargo which would have been lost, or repairs to ship which would have been necessitated by the danger) is deducted. Similarly, property which, as a result of the general average act, could have arrived at its originally intended destination,

---
1. *Fletcher* v. *Alexander* (1868) LR 3 CP 375, 382, per Bovill CJ.
2. *Fletcher* v. *Alexander* (1868) LR 3 CP 375, 386–387, per Montague Smith J.
3. See *Fletcher* v. *Alexander* (1868) LR 3 CP 375, 383, per Bovill CJ.

but which is separated from the adventure early, should be valued at the contributory value it would have had if it had completed the adventure, less any special charges which would have been incurred in bringing that situation about.[4]

2. The parties' interests are generally valued at the end of the voyage

The end of the voyage

In a leading case on the adjustment of general average, Bovill CJ said that "The rules as to contribution and adjustment ... depend upon the probable state of things at, and to have reference to, the time and place of adjustment, that is to say, when and where the adjustment ought to take place."[5] This statement reflects the earlier practice of making the adjustment at the place at which the common adventure terminates. This may, of course, still occur. However, in modern times it is the exception rather than the rule. It is not necessary that the adjuster should be based at or carry out his work at the place with respect to which general average is to be adjusted.[6] Indeed, a foreign adjustment only binds where the parties agree that it should.[7] The fact that there may be a difference between the place with respect to which rights and liabilities in general average are to be adjusted and the place of statement of general average is recognised in Rule G of the York-Antwerp Rules 1994:

"General average shall be adjusted as regards both loss and contribution upon the basis of values at the time and place when and where the adventure ends.
This rule shall not affect the determination of the place at which the average statement is to be made up."

The term "place of adjustment" would be a convenient description of the place with respect to which rights and liabilities are adjusted. However, in practice it is used to refer to the place where the adjuster in fact makes his adjustment.

One effect of fixing the place where the voyage terminates as the place for valuation is that property of value at the time of a general average act may change in value by the time the voyage terminates. For example, a casualty occurring after the general average act may diminish or eliminate the value of a (potential) contributory interest, so reducing or extinguishing the liability of the owner of that interest and increasing (up to the full amount) the burden which the other interested parties must bear.[8] The risk that the value of a claim for a

---

4. For more precise consideration of contributory values, see *infra*, §7, which includes discussion of Rule XVII ("contributory values") of the York-Antwerp Rules 1994.
5. See *Fletcher* v. *Alexander* (1868) LR 3 CP 375, 383, per Bovill CJ.
6. *Wavertree SS Co Ltd* v. *Love* [1897] AC 373. See also *Mavro* v. *Ocean Marine Insurance Co* (1875) 2 Asp MLC 590, 592, per Blackburn J (cf (1875) LR 10 CP 414, 419).
7. *Green Star Shipping Co Ltd* v. *The London Assurance (The Andree)* [1933] 1 KB 378, 389.
8. *Chellew* v. *Royal Commission on the Sugar Supply* [1921] 2 KB 627, affd [1922] 1 KB 12; *Green Star Shipping Co Ltd* v. *London Assurance (The Andree)* [1933] 1 KB 378. The effect of a second general average act in *The Andree* was that, when the general average expenditure was deducted from the value of the interests for which it was incurred (as is required by Rule XVII of the

general average contribution may be so reduced or extinguished is insurable,[9] the cost of insurance being itself allowable as a general average expenditure.

Valuation of sacrifices, expenditures and contributory interests

It was established at common law that, in the case of a general average sacrifice, the value of the contributory interests is the value which they in fact have, and the value of the property sacrificed is the value which (but for the sacrifice) it would have had, at the place of termination of the adventure.[10] In the case of a general average expenditure, the value of such expenditure is fixed where and when it is incurred.[11] However, the place for determining the value of the contributory interests in the case of a general average expenditure was undecided at common law.

Under the York-Antwerp Rules 1994 a uniform rule is applied to the valuation of contributory interests and property sacrificed. Subject to contrary provision,[12] Rule G of the York-Antwerp Rules 1994 provides, in its first paragraph,[13] that:

"General average shall be adjusted as regards both loss and contribution upon the basis of values at the time and place when and where the adventure ends."

It is generally assumed that the relevant amount of expenditure remains the amount actually incurred at the time it was incurred. Rule G could conceivably be interpreted to mean that the sum in question should be converted to its equivalent value at the place where the adventure ends; but this would be wrong in principle. The commercial value of property involved in a common adventure, whether it be the property sacrificed or the property preserved, is the value to its owners at the intended destination; but the loss suffered in a case of expenditure is the amount actually expended at the time of the general average act.

3. Determining the place at which contributory values are assessed

Reflecting the failure of the common law to settle the issue clearly, there is no provision in the York-Antwerp Rules for determining the place of termination

---

York-Antwerp Rules 1994: see *infra*, 97), those interests had no value remaining for the purposes of the first general average act.

9. *Chellew* v. *Royal Commission on the Sugar Supply* [1922] 1 KB 12, 20, per Scrutton LJ. See NG Hudson, "The Insurance of Average Disbursements" [1987] LMCLQ 443; DJ Wilson, *Insurance of Average Disbursements* (Association of Average Adjusters, 1988).

10. *Fletcher* v. *Alexander* (1868) LR 3 CP 375. Cf *Anglo-Grecian Steam Trading Co Ltd* v. *T Beynon & Co* (1926) 24 Ll L Rep 122, 125, where Roche J valued the ship at the date of abandonment of the adventure.

11. This will also be the date for fixing the rate of exchange if necessary: see *Food Corporation of India* v. *Carras* [1980] 2 Lloyd's Rep 577.

12. Of course, Rule G is a lettered Rule, and therefore gives way to any relevant numbered Rule.

13. The second clause is stated *supra*, 88, and the third and fourth clauses are stated *infra*, 91–92.

of the adventure or other place with respect to which general average should be adjusted. At common law, it was held that such place may be either the originally intended destination or an earlier place of termination of the voyage:

"The adjustment must be made at the port of destination, if it be reached, but if the voyage is interrupted by some supervening cause, which necessitates or justifies its termination at some intermediate place, that place is the proper place of adjustment."[14]

The adventure may terminate in accordance with the parties' original intentions. Thus, where all the cargo is destined for a single port of discharge, it will terminate at that port. Where different cargoes are bound for different ports, the adventure will terminate in respect of each parcel at the port at which it is discharged. Alternatively, the adventure may terminate earlier than originally contemplated, for example, where the contract of carriage has been frustrated by the events giving rise to the general average act, so that the shipowner is unable to have the cargo carried from the port of refuge to the destination agreed under the original contract.

If the adventure does in fact terminate at a port of refuge and an interest—in practice, cargo—is subsequently brought to the originally intended destination, the on-carriage and its consequences are in principle outside general average. The cargo owner may be entitled to terminate the adventure at the port of discharge and be freed of all subsequent[15] liability to the carrier, for example, if the carrier is incapable of arranging for the on-carriage of the cargo under the contractual relationship. However, termination of the voyage will not necessarily follow from the fact that the voyage has been interrupted. Thus, the carrier may have a right to choose whether to abandon the voyage or to complete it, either in the original vessel or by alternative means.[16] Where a substitute vessel is used, the original adventure will terminate at the port of refuge so far as the ship is concerned (the original carrying vessel no longer being involved) but the carrier will be entitled to enforce his lien for general average at the final destination, which is in practice treated as the place at which the cargo's contributory value is assessed.[17]

If at a port of refuge the cargo owner took back his cargo and made his own arrangements to have it carried on to destination, this would mean a

---

14. *Mavro* v. *Ocean Marine Insurance Co* (1875) LR 10 CP 414, 416, per Cockburn CJ; *Fletcher* v. *Alexander* (1868) LR 3 CP 375 (vessel returned to port of loading). Cf *Tudor* v. *Macomber* (1833) 14 Pickering 34. Of course, as noted above, Cockburn CJ's reference to "place of adjustment" must be interpreted as referring to the place with respect to which, not at which, the adjustment is made.

15. He will remain liable for accrued liability, e.g., for a general average contribution which has yet to be assessed.

16. This may give rise to a claim by the carrier for substituted expenses under Rule F of the York-Antwerp Rules 1994: see *supra*, 59–61.

17. See *Hudson*, 92. Although it is right for the carrier's lien to survive while the cargo remains in his possession, it may seem odd to treat the final destination as the place with respect to which the adjustment should be made, if the common adventure between the cargo and original carrying vessel has ceased. One explanation might be that the cargo is involved in a common adventure with whichever happens to be the carrying vessel (including substitutes); but this is not the conventional rule, and it could obviously lead to complications as regards contributory values and liens. A proper

termination of the common adventure and so might deprive the carrier of a claim in respect of expenditure incurred as a result of the relevant danger and with a view to completing the voyage himself. The cargo owner might be entitled to do this without being under any liability to the carrier.[18] But in most cases the carrier would be entitled to retain the cargo with a view to completing the voyage and to enforcing a lien. Accordingly, it would in principle be open to the carrier to relinquish his rights in return for a contractually binding promise by the cargo owner to put up security and to pay him in respect of general average claims which would have been enforceable against him if the common adventure had continued. Such an arrangement came to be embodied in a "Non-Separation Agreement". Furthermore, to limit the cargo owner's liability where forwarding was carried out by the carrier but could have been carried out more cheaply by the cargo owner, a "Bigham Clause"[19] could be added. In practice, it is no longer necessary to negotiate for such provisions, because they have been incorporated into the York-Antwerp Rules 1994, which themselves are incorporated into most carriage contracts and charterparties. This also means that, whether or not the cargo owner could claim to take back his cargo free of the obligations in such agreements, he will have agreed at the time of contracting to abide by their terms.[20] A non-separation wording with a Bigham clause now appear in the third and fourth paragraphs of both Rules G[21] and XVII ("contributory values")[22] of the York-Antwerp Rules 1994. Rule G provides[23]:

"[3] When a ship is at any port or place in circumstances which would give rise to an allowance in general average under the provisions of Rules X[24] and XI,[25] and the cargo or part thereof is forwarded to destination by other means, rights and liabilities in general average shall, subject to cargo interests being notified if practicable, remain as nearly as possible the same as they would have been in the absence of such forwarding, as if the adventure had continued in the original ship for so long as justifiable under the contract of affreightment and the applicable law.

---

explanation would be that, although the original carrying vessel has ceased to participate, there remains a common adventure between the cargo and the freight, which is a separate interest: see *supra*, 14–15. See further *Barnard* v. *Adams* (1850) 10 How 270, 307; *McLoon* v. *Cummings* (1873) 73 Penn St Rep 98; *Bradley* v. *Cargo of Lumber* (1886) 29 Fed Rep 648.

18. E.g., if the carrier's fault necessitated calling at the port of refuge: see *supra*, 66–76.

19. Known after the name of the firm which originally drafted it.

20. The precise import of this is unclear. If a cargo owner were entitled to take back his cargo at the port of refuge free of actual or potential "future" general average liabilities (as is the case in Canada and the USA: see *Ellerman Lines* v. *Gibbs (Canada) (The City of Colombo)* (1986) 26 DLR (4th) 161; [1986] AMC 2217; noted PJ Cullen [1987] LMCLQ 160; cf *The Julia Blake* (1882) 107 US 418; *The Dominic de Larrinaga* [1928] AMC 64), the non-separation clause increases his liability. If not (because the carrier still retains the contractual right to earn freight and claim all attendant expenses: cf *The Blenheim* (1886) 10 PD 167), the liabilities would have been incurred anyway.

21. The first and second clauses are stated *supra*, 88.

22. See generally *infra*, 100–101.

23. Paragraph numbers have been inserted for convenience.

24. "Expenses at port of refuge, etc.": see *supra*, 56–59.

25. "Wages and maintenance of crew and other expenses bearing up for and in a port of refuge, etc.": see *supra*, 56–59.

[4] The proportion attaching to cargo of the allowances made in general average by reason of applying the third paragraph of this Rule shall not exceed the cost which would have been borne by the owners of cargo if the cargo had been forwarded at their expense."

Rule XVII states[26]:

"[3] In the circumstances envisaged in the third paragraph of Rule G, the cargo and other property shall contribute on the basis of its value upon delivery at original destination unless sold or otherwise disposed of short of that destination, and the ship shall contribute upon its actual net value at the time of completion of discharge of cargo.

[4] When cargo is sold short of destination, however, it shall contribute upon the actual net proceeds of sale, with the addition of any amount made good as general average."

Where the adventure justifiably terminates for different interests at different places (e.g., part of the cargo is discharged at one port and part at a later port), it seems that the value of a contributor's interest and the extent of his liability are determined at, and by the rules applicable at, the place where the adventure terminates in respect of his interest.[27] However, where it cannot be shown that the adventure has justifiably been determined (e.g., by agreement or necessity) short of destination for a particular interest (e.g., part of the cargo was sold at a port of refuge though the remainder of the cargo was carried on to destination), at common law, all interests will be valued in accordance with their actual or presumed values at the originally intended destination.[28]

4. Average adjusters

Each party is entitled to appoint an average adjuster.[29] In practice, the average adjuster carries out a detailed and often lengthy assessment of the rights and liabilities of all interested parties in order to calculate the contributions due. Moreover, the complexity of settling general average is such that it is often convenient for the adjuster to collect and distribute contributions. However,

---

26. Paragraph numbers have been inserted for convenience.
27. *Lowndes & Rudolf*, paras 30.13–30.14.
28. *Hill* v. *Wilson* (1879) 4 CPD 329. This is also the tenor of Roche J's judgment in *Green Star Shipping Co Ltd* v. *The London Assurance (The Andree)* [1933] 1 KB 378, where cargo taken off at the port of refuge appears to have been valued there rather than at the intended or actual place of termination of the adventure. See the account of the case *infra*, 112–113.
29. For early references to the profession, see *Crofts* v. *Marshall* (1836) 7 C & P 597, 606 ("a settler of averages"); *Pirie* v. *Steele* (1837) 8 C & P 200, 203 ("a taker of averages"). See also *Chandris* v. *Argo Ins Co Ltd* [1963] 2 Lloyd's Rep 65, 75; *Eisernz GmbH* v. *Federal Commerce & Navigation Co Ltd (The Oak Hill)* [1970] 2 Lloyd's Rep 332 (Can Ex Ct) and the cases collected by N Kouladis, "The Legal Status of Average Adjusters" [1994] JBL 488. It is at least arguable that a shipowner is, under the contract of carriage, obliged to appoint an average adjuster: see *The Potoi Chau* [1984] AC 226, 237B–C (PC: per Lord Diplock); cf *Wavertree SS Co Ltd* v. *Love* [1897] AC 373 (PC); *Crooks* v. *Allen* (1879) 5 QBD 38. Enforcement of a claim for general average under an insurance policy is dependent on the assured's establishing his entitlement, and not on the appointment of a professional average adjuster, though this is the usual practice: see *Chandris* v. *Argo Ins Co Ltd* [1963] 2 Lloyd's Rep 65. Where an average adjuster has been appointed by both parties, he is in the

unless otherwise agreed, his adjustment is not binding on the parties[30] and his appointment will not therefore impose on the contributor an obligation to make payment at the place of adjustment.[31]

5. Jurisdiction

A tribunal will have jurisdiction over a dispute if the parties so agree (e.g. by an arbitration agreement or by submission to the court's jurisdiction) or if the court has jurisdiction by law (i.e. provided that service, or notice of service, of a writ can be effected under the Rules of the Supreme Court,[32] and subject to the provisions of the Civil Jurisdiction and Judgments Act 1982).[33]

The Civil Jurisdiction and Judgments Act 1982 implements the Brussels Convention on Jurisdiction and the Enforcement of Judgments in Civil and Commercial Matters 1968. The Convention provides that, as a general rule, persons domiciled in a Contracting State shall be sued in the courts of that State.[34] However, if the Convention's provisions for "special jurisdiction" apply, they may be sued elsewhere, for example, if one of the parties is domiciled in a Contracting State and the parties have agreed that the courts of another Contracting State are to have jurisdiction[35] or "in matters relating to a contract, in the courts for the place of performance of the obligation in question".[36] However, an agreement that general average shall be "adjusted" in a Contracting State does not create special jurisdiction under these provisions.[37] It does not mean that there has been a submission to the courts of that State; nor does it mean that the obligation to pay a general average contribution has to be performed there, although that may be the case if it is provided that general average is to be "settled" and/or "paid" there.[38]

---

position of an arbitrator and not liable to them for negligence: *Tharsis Sulphur & Copper Co Ltd* v. *Jones* (1872) LR 8 CP 1, applying *Pappa* v. *Rose* (1872) LR 7 CP 525; but cf *Sutcliffe* v. *Thakrah* [1974] AC 727; *Arenson* v. *Casson Beckman Rutley & Co* [1977] AC 405. For his liability in negligence to a party who has not engaged him to make an average adjustment, see *Henderson* v. *Merrett Syndicates Ltd* [1995] 2 AC 145; *White* v. *Jones* [1995] 2 AC 207; cf *Spring* v. *Guardian Assurance plc* [1995] 2 AC 296.

30. *Wavertree SS Co Ltd v Love* [1897] AC 373 (PC); *Attaleia Marine Co Ltd* v. *Bimeh Iran (Iran Insurance Co) (The Zeus)* [1993] 2 Lloyd's Rep 497; *Sameon Co SA* v. *NV Petrofina (The World Hitachi Zosen)* [1996] 5 CL 114; affd (May 1997) Unreported (CA).
31. *The World Hitachi Zosen*, ibid.
32. See RSC, Ords 10–11, 75.
33. See further A Briggs, *Civil Jurisdiction and Judgments*, 2nd ed. (1997); DC Jackson, *Enforcement of Maritime Claims*, 2nd ed. (1996); N Meeson, *Admiralty Jurisdiction and Practice* (1993).
34. Civil Jurisdiction and Judgments Act 1982, s.2(2), Sched. 1, art. 2.
35. *Ibid.*, art. 17.
36. *Ibid.*, art. 5(1).
37. *Sameon Co SA* v. *NV Petrofina SA (The World Hitachi Zosen)* [1996] 6 CL 114; affd (May 1996) Unreported (CA).
38. See *The World Hitachi Zosen* [1996] 5 CL 114, per Langley J. See further *infra*, 94.

Where the High Court has jurisdiction over a general average dispute, it falls within its admiralty jurisdiction.[39]

6. Governing law and practice

In the absence of clear words, there is a presumption that general average disputes are to be determined by the same regime as other disputes between the parties.[40] However, general average should normally be adjusted in relation to the time and place where the adventure ends,[41] albeit it is not necessary to employ a local adjuster[42] unless the contract requires the statement to be made there. In the absence of contrary provision, therefore, the parties will be bound by the law and practice at the place where the adventure ends.[43] If they agree to be bound by a custom contradicting the prevailing law, their intention will be given effect provided the alleged contradiction is proved.[44] A contractual provision "to be settled in London" means to be adjusted in accordance with an adjustment prepared in London and conforming with English law and practice, and probably also means "to be paid in London".[45]

"The words 'to be settled in London' are words which provide a contractual agreement for the place at which the adjustment is to be drawn up and carry the implication that the law governing the adjustment shall be the law of that place and that the adjusters shall follow the practice of adjusters at that place."[46]

A provision that a contract, whether of affreightment or insurance, is to be governed by English law, or by English law and practice,[47] should normally be

---

39. By virtue of the Supreme Court Act 1981, ss.20–24. See in particular s.20(2)(q) ("any claim arising out of an act which is or which is claimed to be a general average act"), though a relevant claim may also fall under other heads. See also County Courts Act 1984, ss.26–31.

40. *Swiss Bank Corp* v. *Novorossiysk Shipping Co (The Petr Schmidt)* [1995] 1 Lloyd's Rep 202; *Transamerican Ocean Contractors Inc* v. *Transchemical Rotterdam BV (The Ioanna)* [1978] 1 Lloyd's Rep 238.

41. See *Union of India* v. *EB Aaby's Rederi A/S (The Evje)* [1975] AC 797, 817, per Lord Salmon; York-Antwerp Rules 1994 Rule G; and *supra*, 88–92.

42. See *supra*, 88.

43. *Simonds* v. *White* (1824) 2 B & C 805; *Dalglish* v. *Davidson* (1824) 5 Dowl & Ry KB 6; *Lloyd* v. *Guibert* (1865) LR 1 QB 115; *Fletcher* v. *Alexander* (1868) LR 3 CP 375, 362. The parties may also expressly agree to foreign adjustment. An agreement for adjustment to take place somewhere other than where the adventure terminates may indicate that the adjustment is to be governed by the law of the place where it is carried out: see *Wavertree Sailing Ship Co Ltd* v. *Love* [1897] AC 373. A payment required under an applicable foreign rule on general average cannot be recovered on the ground that it would not have been required under English law: *Simonds* v. *White* (1824) 2 B & C 805; *Dalglish* v. *Davidson* (1824) 5 Dowl & Ry KB 6. Langley J's dictum in *Sameon Co SA* v. *NV Petrofina (The World Hitachi Zosen)* [1996] CL 114; affd (May 1997) Unreported (CA) that "The major purpose of providing for a single place of adjustment is to fix a single law to be applied to questions of general average" obviously has to be treated with caution.

44. *Stewart* v. *West India and Pacific Steamship Co* (1873) LR 8 QB 88, 362; *Achard* v. *Ring* (1874) 2 Asp MLC 422.

45. See *Union of India* v. *EB Aaby's Rederi A/S (The Evje)* [1975] AC 797, 808–809, per Lord Morris of Borth-y-Gest, 817B–C, per Lord Salmon; *Sameon Co SA* v. *NV Petrofina (The World Hitachi Zosen)* [1996] CL 114; affd (May 1997) Unreported (CA).

46. *Marida Ltd* v. *Oswal Steel (The Bijela)* [1992] 1 Lloyd's Rep 636, 642, per Hobhouse J.

47. This is the general rule in marine insurance contracts.

taken to incorporate the rule of English law that general average should be adjusted according to the law and practice prevailing at the place where the adventure terminates. Such a construction, which can also be applied to other choice of law clauses, will justifiably reduce tension between the law generally governing the contract and the general rule in general average law and practice that adjustment should be according to the law and practice of the place where the adventure ends.

The position expressed in the previous paragraph seems to be the effect of *Schothorst & Schuitema* v. *Franz Dauter GmbH (The Nimrod)*[48] and *Armar Shipping Co Ltd* v. *Caisse Algérienne d'Assurance et de Réassurance (The Armar)*.[49] In *The Nimrod*, Kerr J thought that an average bond was governed by the (in that case, English) law governing the bill of lading contract rather than by the (Belgian) law applying at the place where the adventure terminated. His view was not followed in *The Armar*. The *Armar* was chartered to the defendant Cuban charterers under a contract providing for arbitration and adjustment of general average in London. Cargo was shipped under a bill of lading, entitling the plaintiff Cypriot shipowners to choose the place where adjustment of general average was to be made. This right had not been exercised at the time an average bond was concluded in Algeria between the plaintiffs and the Algerian consignee's insurers, an Algerian company. Subsequently, the plaintiffs arranged for general average to be adjusted in London. It was held that the proper law of the bond had to be decided when the contract between the shipowners and the insurers was made, and could not float until the plaintiffs exercised their right under the bill of lading contract. Consequently the average bond was not governed by English law, and an order for leave to serve the writ outside the jurisdiction had to be set aside.

The facts of *The Armar* reflect the perennial problem that, though a single set of facts may underlie a framework of different contractual relationships, whatever the merits of deciding disputes with reference to a single jurisdiction and/or legal system, in principle the relationships under individual contracts should be decided by the terms of the contract in question (which may or may not incorporate terms from other contracts). In practice, potential problems are minimised by common use of the current version of the same set of relevant rules (e.g., the York-Antwerp Rules 1994) and by clauses incorporating the relevant terms of related contracts by reference. Even so, it is perhaps surprising that the different types of problem that might arise do not seem to have provoked much litigation. No doubt it would not take much ingenuity to hold that, although two different cargo owners are bound, by separate contracts, with the shipowner to have the question of general average settled according to the York-Antwerp Rules 1994, they are not entitled to have the question settled as between themselves by the common law on the ground that the contracts of

---

48. [1973] 2 Lloyd's Rep 91.
49. [1981] 1 WLR 207. See also *Star Shipping AS* v. *China National Foreign Trade Transportation Corp (The Star Texas)* [1993] 2 Lloyd's Rep 445.

carriage do not bind them *inter se*. But the question would not be so easily resolved between charterer and cargo owner where the charterparty incorporated an earlier version of the York-Antwerp Rules than is incorporated into the bill of lading contract.[50]

Identifying the proper law which generally governs the relationship between parties and the law which (according to that proper law) governs the adjustment still leaves the possibility that the two laws may produce different results on a particular issue. Such divergence might be resolved by a rule to the effect that issues the significance of which is not limited to general average (e.g., whether there is actionable fault) should be decided according to the proper law of the main contract,[51] whereas issues of general average (e.g., whether actionable fault bars a claim to a general average contribution) should be decided according to the law governing the adjustment.[52]

Where a contract is governed by the Rome Convention,[53] the parties may agree that different parts of their contract should be governed by different laws (including a "floating law"—to be determined in events which are to occur)[54] but the Convention forbids *renvoi*, so *prima facie* excluding reference by the applicable law to a different law at the place of adjustment.

If general average is to survive and to reduce the uncertainty and consequent expense of settling the divergent rules in different legal systems, there is surely a case for the York-Antwerp Rules to be more comprehensive and, arguably, to be enforced by means of an international convention.

---

50. In addition to *Schothorst & Schuitema* v. *Franz Dauter GmbH (The Nimrod)* [1973] 2 Lloyd's Rep 91 and *Armar Shipping Co Ltd* v. *Caisse Algérienne d'Assurance et de Réassurance (The Armar)* [1981] 1 WLR 207, cf *Clarke* v. *Earl of Dunraven (The Satanita)* [1897] AC 59, *Grange & Co* v. *Taylor* (1904) 9 Com Cas 223, *US Shipping Board* v. *R Durell & Co Ltd* [1923] 2 KB 739, *Berry, Barclay* v. *Louis Dreyfus* (1929) 35 Ll L Rep 173 and *New Zealand Shipping Co Ltd* v. *AM Satterthwaite & Co Ltd (The Eurymedon)* [1975] AC 154.

51. See *Drew Brown Ltd* v. *The Orient Trader and her Owners (The Orient Trader)* [1974] SCR 1286; (1973) 34 DLR (3d) 339; [1973] 2 Lloyd's Rep 174 (Can SC). After an unjustifiable deviation but not as a result of it, a fire broke out destroying the ship and damaging the cargo. The shipowners claimed a general average contribution. Under the US proper law, the shipowners' liability for fire was excepted by statute. The cargo owners argued that the effect of the deviation was to terminate the contract, so that the parties' rights were to be determined by the Canadian common law, free of the US statutory protection, and the shipowner could not claim a contribution. It was held that the US proper law governed the parties' relationship, and by that law the shipowners were entitled to succeed regardless of the deviation. Cf *Burton & Co* v. *English & Co* (1883) 12 QBD 218 (shipment of deck cargo "at merchant's risk" did not disentitle charterers from a general average contribution for jettison). *Lowndes & Rudolf*, para 30.33, criticise *Hill* v. *Wilson* (1879) 4 CPD 329 for deciding that a shipowner's entitlement to pro rata freight was a matter for the law of the place where the adventure terminated, but the judgment treats it as a matter for the parties' agreement.

52. This is the view of *Lowndes & Rudolf*, paras 30.32–30.35.

53. EEC Convention on the Law Applicable to Contractual Obligations 1980. See Contracts (Applicable Law) Act 1990, Sched. 1.

54. See *supra*, 95.

7. Valuation

The process of adjustment in essence requires the quantification of: the *contributory values* of interests involved in the common adventure, including both those sacrificed and those preserved; and the amount of *allowances* for which contributions must be made, namely general average *expenditure* and disbursements.

The discussion on valuation has so far proceeded on the basis of the general principles of the common law and the general principle in Rule G of the York-Antwerp Rules 1994. However, the lettered Rule, in accordance with the Rule of Interpretation in the York-Antwerp Rules 1994,[55] is subject to several numbered Rules.

(a) General rule

As a general rule, the contributory value of a subject of general average, whether belonging to the plaintiff or the defendant, is the net value which the property has (or, in the case of sacrificed property, would have had) at the end of the voyage (i.e., its value at that place less any expense of achieving that value).[56]

Rule XVII of the York-Antwerp Rules 1994, which makes provision for contributory values, begins by stating that: "The contribution to a general average shall be made upon the actual values of the property at the termination of the adventure." Rule XVII then provides specifically for valuation of cargo[57] and ship,[58] then continues:

"To these values shall be added the amount made good as general average for property sacrificed, if not already included, deduction being made from the freight and passage money at risk of such charges and crew's wages as would not have been incurred in earning the freight had the ship and cargo been totally lost at the date of the general average act and have not been allowed as general average; deduction being also made from the value of the property of all extra charges incurred in respect thereof subsequently to the general average act, except such charges as are allowed in general average or fall upon the ship by virtue of an award for special compensation under Article 14 of the International Convention on Salvage 1989[59] or under any other provision similar in substance."

If cargo is so damaged as to be useless and have nil contributory value but the damage is made good in general average under Rule XVII, it will then have a contributory value.[60]

---

55. See *supra*, 11.
56. See *supra*, 87.
57. See *infra*, 100–101.
58. See *infra*, 100.
59. See *supra*, 53.
60. *Republic of India* v. *India Steamship Co Ltd (No 2) (The Indian Endurance)* [1997] 2 WLR 538, 544H.

(b) Ship: the general rule

The value of a ship at common law is its value to its owner at the time and place at which the adventure terminates. Its contributory value is this sum plus any sum made good in general average for general average losses, less any extra charges incurred in respect thereof (e.g., the cost of particular average repairs carried out at the port of refuge) after the general average act.[61] Where the ship is sold, the sale price is *prima facie* evidence of her value.[62] Except where the context otherwise requires, for the construction of marine insurance policies, the Marine Insurance Act 1906 provides[63] that:

"The term 'ship' includes the hull, materials and outfit, stores and provisions for the officers and crew, and, in the case of vessels engaged in a special trade, the ordinary fittings requisite for the trade, and also, in the case of a steamship, the machinery, boilers, and coals and engine stores, if owned by the assured."

The valuation of the ship will not include things which are on board for the purpose of the voyage but which are not regarded as part of the ship, such as bunkers, wireless and navigational equipment, and containers.[64]

In similar, though not identical, terms to the provision for the rules for measure of indemnity in the case of partial loss of ship in the Marine Insurance Act 1906, s.69,[65] Rule XVIII of the York-Antwerp Rules 1994, ostensibly applying to "damage to ship" but also referring to actual total loss, provides:

"The amount to be allowed as general average for damage or loss to the ship, her machinery and/or gear caused by a general average act shall be as follows:
  (a) When repaired or replaced,
      The actual reasonable cost of repairing or replacing such damage or loss, subject to deductions in accordance with Rule XIII[66];
  (b) When not repaired or replaced,
      The reasonable depreciation arising from such damage or loss, but not exceeeding the estimated cost of repairs. But where the ship is an actual total loss or when the cost of repairs of the damage would exceed the value of the ship when repaired,[67] the amount to be allowed as general average shall be the difference between the estimated sound value of the ship after deducting therefrom the estimated cost of repairing damage which is not general average and the value of the ship in her damaged state which may be measured by the net proceeds of the sale, if any."

Rule XVIII is based, in part at least, on *Henderson v. Shankland*.[68] During a storm on a voyage from Chittagong to Dundee, the ship suffered considerable

---

61. Cf *African Steamship Co* v. *Swanzy* (1856) 2 K & J 660; *Grainger* v. *Martin* (1863) 4 B & S 9.
62. *Bell* v. *Smith* (1806) 2 Johnson R 98.
63. Marine Insurance Act 1906, Sched. "Rules for Construction of Policy", Rule 15.
64. See *infra*, 103.
65. See Appx 1.
66. York-Antwerp Rules 1994, Rule XIII ("Deductions from cost of repairs") is discussed *infra*, 99.
67. I.e., it is a constructive total loss. See Marine Insurance Act 1906, s.60.
68. [1896] 1 QB 525.

damage. The ship being on her beam ends, in order to avert probable loss of both ship and cargo, her mainmast and foremast were cut away. She was then towed to Calcutta. Since the cost of repairing her would have exceeded her value when repaired, she was condemned and sold as a constructive total loss. Rejecting the arguments that the ship should be valued either at the date of commencement of the voyage or at the beginning of the storm (i.e. before either a particular average loss or a general average loss was incurred), the Court of Appeal held that the ship should be valued at the difference between its undamaged value[69] less the estimated cost of repairing particular average damage, and that there should be no deduction of "one third, new for old", since no repairs were effected and therefore no one benefited from them.[70]

(c) Ship—deductions from cost of repairs

Under current practice, no deduction "new for old" shall be made from the cost of temporary repairs allowable as general average.[71] However, general provision for deductions from cost of repairs is made by Rule XIII of the York-Antwerp Rules 1994,[72] which provides:

"Repairs to be allowed in general average shall not be subject to deductions in respect of 'new for old' where old material or parts are replaced by new unless the ship is over fifteen years old in which case there shall be a deduction of one third. The deductions shall be regulated by the age of the ship from the 31st December of the year of completion of construction to the date of the general average act, except for insulation, life and similar boats, communications and navigational apparatus and equipment, machinery and boilers for which the deductions shall be regulated by the age of the particular parts to which they apply.

The deductions shall be made only from the cost of the new materials or parts when finished and ready to be installed in the ship.

No deduction shall be made in respect of provisions, stores, anchors and chain cables.

Drydock and slipway dues and costs of shifting the ship shall be allowed in full.

The costs of cleaning, painting or coating the bottom shall not be allowed in general average unless the bottom has been painted or coated within the twelve months preceding the date of the general average act in which case one half of such costs shall be allowed."

It is not clear at common law whether the value of a ship should be her value on the open market, her value to her owners taking account of any charterparties

---

69. The Court of Appeal in fact purported to take her value immediately before the general average sacrifice took place.
70. The logic of this disallowal is doubted in *Arnould*, para 980 n. 25.
71. York-Antwerp Rules 1994, Rule XIV. On temporary repairs generally, see *supra*, 61–63.
72. See also Rules of Practice of the Association of Average Adjusters, Rule F19, which is in identical terms.

to which they are committed (which, it is submitted, is the correct approach), or whichever is the higher of those values.[73] The solution provided by Rule XVII of the York-Antwerp Rules 1994[74] is that:

"The value of the ship shall be assessed without taking into account the beneficial or detrimental effect of any demise or time charterparty to which the ship may be committed."

(d) Cargo: the general rule

The general principle at common law is that cargo is valued on the net value it has, or but for its sacrifice would have had, at the end of the voyage (i.e. its *market* value there less the cost of achieving that value, e.g. landing charges, freight, and salvage[75]); this will be its sound or damaged value depending on the condition in which it would have arrived but for the general average act.[76] This principle has, however, been modified by the York-Antwerp Rules 1994, which use the *invoice* or *shipped* value as the basis for calculation. Thus, so far as concerns claims *by* cargo, Rule XVI ("amount to be made good for cargo lost or damaged by sacrifice") begins by stating that "The amount to be made good as general average for damage to or loss of cargo sacrificed shall be the loss which has been sustained thereby based on the value at the time of discharge." Similarly, in relation to claims *against* cargo, Rule XVII ("contributory values") begins by stating that "The contribution to a general average shall be made upon the actual net values of the property at the termination of the adventure except that the value of cargo shall be the value at the time of discharge." The value at the time of discharge is then stated by Rule XVII (to which Rule XVI is similar) to be[77]:

"ascertained from the commercial invoice rendered to the receiver or if there is no such invoice from the shipped value. The value *of the cargo*[78] shall include the cost of insurance and freight *unless and*[79] insofar as such freight is at the risk of interests other than the cargo, *deducting therefrom any loss or damage suffered by the cargo prior to or at the time of discharge.*"[80]

---

73. In *The San Onofre* [1917] P 96 Sir Samuel Evans P disregarded a non-profitable charterparty. In *The Castor* [1932] P 142 Lord Merrivale P took into account a profitable charterparty. See further *The Harmonides* [1903] P 1; *The Hohenzollern* [1906] P 339; MN Howard, "Valuation in Salvage Cases—Damage, Damages and Remoteness" (1975) LQR 502; *Kennedy*, paras 1050–1059.
74. See also Rules of Practice of the Association of Average Adjusters, Rules B27–B28.
75. *The Eliza Lines* (1902) 114 Fed Rep 307.
76. *Fletcher* v. *Alexander* (1868) LR 3 CP 375. Where the cargo is returned to the port from which the voyage began and the voyage is there broken up, so that that is the place with respect to which adjustment is to be made, then, since the value of the goods has not been increased, the value of the goods has been taken to be their value on board (i.e. including loading charges but without charges, such as insurance and advance freight, which add nothing to its value there): *ibid*. However, if goods upon which freight has been pre-paid would there have been reshipped, advance freight would have added to their value and so should be included: *ibid.*, 385, per Bovill CJ.
77. Italics added. The italicised words appear in Rule XVII but not in Rule XVI.
78. In Rule XVI "at the time of discharge" appears instead of the italicised words.
79. In Rule XVI "except" appears instead of the italicised words.
80. The italicised words do not appear in Rule XVI.

(e) Sale of cargo

The sale of cargo may constitute a general average loss.[81] At common law, the loss suffered by the owners of the cargo sold is in principle the actual or estimated value of the cargo at the originally intended destination less the freight which would have been payable. However, the value at the place of sale has been allowed[82]; this may exceed the value at destination, particularly since pro rata freight is not generally payable for an uncompleted voyage.[83]

The York-Antwerp Rules 1994 contain several, not clearly related, provisions for cargo which is sold. Rule XVII contains the general rule on contributory values, that: "Where cargo is sold short of destination, however, it shall contribute upon the actual net proceeds of sale, with the addition of any amount made good as general average."

However, Rule XX, on "provision of funds", provides that: "The capital loss sustained by the owners of goods sold for the purpose of raising funds to defray general average disbursements shall be allowed in general average."

It is said[84] that the cargo owner is also entitled to the two per cent commission allowed by Rule XX on general average disbursements,[85] though this is not specifically stated in the Rule.

Where cargo has been sacrificed for purposes of general average, damaged and then sold, Rule XVI provides that:

"When cargo so damaged [i.e., by general average sacrifice] is sold and the amount of the damage has not been otherwise agreed, the loss to be made good in general average shall be the difference between the net proceeds of sale and the net sound value as computed in the first paragraph of this Rule [XVI]."[86]

---

81. *The Gratitudine* (1801) 3 C Rob 240 (sale of all of the cargo would not benefit more than one interest); *Richardson* v. *Nourse* (1819) 3 B & Ald 237. Loss by sale of cargo is allowable under Rule F16 of the Rules of Practice of the Association of Average Adjusters. A sale of cargo prompted by the necessity of financing the repair of the ship and completion of the adventure is treated as a justifiable forced loan. Given modern methods of communication, raising finance in this way is in practice obsolete. Even were it to occur, there are practical difficulties in recovering contribution, namely: demonstrating that there is a danger to the common adventure (the cargo itself presumably being in safety at the time of sale) and not merely particular average suffered by the ship (*Hallett* v. *Wigram* (1850) 9 CB 580); demonstrating that the sale is for the purposes of the common adventure, and not merely due to the shipowner's general impecuniosity or to defray expenses for which he is liable (*Dobson* v. *Wilson* (1813) 3 Camp 480; cf *Powell* v. *Gudgeon* (1816) 5 M & S 431; *Sarquy* v. *Hobson* (1827) 4 Bing 131); and the fact that cargo can only lawfully be sold with its owners' consent, which means in practice that the matter should be covered by agreement (see *The Minnetonka* (1905) 10 Asp MLC 142). Of course, if the ship fails to arrive at destination it is not a case of general average (see *supra*, 39–45) and the loss will have been incurred on behalf of and indemnifiable by the shipowner alone (*Atkinson* v. *Stephens* (1852) 7 Ex 567).
82. *Richardson* v. *Nourse* (1819) 3 B & Ald 237 (explicable on the ground that the court was reluctant to interfere with a decision by arbitrators); *Hopper* v. *Burness* (1876) 1 CPD 137.
83. *Hopper* v. *Burness* (1876) 1 CPD 137.
84. *Hudson*, 253.
85. See *infra*, 103.
86. For the first paragraph, see *supra*, 100.

(f) Where cargo forwarded from port of refuge to destination by other means

When a ship is at a place which would give rise to an allowance for port of refuge expenses under Rules X–XI of the York-Antwerp Rules 1994,[87] and cargo is forwarded to destination by other means, as nearly as possible rights and liabilities shall remain as if the adventure had continued in the original ship,[88] with the result that:

"the cargo and other property shall contribute on the basis of its value upon delivery at original destination unless sold or otherwise disposed of short of that destination, and the ship shall contribute upon its actual net value at the time of completion of discharge of cargo."[89]

(g) Freight

Reflecting the principle that net values should be employed (i.e. the gross freight less the cost of earning it), Rule XV of the York-Antwerp Rules 1994 provides[90] that:

"Deduction shall be made from the amount of gross freight lost, of the charges which the owner thereof would have incurred to earn such freight, but has, in consequence of the sacrifice, not incurred."

However, Rule B28 ("Deductions from freight at charterer's risk") of the Rules of Practice of the Association of Average Adjusters provides:

"That freight at the risk of the charterer shall be subject to no deduction for wages and charges, except in the case of charters in which the wages or charges are payable by the charterer, in which case such freight shall be governed by the same rule as freight at the risk of the shipowner."[91]

(h) Hire

The Rules of Practice of the Association of Average Adjusters state, in Rule B26, that: "In practice neither time charter hire, as such, nor time charterer's voyage freight shall contribute to general average." In fact, this misrepresents the situation. In current practice, if time charterer's bill of lading freight is at risk, it pays a general average contribution; and, if the time charter does not contain the expression "hire not to contribute" or words to similar effect, that contribution is sub-divided between time charterer's bill of lading freight at risk and shipowners' time charter hire at risk.

---

87. See 56–59.
88. York-Antwerp Rules 1994, Rule G. See *supra*, 88.
89. York-Antwerp Rules 1994, Rule XVII. Presumably this is subject to cargo having, if practicable, been notified of the forwarding.
90. See also Rules of Practice of the Association of Average Adjusters, Rule F22.
91. See further Rules of Practice of the Association of Average Adjusters, Rule B29 ("forwarding charges on advance freight").

(i) Other interests

In the adventure property of a commercial nature that is not part of the ship or cargo—such as bunkers, wireless and navigational equipment, and containers—forms subjects of general average and must be separately valued. Mails and property of a non-commercial nature do not contribute.[92]

(j) General average disbursements

The term "general average disbursement" includes both sums paid as general average expenditure and payments made consequential on general average acts (e.g., for ship repairs or reconditioning of cargo as a result of a general average loss). Historically, a master without funds has been entitled to raise money, in descending order of necessity: on the ship and freight, by bottomry bond; otherwise, on the cargo, by respondentia bond; otherwise, by sale of cargo. Given the strict requirements to be satisfied before such action is allowed and the unlikelihood in modern times that they will be satisfied, such methods of raising finance are now of minimal practical significance.

As noted above, the value of general average expenditure is taken to be the amount of expenditure actually incurred.[93] Where finance is raised for general average purposes, the amount for which contribution is due will include interest, the amount of discount on bills of exchange, and losses caused by the rate of exchange.[94]

In addition, under the heading "provision of funds", Rule XX of the York-Antwerp Rules 1994 provides:

"A commission of 2 per cent on general average disbursements, other than the wages and maintenance of master, officers and crew and fuel and stores not replaced during the voyage, shall be allowed in general average."

---

92. York-Antwerp Rules 1994, Rule XVII. See *supra*, 13–14.
93. *Supra*, 89.
94. See *Arnould*, para 980.

CHAPTER 7

INSURANCE CONTRACTS

An assured is entitled to claim from his insurer an indemnity for an insured loss according to the terms of the policy. The fact that a person suffers a loss in consequence of a general average act does not mean that he will be able to recover in full from a single insurer, for: his entitlement to claim will be governed, not only by the general law, but in particular by the terms of the policy; and provision may be made for different losses by different insurance contracts.

For present purposes, the types of loss generally recoverable under insurance contracts may be divided into three groups.[1] First, the loss may be one of the losses specifically insured under the policy, albeit one in respect of which the insured (and, by subrogation, his insurer) may be entitled to claim contribution from interests benefiting from the loss. This group includes general average sacrifices and expenditures.

Secondly, the insured may not suffer from the general average act but benefit from it, in which case he will come under a liability to contribute in general average: the contribution for which he is liable may also be indemnifiable by his insurer.

Thirdly, the loss may result from steps taken to avert or minimise an insured loss for which the insured is entitled to recover an additional indemnity under suing and labouring provisions.[2] The Institute hulls and cargo clauses require the assured to take steps to avert or minimise insured losses, in return for which the insurer agrees to indemnify the assured for charges properly and reasonably incurred.[3] The hulls clauses specifically add that:

---

1. See also the discussion on the classification of partial losses *supra*, 3–5.
2. Marine Insurance Act 1906, s.78. See generally FD Rose, "Aversion and Minimisation of Loss", Chap. 7 of DR Thomas (ed.), *The Modern Law of Marine Insurance* (1996); and *supra*, 4.
It should also be noted that there is a practice for underwriters to pay the cost of temporary repairs: regardless of any resultant saving in the total cost of repairs, in the case of passenger vessels running on advertised schedules and cargo vessels committed to regular advertised sailing dates; and in addition to later permanent repairs, where incurred in lieu of more expensive permanent repairs (the cost of which fixes the upper limit of what the underwriter will pay).
3. Institute Time Clauses (Hulls) 1/11/95, cl.11; Institute Voyage Clauses (Hulls) 1/11/95, cl.9; Institute Cargo Clauses, cls 16–17.

"General average, salvage charges (except as provided for in [the case of total loss of vessel][4]), special compensation and expenses as referred to in [sub-clause 5 of the General Average and Salvage Clause][5] and collision defence or attack costs are not recoverable under this [Duty of Assured (Sue and Labour) Clause]."[6]

Liability to contribute determined independently of insurance

In accordance with general principle, Gorell Barnes J stated in *The Brigella*[7] that:

"the obligation to contribute in general average exists between the parties to the adventure, whether they are insured or not. The circumstance of a party being insured can have no influence upon the adjustment of general average, the rules of which . . . are entirely independent of insurance."

Thus, "no more contribution is exigible from the owner of a parcel of goods that are insured than from the owner of a parcel that is not insured."[8]

Assured with more than one interest

Liability for general average is initially assessed not only without regard to whether or not the interests are insured, but also as if each interest involved in the adventure is owned by a separate person. Then, once the *prima facie* rights and liabilities to contribution have been determined, the owner of an individual interest is entitled to claim from his insurer an indemnity in respect of his *prima facie* liability to contribute.[9] A particular aspect of this rule appears in the Marine Insurance Act 1906, s.66(7), which provides that:

"Where ship, freight and cargo, or any two of those interests, are owned by the same assured, the liability of the insurer in respect of general average losses or contributions is to be determined as if those subjects were owned by different persons."

Thus, an insurer is not entitled to deny liability by arguing that the assured is the owner of both the interest suffering the loss and the interest liable to contribute, so that he is unable to sue himself for a general average contribution and the underwriter has no effective right of subrogation.

However, though the insurer's *prima facie* liability is assessed independently of the fact that the assured is also the owner of a different interest, the amount

---

4. See *supra*, 44, n. 227.
5. See *infra*, 113–114.
6. Institute Time Clauses (Hulls) 1/11/95, cl.11.2; Institute Voyage Clauses (Hulls) 1/11/95, cl.9.2.
7. [1893] P 189, 195–196. Cf *Morrison Steamship Co Ltd* v. *Greystoke Castle (Cargo Owners)* [1947] AC 265, 296–297, per Lord Porter.
8. *Anderson Tritton & Co* v. *Ocean Steamship Co* (1884) 10 App Cas 107, 113, per Lord Blackburn.
9. Marine Insurance Act 1906, s.66(7); enacting *Montgomery & Co* v. *Indemnity Mutual Marine Insurance Co Ltd* [1902] 1 KB 734 (which overruled *The Brigella* [1893] P 189). See also *Oppenheim* v. *Fry* (1863) 3 B & S 874, 884, per Blackburn J (affd (1864) 5 B & S 348); *Carisbrook Steamship Co* v. *London & Provincial Marine & General Insurance Co* [1901] 2 KB 861 (ship and voyage freight separate interests). But cf *Simpson* v. *Thomson* (1877) 3 App Cas 279; Institute Time Clauses (Hulls) 1/11/95, cl.9 and Institute Time Clauses (Freight) 1/11/95, cl.10 ("Sistership" clause).

which the insurer is bound to pay the assured is diminished by the contribution which the assured is entitled to recover from himself in his other capacity, for the assured is deemed to have such a contribution in his pocket already[10]; the assured should claim for such contribution from the insurers of the relevant interest. Thus, where the assured owns both ship and cargo, and freight is at his risk as shipowner, if he claims for a general average sacrifice of ship's materials under the hull policy, the hull insurer is liable to pay for the loss, subject to deductions for the cargo's and the freight's liabilities to contribute, for which the cargo and freight insurers will be liable respectively—and even if the hull, cargo and freight insurers are the same person. A different approach (though it could be reflected in a reduction in premiums) would mean that the assured would be uninsured, and the insurer arguably unjustly enriched, whenever an assured owned more than one interest.

Voyage charterparty freight is a separate interest from the vessel itself[11] but there is no decision at common law as to whether time charter hire is a separate interest for this purpose or is included within the value of the vessel. A similar, unresolved question is whether voyage freight due to a time charterer constitutes a separate interest. In principle, both voyage charter freight and time charter hire are capable of being separate interests and should be treated as such—rather than counted twice or not at all—for purposes of general average.[12]

Insurer's liability

(a) Subject-matter and peril insured

In principle, an insurer's liability in respect of general average is limited to the subject-matter insured by the policy and the perils against which it is insured.[13] The general principle is that an insurer is liable to indemnify the assured for a general average loss to the extent that the general average act was done to avoid an insured peril. As Bovill CJ put it in *Harris v. Scaramanga*[14]:

"If the sacrifice or loss which occasioned the general average arose from any of the perils insured against or the consequences of them, or from proper endeavours to avert such perils or their consequences, to that extent the underwriters would, under the terms of an ordinary policy, and according to well-known maritime usage, be liable to indemnify the assured, though, as between the shipowner and the owner of the cargo, matters might be introduced into the statement of general average for which the underwriters, upon the ordinary form of policy, would not be liable. . . ."

10. *Montgomery & Co* v. *Indemnity Mutual Marine Insurance Co Ltd* [1902] 1 KB 734.
11. *Carisbrook Steamship Co* v. *London & Provincial Marine & General Insurance Co* [1901] 2 KB 861.
12. Cf York-Antwerp Rules 1994, Rule XVII (*supra*, 100); Rules of Practice of the Association of Average Adjusters, Rule B26.
13. *Hick* v. *London Assurance* (1895) 1 Com Cas 244, where Mathew J observed, at 250, that "The underwriters on ship do not guarantee that owners of cargo will pay their contribution to general average."
14. (1872) LR 7 CP 481, 488, 496.

"... I think that, according to English and American law, the underwriter of a policy in the ordinary form is not liable to indemnify against any general average loss or contribution, whether it be general according to the law of his country or according to the law of the foreign country in which the voyage terminates, or whether the adjustment be made according to his domestic or according to the foreign law, if the general average loss be not incurred, or the general average contribution be not made, in order to avert loss by a peril insured against."

This rule is now embodied in the Marine Insurance Act 1906, s.66(6), which provides:

"In the absence of express stipulation, the insurer is not liable for any general average loss or contribution where the loss was not incurred for the purpose of avoiding, or in connection with the avoidance of, a peril insured against."

This rule is emphasised in the General Average and Salvage Clause of the Institute hulls and freight clauses, which provides[15]: "No claim under this Clause [...[16]] shall in any case be allowed where the loss was not incurred to avoid or in connection with the avoidance of a peril insured against."

However, the rule can be overridden by contract.[17] Thus, recognising the practical inability of cargo owners to resist liability for general average contributions, the General Average Clause in the Institute Cargo Clauses provides:

"This insurance covers general average and salvage charges, adjusted or determined according to the contract of affreightment and/or the governing law and practice, incurred to avoid or in connection with the avoidance of loss *from any cause* except those excluded in Clauses 4, 5, 6 and 7 or elsewhere in this insurance."[18]

In interpreting the effect of an earlier version of this clause[19] in *Brandeis, Goldschmidt & Co v. Economic Insurance Co Ltd*,[20] Bailhache J held: that the insurer's liability to pay general average arose not from the contract but from the Marine Insurance Act 1906; under the Act the insurer is liable for a general average sacrifice immediately it occurs but only liable for the assured's share of an expenditure made or for a contribution due from the assured once the amount has been assessed; so that, if an adjustment is made a condition of the insurer's liability (which he held to be the effect of the general average clause), no liability arises where no adjustment is made, something which the shipowner in that case declined to arrange. Bailhache J confessed his lack of confidence in dealing with the issues in that case. However, in practice insurers commonly pay

---

15. Institute Time Clauses (Hulls) 1/11/95, cl.10.4; Institute Voyage Clauses (Hulls) 1/11/95, cl.8.4; Institute Time Clauses (Freight) 1/11/95, cl.11.3; Institute Voyage Clauses (Freight) 1/11/95, cl.8.3.
16. The number of the relevant clause is stated here.
17. Marine Insurance Act 1906, s.87.
18. Institute Cargo Clauses (A), (B) and (C), cl.2 (emphasis added). The specified exceptions are: cl.4, general exclusions; cl.5, unseaworthiness and unfitness; cl.6, war; and cl.7, strikes.
19. "General average and salvage charges payable according to foreign statement or per York-Antwerp rules if in accordance with the contract of affreightment."
20. (1922) 11 Ll L Rep 42.

indemnities for reasonably paid cash deposits, so it has proved unnecessary to determine conclusively: whether such deposits are a proper subject of indemnity; exactly when or why an assured should recover from his insurer without being able to prove the precise amount which should be indemnified; and the extent to which an insurer can make his liability conditional on a foreign adjustment which the shipowner can decline to make.

(b) Value insured

The insurer's liability is also measured by the insured value under the policy (i.e., the insurable value in the case of an unvalued policy or the agreed value in the case of a valued policy), whereas general average contributions are generally assessed on values at the end of the voyage.[21] Accordingly, the amount of the insurer's liability for the general average loss or contribution is the proportion which the insured value bears to the contributory value of the insured subject-matter.[22]

(I) UNDER-INSURANCE

In the case of full insurance, whether under an unvalued policy or under a valued policy with a valuation equalling or exceeding the sound market value of the subject-matter, the assured will recover a full indemnity for any insured loss. Where the subject-matter is under-insured and the assured suffers a general average sacrifice, the assured can recover in full up to the insured value. In other cases of under-insurance (i.e., general average expenditures and general average contributions), the insurer is liable for a proportion of the loss.[23]

(II) EXCESS LIABILITIES

In the case of under-insurance (i.e., in respect of the excess value of general average sacrifices beyond the insured amount and the proportion of general average expenditure, general average contribution, salvage and sue and labour charges for which the insurer is not liable under the main policy), the assured may effect additional "excess liabilities" insurance.[24] Unless the policy otherwise provides, the general rule, laid down in *Holman & Sons Ltd, for Owners of the SS Nefeli* v. *Merchants' Marine Insurance Co Ltd*,[25] is that the excess liabilities insurer is not liable for all the loss not covered by the main policy,[26] but only for

---

21. See *supra*, 88–89.
22. *Anderson Tritton & Co* v. *Ocean SS Co* (1884) 10 App Cas 107. Of course, the proportion will not exceed 100 per cent; in respect of general averages exceeding 100 per cent of contributory values, see *supra*, 88–89.
23. See further *infra*, 114–116.
24. The position in Scandinavian insurance systems is different.
25. [1919] 1 KB 383.
26. Sankey J distinguished *Joyce* v. *Kennard* (1871) LR 7 QB 78 and *Cunard Steamship Co* v. *Marten* [1902] 2 KB 624 as exceptional instances of an insurance against liability.

such proportion thereof as the amount insured under the excess liabilities policy bears to the total excess valuation and total excess contributory value of the subject-matter respectively. Excess liabilities insurance is common in the case of insurance on hull and machinery. Thus, the Institute Time Clauses—Hulls: Excess Liabilities 1/11/95, cl. 1.1.1[27] (which incorporates the rule in *The Nefeli*) provides:

> "**General Average, Salvage and Salvage Charges** not recoverable in full under the insurances on hull and machinery by reason of the difference between the insured value of the Vessel as stated therein (or any reduced value arising from the deduction therefrom in process of adjustment of any claim which law or practice or the terms of the insurances covering hull and machinery may have required) and the value of the Vessel adopted for the purpose of contribution to general average, salvage or salvage charges, the liability under this insurance being for such proportion of the amount not recoverable as the amount insured hereunder bears to the said difference or to the total sum insured against excess liabilities if it exceeds such difference."[28]

(c) Loss suffered

An insurer is in general obliged to indemnify his insured for a loss actually suffered, not for a potential loss. Accordingly, an insured who has borne a general average sacrifice or expenditure may claim an indemnity immediately. But an insured who is the beneficiary of a general average act, and who therefore incurs a liability to contribute, in one sense does not actually suffer a loss until the extent of his liability has been assessed and discharged by payment. Nonetheless, the general rule is that, where an assured is liable to contribute in general average in respect of the subject-matter of an insurance contract, he can claim against his insurer in accordance with the terms of the policy, whether or not he has yet satisfied his liability to contribute. Section 66(5) of the Marine Insurance Act 1906 provides[29] that:

> "Subject to any express provision in the policy, where the assured has paid, or is liable to pay, a general average contribution in respect of the subject insured, he may recover therefor from the insurer."

However, in practice the cargo insurer will have given an average guarantee[30] and will be called upon to pay his assured's contribution in accordance with the terms of the guarantee, irrespective of the terms or valuation in the policy.

---

27. See also the Institute Time Clauses—Hulls: Disbursements and Increased Value (Total Loss only, including Excess Liabilities)—1/11/95, cl.6.4.1.
28. The last fourteen words appear to provide for the possibility of there being more than one excess liabilities policy: see *Arnould*, para 1008 n. 53.
29. See also Marine Insurance Act 1906, s.73.
30. See *supra*, 82.

Insured's rights to indemnity and contribution

Obviously, an assured who suffers a loss may have claims against two potential defendants: his insurer, and a third party (e.g., because the third party is liable for the loss or for a general average contribution). In theory, this raises three possible issues: that each defendant may argue that his liability is diminished by the amount which the assured can recover from the other; that the premium for the insurance policy can be calculated at different rates depending on whether the insurer can plead the third party's liability in reduction of his own; and that the assured could pay a premium on the basis of the insurer's full liability but be uninsured, and the insurer unjustly enriched, if the insurer's liability is in fact reduced in whole or in part by the amount of the third party's liability.

In principle these issues are resolved as follows. First, as seen above, parties' rights and liabilities are calculated independently of whether or not either or both of them are insured.[31] Secondly, regardless of a third party's liability, an insurer must pay a full indemnity where the assured suffers a loss resulting from an insured peril; and, having paid, is then entitled to be subrogated to the assured's rights against third parties in respect of the loss.[32] However, as will be seen, practical considerations have influenced the detailed rules giving expression to these principles.

Thus, an insurer is liable in full for an insured loss, but the extent of that liability differs according to whether the loss arises from a general average sacrifice of the assured's property (for which his insurer will be liable with respect to the full amount) or from a general average expenditure (for which his insurer will be liable only for the amount expended in respect of the assured's interest).[33]

(a) General average sacrifice

The Marine Insurance Act 1906, s.66(4) provides[34] that,

"Subject to any express provisions in the policy, ... in the case of a general average sacrifice, he [i.e., the assured] may recover from the insurer in respect of the whole loss without having enforced his right of contribution from the other parties liable to contribute."

(b) General average expenditure

The mere fact that the assured is the appropriate person to incur expenditure on behalf of the common adventure does not entitle him to claim an indemnity for it in full from his insurer, even if he is unable to recover contributions from other

---

31. *Supra*, 106.
32. *Dickenson* v. *Jardine* (1868) LR 3 CP 639.
33. Marine Insurance Act 1906, s.66(4).
34. Codifying *Dickenson* v. *Jardine* (1868) LR 3 CP 639. See also Rules of Practice of the Association of Average Adjusters, Rules B30–B31.

interests.[35] Since the insurer is only liable for the subject-matter insured, the full extent of his liability in respect of general average expenditure by the assured is for such amount as was spent in respect of the assured's interest.[36] Thus, the Marine Insurance Act 1906, s.66(4) provides:

> "Subject to any express provision in the policy, where the assured has incurred a general average expenditure, he may recover from the insurer in respect of the proportion of the loss which falls upon him ..."

However, provided the sum insured by the policy is sufficiently high, the amount recoverable may exceed the contributory value of the assured's interest.[37]

These principles are illustrated by *Green Star Shipping Co Ltd* v. *The London Assurance (The Andree).*[38]

> During loading at New York a fire broke out. Part of the cargo, worth $18,000, was discharged at New York and not reloaded. The shipowner incurred general average expenditure of $63,000. He took out a special general average disbursements policy to cover the risk that the contributory value of the remaining cargo might subsequently become insufficient for him to recover the contribution which in principle it should make in respect of that expenditure. Later, a collision occurred. The ship and cargo sank, then were salved and taken to Philadelphia, where the voyage was abandoned. General average expenditure of $180,000 was incurred in respect of the second incident. The contributory values of the ship and cargo salved were $116,000 and $26,000 respectively; i.e., $142,000 in total. Thus, after deducting the salved values of the ship and cargo from the general average expenditure at Philadelphia, the shipowner was out of pocket for that general average expenditure to the sum of ($180,000 − $142,000 =) $38,000, and the property salved at Philadelphia had no remaining contributory value for the purposes of the general average expenditure at New York. Contribution was therefore due for the New York expenditure only from the property unloaded there (worth $18,000), leaving $45,000 outstanding. The amount recoverable under the special risks policy was held to be deductible from this sum. The balance of that expenditure was therefore due from the hull underwriters, even though it exceeded the then value of the ship. (In consequence, nothing was due

---

35. *The Mary Thomas* [1894] P 108 (owing to their negligence, the assured shipowners were unable to recover a general average contribution from cargo interests under the law of the place where the adventure terminated: see *supra*, 66–76); *Green Star Shipping Co Ltd* v. *The London Assurance (The Andree)* [1933] 1 KB 378 (the effect of a second general average incident was to reduce the contribution which would have been payable by cargo in respect of the first general average incident).

36. Marine Insurance Act 1906, s.66(4), codifying *The Mary Thomas* [1894] P 108.

37. *Green Star Shipping Co Ltd* v. *The London Assurance (The Andree)* [1933] 1 KB 378.

38. [1933] 1 KB 378. The sums stated are a slightly simplified version of those assumed by the court for the purpose of determining the issues of principle.

from the ship's club on the basis of liability for cargo's proportion of general average not otherwise recoverable.)

The current version of the Institute hulls clauses[39] covers the vessel's proportion[40] of general average, but reduced in respect of any under-insurance.

(c) Institute clauses

Loss of or damage to the subject-matter insured caused by general average sacrifice and/or jettison is covered specifically by the Institute Cargo Clauses (B) and (C)[41] and generally under "all risks" by the Institute Cargo Clauses (A). All three sets of cargo clauses cover "general average and salvage charges".[42] The Institute hulls and freight clauses also specifically cover jettison.[43] Otherwise, general average sacrifice is only mentioned incidentally (in the hulls clauses) in the general provision for general average. Thus, the Institute hulls clauses[44] (and, with appropriate modification, the freight clauses)[45] provide:

"This insurance covers the Vessel's proportion of salvage, salvage charges and/or general average, reduced in respect of any under-insurance, but in case of general average sacrifice of the Vessel the Assured may recover in respect of the whole loss without first enforcing their right of contribution from other parties."

(d) Salvage and the environment

The Institute hulls and freight clauses provide (with different numbering)[46]:

"10.5 No claim under this Clause 10 shall in any case be allowed for or in respect of
10.5.1 special compensation payable to a salvor under Article 14 of the International Convention on Salvage, 1989 or under any other provision in any statute, rule, law or contract which is similar in substance
10.5.2 expenses or liabilities incurred in respect of damage to the environment, or the threat of such damage, or as a consequence of the escape or release of pollutant substances from the Vessel, or the threat of such escape or release.

---

39. Institute Time Clauses (Hulls) 1/11/95, cl.10.1; Institute Voyage Clauses (Hulls) 1/11/95, cl.8.1. See *infra*, 113–114.

40. NG Hudson and JC Allen, *The Institute Clauses*, 2nd ed. (1995), 106, remark that "the coverage is against only the *vessel's* proportion of ... general average, which should be differentiated from the proportion of loss which falls upon the *shipowner*. *So far as the authors are aware*, there was no intention when redrafting this clause to alter the position under English law."

41. Institute Cargo Clauses (B) and (C), cls 1.2.1 and 1.2.2.

42. See *supra*, 3–5.

43. Institute Time Clauses (Hulls) 1/11/95, cl.6.1.4; Institute Voyage Clauses (Hulls) 1/11/95, cl.4.1.4; Institute Time Clauses (Freight) 1/11/95, cl.7.1.4; Institute Voyage Clauses (Freight), cl.4.1.4.

44. Institute Time Clauses (Hulls) 1/11/95, cl.10.1; Institute Voyage Clauses (Hulls) 1/11/95, cl.8.1.

45. Institute Time Clauses (Freight) 1/11/95, cl.11.1; Institute Voyage Clauses (Freight) 1/11/95, cl.8.1: "This insurance covers the proportion of general average, salvage and/or salvage charges attaching to freight at risk of the Assured, reduced in respect of any under-insurance."

46. Institute Time Clauses (Hulls) 1/11/95, cl.10.5–10.6; Institute Voyage Clauses (Hulls) 1/11/95, cl.8.5–8.6; Institute Time Clauses (Freight) 1/11/95, cl.11.4–11.5; Institute Voyage Clauses (Freight) 1/11/95, cl.8.4–8.5.

10.6 Clause 10.5 shall not however exclude any sum which the Assured shall pay to salvors for or in respect of salvage remuneration in which the skill and efforts of the salvors in preventing or minimising damage to the environment as is referred to in Article 13 paragraph 1(b) of the International Convention on Salvage, 1989 have been taken into account."

These provisions are not entirely consistent with the provision in the York-Antwerp Rules 1994 for salvage and related liability. Clause 10.5.2 was inserted in the new Institute clauses against the spirit of the compromise which underlies Rule C and XI(d) of the York-Antwerp Rules 1994.[47] Perhaps significantly, the Norwegian Insurance Plan of 1996 takes the opposite position and thereby avoids the need for average adjusters to "unpick" any adjustment under the 1994 Rules where expenditure is allowed under Rule XI(d).

Measure of indemnity: insurer's liability proportionate to insured amount

Section 73 of the Marine Insurance Act 1906 provides:

"(1) Subject to any express provision in the policy, where the assured has paid, or is liable for, any general average contribution, the measure of indemnity is the full amount of such contribution, if the subject-matter liable to contribution is insured for its full contributory value; but, if such subject-matter be not insured for its full contributory value, or if only part of it be insured, the indemnity payable by the insurer must be reduced in proportion to the under insurance, and where there has been a particular average loss, which constitutes a deduction from the contributory value, and for which the insurer is liable, that amount must be deducted from the insured value in order to ascertain what the insurer is liable to contribute.

(2) Where the insurer is liable for salvage charges the extent of his liability must be determined on the like principle."

In practice, section 73 must be considered together with Rule B33 of the Rules of Practice of the Association of Average Adjusters. Rule B33 provides as follows:

"If the ship or cargo be insured for more than its contributory value, the underwriter pays what is assessed on the contributory value. But where insured for less than the contributory value, the underwriter pays on the insured value; and when there has been a particular average for damage which forms a deduction from the contributory value of the ship that must be deducted from the insured value to find upon what the underwriter contributes.

This rule does not apply to foreign adjustments, when the basis of contribution is something other than the net value of the thing insured.

That in practice, in applying the above rule for the purpose of ascertaining the liability of underwriters for contribution to general average and salvage charges, deduction shall be made from the insured value of all losses and charges for which underwriters are liable and which have been deducted in arriving at the contributory value.

In adjusting the liability of underwriters on freight for general average contribution and salvage charges, effect shall be given to section 73 of the Marine Insurance Act 1906,

---

47. See York-Antwerp Rules 1994, Rules C and VI, discussed *supra*, 51–54.

by comparing the gross and not the net amount of freight at risk with the insured value in the case of a valued policy or the insurable value in the case of an unvalued policy."

The effect of these provisions is as follows. First, the relevant values must be determined. Where no value is agreed for the purposes of insurance, the *insured value* of the subject-matter of the insurance will be its "true" value in the form of its *insurable value* determined in accordance with the general law on marine insurance[48] (which may, though will not necessarily be, identical with its contributory value).[49] However, it is more common for insurance to be effected under valued policies, i.e., with the insured value being the *agreed value* fixed in the insurance contract. The valuation in a valued policy generally fixes the upper limit of the insurer's liability. It must further be noted that, however the insured value is determined, the amount agreed to be insured may be less than the insured value: i.e., the insurer may only accept the risk for part of the insured value, so the subject-matter will be under-insured.

The *contributory value* of the subject-matter of the insurance is in principle its value for the purposes of the average adjustment. However, the statute uses the expression "full contributory value", thereby raising the question of the significance of the adjective "full".[50] *Arnould*[51] argues that it means the gross sound value at the port of destination, without deduction for damage, deterioration or expenses, since: the adjective would otherwise be superfluous and misleading; "full contributory value" cannot mean less than "contributory value", which is used later in section 73 to mean gross value; and it fulfils the object of providing the assured with a full, though no more than a full, indemnity.[52] In practice, "contributory value" is used to mean the *net* value on which an interest contributes and "full contributory value" is taken to mean the gross sound value of the interest before deductions for damage or charges for which insurers are liable.

Where the assured's liability for a general average contribution is equal to or exceeds the amount insured, the insurer must in principle pay the full amount. But, where the amount insured is less than the contributory value, the insurer is only bound to indemnify the assured for a proportion of his liability. In that

---

48. See in particular the Marine Insurance Act 1906, s.16 ("insurable value").

49. Thus, under the Marine Insurance Act 1906, s.16(1), the insurable value of a ship is basically its value at the commencement of the risk, whereas its contributory value for the purposes of general average adjustment will be its value at the end of the voyage: see *supra*, 98–99.

50. Close to the passing of the codifying Marine Insurance Act 1906, in *Steamship Balmoral Co Ltd* v. *Marten* [1902] AC 511, 522, Lord Lindley intimated that the word was superfluous: "If the word 'fully' is introduced, it must be qualified so as to show its true meaning, i.e., fully for a ship of the value mentioned in the policy."

51. *Arnould*, para 1007.

52. *Arnould*, para 1007 states: "the object of section 73(1) ... is to ensure that the assured shall receive a full, but no more than a full, indemnity; in other words, that underwriters' liability shall in no case exceed the agreed or insurable value, as the case may be, of the subject-matter insured. If the provisions as to under-insurance were not to be applied in cases where the insured value, though greater than the value on which the subject-matter in fact contributed, was less than its maximum potential contributory value, this object would not necessarily be achieved."

case, the relevant proportion is the proportion which the amount insured bears to the contributory value. Thus, if the contributory value is £100,000 and the insured value under a valued policy is £90,000, the insurer will be liable for 90 per cent of the assured's contribution to general average.[53] Similarly, if on the same facts the policy further provides that the insurer is only liable for 80 per cent of the assured's loss (i.e., the subject-matter is partly insured), the insurer will only be liable for 80 per cent of the 90 per cent contribution.

The final part of section 73(1) deals with particular average. It provides that in a case of under-insurance, if the underwriter is also liable for a particular average loss, and the contributory value of the assured's interest is reduced by that particular average loss, then the amount of the particular average loss (or the proportion of the particular average loss for which the insurer is liable) must be deducted from the insured value, and the proportion between the resulting amount and the net contributory value is the proportion of the general average contribution for which the insurer is liable.

Adjustment regime; place of adjustment; foreign adjustment

In principle, general average should be adjusted at the place of termination of the adventure.[54] The parties to the adventure may agree to adjustment at a different place, and that agreement will normally be binding upon them. But obviously, if an insurer is not a party to such an agreement, it will not bind him.[55] However, it is of course open to the parties to an insurance contract to make a specific agreement as to adjustment[56]; and an insurer may agree, either in the insurance contract or independently, for his liability to be determined in

---

53. *Steamship Balmoral Co Ltd* v. *Marten* [1902] AC 511; 1 Magens 245, Case XIX. In the *Balmoral* case [1902] AC 511, 514–515, Lord Macnaghten thought that a more logical rule would be the amount that would have been assessed against the ship if the agreed value had been employed in the adjustment as the contributory value; but he regarded the rule as too settled to decide otherwise. The stimulus for taking such an arguably simple and obvious point to the House of Lords may have been the existence of the contradictory US rule. It was held in the US that insurers on ship were liable in full for the ship's contribution to general average, regardless of the insured value: see *International Navigation Co* v. *Atlantic Mutual Insurance Co* (1900) 100 Fed Rep 304, affd (1901) 108 Fed Rep 988; *International Navigation Co* v. *Sea Insurance Co* (1904) 129 Fed Rep 13; *Maldonado* v. *British & Foreign Marine Insurance Co* (1910) 182 Fed Rep 744. The English rule in the *Balmoral* case was followed, in a case of cargo insurance, in *Gulf Refining Co* v. *Atlantic Mutual Insurance Co* (1929) 279 US 708; 35 Ll L Rep 21. In practice, the English rule is commonly applied to ship insurances by contract. But see the Scandinavian systems for a contrary practice.

54. See *supra*, 88–92.

55. Cf the discussion by *Arnould*, para 1002, on whether an insurer is bound by an adjustment abroad on an estimate of damage sustained.

56. The effect of such an agreement will be a matter of construction. In *The Brigella* [1893] P 189 —the actual decision in which (on another point) was disapproved in *Montgomery & Co* v. *Indemnity Mutual Marine Insurance Co Ltd* [1902] 1 KB 734—a clause providing that general average was payable "as per foreign statement if required" was held inapplicable to an average adjustment obtained by the assured on the general ground that a foreign adjustment clause has no relation to a case "... where there has been no necessity for any foreign adjustment nor any compulsion to pay general average according to foreign law, nor any contribution in fact in general average": [1893] P 189, 200.

accordance with an agreement between the assured and his co-adventurers, or that foreign adjustment is a condition precedent of his liability.[57]

If the insurance contract provides for insurance to be adjusted according to foreign law and/or practice, this will increase the liability of the insurer beyond that otherwise provided by the policy if the foreign adjustment permits greater liability than under English law and practice, unless the policy specifically excludes the relevant peril or, perhaps, the loss arises from a peril not specifically insured under the policy.[58]

> In *Harris* v. *Scaramanga*,[59] the vessel encountered bad weather, so had to put into port for repairs, to raise money for which the master gave bottomry bonds on ship, freight and cargo. At destination, Bremen, the master having no funds, the cargo consignees paid the whole amount due on the bonds to obtain delivery of the cargo. They then procured the ship's sale, which realised £663 less than the ship's proportion of liability on the bonds. A Bremen adjuster stated this additional bottomry debt to be at Bremen a general average loss. The insurers were therefore liable for this loss as the parties had agreed, by the foreign adjustment clause in the cargo insurance contract, to accept the foreign adjuster's statement on matters of principle and detail.

Similarly, the effect of a foreign adjustment clause may be to decrease the liability to which the insurer would otherwise be subject.[60] The effect of a foreign adjustment clause, therefore, may be to make a foreign adjuster's statement conclusive as to the propriety of particular items giving rise to claims in general average (e.g., as opposed to particular average), the correctness of the apportionment and even the correctness of the relevant foreign law.

The Institute cargo clauses General Average Clause[61] provides: "This insurance covers general average and salvage charges, adjusted or determined according to the contract of affreightment and/or the governing law and practice . . ."

The Institute hulls and freight clauses General Average and Salvage Clause provides that, so far as concerns the insurance contract, general average shall be

---

57. *Brandeis, Goldschmidt & Co* v. *Economic Insurance Co Ltd* (1922) 11 Ll L Rep 42 (interpreting the then applicable version of the general average clause in the Institute Cargo Clauses).
58. *Harris* v. *Scaramanga* (1872) LR 7 CP 481; *Hendricks* v. *Australian Insurance Co* (1874) LR 9 CP 460; *Mavro* v. *Ocean Marine Insurance Co* (1875) LR 10 CP 414 (insurer liable under policy excluding particular average for loss treated as particular average in English law but general average under the foreign law); *De Hart* v. *Compania Anonima Aurora* [1903] 1 KB 109. The assured in *Harris* v. *Scaramanga* succeeded despite the insurers' argument that the loss arose from an uninsured peril (the master's insolvency), though *Arnould*, para 999, criticises this argument on the basis that the real argument was over the apportionment of losses admitted to be general average losses at the port of adjustment—a not entirely convincing point if the reason for increasing the assured's proportion of the loss was an otherwise uninsured peril. On restriction of the insurer's liability to losses arising from insured perils, see further *supra*, 107–109.
59. (1872) LR 7 CP 481.
60. *The Mary Thomas* [1894] P 108 (CA).
61. Institute Cargo Clauses (A), (B) and (C), cl.2.

adjusted according to the York-Antwerp Rules if so provided by the contract of affreightment; otherwise, it must be adjusted according to the law and practice prevailing at the place where the adventure ends, and not otherwise. The clause provides[62]:

"Adjustment to be according to the law and practice obtaining at the place where the adventure ends, as if the contract of affreightment contained no special terms upon the subject; but where the contract of affreightment so provides the adjustment shall be according to the York-Antwerp Rules."

In the case of a vessel under ballast not under charter, the hulls and freight clauses provide[63]:

"Where the Vessel sails in ballast, not under charter, the provisions of the York-Antwerp Rules, 1994 (excluding Rules XI(d),[64] XX[65] and XXI[66]) shall be applicable, and the voyage for this purpose shall be deemed to continue from the port or place of departure until the arrival of the Vessel at the first port or place thereafter other than a port or place of refuge or a port or place of call for bunkering only. If at any such intermediate port or place there is an abandonment of the adventure originally contemplated the voyage shall thereupon be deemed to be terminated."

Protection and indemnity association cover

Losses for which shipowners are uninsured on the insurance market are commonly covered by mutual insurance arrangements within protection and indemnity associations (commonly known as "P & I clubs").[67] The terms of such arrangements are obviously a matter of construction of the relevant club rules. They usually provide for two types of cover. First, where the ship's proportion of contribution to general average has been assessed at a sound value in excess of the insured value, the club will generally be liable for the amount of the ship's proportion which would not have been recoverable under the hull policy if the ship had been insured thereunder at its proper market value. Secondly, the club may pay for general average contributions not recoverable by the member from other interests in the adventure by virtue of the member's breach of contract.[68] There is commonly a right or discretion to refuse such an indemnity so far as the member could have protected his *prima facie* right to contribution, for example by qualifying his liability as permitted by the Hague-Visby Rules[69] or enforcing his rights by legal remedies.

---

62. Institute Time Clauses (Hulls) 1/11/95, cl.10.2; Institute Voyage Clauses (Hulls) 1/11/95, cl.8.2; Institute Time Clauses (Freight) 1/11/95, cl.11.2; Institute Voyage Clauses (Freight) 1/11/95, cl.8.2.
63. Institute Time Clauses (Hulls) 1/11/95, cl.10.3; Institute Voyage Clauses (Hulls) 1/11/95, cl.8.3. See also Rules of Practice of the Association of Average Adjusters, Rule B26.
64. *Supra*, 53.
65. *Supra*, 101, 103.
66. *Supra*, 85.
67. See generally SJ Hazelwood, *P. & I. Clubs: Law and Practice*, 2nd ed. (1994).
68. See *supra*, 66–76.
69. See Carriage of Goods by Sea Act 1971, Sched.

APPENDIX 1

STATUTES[1]

MARINE INSURANCE ACT 1906
(6 Edw. 7, c. 41)

An Act to codify the Law relating to Marine Insurance. [21st December 1906]

Marine insurance

1. Marine insurance defined
A contract of marine insurance is a contract whereby the insurer undertakes to indemnify the assured, in manner and to the extent thereby agreed, against marine losses, that is to say, the losses incident to marine adventure.

2. Mixed sea and land risks
(1) A contract of marine insurance may, by its express terms, or by usage of trade, be extended so as to protect the assured against losses on inland waters or on any land risk which may be incidental to any sea voyage.

(2) Where a ship in course of building, or the launch of a ship, or any adventure analogous to marine adventure, is covered by a policy in the form of a marine policy, the provisions of this Act, in so far as applicable, shall apply thereto; but, except as by this section provided, nothing in this Act shall alter or affect any rule of law applicable to any contract of insurance other than a contract of marine insurance as by this Act defined.

3. Marine adventure and maritime perils defined
(1) Subject to the provisions of this Act, every lawful marine adventure may be the subject of marine insurance.

(2) In particular there is a marine adventure where—

(a) Any ship goods or other moveables are exposed to maritime perils. Such property is in this Act referred to as "insurable property";

(b) The earning or acquisition of any freight, passage money, commission, profit, or other pecuniary benefit, or the security for any advances, loan or disbursements, is endangered by the exposure of insurable property to maritime perils;

(c) Any liability to a third party may be incurred by the owner of, or other person interested in or responsible for, insurable property, by reason of maritime perils.

"Maritime perils" means the perils consequent on, or incidental to, the navigation of the sea, that is to say, perils of the seas, fire, war perils, pirates, rovers, thieves, captures,

---

1. The statutes are reproduced as amended.

seisures, restraints, and detainments of princes and peoples, jettisons, barratry, and any other perils, either of the like kind or which may be designated by the policy.

Insurable interest

4. Avoidance of wagering or gaming contracts
(1) Every contract of marine insurance by way of gaming or wagering is void.

(2) A contract of marine insurance is deemed to be a gaming or wagering contract—

(a) Where the assured has not an insurable interest as defined by this Act, and the contract is entered into with no expectation of acquiring such an interest; or

(b) Where the policy is made "interest or no interest," or "without further proof of interest than the policy itself," or "without benefit of salvage to the insurer," or subject to any other like term:

Provided that, where there is no possibility of salvage, a policy may be effected without benefit of salvage to the insurer.

5. Insurable interest defined
(1) Subject to the provisions of this Act, every person has an insurable interest who is interested in a marine adventure.

(2) In particular a person is interested in a marine adventure where he stands in any legal or equitable relation to the adventure or to any insurable property at risk therein, in consequence of which he may benefit by the safety or due arrival of insurable property, or may be prejudiced by its loss, or damage thereto, or by the detention thereof, or may incur liability in respect thereof.

6. When interest must attach
(1) The assured must be interested in the subject-matter insured at the time of the loss though he need not be interested when the insurance is effected:

Provided that where the subject-matter is insured "lost or not lost," the assured may recover although he may not have acquired his interest until after the loss, unless at the time of effecting the contract of insurance the assured was aware of the loss, and the insurer was not.

(2) Where the assured has no interest at the time of the loss, he cannot acquire interest by any act or election after he is aware of the loss.

7. Defeasible or contingent interest
(1) A defeasible interest is insurable, as also is a contingent interest.

(2) In particular, where the buyer of goods has insured them, he has an insurable interest, notwithstanding that he might, at his election, have rejected the goods, or have treated them as at the seller's risk, by reason of the latter's delay in making delivery or otherwise.

8. Partial interest
A partial interest of any nature is insurable.

9. Re-insurance
(1) The insurer under a contract of marine insurance has an insurable interest in his risk, and may re-insure in respect of it.

(2) Unless the policy otherwise provides, the original assured has no right or interest in respect of such re-insurance.

10. Bottomry
The lender of money on bottomry or respondentia has an insurable interest in respect of the loan.

11. Master's and seamen's wages
The master or any member of the crew of a ship has an insurable interest in respect of his wages.

12. Advance freight
In the case of advance freight, the person advancing the freight has an insurable interest, in so far as such freight is not repayable in case of loss.

13. Charges of insurance
The assured has an insurable interest in the charges of any insurance which he may effect.

14. Quantum of interest
(1) Where the subject-matter insured is mortgaged, the mortgagor has an insurable interest in the full value thereof, and the mortgagee has an insurable interest in respect of any sum due or to become due under the mortgage.

(2) A mortgagee, consignee, or other person having an interest in the subject-matter insured may insure on his own behalf and for the benefit of other persons interested as well as for his own benefit.

(3) The owner of insurable property has an insurable interest in respect of the full value thereof, notwithstanding that some third person may have agreed, or be liable, to indemnify him in case of loss.

15. Assignment of interest
Where the assured assigns or otherwise parts with his interest in the subject-matter insured, he does not thereby transfer to the assignee his rights under the contract of insurance, unless there be an express or implied agreement with the assignee to that effect.

But the provisions of this section do not affect a transmission of interest by operation of law.

Insurable value

16. Measure of insurable value
Subject to any express provision or valuation in the policy, the insurable value of the subject-matter insured must be ascertained as follows:—

(1) In insurance on ship, the insurable value is the value, at the commencement of the risk, of the ship, including her outfit, provisions and stores for the officers and crew, money advanced for seamen's wages, and other disbursements (if any) incurred to make the ship fit for the voyage or adventure contemplated by the policy, plus the charges of insurance upon the whole:

The insurable value, in the case of a steamship, includes also the machinery, boilers, and coals and engine stores if owned by the assured, and, in the case of a ship engaged in a special trade, the ordinary fittings requisite for that trade:

(2) In insurance on freight, whether paid in advance or otherwise, the insurable value is the gross amount of freight at the risk of the assured, plus the charges of insurance:

(3) In insurance on goods or merchandise, the insurable value is the prime cost of the property insured, plus the expenses of and incidental to shipping and the charges of insurance upon the whole:

(4) In insurance on any other subject-matter, the insurable value is the amount at the risk of the assured when the policy attaches, plus the charges of insurance.

Disclosure and representations

17. Insurance is uberrimae fidei
A contract of marine insurance is a contract based upon the utmost good faith, and, if the utmost good faith is not observed by either party, the contract may be avoided by the other party.

18. Disclosure by assured
(1) Subject to the provisions of this section, the assured must disclose to the insurer, before the contract is concluded, every material circumstance which is known to the assured, and the assured is deemed to know every circumstance which, in the ordinary course of business, ought to be known by him. If the assured fails to make such disclosure, the insurer may avoid the contract.

(2) Every circumstance is material which would influence the judgment of a prudent insurer in fixing the premium, or determining whether he will take the risk.

(3) In the absence of inquiry the following circumstances need not be disclosed, namely:—

(a) Any circumstance which diminishes the risk;

(b) Any circumstance which is known or presumed to be known to the insurer. The insurer is presumed to know matters of common notoriety or knowledge, and matters which an insurer in the ordinary course of his business, as such, ought to know;

(c) Any circumstance as to which information is waived by the insurer;

(d) Any circumstance which it is superfluous to disclose by reason of any express or implied warranty.

(4) Whether any particular circumstance, which is not disclosed, be material or not is, in each case, a question of fact.

(5) The term "circumstance" includes any communication made to, or information received by, the assured.

19. Disclosure by agent effecting insurance
Subject to the provisions of the preceding section as to circumstances which need not be disclosed, where an insurance is effected for the assured by an agent, the agent must disclose to the insurer—

(a) Every material circumstance which is known to himself, and an agent to insure is deemed to know every circumstance which, in the ordinary course of business, ought to be known by, or to have been communicated to, him; and

(b) Every material circumstance which the assured is bound to disclose, unless it came to his knowledge too late to communicate it to the agent.

20. Representations pending negotiation of contract
(1) Every material representation made by the assured or his agent to the insurer during the negotiations for contract, and before the contract is concluded, must be true. If it be untrue the insurer may avoid the contract.

(2) A representation is material which would influence the judgment of a prudent insurer in fixing the premium, or determining whether he will take the risk.

(3) A representation may be either a representation as to a matter of fact, or as to a matter of expectation or belief.

(4) A representation as to matter of fact is true, if it be substantially correct, that is to say, if the difference between what is represented and what is actually correct would not be considered material by a prudent insurer.

(5) A representation as to a matter of expectation or belief is true if it be made in good faith.

(6) A representation may be withdrawn or corrected before the contract is concluded.

(7) Whether a particular representation be material or not is, in each case, a question of fact.

21. When contract is deemed to be concluded

A contract of marine insurance is deemed to be concluded when the proposal of the assured is accepted by the insurer, whether the policy be then issued or not; and, for the purpose of showing when the proposal was accepted, reference may be made to the slip or covering note or other customary memorandum of the contract, [...]

The policy

22. Contract must be embedded in policy

Subject to the provisions of any statute, a contract of marine insurance is inadmissible in evidence unless it is embodied in a marine policy in accordance with this Act. The policy may be executed and issued either at the time when the contract is concluded or afterwards.

23. What policy must specify

A marine policy must specify—

(1) The name of the assured, or of some person who effects the insurance on his behalf: [...]

24. Signature of insurer

(1) A marine policy must be signed by or on behalf of the insurer, provided that in the case of a corporation the corporate seal may be sufficient, but nothing in this section shall be construed as requiring the subscription of a corporation to be under seal.

(2) Where a policy is subscribed by or on behalf of two or more insurers, each subscription, unless the contrary be expressed, constitutes a distinct contract with the assured.

25. Voyage and time policies

(1) Where the contract is to insure the subject-matter "at and from", or from one place to another or others, the policy is called a "voyage policy", and where the contract is to insure the subject-matter for a definite period of time the policy is called a "time policy". A contract for both voyage and time may be included in the same policy.

[...]

26. Designation of subject-matter

(1) The subject-matter insured must be designated in a marine policy with reasonable certainty.

(2) The nature and extent of the interest of the assured in the subject-matter insured need not be specified in the policy.

(3) Where the policy designates the subject-matter insured in general terms, it shall be construed to apply to the interest intended by the assured to be covered.

(4) In the application of this section regard shall be had to any usage regulating the designation of the subject-matter insured.

27. Valued policy

(1) A policy may be either valued or unvalued.

(2) A valued policy is a policy which specifies the agreed value of the subject-matter insured.

(3) Subject to the provisions of this Act, and in the absence of fraud, the value fixed by the policy is, as between the insurer and the assured, conclusive of the insurable value of the subject intended to be insured, whether the loss be total or partial.

(4) Unless the policy otherwise provides, the value fixed by the policy is not conclusive for the purpose of determining whether there has been a constructive total loss.

28. Unvalued policy

An unvalued policy is a policy which does not specify the value of the subject-matter insured, but, subject to the limit of the sum insured, leaves the insurable value to be subsequently ascertained, in the manner herein-before specified.

29. Floating policy by ship or ships

(1) A floating policy is a policy which describes the insurance in general terms, and leaves the name of the ship or ships and other particulars to be defined by subsequent declaration.

(2) The subsequent declaration or declarations may be made by indorsement on the policy, or in other customary manner.

(3) Unless the policy otherwise provides, the declarations must be made in the order of dispatch or shipment. They must, in the case of goods, comprise all consignments within the terms of the policy, and the value of the goods or other property must be honestly stated, but an omission or erroneous declaration may be rectified even after loss or arrival, provided the omission or declaration was made in good faith.

(4) Unless the policy otherwise provides, where a declaration of value is not made until after notice of loss or arrival, the policy must be treated as an unvalued policy as regards the subject-matter of that declaration.

30. Construction of terms in policy

(1) A policy may be in the form in the First Schedule to this Act.

(2) Subject to the provisions of this Act, and unless the context of the policy otherwise requires, the terms and expressions mentioned in the First Schedule to this Act shall be construed as having the scope and meaning in that schedule assigned to them.

31. Premium to be arranged

(1) Where an insurance is effected at a premium to be arranged, and no arrangement is made, a reasonable premium is payable.

(2) Where an insurance is effected on the terms that an additional premium is to be arranged in a given event, and that event happens but no arrangement is made, then a reasonable additional premium is payable.

Double insurance

32. Double insurance

(1) Where two or more policies are effected by or on behalf of the assured on the same adventure and interest or any part thereof, and the sums insured exceed the indemnity allowed by this Act, the assured is said to be over-insured by double insurance.

(2) Where the assured is over-insured by double insurance—

(a) The assured, unless the policy otherwise provides, may claim payment from the insurers in such order as he may think fit, provided that he is not entitled to receive any sum in excess of the indemnity allowed by this Act;

(b) Where the policy under which the assured claims is a valued policy, the assured must give credit as against the valuation for any sum received by him under any other policy without regard to the actual value of the subject-matter insured;

(c) Where the policy under which the assured claims is an unvalued policy he must give credit, as against the full insurable value, for any sum received by him under any other policy.

(d) Where the assured receives any sum in excess of the indemnity allowed by this Act, he is deemed to hold such sum in trust for the insurers, according to their right of contribution among themselves.

Warranties, etc.

33. Nature of warranty

(1) A warranty, in the following sections relating to warranties, means a promissory warranty, that is to say, a warranty by which the assured undertakes that some particular thing shall or shall not be done, or that some condition shall be fulfilled, or whereby he affirms or negatives the existence of a particular state of facts.

(2) A warranty may be express or implied.

(3) A warranty, as above defined, is a condition which must be exactly complied with, whether it be material to the risk or not. If it be not so complied with, then, subject to any express provision in the policy, the insurer is discharged from liability as from the date of the breach of warranty, but without prejudice to any liability incurred by him before that date.

34. When breach of warranty excused

(1) Non-compliance with a warranty is excused when, by reason of a change of circumstances, the warranty ceases to be applicable to the circumstances of the contract, or when compliance with the warranty is rendered unlawful by any subsequent law.

(2) Where a warranty is broken, the assured cannot avail himself of the defence that the breach has been remedied, and the warranty complied with, before loss.

(3) A breach of warranty may be waived by the insurer.

35. Express warranties

(1) An express warranty may be in any form of words from which the intention to warrant is to be inferred.

(2) An express warranty must be included in, or written upon, the policy, or must be contained in some document incorporated by reference into the policy.

(3) An express warranty does not exclude an implied warranty, unless it be inconsistent therewith.

36. Warranty of neutrality

(1) Where insurable property, whether ship or goods, is expressly warranted neutral, there is an implied condition that the property shall have a neutral character at the commencement of the risk, and that, so far as the assured can control the matter, its neutral character shall be preserved during the risk.

(2) Where a ship is expressly warranted "neutral" there is also an implied condition that, so far as the assured can control the matter, she shall be properly documented, that is to say, that she shall carry the necessary papers to establish her neutrality, and that she shall not falsify or suppress her papers, or use simulated papers. If any loss occurs through breach of this condition, the insurer may avoid the contract.

37. No implied warranty of nationality

There is no implied warranty as to the nationality of a ship, or that her nationality shall not be changed during the risk.

38. Warranty of good safety
Where the subject-matter insured is warranted "well" or "in good safety" on a particular day, it is sufficient if it be safe at any time during that day.

39. Warranty of seaworthiness of ship
(1) In a voyage policy there is an implied warranty that at the commencement of the voyage the ship shall be seaworthy for the purpose of the particular adventure insured.

(2) Where the policy attaches while the ship is in port, there is also an implied warranty that she shall, at the commencement of the risk, be reasonably fit to encounter the ordinary perils of the port.

(3) Where the policy relates to a voyage which is performed in different stages, during which the ship requires different kinds of or further preparation or equipment, there is an implied warranty that at the commencement of each stage the ship is seaworthy in respect of such preparation or equipment for the purposes of that stage.

(4) A ship is deemed to be seaworthy when she is reasonably fit in all respects to encounter the ordinary perils of the seas of the adventure insured.

(5) In a time policy there is no implied warranty that the ship shall be seaworthy at any stage of the adventure, but where, with the privity of the assured, the ship is sent to sea in an unseaworthy state, the insurer is not liable for any loss attributable to unseaworthiness.

40. No implied warranty that goods are seaworthy
(1) In a policy on goods or other moveables there is no implied warranty that the goods or moveables are seaworthy.

(2) In a voyage policy on goods or other moveables there is an implied warranty that at the commencement of the voyage the ship is not only seaworthy as a ship, but also that she is reasonably fit to carry the goods or other moveables to the destination contemplated by the policy.

41. Warranty of legality
There is an implied warranty that the adventure insured is a lawful one, and that, so far as the assured can control the matter, the adventure shall be carried out in a lawful manner.

The voyage

42. Implied condition as to commencement of risk
(1) Where the subject-matter is insured by a voyage policy "at and from" or "from" a particular place, it is not necessary that the ship should be at that place when the contract is concluded, but there is an implied condition that the adventure shall be commenced within a reasonable time, and that if the adventure be not so commenced the insurer may avoid the contract.

(2) The implied condition may be negatived by showing that the delay was caused by circumstances known to the insurer before the contract was concluded, or by showing that he waived the condition.

43. Alteration of port of departure
Where the place of departure is specified by the policy, and the ship instead of sailing from that place sails from any other place, the risk does not attach.

44. Sailing for different destination
Where the destination is specified in the policy, and the ship, instead of sailing for that destination, sails for any other destination, the risk does not attach.

45. Change of voyage

(1) Where, after the commencement of the risk, the destination of the ship is voluntarily changed from the destination contemplated by the policy, there is said to be a change of voyage.

(2) Unless the policy otherwise provides, where there is a change of voyage, the insurer is discharged from liability as from the time of the change, that is to say, as from the time when the determination to change it is manifested; and it is immaterial that the ship may not have left the course of voyage contemplated by the policy when the loss occurs.

46. Deviation

(1) Where a ship, without lawful excuse, deviates from the voyage contemplated by the policy, the insurer is discharged from liability as from the time of deviation, and it is immaterial that the ship may have regained her route before any loss occurs.

(2) There is a deviation from the voyage contemplated by the policy—

(a) Where the course of the voyage is specifically designated by the policy, and that course is departed from; or

(b) Where the course of the voyage is not specifically designated by the policy, but the usual and customary course is departed from.

(3) The intention to deviate is immaterial; there must be a deviation in fact to discharge the insurer from his liability under the contract.

47. Several ports of discharge

(1) Where several ports of discharge are specified by the policy, the ship may proceed to all or any of them, but, in the absence of any usage or sufficient cause to the contrary, she must proceed to them, or such of them as she goes to, in the order designated by the policy. If she does not there is a deviation.

(2) Where the policy is to "ports of discharge", within a given area, which are not named, the ship must, in the absence of any usage or sufficient cause to the contrary, proceed to them, or such of them as she goes to, in their geographical order. If she does not there is a deviation.

48. Delay in voyage

In the case of a voyage policy, the adventure insured must be prosecuted throughout its course with reasonable dispatch, and, if without lawful excuse it is not so prosecuted, the insurer is discharged from liability as from the time when the delay becomes unreasonable.

49. Excuses for deviation or delay

(1) Deviation or delay in prosecuting the voyage contemplated by the policy is excused—

(a) Where authorised by any special term in the policy; or

(b) Where caused by circumstances beyond the control of the master and his employer; or

(c) Where reasonably necessary in order to comply with an express or implied warranty; or

(d) Where reasonably necessary for the safety of the ship or subject-matter insured; or

(e) For the purpose of saving human life, or aiding a ship in distress where human life may be in danger; or

(f) Where reasonably necessary for the purpose of obtaining medical or surgical aid for any person on board the ship; or

(g) Where caused by the barratrous conduct of the master or crew, if barratry be one of the perils insured against.

(2) When the cause excusing the deviation or delay ceases to operate, the ship must resume her course, and prosecute her voyage, with reasonable dispatch.

Assignment of policy

50. When and how policy is assignable
(1) A marine policy is assignable unless it contains terms expressly prohibiting assignment. It may be assigned either before or after loss.

(2) Where a marine policy has been assigned so as to pass the beneficial interest in such policy, the assignee of the policy is entitled to sue thereon in his own name; and the defendant is entitled to make any defence arising out of the contract which he would have been entitled to make if the action had been brought in the name of the person by or on behalf of whom the policy was effected.

(3) A marine policy may be assigned by indorsement thereon or in other customary manner.

51. Assured who has no interest cannot assign
Where the assured has parted with or lost his interest in the subject-matter insured, and has not, before or at the time of so doing, expressly or impliedly agreed to assign the policy, any subsequent assignment of the policy is inoperative:

Provided that nothing in this section affects the assignment of a policy after loss.

The premium

52. When premium payable
Unless otherwise agreed, the duty of the assured or his agent to pay the premium, and the duty of the insurer to issue the policy to the assured or his agent, are concurrent conditions, and the insurer is not bound to issue the policy until payment or tender of the premium.

53. Policy effected through broker
(1) Unless otherwise agreed, where a marine policy is effected on behalf of the assured by a broker, the broker is directly responsible to the insurer for the premium, and the insurer is directly responsible to the assured for the amount which may be payable in respect of losses, or in respect of returnable premium.

(2) Unless otherwise agreed, the broker has, as against the assured, a lien upon the policy for the amount of the premium and his charges in respect of effecting the policy; and, where he has dealt with the person who employs him as a principal, he has also a lien on the policy in respect of any balance on any insurance account which may be due to him from such person, unless when the debt was incurred he had reason to believe that such person was only an agent.

54. Effect of receipt on policy
Where a marine policy effected on behalf of the assured by a broker acknowledges the receipt of the premium, such acknowledgement is, in the absence of fraud, conclusive as between the insurer and the assured, but not as between the insurer and broker.

Loss and abandonment

55. Included and excluded losses
(1) Subject to the provisions of this Act, and unless the policy otherwise provides, the insurer is liable for any loss proximately caused by a peril insured against, but, subject as

aforesaid, he is not liable for any loss which is not proximately caused by a peril insured against.

(2) In particular,—

(a) The insurer is not liable for any loss attributable to the wilful misconduct of the assured, but, unless the policy otherwise provides, he is liable for any loss proximately caused by a peril insured against, even though the loss would not have happened but for the misconduct or negligence of the master or crew;

(b) Unless the policy otherwise provides, the insurer on ship or goods is not liable for any loss proximately caused by delay, although the delay be caused by a peril insured against.

(c) Unless the policy otherwise provides, the insurer is not liable for ordinary wear and tear, ordinary leakage and breakage, inherent vice or nature of the subject-matter insured, or for any loss proximately caused by rats or vermin, or for any injury to machinery not proximately caused by maritime perils.

56. Partial and total loss

(1) A loss may be either total or partial. Any loss other than a total loss, as herein-after defined, is a partial loss.

(2) A total loss may be either an actual total loss, or a constructive total loss.

(3) Unless a different intention appears from the terms of the policy, an insurance against total loss includes a constructive, as well as an actual, total loss.

(4) Where the assured brings an action for a total loss and the evidence proves only a partial loss, he may, unless the policy otherwise provides, recover for a partial loss.

(5) Where goods reach their destination in specie, but by reason of obliteration of marks, or otherwise, they are incapable of identification, the loss, if any, is partial, and not total.

57. Actual total loss

(1) Where the subject-matter insured is destroyed, or so damaged as to cease to be a thing of the kind insured, or where the assured is irretrievably deprived thereof, there is an actual total loss.

(2) In the case of an actual total loss no notice of abandonment need be given.

58. Missing ship

Where the ship concerned in the adventure is missing, and after the lapse of a reasonable time no news of her has been received, an actual total loss may be presumed.

59. Effect of transhipment, etc.

Where, by a peril insured against, the voyage is interrupted at any intermediate port or place, under such circumstances as apart from any special stipulation in the contract of affreightment, to justify the master in landing and re-shipping the goods or other moveables, or in transhipping them, and sending them on to their destination, the liability of the insurer continues, notwithstanding the landing or transhipment.

60. Constructive total loss defined

(1) Subject to any express provision in the policy, there is a constructive total loss where the subject-matter insured is reasonably abandoned on account of its total loss appearing to be unavoidable, or because it could not be preserved from the actual total loss without an expenditure which would exceed its value when the expenditure had been incurred.

(2) In particular, there is a constructive total loss—

(i) Where the assured is deprived of the possession of his ship or goods by a peril insured against, and (a) it is unlikely that he can recover the ship or goods, as the case may be, or (b) the cost of recovering the ship or goods, as the case may be, would exceed their value when recovered; or

(ii) In the case of damage to a ship, where she is so damaged by a peril insured against that the cost of repairing the damage would exceed the value of the ship when repaired.

In estimating the cost of repairs, no deduction is to be made in respect of general average contributions to those repairs payable by other interests, but account is to be taken of the expense of future salvage operations and of any future general average contributions to which the ship would be liable if repaired; or

(iii) In the case of damage to goods, where the cost of repairing the damage and forwarding the goods to their destination would exceed their value on arrival.

61. Effect of constructive total loss

Where there is a constructive total loss the assured may either treat the loss as a partial loss, or abandon the subject-matter insured to the insurer and treat the loss as if it were an actual total loss.

62. Notice of abandonment

(1) Subject to the provisions of this section, where the assured elects to abandon the subject-matter insured to the insurer, he must give notice of the abandonment. If he fails to do so the loss can only be treated as a partial loss.

(2) Notice of abandonment may be given in writing, or by word of mouth, or partly in writing and partly by word of mouth, and may be given in terms which indicate the intention of the assured to abandon his insured interest in the subject-matter insured unconditionally to the insurer.

(3) Notice of abandonment must be given with reasonable diligence after the receipt of reliable information of the loss, but where the information is of a doubtful character the assured is entitled to a reasonable time to make inquiry.

(4) Where notice of abandonment is properly given, the rights of the assured are not prejudiced by the fact that the insurer refuses to accept the abandonment.

(5) The acceptance of an abandonment may be either express or implied from the conduct of the insurer. The mere silence of the insurer after notice is not an acceptance.

(6) Where a notice of abandonment is accepted the abandonment is irrevocable. The acceptance of the notice conclusively admits liability for the loss and the sufficiency of the notice.

(7) Notice of abandonment is unnecessary where, at the time when the assured receives information of the loss, there would be no possibility of benefit to the insurer if notice were given to him.

(8) Notice of abandonment may be waived by the insurer.

(9) Where an insurer has re-insured his risk, no notice of abandonment need be given by him.

63. Effect of abandonment

(1) Where there is a valid abandonment the insurer is entitled to take over the interest of the assured in whatever may remain of the subject-matter insured, and all proprietary rights incidental thereto.

(2) Upon the abandonment of a ship, the insurer thereof is entitled to any freight in course of being earned, and which is earned by her subsequent to the casualty causing the loss, less the expenses of earning it incurred after the casualty; and, where a ship is carrying the owner's goods, the insurer is entitled to a reasonable remuneration for the carriage of them subsequent to the casualty causing the loss.

Partial losses (including salvage and general average and particular charges)

64. Particular average loss

(1) A particular average loss is a partial loss of the subject-matter insured, caused by a peril insured against, and which is not a general average loss.

(2) Expenses incurred by or on behalf of the assured for the safety or preservation of the subject-matter insured, other than general average and salvage charges, are called particular charges. Particular charges are not included in particular average.

65. Salvage charges

(1) Subject to any express provision in the policy, salvage charges incurred in preventing a loss by perils insured against may be recovered as a loss by those perils.

(2) "Salvage charges" means the charges recoverable under maritime law by a salvor independently of contract. They do not include the expenses of services in the nature of salvage rendered by the assured or his agents, or any person employed for hire by them, for the purpose of averting a peril insured against. Such expenses, where properly incurred, may be recovered as particular charges or as a general average loss, according to the circumstances under which they were incurred.

66. General average loss

(1) A general average loss is a loss caused by or directly consequential on a general average act. It includes a general average expenditure as well as a general average sacrifice.

(2) There is a general average act where any extraordinary sacrifice or expenditure is voluntarily and reasonably made or incurred in the time of peril for the purpose of preserving the property imperilled in the common adventure.

(3) Where there is a general average loss, the party on whom it falls is entitled, subject to the conditions imposed by maritime law, to a rateable contribution from the other parties interested, and such contribution is called a general average contribution.

(4) Subject to any express provision in the policy, where the assured has incurred a general average expenditure, he may recover from the insurer in respect of the proportion of the loss which falls upon him; and, in the case of a general average sacrifice, he may recover from the insurer in respect of the whole loss without having enforced his right of contribution from the other parties liable to contribute.

(5) Subject to any express provision in the policy, where the assured has paid, or is liable to pay, a general average contribution in respect of the subject insured, he may recover therefor from the insurer.

(6) In the absence of express stipulation, the insurer is not liable for any general average loss or contribution where the loss was not incurred for the purpose of avoiding, or in connexion with the avoidance of, a peril insured against.

(7) Where ship, freight, and cargo, or any two of those interests, are owned by the same assured, the liability of the insurer in respect of general average losses or contributions is to be determined as if those subjects were owned by different persons.

Measure of indemnity

67. Extent of liability of insurer for loss

(1) The sum which the assured can recover in respect of a loss on a policy by which he is insured, in the case of an unvalued policy to the full extent of the insurable value, or in the case of a valued policy to the full extent of the value fixed by the policy, is called the measure of indemnity.

(2) Where there is a loss recoverable under the policy, the insurer, or each insurer if there be more than one, is liable for such proportion of the measure of indemnity as the

amount of his subscription bears to the value fixed by the policy in the case of a valued policy, or to the insurable value in the case of an unvalued policy.

68. Total loss
Subject to the provisions of this Act and to any express provision in the policy, where there is a total loss of the subject-matter insured,—

(1) If the policy be a valued policy, the measure of indemnity is the sum fixed by the policy:

(2) If the policy be an unvalued policy, the measure of indemnity is the insurable value of the subject-matter insured.

69. Partial loss of ship
Where a ship is damaged, but not totally lost, the measure of indemnity, subject to any express provision in the policy, is as follows:—

(1) Where the ship has been repaired, the assured is entitled to the reasonable cost of the repairs, less the customary deductions, but not exceeding the sum insured in respect of any one casualty:

(2) Where the ship has been only partially repaired, the assured is entitled to the reasonable cost of such repairs, computed as above, and also to be indemnified for the reasonable depreciation, if any, arising from the unrepaired damage, provided that the aggregate amount shall not exceed the cost of repairing the whole damage, computed as above:

(3) Where the ship has not been repaired, and has not been sold in her damaged state during the risk, the assured is entitled to be indemnified for the reasonable depreciation arising from the unrepaired damage, but not exceeding the reasonable cost of repairing such damage, computed as above.

70. Partial loss of freight
Subject to any express provision in the policy, where there is a partial loss of freight, the measure of indemnity is such proportion of the sum fixed by the policy in the case of a valued policy, or of the insurable value in the case of an unvalued policy, as the proportion of freight lost by the assured bears to the whole freight at the risk of the assured under the policy.

71. Partial loss of goods, merchandise, etc.
Where there is a partial loss of goods, merchandise, or other moveables, the measure of indemnity, subject to any express provision in the policy, is as follows:—

(1) Where part of the goods, merchandise, or other moveables insured by a valued policy is totally lost, the measure of indemnity is such proportion of the sum fixed by the policy as the insurable value of the part lost bears to the insurable value of the whole, ascertained as in the case of an unvalued policy:

(2) Where part of the goods, merchandise, or other moveables insured by an unvalued policy is totally lost, the measure of indemnity is the insurable value of the part lost, ascertained as in the case of total loss:

(3) Where the whole or any part of the goods or merchandise insured has been delivered damaged at its destination, the measure of indemnity is such proportion of the sum fixed by the policy in the case of a valued policy, or of the insurable value in the case of an unvalued policy, as the difference between the gross sound and damaged values at the place of arrival bears to the gross sound value:

(4) "Gross value" means the wholesale price or, if there be no such price, the estimated value, with, in either case, freight, landing charges, and duty paid beforehand; provided

that, in the case of goods or merchandise customarily sold in bond, the bonded price is deemed to be the gross value. "Gross proceeds" means the actual price obtained at a sale where all charges on sale are paid by the sellers.

72. Apportionment of valuation

(1) Where different species of property are insured under a single valuation, the valuation must be apportioned over the different species in proportion to their respective insurable values, as in the case of an unvalued policy. The insured value of any part of a species is such proportion of the total insured value of the same as the insurable value of the part bears to the insurable value of the whole, ascertained in both cases as provided by this Act.

(2) Where a valuation has to be apportioned, and particulars of the prime cost of each separate species, quality, or description of goods cannot be ascertained, the division of the valuation may be made over the net arrived sound values of the different species, qualities, or descriptions of goods.

73. General average contributions and salvage charges

(1) Subject to any express provision in the policy, where the assured has paid, or is liable for, any general average contribution, the measure of indemnity is the full amount of such contribution, if the subject-matter liable to contribution is insured for its full contributory value; but, if such subject-matter be not insured for its full contributory value, or if only part of it be insured, the indemnity payable by the insurer must be reduced in proportion to the under insurance, and where there has been a particular average loss which constitutes a deduction from the contributory value, and for which the insurer is liable, that amount must be deducted from the insured value in order to ascertain what the insurer is liable to contribute.

(2) Where the insurer is liable for salvage charges the extent of his liability must be determined on the like principle.

74. Liabilities to third parties

Where the assured has effected an insurance in express terms against any liability to a third party, the measure of indemnity, subject to any express provision in the policy, is the amount paid or payable by him to such third party in respect of such liability.

75. General provisions as to measure of indemnity

(1) Where there has been a loss in respect of any subject-matter not expressly provided for in the foregoing provisions of this Act, the measure of indemnity shall be ascertained, as nearly as may be, in accordance with those provisions, in so far as applicable to the particular case.

(2) Nothing in the provisions of this Act relating to the measure of indemnity shall affect the rules relating to double insurance, or prohibit the insurer from disproving interest wholly or in part, or from showing that at the time of the loss the whole or any part of the subject-matter insured was not at risk under the policy.

76. Particular average warranties

(1) Where the subject-matter insured is warranted free from particular average, the assured cannot recover for a loss of part, other than a loss incurred by a general average sacrifice, unless the contract contained in the policy be apportionable; but, if the contract be apportionable, the assured may recover for a total loss of any apportionable part.

(2) Where the subject-matter insured is warranted free from particular average, either wholly or under a certain percentage, the insurer is nevertheless liable for salvage charges, and for particular charges and other expenses properly incurred pursuant to the provisions of the suing and labouring clause in order to avert a loss insured against.

(3) Unless the policy otherwise provides, where the subject-matter is warranted free from particular average under a specified percentage, a general average loss cannot be added to a particular average loss to make up the specified percentage.

(4) For the purpose of ascertaining whether the specified percentage has been reached, regard shall be had only to the actual loss suffered by the subject-matter insured. Particular charges and the expenses of and incidential to ascertaining and proving the loss must be excluded.

77. Successive losses

(1) Unless the policy otherwise provides, and subject to the provisions of this Act, the insurer is liable for successive losses, even though the total amount of such losses may exceed the sum insured.

(2) Where, under the same policy, a partial loss, which has not been repaired or otherwise made good, is followed by a total loss, the assured can only recover in respect of the total loss:

Provided that nothing in this section shall affect the liability of the insurer under the suing and labouring clause.

78. Suing and labouring clause

(1) Where the policy contains a suing and labouring clause, the engagement thereby entered into is deemed to be supplementary to the contract of insurance, and the assured may recover from the insurer any expenses properly incurred pursuant to the clause, notwithstanding that the insurer may have paid for a total loss, or that the subject-matter may have been warranted free from particular average, either wholly or under a certain percentage.

(2) General average losses and contributions and salvage charges, as defined by this Act, are not recoverable under the suing and labouring clause.

(3) Expenses incurred for the purpose of averting or diminishing any loss not covered by the policy are not recoverable under the suing and labouring clause.

(4) It is the duty of the assured and his agents, in all cases, to take such measures as may be reasonable for the purpose of averting or minimising a loss.

Rights of insurer on payment

79. Right of subrogation

(1) Where the insurer pays for a total loss, either of the whole, or in the case of goods of any apportionable part, of the subject-matter insured, he thereupon becomes entitled to take over the interest of the assured in whatever may remain of the subject-matter so paid for, and he is thereby subrogated to all the rights and remedies of the assured in and in respect of that subject-matter as from the time of the casualty causing the loss.

(2) Subject to the foregoing provisions, where the insurer pays for a partial loss, he acquires no title to the subject-matter insured, or such part of it as may remain, but he is thereupon subrogated to all rights and remedies of the assured in and in respect of the subject-matter insured as from the time of the casualty causing the loss, in so far as the assured has been indemnified, according to this Act, by such payment for the loss.

80. Right of contribution

(1) Where the assured is over-insured by double insurance, each insurer is bound, as between himself and the other insurers, to contribute rateably to the loss in proportion to the amount for which he is liable under his contract.

(2) If any insurer pays more than his proportion of the loss, he is entitled to maintain an action for contribution against the other insurers, and is entitled to the like remedies as a surety who has paid more than his proportion of the debt.

81. Effect of under insurance
Where the assured is insured for an amount less than the insurable value or, in the case of a valued policy, for an amount less than the policy valuation, he is deemed to be his own insurer in respect of the uninsured balance.

Return of premium

82. Enforcement of return
Where the premium or a proportionate part thereof is, by this Act, declared to be returnable,—
    (a) If already paid, it may be recovered by the assured from the insurer; and
    (b) If unpaid, it may be retained by the assured or his agent.

83. Return by agreement
Where the policy contains a stipulation for the return of the premium, or a proportionate part thereof, on the happening of a certain event, and that event happens, the premium, or, as the case may be, the proportionate part thereof, is thereupon returnable to the assured.

84. Return for failure of consideration
(1) Where the consideration for the payment of the premium totally fails, and there has been no fraud or illegality on the part of the assured or his agents, the premium is thereupon returnable to the assured.

(2) Where the consideration for the payment of the premium is apportionable and there is a total failure of any apportionable part of the consideration, a proportionate part of the premium is, under the like conditions, thereupon returnable to the assured.

(3) In particular—
    (a) Where the policy is void, or is avoided by the insurer as from the commencement of the risk, the premium is returnable, provided that there has been no fraud or illegality on the part of the assured; but if the risk is not apportionable, and has once attached, the premium is not returnable;
    (b) Where the subject-matter insured, or part thereof, has never been imperilled, the premium, or, as the case may be, a proportionate part thereof, is returnable:
    Provided that where the subject-matter has been insured "lost or not lost" and has arrived in safety at the time when the contract is concluded, the premium is not returnable unless, at such time, the insurer knew of the safe arrival.
    (c) Where the assured has no insurable interest throughout the currency of the risk, the premium is returnable, provided that this rule does not apply to a policy effected by way of gaming or wagering;
    (d) Where the assured has a defeasible interest which is terminated during the currency of the risk, the premium is not returnable;
    (e) Where the assured has over-insured under an unvalued policy, a proportionate part of the premium is returnable;
    (f) Subject to the foregoing provisions, where the assured has over-insured by double insurance, a proportionate part of the several premiums is returnable:
    Provided that, if the policies are effected at different times, and any earlier policy has at any time borne the entire risk, or if a claim has been paid on the policy in respect of the full sum insured thereby, no premium is returnable in respect of that policy, and when the double insurance is effected knowingly by the assured no premium is returnable.

Mutual insurance

85. Modification of Act in case of mutual insurance

(1) Where two or more persons mutually agree to insure each other against marine losses there is said to be a mutual insurance.

(2) The provisions of this Act relating to the premium do not apply to mutual insurance, but a guarantee, or such other arrangement as may be agreed upon, may be substituted for the premium.

(3) The provisions of this Act, in so far as they may be modified by the agreement of the parties, may in the case of mutual insurance be modified by the terms of the policies issued by the association, or by the rules and regulations of the association.

(4) Subject to the expectations mentioned in this section, the provisions of this Act apply to a mutual insurance.

Supplemental

86. Ratification by assured

Where a contract of marine insurance is in good faith effected by one person on behalf of another, the person on whose behalf it is effected may ratify the contract even after he is aware of a loss.

87. Implied obligations varied by agreement or usage

(1) Where any right, duty, or liability would arise under a contract of marine insurance by implication of law, it may be negatived or varied by express agreement or by usage, if the usage be such as to bind both parties to the contract.

(2) The provisions of this section extend to any right, duty, or liability declared by this Act which may be lawfully modified by agreement.

88. Reasonable time, etc, a question of fact

Where by this Act any reference is made to reasonable time, reasonable premium, or reasonable diligence, the question what is reasonable is a question of fact.

89. Slip as evidence

Where there is a duly stamped policy, reference may be made, as heretofore, to the slip or covering note, in any legal proceeding.

90. Interpretation of terms

In this Act, unless the context or subject-matter otherwise requires,—

"Action" includes counter-claim and set off:

"Freight" includes the profit derivable by a shipowner from the employment of his ship to carry his own goods or moveables, as well as freight payable by a third party, but does not include passage money:

"Moveables" means any moveable tangible property, other than the ship, and includes money, valuable securities, and other documents.

"Policy" means a marine policy.

91. Savings

(1) Nothing in this Act, or in any repeal effected thereby, shall affect—

(a) The provisions of the Stamp Act 1891, or any enactment for the time being in force relating to the revenue;

(b) The provisions of the Companies Act 1862, or any enactment amending or substituted for the same;

(c) The provisions of any statute not expressly repealed by this Act.

(2) The rules of the common law including the law merchant, save in so far as they are inconsistent with the express provisions of this Act, shall continue to apply to contracts of marine insurance.

94. Short title
This Act may be cited as the Marine Insurance Act 1906.

SCHEDULES

Section 30 SCHEDULE 1

FORM OF POLICY

BE IT KNOWN THAT .... as well in .... own name as for and in the name and names of all and every other person or persons to whom the same doth, may, or shall appertain, in part or in all doth make assurance and cause and them, and every of them, to be insured lost or not lost, at and from ....

Upon any kind of goods and merchandise, and also upon the body, tackle, apparel, ordnance, munition, artillery, boat, and other furniture, of and in the good ship or vessel called the .... whereof is master under God, for this present voyage, ... or whosoever else shall go for master in the said ship, or by whatsoever other name or names the said ship, or the master thereof, is or shall be named or called; beginning the adventure upon the said goods and merchandises from the loading thereof aboard the said ship, upon the said ship, etc.

and so shall continue and endure, during her abode there, upon the said ship, etc.

And further, until the said ship, with all her ordnance, tackle, apparel, etc., and goods and merchandises whatsoever shall be arrived at .... upon the said ship, etc., until she hath moored at anchor for twenty-four hours in good safety; and upon the goods and merchandises, until the same be there discharged and safely landed. And it shall be lawful for the said ship, etc., in this voyage to proceed and sail to and touch and stay at any ports or places whatsoever without prejudice to this insurance. The said ship, etc., goods and merchandises, etc., for so much as concerns the assured by agreement between the assured and assurers in this policy, are and shall be valued at ....

Touching the adventures and perils which we the assurers are contented to bear and do take upon us in this voyage: they are of the seas, men of war, fire, enemies, pirates, rovers, thieves, jettisons, letters of mart and countermart, surprisals, takings at sea, arrests, restraints, and detainments of all kings, princes, and people, of what nation, condition, or quality soever, barratry of the master and mariners, and of all other perils, losses, and misfortunes, that have or shall come to the hurt, detriment, or damage of the said goods and merchandises, and ship, etc., or any part thereof. And in case of any loss or misfortune it shall be lawful to the assured, their factors, servants and assigns, to sue, labour, and travel for, in and about the defence, safeguards, and recovery of the said goods and merchandises, and ship, etc., or any part thereof, without prejudice to this insurance; to the charges whereof we, the assurers, will contribute each one according to the rate and quantity of his sum herein assured. And it is especially declared and agreed that no acts of the insurer or insured in recovering, saving, or preserving the property insured shall be considered as a waiver, or acceptance of abandonment. And it is agreed by us, the insurers, that this writing or policy of assurance shall be of as much force and effect as the surest writing or policy of assurance heretofore made in Lombard Street, or in the Royal Exchange, or elsewhere in London. And so we, the assurers, are contented, and do hereby promise and bind ourselves, each one for his own part, our heirs, executors, and goods to the assured, their executors, administrators, and assigns, for the true performance of the premises, confessing ourselves paid the consideration due unto us for this assurance by the assured, at and after the rate of ....

IN WITNESS whereof we, the assurers, have subscribed our names and sums assured in London.

N.B.—Corn, fish, salt, fruit, flour, and seed are warranted free from average, unless general, or the ship be stranded—sugar, tobacco, hemp, flax, hides and skins are warranted free from average, under five pounds per cent, and all other goods, also the ship and freight, are warranted free from average, under three pounds per cent unless general, or the ship be stranded.

Rules for construction of policy

The following are the rules referred to by this Act for the construction of a policy in the above or other like form, where the context does not otherwise require:—

1. Where the subject-matter is insured "lost or not lost," and the loss has occurred before the contract is concluded, the risk attaches, unless at such time the assured was aware of the loss, and the insurer was not.

2. Where the subject-matter is insured "from" a particular place, the risk does not attach until the ship starts on the voyage insured.

3. (a) Where a ship is insured "at and from" a particular place, and she is at that place in good safety when the contract is concluded, the risk attaches immediately.

(b) If she be not at that place when the contract is concluded, the risk attaches as soon as she arrives there in good safety, and, unless the policy otherwise provides, it is immaterial that she is covered by another policy for a specified time after arrival.

(c) Where chartered freight is insured "at and from" a particular place, and the ship is at that place in good safety when the contract is concluded the risk attaches immediately. If she be not there when the contract is concluded, the risk attaches as soon as she arrives there in good safety.

(d) Where freight, other than chartered freight, is payable without special conditions and is insured "at and from" a particular place, the risk attaches pro rata as the goods or merchandise are shipped; provided that if there be cargo in readiness which belongs to the shipowner, or which some other person has contracted with him to ship, the risk attaches as soon as the ship is ready to receive such cargo.

4. Where goods or other moveables are insured "from the loading thereof," the risk does not attach until such goods or moveables are actually on board, and the insurer is not liable for them while in transit from shore to ship.

5. Where the risk on goods or other moveables continues until they are "safely landed," they must be landed in the customary manner and within a reasonable time after arrival at the port of discharge, and if they are not so landed the risk ceases.

6. In the absence of any further license or usage, the liberty to touch and stay "at any port or place whatsoever" does not authorise the ship to depart from the course of her voyage from the port of departure to the port of destination.

7. The term "perils of the seas," refers only to fortuitous accidents or casualties of the seas. It does not include the ordinary action of the winds and waves.

8. The term "pirates" includes passengers who mutiny and rioters who attach the ship from the shore.

9. The term "thieves" does not cover clandestine theft or a theft committed by anyone of the ship's company, whether crew or passengers.

10. The term "arrests, etc., of kings, princes, and people" refers to political or executive acts, and does not include a loss caused by riot or by ordinary judicial process.

11. The term "barratry" includes every wrongful act wilfully committed by the master or crew to the prejudice of the owner, or, as the case may be, the charterer.

12. The term "all other perils" includes only perils similar in kind to the perils specifically mentioned in the policy.

13. The term "average unless general" means a partial loss of the subject-matter insured other than a general average loss, and does not include "particular charges."

14. Where the ship has stranded, the insurer is liable for the expected losses, although the loss is not attributable to the stranding, provided that when the stranding takes place the risk has attached and, if the policy be on goods, that the damaged goods are on board.

15. The term "ship" includes the hull, materials and outfit, stores and provisions for the officers and crew, and, in the case of vessels engaged in a special trade, the ordinary fittings requisite for the trade, and also, in the case of a steamship, the machinery, boilers, and coals and engine stores, if owned by the assured.

16. The term "freight" includes the profit derivable by a shipowner from the employment of his ship to carry his own goods or moveables, as well as freight payable by a third party, but does not include passage money.

17. The term "goods" means goods in the nature of merchandise, and does not include personal effects or provisions and stores for use on board.

In the absence of any usage to the contrary, deck cargo and living animals must be insured specifically, and not under the general denomination of goods.

SUPREME COURT ACT 1981
(1981, c. 54)

Admiralty jurisdiction

20. Admiralty jurisdiction of High Court

(1) The Admiralty jurisdiction of the High Court shall be as follows, that is to say—

   (a) jurisdiction to hear and determine any of the questions and claims mentioned in subsection (2);
   (b) jurisdiction in relation to any of the proceedings mentioned in subsection (3);
   (c) any other Admiralty jurisdiction which it had immediately before the commencement of this Act; and
   (d) any jurisdiction connected with ships or aircraft which is vested in the High Court apart from this section and is for the time being by rules of court made or coming into force after the commencement of this Act assigned to the Queen's Bench Division and directed by the rules to be exercised by the Admiralty Court.

(2) The questions and claims referred to in subsection (1)(a) are—

   (a) any claim to the possession or ownership of a ship or to the ownership of any share therein;
   (b) any question arising between the co-owners of a ship as to possession, employment or earnings of that ship;
   (c) any claim in respect of a mortgage of or charge on a ship or any share therein;
   (d) any claim for damage received by a ship;
   (e) any claim for damage done by a ship;
   (f) any claim for loss of life or personal injury sustained in consequence of any defect in a ship or in her apparel or equipment, or in consequence of the wrongful act, neglect or default of—
      (i) the owners, charterers or persons in possession or control of a ship; or
      (ii) the master or crew of a ship, or any other person for whose wrongful acts, neglects or defaults the owners, charterers or persons in possession or control of a ship are responsible,

being an act, neglect or default in the navigation or management of the ship, in the loading, carriage or discharge of goods on, in or from the ship, or in the embarkation, carriage or disembarkation of persons on, in or from the ship;
- (g) any claim for loss of or damage to goods carried in a ship;
- (h) any claim arising out of any agreement relating to the carriage of goods in a ship or to the use or hire of a ship;
- (j) any claim—
    - (i) under the Salvage Convention 1989;
    - (ii) under any contract for or in relation to salvage services; or
    - (iii) in the nature of salvage not falling within (i) or (ii) above;
  or any corresponding claim in connection with an aircraft;
- (k) any claim in the nature of towage in respect of a ship or an aircraft;
- (l) any claim in the nature of pilotage in respect of a ship or an aircraft;
- (m) any claim in respect of goods or materials supplied to a ship for her operation or maintenance;
- (n) any claim in respect of the construction, repair or equipment of a ship or in respect of dock charges or dues;
- (o) any claim by a master or member of the crew of a ship for wages (including any sum allotted out of wages or adjudged by a superintendent to be due by way of wages),
- (p) any claim by a master, shipper, charterer or agent in respect of disbursements made on account of a ship;
- (q) any claim arising out of an act which is or is claimed to be a general average act;
- (r) any claim arising out of bottomry;
- (s) any claim for the forfeiture or condemnation of a ship or of goods which are being or have been carried, or have been attempted to be carried, in a ship, or for the restoration of a ship or any such goods after seizure, or for droits of Admiralty.

(3) The proceedings referred to in subsection (1)(b) are—

- (a) any application to the High Court under the Merchant Shipping Act 1995;
- (b) any action to enforce a claim for damage, loss of life or personal injury arising out of—
    - (i) a collision between ships; or
    - (ii) the carrying out of or omission to carry out a manoeuvre in the case of one or more of two or more ships; or
    - (iii) non-compliance, on the part of one or more of two or more ships, with the collision regulations;
- (c) any action by shipowners or other persons under the Merchant Shipping Act 1995 for the limitation of the amount of their liability in connection with a ship or other property.

(4) The jurisdiction of the High Court under subsection (2)(b) includes power to settle any account outstanding and unsettled between the parties in relation to the ship, and to direct that the ship, or any share thereof, shall be sold, and to make such other order as the court thinks fit.

(5) Subsection (2)(e) extends to—

- (a) any claim in respect of a liability incurred under Chapter III of Part VI of the Merchant Shipping Act 1995;
- (b) any claim in respect of a liability falling on the International Oil Pollution Compensation Fund or on the International Oil Pollution Compensation Fund 1984 under Chapter VI of Part VI of the Merchant Shipping Act 1995.

(6) In subsection (2)(j)—

(a) the "Salvage Convention 1989" means the International Convention on Salvage, 1989 as it has effect under section 224 of the Merchant Shipping Act 1995;
(b) the reference to salvage services includes services rendered in saving life from a ship and the reference to any claim under any contract for or in relation to salvage services includes any claim arising out of such a contract whether or not arising during the provision of the services;
(c) the reference to a corresponding claim in connection with an aircraft is a reference to any claim corresponding to any claim mentioned in sub-paragraph (i) or (ii) of paragraph (j) which is available under section 87 of the Civil Aviation Act 1982.

(7) The preceding provisions of this section apply—

(a) in relation to all ships or aircraft, whether British or not and whether registered or not and wherever the residence or domicile of their owners may be;
(b) in relation to all claims, wherever arising (including, in the case of cargo or wreck salvage, claims in respect of cargo or wreck found on land); and
(c) so far as they relate to mortgages and charges, to all mortgages or charges, whether registered or not and whether legal or equitable, including mortgages and charges created under foreign law:

Provided that nothing in this subsection shall be construed as extending the cases in which money or property is recoverable under any of the provisions of the Merchant Shipping Act 1995.

21. Mode of exercise of Admiralty jurisdiction

(1) Subject to section 22, an action in personam may be brought in the High Court in all cases within the Admiralty jurisdiction of that court.

(2) In the case of any such claim as is mentioned in section 20(2)(a)(c) or (s) or any such question as is mentioned in section 20(2)(b), an action in rem may be brought in the High Court against the ship or property in connection with which the claim or question arises.

(3) In any case in which there is maritime lien or other charge on any ship, aircraft or other property for the amount claimed, an action in rem may be brought in the High Court against that ship, aircarft or property.

(4) In the case of any such claim as is mentioned in section 2((2)(e) to (r), where—

(a) the claim arises in connection with a ship; and
(b) the person who would be liable on the claim in an action in personam ("the relevant person") was, when the cause of action arose, the owner or charterer of, or in possession or in control of, the ship,

an action in rem may (whether or not the claim gives rise to a maritime lien on that ship) be brought in the High Court against—

(i) that ship, if at the time when the action is brought the relevant person is either the beneficial owner of that ship as respects all the shares in it or the charterer of it under a charter by demise; or
(ii) any other ship of which, at the time when the action is brought, the relevant person is the beneficial owner as respects all the shares in it.

(5) In the case of a claim in the nature of towage or pilotage in respect of an aircraft, an action in rem may be brought in the High Court against that aircraft if, at the time when

the action is brought, it is beneficially owned by the person who would be liable on the claim in an action in personam.

(6) Where, in the exercise of its Admiralty jurisdiction, the High Court orders any ship, aircraft or other property to be sold, the court shall have jurisdiction to hear and determine any question arising as to the title to the proceeds of sale.

(7) In determining for the purposes of subsections (4) and (5) whether a person would be liable on a claim in an action in personam it shall be assumed that he has his habitual residence or a place of business within England or Wales.

(8) Where, as regards any such claim as is mentioned in section 20(2)(e) to (r), a ship has been served with a writ or arrested in an action in rem brought to enforce that claim, no other ship may be served with a writ or arrested in that or any other action in rem brought to enforce that claim; but this subsection does not prevent the issue, in respect of any one such claim, of a writ naming more than one ship or of two or more writs each naming a different ship.

22. Restrictions on entertainment of actions in personam in collision and other similar cases

(1) This section applies to any claim for damage, loss of life or personal injury arising out of—

- (a) a collision between ships; or
- (b) the carrying out of, or omission to carry out, a manoeuvre in the case of one or more of two or more ships; or
- (c) non-compliance, on the part of one or more of two or more ships, with the collision regulations.

(2) The High Court shall not entertain any action in personam to enforce a claim to which this section applies unless—

- (a) the defendant has his habitual residence or a place of business within England or Wales; or
- (b) the cause of action arose within inland waters of England or Wales or within the limits of a port of England or Wales; or
- (c) an action arising out of the same incident or series of incidents is proceeding in the court or has been heard and determined in the court.

In this subsection—

"inland waters" includes any part of the sea adjacent to the coast of the United Kingdom certified by the Secretary of State to be waters falling by international law to be treated as within the territorial sovereignty of Her Majesty apart from the operation of that law in relation to territorial waters;

"port" means any port, harbour, river, estuary, haven, dock, canal or other place so long as a person or body of persons is empowered by or under an Act to make charges in respect of ships entering it or using the facilities therein, and "limits of a port" means the limits thereof as fixed by or under the Act in question or, as the case may be, by the relevant charter or custom;

"charges" means any charges with the exception of light dues, local light dues and any other charges in respect of lighthouses, buoys or beacons and of charges in respect of pilotage.

(3) The High Court shall not entertian any action in personam to enforce a claim to which this section applies until any proceedings previously brought by the plaintiff in any

court outside England and Wales against the same defendant in respect of the same incident or series of incidents have been discontinued or otherwise come to an end.

(4) Subsections (2) and (3) shall apply to counterclaims (except counterclaims in proceedings arising out of the same incident or series of incidents) as they apply to actions, the references to the plaintiff and the defendant being for this purpose read as references to the plaintiff on the counterclaim and the defendant to the counterclaim respectively.

(5) Subsections (2) and (3) shall not apply to any action or counterclaim if the defendant thereto submits or has agreed to submit to the jurisdiction of the court.

(6) Subject to the provisions of subsection (3), the High Court shall have jurisdiction to entertain an action in personam to enforce a claim to which this section applies whenever any of the conditions specified in subsection (2)(a) to (c) is satisfied, and the rules of court relating to the service of process outside the jurisdiction shall make such provision as may appear to the rule-making authority to be appropriate having regard to the provisions of this subsection.

(7) Nothing in this section shall prevent an action which is brought in accordance with the provisions of this section in the High Court being transferred, in accordance with the enactments in that behalf, to some other court.

(8) For the avoidance of doubt it is hereby declared that this section applies in relation to the jurisdiction of the High Court not being Admiralty jurisdiction, as well as in relation to its Admiralty jurisdiction.

23. High Court not to have jurisdiction in cases within Rhine Convention

The High Court shall not have jurisdiction to determine any claim or question certified by the Secretary of State to be a claim or question which, under the Rhine Navigation Convention, falls to be determined in accordance with the provisions of that Convention; and any proceedings to enforce such a claim which are commenced in the High Court shall be set aside.

24. Supplementary provisions as to Admiralty jurisdiction

(1) In sections 20 to 23 and this section, unless the context otherwise requires—

"collision regulations" means safety regulations under section 85 of the Merchant Shipping Act 1995;

"goods" includes baggage;

"master" has the same meaning as in the Merchant Shipping Act 1995, and accordingly includes every person (except a pilot) having command or charge of a ship;

"the Rhine Navigation Convention" means the Convention of the 7th October 1868 as revised by any subsequent Convention;

"ship" includes any description of vessel used in navigation and (except in the definition of "port" in section 22(2) and in subsection (2)(c) of this section) includes, subject to section 2(3) of the Hovercraft Act 1968, a hovercraft;

"towage" and "pilotage", in relation to an aircraft, mean towage and pilotage while the aircraft is water-borne.

(2) Nothing in sections 20 to 23 shall—

(a) be construed as limiting the jurisdiction of the High Court to refuse to entertain an action for wages by the master or a member of the crew of a ship, not being a British ship;

(b) affect the provisions of section 226 of the Merchant Shipping Act 1995 (power of a receiver of wreck to detain a ship in respect of a salvage claim); or

(c) authorise proceedings in rem in respect of any claim against the Crown, or the arrest, detention or sale of any of Her Majesty's ships or Her Majesty's aircraft, or, subject to section 2(3) of the Hovercraft Act 1968, Her Majesty's hovercraft, or of any cargo or other property belonging to the Crown.

(3) In this section—

"Her Majesty's ships" and "Her Majesty's aircraft" have the meanings given by section 38(2) of the Crown Proceedings Act 1947;

"Her Majesty's hovercraft" means hovercraft belonging to the Crown in right of Her Majesty's Government in the United Kingdom or Her Majesty's Government in Northern Ireland.

APPENDIX 2

YORK-ANTWERP RULES*

YORK-ANTWERP RULES 1974
(As amended 1990)

Rule of Interpretation

In the adjustment of general average the following lettered and numbered Rules shall apply to the exclusion of any Law and Practice inconsistent therewith.

Except as provided by the numbered Rules, general average shall be adjusted according to the lettered Rules.

Rule A

There is a general average act when, and only when, any extraordinary sacrifice or expenditure is intentionally and reasonably made or incurred for the common safety for the purpose of preserving from peril the property involved in a common maritime adventure.

Rule B

General average sacrifices and expenses shall be borne by the different contributing interests on the basis hereinafter provided.

Rule C

Only such losses, damages or expenses which are the direct consequence of the general average act shall be allowed as general average.

Loss or damage sustained by the ship or cargo through delay, whether on the voyage or subsequently, such as demurrage, and any indirect loss whatsoever, such as loss of market, shall not be admitted as general average.

Rule D

Rights to contribution in general average shall not be affected, though the event which gave rise to the sacrifice or expenditure may have been due to the fault of one of the parties to the adventure, but this shall not prejudice any remedies or defences which may be open against or to that party in respect of such fault.

Rule E

The onus of proof is upon the party claiming in general average to show that the loss or expense claimed is properly allowable as general average.

Rule F

Any extra expense in place of another expense which would have been allowable as general average shall be deemed to be general average and so allowed without regard to the saving, if any, to other interests, but only up to the amount of the general average expense avoided.

---

* Reproduced with the kind permission of the Comité Maritime International.

Rule G

General average shall be adjusted as regards both loss and contribution upon the basis of values at the time and place when and where the adventure ends.

This rule shall not affect the determination of the place at which the average statement is to be made up.

Rule I

Jettison of Cargo

No jettison of cargo shall be made good as general average, unless such cargo is carried in accordance with the recognised custom of the trade.

Rule II

Damage by Jettison and Sacrifice for the Common Safety

Damage done to a ship and cargo, or either of them, by or in consequence of a sacrifice made for the common safety, and by water which goes down a ship's hatches opened or other opening made for the purpose of making a jettison for the common safety, shall be made good as general average.

Rule III

Extinguishing Fire on Shipboard

Damage done to a ship and cargo, or either of them, by water or otherwise, including damage by beaching or scuttling a burning ship, in extinguishing a fire on board the ship, shall be made good as general average; except that no compensation shall be made for damage by smoke or heat however caused.

Rule IV

Cutting Away Wreck

Loss or damage sustained by cutting away wreck or parts of the ship which have been previously carried away or are effectively lost by accident shall not be made good as general average.

Rule V

Voluntary Stranding

When a ship is intentionally run on shore for the common safety, whether or not she might have been driven on shore, the consequent loss or damage shall be allowed in general average.

Rule VI [as amended 1990]

Salvage

(a) Expenditure incurred by the parties to the adventure in the nature of salvage, whether under contract or otherwise, shall be allowed in general average provided that the salvage operations were carried out for the purpose of preserving from peril the property involved in the common maritime adventure.

Expenditure allowed in general average shall include any salvage remuneration in which the skill and efforts of the salvors in preventing or minimising damage to the environment such as is referred to in Art. 13 paragraph 1(b) of the International Convention on Salvage, 1989 have been taken into account.

(b) Special compensation payable to a salvor by the shipowner under Art. 14 of the said Convention to the extent specified in paragraph 4 of that Article or under any other provision similar in substance shall not be allowed in general average.

Rule VII

Damage to Machinery and Boilers

Damage caused to any machinery and boilers of a ship which is ashore and in a position of peril, in endeavouring to refloat, shall be allowed in general average when shown to have arisen from an actual intention to float the ship for the common safety at the risk of such damage; but where a ship is afloat no loss or damage caused by working the propelling machinery and boilers shall in any circumstances be made good as general average.

Rule VIII

Expenses Lightening a Ship When Ashore and Consequent Damage

When a ship is ashore and cargo and ship's fuel and stores or any of them are discharged as a general average act, the extra cost of lightening, lighter hire and reshipping if incurred and the loss or damage sustained thereby, shall be admitted as general average.

Rule IX

Ship's Materials and Stores Burnt for Fuel

Ship's materials and stores, or any of them, necessarily burnt for fuel for the common safety at a time of peril, shall be admitted as general average, when and only when an ample supply of fuel had been provided; but the estimated quantity of fuel that would have been consumed, calculated at the price current at the ship's last port of departure at the date of her leaving, shall be credited to the general average.

Rule X

Expenses at Port of Refuge, etc.

(a) When a ship shall have entered a port of refuge, or shall have returned to her port or place of loading in consequence of accident, sacrifice or other extraordinary circumstances, which render that necessary for the common safety, the expenses of entering such port or place shall be admitted as general average; and when she shall have sailed thence with her original cargo, or a part of it, the corresponding expenses of leaving such port or place consequent upon such entry or return shall likewise be admitted as general average.

When a ship is at any port or place of refuge and is necessarily removed to another port or place because repairs cannot be carried out in the first port or place, the provisions of this Rule shall be applied to the second port or place as if it were a port or place of refuge and the cost of such removal including temporary repairs and towage shall be admitted as general average. The provisions of Rule XI shall be applied to the prolongation of the voyage occasioned by such removal.

(b) The cost of handling on board or discharging cargo, fuel or stores whether at a port or place of loading, call or refuge shall be admitted as general average, when the handling or discharge was necessary for the common safety or to enable damage to the ship caused by sacrifice or accident to be repaired, if the repairs were necessary for the safe prosecution of the voyage, except in cases where the damage to the ship is discovered at a port or place of loading or call without any accident or other extraordinary circumstances connected with such damage having taken place during the voyage.

The cost of handling on board or discharging cargo, fuel or stores shall not be admissible as general average when incurred solely for the purpose of re-stowage due to shifting during the voyage unless such re-stowage is necessary for the common safety.

(c) Whenever the cost of handling or discharging cargo, fuel or stores is admissible as general average, the costs of storage, including insurance if reasonably incurred, reloading and stowing of such cargo, fuel or stores shall likewise be admitted as general average.

But when the ship is condemned or does not proceed on her original voyage, storage expenses shall be admitted as general average only up to the date of the ship's condemnation or of the abandonment of the voyage or up to the date of completion of discharge of cargo if the condemnation or abandonment takes place before that date.

Rule XI

Wages and Maintenance of Crew and Other Expenses Bearing up for and in a Port of Refuge, etc.

(a) Wages and maintenance of masters, officers and crew reasonably incurred and fuel and stores consumed during the prolongation of the voyage occasioned by a ship entering a port or place of refuge or returning to her port or place of loading shall be admitted as general average when the expenses of entering such port or place are allowable in general average in accordance with Rule X(a).

(b) When a ship shall have entered or been detained in any port or place in consequence of accident, sacrifice or other extraordinary circumstances which render that necessary for the common safety, or to enable damage to the ship caused by sacrifice or accident to be repaired, if the repairs were necessary for the safe prosecution of the voyage, the wages and maintenance of the master, officers and crew reasonably incurred during the extra period of detention in such port or place until the ship shall or should have been made ready to proceed upon her voyage, shall be admitted in general average.

Provided that when damage to the ship is discovered at a port or place of loading or call without any accident or other extraordinary circumstance connected with such damage having taken place during the voyage, then the wages and maintenance of master, officers and crew and fuel and stores consumed during the extra detention for repairs to damages so discovered shall not be admissible as general average, even if the repairs are necessary for the safe prosecution of the voyage.

When the ship is condemned or does not proceed on her original voyage, wages and maintenance of the master, officers and crew and fuel and stores consumed shall be admitted as general average only up to the date of the ship's condemnation or of the abandonment of the voyage or up to the date of completion of discharge of cargo if the condemnation or abandonment takes place before that date.

Fuel and stores consumed during the extra period of detention shall be admitted as general average, except such fuel and stores as are consumed in effecting repairs not allowable in general average.

Port charges incurred during the extra period of detention shall likewise be admitted as general average except such charges as are incurred solely by reason of repairs not allowable in general average.

(c) For the purpose of this and the other Rules wages shall include all payments made to or for the benefit of the master, officers and crew, whether such payments be imposed by law upon the shipowners or be made under the terms or articles of employment.

(d) When overtime is paid to the master, officers or crew for maintenance of the ship or repairs, the cost of which is not allowable in general average, such overtime shall be allowed in general average only up to the saving in expense which would have been incurred and admitted as general average, had such overtime not been incurred.

Rule XII

Damage to Cargo in Discharging, etc.

Damage to or loss of cargo, fuel or stores caused in the act of handling, discharging, storing, reloading and stowing shall be made good as general average, when and only when the cost of those measures respectively is admitted as general average.

Rule XIII

Deductions From Cost of Repairs

Repairs to be allowed in general average shall not be subject to deductions in respect of "new for old" where old material or parts are replaced by new unless the ship is over fifteen years old in which case there shall be a deduction of one third. The deductions shall be regulated by the age of the ship from 31 December of the year of completion of construction to the date of the general average act, except for insulation, life and similar boats, communications and navigational apparatus and equipment, machinery and boilers for which the deductions shall be regulated by the age of the particular parts to which they apply. The deductions shall be made only from the cost of the new material or parts when finished and ready to be installed in the ship.

No deduction shall be made in respect of provisions, stores, anchors and chain cables.

Drydock and shipway dues and costs of shifting the ship shall be allowed in full.

The costs of cleaning, painting or coating of bottom shall not be allowed in general average unless the bottom has been painted or coated within the twelve months preceding the date of the general average act in which case one half of such costs shall be allowed.

Rule XIV

Temporary Repairs

Where temporary repairs are effected to a ship at a port of loading, call or refuge, for the common safety, or of damage caused by general average sacrifice, the cost of such repairs shall be admitted as general average.

Where temporary repairs of accidental damage are effected in order to enable the adventure to be completed, the cost of such repairs shall be admitted as general average without regard to the saving, if any, to other interests, but only up to the saving in expenses which would have been incurred and allowed in general average if such repairs had not been effected there.

No deductions "new for old" shall be made from the cost of temporary repairs allowable as general average.

Rule XV

Loss of Freight

Loss of freight arising from damage to or loss of cargo shall be made good as general average, either when caused by a general average act, or when the damage to or loss of cargo is so made good.

Deduction shall be made from the amount of gross freight lost, of the charges which the owner thereof would have incurred to earn such freight, but has, in consequence of the sacrifice, not incurred.

Rule XVI

Amount to be Made Good for Cargo Lost or Damaged by Sacrifice

The amount to be made good as general average for damage to or loss of cargo sacrificed shall be the loss which has been sustained thereby based on the value at the time of discharge, ascertained from the commercial invoice rendered to the receiver or if there is no such invoice from the shipped value. The value at the time of discharge shall include the cost of insurance and freight except in so far as such freight is at the risk of interests other than the cargo.

When cargo so damaged is sold and the amount of the damage has not been otherwise agreed, the loss to be made good in general average shall be the difference between the net proceeds of sale and the net proceeds of sound value as computed in the first paragraph of this Rule.

Rule XVII

Contributory Values

The contribution to a general average shall be made upon the actual net values of the property at the termination of the adventure except that the value of cargo shall be the value at the time of discharge ascertained from the commercial invoice rendered to the receiver or if there is no such invoice from the shipped value. The value of the cargo shall include the cost of insurance and freight unless and in so far as such freight is at the risk of interests other than the cargo, deducting therefrom any loss or damage suffered by the cargo prior to or at the time of discharge. The value of the ship shall be assessed without taking into account the beneficial or detrimental effect of any demise or time charterparty to which the ship may be committed.

To these values shall be added the amount made good as general average for property sacrificed, if not already included, deductions being made from the freight and passage money at risk of such charges and crew's wages as would not have been incurred in earning the freight had the ship and cargo been totally lost at the date of the general average act and have not been allowed as general average, deduction being also made from the value of the property of all extra charges incurred in respect thereof subsequently to the general average act, except such charges as are allowed in general average.

Where cargo is sold short of destination, however, it shall contribute upon the actual net proceeds of sale, with the addition of any amount made good as general average.

Passengers' luggage and personal effects not shipped under Bill of Lading shall not contribute in general average.

Rule XVIII

Damage to Ship

The amount to be allowed as general average for damage or loss to the ship, her machinery and/or gear caused by a general average act shall be as follows:

(a) When repaired or replaced, the actual reasonable cost of repairing or replacing such damage or loss, subject to deduction in accordance with Rule XIII.

(b) When not repaired or replaced, the reasonable depreciation arising from such damage or loss, but not exceeding the estimated cost of repairs. But where the ship is an actual total loss or when the cost of repairs of the damage would exceed the value of the ship when repaired, the amount to be allowed as general average shall be the difference between the estimated sound value of the ship after deducting therefrom the estimated cost of repairing damage which is not general average and the value of the ship in her damaged state which may be measured by the net proceeds of sale, if any.

Rule XIX

Undeclared or Wrongfully Declared Cargo

Damage or loss caused to goods loaded without the knowledge of the shipowner or his agent or to goods wilfully misdescribed at time of shipment shall not be allowed as general average, but such goods shall remain liable to contribute, if saved.

Damage or loss caused to goods which have been wrongfully declared on shipment at a value which is lower than their real value shall be contributed for at the declared value, but such goods shall contribute upon their actual value.

Rule XX

Provision of Funds

A commission of 2 per cent on general average disbursements, other than the wages and maintenance of master, officers and crew and fuel and stores not replaced during the voyage shall be allowed in general average, but when the funds are not provided by any of the contributing interests, the necessary cost of obtaining the funds required by means of a bottomry bond or otherwise, or the loss sustained by owners of goods sold for the purpose, shall be allowed in general average.

The cost of insuring money advanced to pay for general average disbursements shall be allowed in general average.

Rule XXI

Interest on Losses Made Good in general average

Interest shall be allowed on expenditure, sacrifices and allowances charged to general average at the rate of 7 per cent per annum, until the date of the general average statement, due allowance being made for any interim reimbursement from the contributory interests or from the general average deposit fund.

Rule XXII

Treatment of Cash Deposits

Where cash deposits have been collected in respect of cargo's liability for general average, salvage or special charges, such deposits shall be paid without any delay into a special account in the joint names of a representative nominated on behalf of the shipowner and a representative nominated on behalf of the depositors in a bank to be approved by both. The sum so deposited, together with accrued interest, if any, shall be held as security for payment to the parties entitled thereto of the general average, salvage or special charges payable by cargo in respect to which the deposits have been collected. Payments on account or refund of deposits may be made if certified to in writing by the average adjuster. Such deposits and payments or refunds shall be without prejudice to the ultimate liability of the parties.

THE YORK-ANTWERP RULES 1994

Rule of Interpretation

In the adjustment of general average the following Rules shall apply to the exclusion of any Law and Practice inconsistent therewith.

Except as provided by the Rule Paramount and the numbered Rules, general average shall be adjusted according to the lettered Rules.

Rule Paramount

In no case shall there by any allowance for sacrifice or expenditure unless reasonably made or incurred.

Rule A

There is a general average act when, and only when, any extraordinary sacrifice or expenditure is intentionally and reasonably made or incurred for the common safety for the purpose of preserving from peril the property involved in a common maritime adventure.

General average sacrifices and expenditures shall be borne by the different contributing interests on the basis hereinafter provided.

Rule B

There is a common maritime adventure when one or more vessels are towing or pushing another vessel or vessels, provided that they are all involved in commercial activities and not in a salvage operation.

When measures are taken to preserve the vessels and their cargoes, if any, from a common peril, these Rules shall apply.

A vessel is not in common peril with another vessel or vessels if by simply disconnecting from the other vessel or vessels she is in safety; but if the disconnection is itself a general average act the common maritime adventure continues.

Rule C

Only such losses, damages or expenses which are the direct consequence of the general average act shall be allowed as general average.

In no case shall there be any allowance in general average for losses, damages or expenses incurred in respect of damage to the environment or in consequence of the escape or release of pollutant substances from the property invovled in the common maritime adventure.

Demurrage, loss of market, and any loss or damage sustained or expense incurred by reason of delay, whether on the voyage or subsequently, and any indirect loss whatsoever, shall not be admitted as general average.

Rule D

Rights to contribution in general average shall not be affected, though the event which gave rise to the sacrifice or expenditure may have been due to the fault of one of the parties to the adventure; but this shall not prejudice any remedies or defences which may be open against or to that party in respect of such fault.

Rule E

The onus of proof is upon the party claiming in general average to show that the loss or expense claimed is properly allowable as general average.

All parties claiming in general average shall give notice in writing to the average adjuster of the loss or expense in respect of which they claim contribution within 12 months of the date of the termination of the common maritime adventure.

Failing such notification, or if within 12 months of a request for the same any of the parties shall fail to supply evidence in support of a notified claim, or particulars of value in respect of a contributory interest, the average adjuster shall be at liberty to estimate the extent of the allowance or the contributory value on the basis of the information available to him, which estimate may be challenged only on the ground that it is manifestly incorrect.

Rule F

Any additional expense incurred in place of another expense which would have been allowable as general average shall be deemed to be general average and so allowed without regard to the saving, if any, to other interests, but only up to the amount of the general average expense avoided.

Rule G

General average shall be adjusted as regards both loss and contribution upon the basis of values at the time and place when and where the adventure ends.

This rule shall not affect the determination of the place at which the average statement is to be made up.

When a ship is at any port or place in circumstances which would give rise to an allowance in general average under the provisions of Rules X and XI, and the cargo or part thereof is forwarded to destination by other means, rights and liabilities in general average shall, subject to cargo interests being notified if practicable, remain as nearly as possible the same as they would have been in the absence of such forwarding, as if the adventure had continued in the original ship for so long as justifiable under the contract of affreightment and the applicable law.

The proportion attaching to cargo of the allowances made in general average by reason of applying the third paragraph of this Rule shall not exceed the cost which would have been borne by the owners of cargo if the cargo had been forwarded at their expense.

Rule I. Jettison of Cargo

No jettison of cargo shall be made good as general average, unless such cargo is carried in accordance with the recognised custom of the trade.

Rule II. Loss or Damage by Sacrifices for the Common Safety

Loss of or damage to the property involved in the common maritime adventure by or in consequence of a sacrifice made for the common safety, and by water which goes down a ship's hatches opened or other opening made for the purpose of making a jettison for the common safety, shall be made good as general average.

Rule III. Extinguishing Fire on Shipboard

Damage done to a ship and cargo, or either of them, by water or otherwise, including damage by beaching or scuttling a burning ship, in extinguishing a fire on board the ship, shall be made good as general average; except that no compensation shall be made for damage by smoke however caused or by heat of the fire.

Rule IV. Cutting Away Wreck

Loss or damage sustained by cutting away wreck or parts of the ship which have been previously carried away or are effectively lost by accident shall not be made good as general average.

Rule V. Voluntary Stranding

When a ship is intentionally run on shore for the common safety, whether or not she might have been driven on shore, the consequent loss or damage to the property involved in the common maritime adventure shall be allowed in general average.

Rule VI. Salvage Remuneration

(a) Expenditure incurred by the parties to the adventure in the nature of salvage, whether under contract or otherwise, shall be allowed in general average provided that the salvage operations were carried out for the purpose of preserving from peril the property involved in the common maritime adventure.

Expenditure allowed in general average shall include any salvage remuneration in which the skill and efforts of the salvors in preventing or minimising damage to the environment such as is referred to in Article 13 paragraph 1(b) of the International Convention on Salvage, 1989 have been taken into account.

(b) Special compensation payable to a salvor by the shipowner under Article 14 of the said Convention to the extent specified in paragraph 4 of that Article or under any other provision similar in substance shall not be allowed in general average.

Rule VII. Damage to Machinery and Boilers

Damage caused to any machinery and boilers of a ship which is ashore and in a position of peril, in endeavouring to refloat, shall be allowed in general average when shown to have arisen from an actual intention to float the ship for the common safety at the risk of such damage; but where a ship is afloat no loss or damage caused by working the propelling machinery and boilers shall in any circumstances be made good as general average.

Rule VIII. Expenses Lightening a Ship when Ashore, and Consequent Damage

When a ship is ashore and cargo and ship's fuel and stores or any of them are discharged as a general average act, the extra cost of lightening, lighter hire and reshipping (if incurred), and any loss or damage to the property involved in the common maritime adventure in consequence thereof, shall be admitted as general average.

Rule IX. Cargo, Ship's Materials and Stores for Fuel

Cargo, ship's materials and stores, or any of them, necessarily used for fuel for the common safety at a time of peril shall be admitted as general average, but when such an allowance is made for the cost of ship's materials and stores the general average shall be credited with the estimated cost of the fuel which would otherwise have been consumed in prosecuting the intended voyage.

Rule X. Expenses at Port of Refuge, etc.

(a) When a ship shall have entered a port or place of refuge or shall have returned to her port or place of loading in consequence of accident, sacrifice or other extraordinary circumstances which render that necessary for the common safety, the expenses of entering such port or place shall be admitted as general average; and when she shall have sailed thence with her original cargo, or a part of it, the corresponding expenses of leaving such port or place consequent upon such entry or return shall likewise be admitted as general average.

When a ship is at any port or place of refuge and is necessarily removed to another port or place because repairs cannot be carried out in the first port or place, the provisions of this Rule shall be applied to the second port or place as if it were a port or place of refuge and the cost of such removal including temporary repairs and towage shall be admitted as general average. The provisions of Rule XI shall be applied to the prolongation of the voyage occasioned by such removal.

(b) The cost of handling on board or discharging cargo, fuel or stores whether at a port or place of loading, call or refuge, shall be admitted as general average, when the handling or discharge was necessary for the common safety or to enable damage to the ship caused by sacrifice or accident to be repaired, if the repairs were necessary for the safe prosecution of the voyage, except in cases where the damage to the ship is discovered at a port or place of loading or call without any accident or other extraordinary circumstance connected with such damage having taken place during the voyage.

The cost of handling on board or discharging cargo, fuel or stores shall not be admissible as general average when incurred solely for the purpose of restowage due to shifting during the voyage, unless such restowage is necessary for the common safety.

(c) Whenever the cost of handling or discharging cargo, fuel or stores is admissible as general average, the costs of storage, including insurance if reasonably incurred, reloading and stowing of such cargo, fuel or stores shall likewise be admitted as general average. The provisions of Rule XI shall be applied to the extra period of detention occasioned by such reloading or restowing.

But when the ship is condemned or does not proceed on her original voyage, storage expenses shall be admitted as general average only up to the date of the ship's condemnation or of the abandonent of the voyage or up to the date of completion of discharge of cargo if the condemnation or abandonment takes place before that date.

Rule XI. Wages and Maintenance of Crew and Other Expenses Bearing up for and in a Port of Refuge, etc.

(a) Wages and maintenance of master, officers and crew reasonably incurred and fuel and stores consumed during the prolongation of the voyage occasioned by a ship entering a port or place of refuge or returning to her port or place of loading shall be admitted as general average when the expenses of entering such port or place are allowable in general average in accordance with Rule X(a).

(b) When a ship shall have entered or been detained in any port or place in consequence of accident, sacrifice or other extraordinary circumstances which render that necessary for the common safety, or to enable damage to the ship caused by sacrifice or accident to be repaired, if the repairs were necessary for the safe prosecution of the voyage, the wages and maintenance of the master, officers and crew reasonably incurred during the extra period of detention in such port or place until the ship shall or should have been made ready to proceed upon her voyage, shall be admitted in general average.

Fuel and stores consumed during the extra period of detention shall be admitted as general average, except such fuel and stores as are consumed in effecting repairs not allowable in general average.

Port charges incurred during the extra period of detention shall likewise be admitted as general average except such charges as are incurred solely by reason of repairs not allowable in general average.

Provided that when damage to the ship is discovered at a port or place of loading or call without any accident or other extraordinary circumstance connected with such damage having taken place during the voyage, then the wages and maintenance of master, officers and crew and fuel and stores consumed and port charges incurred during the extra detention for repairs to damages so discovered shall not be admissible as general average, even if the repairs are necessary for the safe prosecution of the voyage.

When the ship is condemned or does not proceed on her original voyage, the wages and maintenance of the master, officers and crew and fuel and stores consumed and port charges shall be admitted as general average only up to the date of the ship's condemnation or of the abandonment of the voyage or up to the date of completion of discharge of cargo if the condemnation or abandonment takes place before that date.

(c) For the purpose of this and the other Rules wages shall include all payments made to or for the benefit of the master, officers and crew, whether such payments be imposed by law upon the shipowners or be made under the terms or articles of employment.

(d) The cost of measures undertaken to prevent or minimise damage to the environment shall be allowed in general average when incurred in any or all of the following circumstances:

(i) as part of an operation performed for the common safety which, had it been undertaken by a party outside the common maritime adventure, would have entitled such party to a salvage reward;
(ii) as a condition of entry into or departure from any port or place in the circumstances prescribed in Rule X(a);
(iii) as a condition of remaining at any port or place in the circumstances prescribed in Rule XI(b), provided that when there is an actual escape or release of pollutant substances the cost of any additional measures required on that account to prevent or minimise pollution or environmental damage shall not be allowed as general average;
(iv) necessarily in connection with the discharging, storing or reloading of cargo whenever the cost of those operations is admissible as general average.

Rule XII. Damage to Cargo in Discharging, etc.

Damage to or loss or cargo, fuel or stores sustained in consequence of their handling, discharging, storing, reloading and stowing shall be made good as general average, when and only when the cost of those measures respectively is admitted as general average.

Rule XIII. Deductions from Cost of Repairs

Repairs to be allowed in general average shall not be subject to deductions in respect of "new for old" where old material or parts are replaced by new unless the ship is over fifteen years old in which case there shall be a deduction of one third. The deductions shall be regulated by the age of the ship from 31 December of the year of completion of construction to the date of the general average act, except for insulation, life and similar boats, communications and navigational apparatus and equipment, machinery and boilers for which the deductions shall be regulated by the age of the particular parts to which they apply. The deductions shall be made only from the cost of the new material or parts when finished and ready to be installed in the ship.

No deduction shall be made in respect of provisions, stores, anchors and chain cables.

Drydock and slipway dues and costs of shifting the ship shall be allowed in full.

The costs of cleaning, painting or coating of bottom shall not be allowed in general average unless the bottom has been painted or coated within the twelve months preceding the date of the general average act in which case one half of such costs shall be allowed.

Rule XIV. Temporary Repairs

Where temporary repairs are effected to a ship at a port of loading, call or refuge, for the common safety, or of damage caused by general average sacrifice, the cost of such repairs shall be admitted as general average.

Where temporary repairs of accidental damage are effected in order to enable the adventure to be completed, the cost of such repairs shall be admitted as general average without regard to the saving, if any, to other interests, but only up to the saving in expense which would have been incurred and allowed in general average if such repairs had not been effected there.

No deductions "new for old" shall be made from the cost of temporary repairs allowable as general average.

Rule XV. Loss of Freight

Loss of freight arising from damage to or loss of cargo shall be made good as general average, either when caused by a general average act, or when the damage to or loss of cargo is so made good.

Deduction shall be made from the amount of gross freight lost, of the charges which the owner thereof would have incurred to earn such freight, but has, in consequence of the sacrifice, not incurred.

Rule XVI. Amount to be Made Good for Cargo Lost or Damaged by Sacrifice

The amount to be made good as general average for damage to or loss of cargo sacrificed shall be the loss which has been sustained thereby based on the value at the time of discharge, ascertained from the commercial invoice rendered to the receiver or if there is no such invoice from the shipped value. The value at the time of discharge shall include the cost of insurance and freight except insofar as such freight is at the risk of interests other than the cargo.

When cargo so damaged is sold and the amount of the damage has not been otherwise agreed, the loss to be made good in general average shall be the difference between the net proceeds of sale and the net sound value as computed in the first paragraph of this Rule.

Rule XVII. Contributory Values

The contribution to a general average shall be made upon the actual net values of the property at the termination of the adventure except that the value of cargo shall be the value at the time of discharge, ascertained from the commercial invoice rendered to the receiver or if there is no such invoice from the shipped value. The value of the cargo shall include the cost of insurance and freight unless and insofar as such freight is at the risk of interests other than the cargo, deducting therefrom any loss or damage suffered by the cargo prior to or at the time of discharge. The value of the ship shall be assessed without taking into account the beneficial or detrimental effect of any demise or time charterparty to which the ship may be committed.

To these values shall be added the amount made good as general average for property sacrificed, if not already included, deduction being made from the freight and passage money at risk of such charges and crew's wages as would not have been incurred in earning the freight had the ship and cargo been totally lost at the date of the general average act and have not been allowed as general average; deduction being also made from the value of the property of all extra charges incurred in respect thereof subsequently to the general average act, except such charges as are allowed in general average or fall upon the ship by virtue of an award for special compensation under Article 14 of the International Convention on Salvage, 1989 or under any other provision similar in substance.

In the circumstances envisaged in the third paragraph of Rule G, the cargo and other property shall contribute on the basis of its value upon delivery at original destination unless sold or otherwise disposed of short of that destination, and the ship shall contribute upon its actual net value at the time of completion of discharge of cargo.

Where cargo is sold short of destination, however, it shall contribute upon the actual net proceeds of sale, with the addition of any amount made good as general average.

Mails, passengers' luggage, personal effects and accompanied private motor vehicles shall not contribute in general average.

Rule XVIII. Damage to Ship

The amount to be allowed as general average for damage or loss to the ship, her machinery and/or gear caused by a general average act shall be as follows:

(a) When repaired or replaced,

The actual reasonable cost of repairing or replacing such damage or loss, subject to deductions in accordance with Rule XIII;

(b) When not repaired or replaced,

The reasonable depreciation arising from such damage or loss, but not exceeding the estimated cost of repairs. But where the ship is an actual total loss or when the cost of repairs of the damage would exceed the value of the ship when repaired, the amount to be allowed as general average shall be the difference between the estimated sound value of the ship after deducting therefrom the estimated cost of repairing damage which is not general average and the value of the ship in her damaged state which may be measured by the net proceeds of sale, if any.

Rule XIX. Undeclared or Wrongfully Declared Cargo

Damage or loss caused to goods loaded without the knowledge of the shipowner or his agent or to goods wilfully misdescribed at time of shipment shall not be allowed as general average, but such goods shall remain liable to contribute, if saved.

Damage or loss caused to goods which have been wrongfully declared on shipment at a value which is lower than their real value shall be contributed for at the declared value, but such goods shall contribute upon their actual value.

Rule XX. Provision of Funds

A commission of 2 per cent on general average disbursements, other than the wages and maintenance of master, officers and crew and fuel and stores not replaced during the voyage, shall be allowed in general average.

The capital loss sustained by the owners of goods sold for the purpose of raising funds to defray general average disbursements shall be allowed in general average.

The cost of insuring general average disbursements shall also be admitted in general average.

Rule XXI. Interest on Losses Made Good in General Average

Interest shall be allowed on expenditure, sacrifices and allowances in general average at the rate of 7 per cent per annum, until three months after the date of issue of the general average adjustment, due allowance being made for any payment on account by the contributory interests or from the general average deposit fund.

Rule XXII. Treatment of Cash Deposits

Where cash deposits have been collected in respect of cargo's liability for general average, salvage or special charges, such deposits shall be paid without any delay into a special account in the joint names of a representative nominated on behalf of the shipowner and a representative nominated on behalf of the depositors in a bank to be approved by both. The sum so deposited, together with accrued interest, if any, shall be held as security for payment to the parties entitled thereto of the general average, salvage or special charges payable by cargo in respect to which the deposits have been collected. Payments on account or refunds of deposits may be made if certified to in writing by the average adjuster. Such deposits and payments or refunds shall be without prejudice to the ultimate liability of the parties.

APPENDIX 3

RULES OF PRACTICE OF THE ASSOCIATION OF AVERAGE ADJUSTERS*

Section A—General Rules

A1 Adjustments for the Consideration of Underwriters

That any claim prepared for the consideration of underwriters shall include a statement of the reasons of the average adjuster for stating such a claim, and when submitted in conjunction with a claim for which underwriters are liable, shall be shown in such a manner as clearly to distinguish the claim for consideration from other claims embodied in the same adjustment.

A2 Interest and Commission for Advancing Funds

That, in practice, interest and commission for advancing funds are only allowable in average when, proper and necessary steps having been taken to make a collection on account, an out-of-pocket expense for interest and/or commission for advancing funds is reasonably incurred.

A3 Agency Commission and Agency

That, in practice, neither commission (excepting bank commission) nor any charge by way of agency or remuneration for trouble is allowed to the shipowner in average, except in respect of services rendered on behalf of cargo when such services are not involved in the contract of affreightment.

A4 Duty of Adjusters in Respect of Cost of Repairs

That in adjusting particular average on ship or general average which includes repairs, it is the duty of the adjuster to satisfy himself that such reasonable and usual precautions have been taken to keep down the cost of repairs as a prudent shipowner would have taken if uninsured.

A5 Claims on Ship's Machinery

That in all claims on ship's machinery for repairs, no claim for a new propeller or new shaft shall be admitted into an adjustment, unless the adjuster shall obtain and insert into his statement evidence showing what has become of the old propeller or shaft.

A6 Water Casks

Water casks or tanks carried on a ship's deck are not paid for by underwriters as general or particular average; nor are warps or other articles when improperly carried on deck.

A7 Adjustment; Policies of Insurance and Names of Underwriters

That no adjustment shall be drawn up showing the amount of payments by or to the underwriters, unless the policies or copies of the policies of insurance or certificates of

---

* Reproduced with the kind permission of the Association of Average Adjusters.

insurance, for which the statement is required, be produced to the average adjusters. Such statement shall set out sufficient details of the underwriters interested and the amounts due on the respective policies produced.

A8 Apportionment of Costs in Collision Cases

That when a vessel sustains and does damage by collision, and litigation consequently results for the purpose of testing liability, the technicality of the vessel having been plaintiff or defendant in the litigation shall not necessarily govern the apportionment of the costs of such litigation, which shall be apportioned between claim and counterclaim in proportion to the amount, excluding interest, which has been or would have been allowed in respect of each in the event of the claim or counterclaim being established; provided that when a claim or counterclaim is made solely for the purpose of defence, and is not allowed, the costs apportioned thereto shall be treated as costs of defence.

A9 Franchise Charges

The expenses of protest, survey, and other proofs of loss, including the commission or other expenses of a sale by auction, are not admitted to make up the percentage of a claim; and are only paid by the underwriters in case the loss amounts to a claim without them.

Section B—General Average
Rules of General Application

Note: In this edition of the Rules of Practice, the Rules relating to the adjustment of general average under English law and practice have been transferred to Section F.

B1 Basis of Adjustment

That in any adjustment of general average not made in accordance with British law it shall be prefaced on what principle or according to what law the adjustment has been made, and the reason for so adjusting the claim shall be set forth.

In all cases the adjuster shall give particulars in a prominent position in the average statement of the clause or clauses contained in the charterparty and/or bills of lading with reference to the adjustment of general average.

B2–B8 inclusive—transferred to section F

B9 Claims Arising out of Deficiency of Fuel

That in adjusting general average arising out of deficiency of fuel, the facts on which the general average is based shall be set forth in the adjustment, including the material dates and distances, and particulars of fuel supplies and consumption.

B10–B23 inclusive—transferred to section F

B24 Contributory Value of Ship

That in any adjustment of general average there shall be set forth the certificate on which the contributory value of the ship is based or, if there be no such certificate, the information adopted in lieu thereof, and any amount made good shall be specified.

B25 Contributory Value of Freight

That in any adjustment of general average there shall be set forth the amount of the gross freight and the freight advanced, if any; also the charges and wages deducted and any amount made good.

The first paragraph of Rule B25, dealing with the basis of adjustment under English law and practice, has been transferred to Section F and renumbered F22.

B26 Vessel in Ballast and under Charter: Contributing Interests

For the purpose of ascertaining the liability of Underwriters on British policies of insurance, the following provisions shall apply:—

When a vessel is proceeding in ballast to load under a voyage charter entered into by the shipowner before the general average act, the interests contributing to the general average shall be the vessel, such items of stores and equipment as belong to parties other than the owners of the vessel (e.g. bunkers, wireless installation and navigational instruments) and the freight earned under the voyage charter computed in the usual way after deduction of contingent expenses subsequent to the general average act. Failing a prior termination of the adventure, the place where the adventure shall be deemed to end and at which the values for contribution to general average shall be calculated is the final port of discharge of the cargo carried under the charter but in the event of the prior loss of the vessel and freight, or either of them, the general average shall attach to any surviving interest or interests including freight advanced at the loading port deducting therefrom contingent expenses subsequent to the general average act.

When a vessel is proceeding in ballast under a time charter alone or a time charter and a voyage charter entered into by the time charterer, the general average shall attach to the vessel and such items of stores and equipment as are indicated above. Failing a prior termination of the adventure, the adventure shall be deemed to end and the values for contribution to general average calculated at the first loading port upon the commencement of loading cargo.

When the charter to which the shipowner is a party provides for York-Antwerp Rules, the general average shall be adjusted in accordance with those Rules and British law and practice and without regard to the law and practice of any foreign port at which the adventure may terminate; and in the interpretation of Rule XI it shall be immaterial whether the extra period of detention takes place at a port of loading, call or refuge, provided that the detention is in consequence of accident, sacrifice or other extraordinary circumstance occurring whilst the vessel is in ballast.

In practice neither time charter hire, as such, nor time charterer's voyage freight shall contribute to general average.

B27 Ulterior Chartered Freight: Contribution to General Average

That when at the time of a general average act the vessel has on board cargo shipped under charterparty or bills of lading, and is also under a separate charter to load another cargo after the cargo then in course of carriage has been discharged, the ulterior chartered freight shall not contribute to the general average.

B28 Deductions from Freight at Charterer's Risk

That freight at the risk of the charterer shall be subject to no deduction for wages and charges, except in the case of charters in which the wages or charges are payable by the charterer, in which case such freight shall be governed by the same rule as freight at the risk of the shipowner.

B29 Forwarding Charges on Advanced Freight

That in case of wreck, the cargo being forwarded to its destination, the charterer, who has paid a lump sum on account of freight, which is not to be returned in the event of the vessel being lost, shall not be liable for any portion of the forwarding freight and charges, when the same are less than the balance of freight payable to the shipowner at the port of destination under the original charterparty.

B30 Sacrifice for the Common Safety: Direct Liability of Underwriters

That in case of general average sacrifice there is, under ordinary policies of insurance, a direct liability of an underwriter on ship for loss of or damage to ship's materials, and of an underwiter on goods or freight, for loss of or damage to goods or loss of freight so sacrificed as a general average loss; that such loss not being particular average is not taken into account in computing the memorandum percentages, and that the direct liability of an underwriter for such loss is consequently unaffected by the memorandum or any other warranty respecting particular average.

B31 Sacrifice of Ship's Stores: Direct Liability of Underwriters

That underwriters insuring ship's stores, bunker coal or fuel, destroyed or used as part of a general average operation, shall only be liable for those articles as a direct claim on the policy when they formed part of the property at risk at the time of the peril giving rise to the general average act.

B32 Enforcement of General Average Lien by Shipowners

That in all cases where general average damage to ship is claimed direct from the underwriters on that interest, the average adjusters shall ascertain whether the shipowners have taken the necessary steps to enforce their lien for general average on the cargo, and shall insert in the average statement a note giving the result of their enquiries.

B33 Underwriter's Liability

If the ship or cargo be insured for more than its contributory value, the underwriter pays what is assessed on the contributory value. But where insured for less than the contributory value, the underwriter pays on the insured value; and when there has been a particular average for damage which forms a deduction from the contributory value of the ship that must be deducted from the insured value to find upon what the underwriter contributes.

This rule does not apply to foreign adjustments, when the basis of contribution is something other than the net value of the thing insured.

That in practice, in applying the above rule for the purpose of ascertaining the liability of underwriters for contribution to general average and salvage charges, deduction shall be made from the insured value of all losses and charges for which underwriters are liable and which have been deducted in arriving at the contributory value.

In adjusting the liability of underwriters on freight for general average contribution and salvage charges, effect shall be given to Section 73 of the Marine Insurance Act, 1906, by comparing the gross and not the net amount of freight at risk with the insured value in the case of a valued policy or the insurable value in the case of an unvalued policy.

B34 The Duty of Adjusters in Cases Involving Refunds of General Average Deposits or Apportionment of Salvage, Collision Recoveries, or other Funds

That in cases of general average where deposits have been collected and it is likely that repayments will have to be made, measures be taken by the adjuster to ascertain the names of underwriters who have reimbursed their assured in respect of such deposits; that the names of any such underwriters be set forth in the adjustment as claimants of refund, if any, to which they are apparently entitled; and that on completion of the adjustment, notice be sent to all underwriters whose names are so set forth as to any refund of which they appear as claimants and as to the steps to be taken in order to obtain payment of the same.

That in cases where the names of any underwriters are not to be ascertained on completion of the adjustment, notice be sent to the Secretary of Lloyd's, to the Institute of London Underwriters, to the Liverpool Underwriters' Association, and to the Association of Underwriters of Glasgow, notifying such interests as have not been appropriated to underwriters.

And that in cases of apportionment of salvage or other funds for distribution, similar measures be taken by the adjuster to safeguard the interests of any underwriters who may be entitled to benefit under the apportionment.

B35 Memorandum to Statements showing Refunds in respect of General Average Deposits

That the following memorandum shall appear at the end of statements which show refunds to be due in respect of General Average Deposits, viz:—
> Memorandum—Refunds of general average deposits shown in this statement should only be paid on production of the original deposit receipts.

B36 Interest on Deposits

That, unless otherwise expressly provided, the interest accrued on deposits on account of salvage and/or general average and/or particular and/or other charges, or on the balance of such deposits after payments on account, if any, have been made, shall be credited to the depositor or those to whom his rights in respect of the deposits have been transferred.

B37 Apportionment of Interest on Amounts Made Good

That in practice (in the absence of express agreement between the parties concerned) interest allowed on amounts made good shall be apportioned between assured and underwriters, taking into account the sums paid by underwriters and the dates when such payments were made, notwithstanding that by the addition of interest the underwriter may receive a larger sum than he has paid.

Section C—York-Antwerp Rules

C1 Salvage Services Rendered under an Agreement

Expenses for salvage services rendered by or accepted under agreement shall in practice be treated as general average provided that such expenses were incurred for the common safety within the meaning of Rule "A" of the York-Antwerp Rules 1924 or York-Antwerp Rules 1950.

C2 Commission Allowed under York-Antwerp Rules

That the commission of 2 per cent allowed on general average disbursements under the York-Antwerp Rules shall be credited in full to the party who has authorised the expenditure and is liable for payment except where the funds for payment are provided in the first instance in whole or in part from the deposit funds, or by other parties to the adventure, or by underwriters, the commission on such advances shall be credited to the deposit funds or to the parties or underwriters providing funds for payment.

C3 York-Antwerp Rules, 1924. Rules X(a) and XX

That, in practice, where a vessel is at any port or place in circumstances in which the wages and maintenance of crew during detention there for the purpose of repairs necessary for the safe prosecution of the voyage would be admissible in general average under Rule XI of the York-Antwerp Rules, 1924, and the vessel is necessarily removed thence to another port or place because such repairs cannot be effected at the first port or place, the provisions of Rule X(a) shall be applied to the second port or place as if it were a port or place of refuge within that Rule and the provisions of Rule XX shall be applied to the prolongation of the voyage occasioned by such removal.

C4 York-Antwerp Rules 1950, 1974 and 1994—Rule X(a)

That in practice, in applying the second paragraph of Rule X(a), a vessel shall be deemed to be at a port or place of refuge when she is at any port or place in circumstances in which the wages and maintenance of the Master, Officers and crew incurred during any extra period of detention there would be admissible in General Average under the provisions of Rule XI.

Section D—Damage and Repairs to Ship

D1 Expenses of Removing a Vessel for Repair

1. For the purpose of ascertaining the reasonable cost of repairs, and subject to any express provisions in the policy, where a vessel is at any port place or location (herinafter referred to as "port") and is necessarily or reasonably removed to some other port for the purpose of repairs, either because the repairs cannot be effected at the first port, or cannot be effected prudently, the additional expenses reasonably incurred by the shipowner in removing the vessel (other than any expenses allowable in general average) shall be treated as part of the reasonable cost of repairs.

2. (a) Where the vessel after repairing forthwith returns to the port from which she was removed, the expenses incurred both in removing the vessel to the port of repair and in returning shall be treated as part of the expenses of removal.

   (b) Where the vessel loads a new cargo at the port of repair or proceeds thence to some other port for the same purpose, the expenses shall be calculated as though, but for the repairs, the vessel had previously been engaged to proceed direct from the port from which she was removed to the loading port.

   (c) Where, immediately following a casualty, or upon completion of the voyage on which the casualty occurred, the vessel is removed solely to enable repairs to be effected which are essential for continued trading, the expenses may, at the owners' option, be calculated only for the single passage to the repair port.

3. (a) The expenses of removal shall include, inter alia, the cost of any necessary temporary repairs, wages and provisions of crew and/or runners, pilotage, towage, extra marine insurance, port charges, bunkers and stores.

   (b) Where by moving the vessel to or from the port of repair any new freight or hire is earned, such net earnings shall be deducted from the expenses of removal.

4. The expenses of removing the vessel for repairs shall be charged as follows:

   (a) Where the vessel is removed to the port of repair as an immediate consequence of damage for the repair of which underwriters are liable, or the vessel is necessarily taken out of service especially to effect repairs arising from that damage, the whole cost of removal shall be treated as part of the cost of repairing that damage, notwithstanding that the shipowner may have taken advantage of the removal to carry out survey for classification purposes or to effect other average repairs or repairs on his own account.

   However, where the vessel is removed for owners' purposes, other than a routine overhaul as in 4(b) below, or as an immediate consequence of damage for which underwriters are not liable, no part of the cost of removal shall be charged to underwriters, notwithstanding that repairs for which they are liable may be carried out at the port of repair.

(b) Where the vessel is removed to the port of repair for routine overhaul at which repairs on both owners' and underwriters' accounts are effected, the expenses of removal shall be apportioned pro rata to the cost (including drydock dues and general services) of all work effected at the port, other than to any damage sustained after the commencement of the removal passage and the cost of any major parts shipped to the repair port from elsewhere.

D2 Fuel and Stores used in Repairs of Damage to the Vessel

That the cost of replacing fuel and stores consumed either in the repair of damage to a vessel, in working the engines or winches to assist in the repairs of damage, or in moving her to a place of repair within the limits of the port where she is lying, shall be treated as part of the cost of repairs.

D3 Rigging Chafed

Rigging injured by straining or chafing is not charged to underwriters, unless such injury is caused by blows of the sea, grounding, or contact; or by displacement, through sea peril, of the spars, channels, bulwarks, or rails.

D4 Sails Split or Blown Away

Sails split by the wind, or blown away while set, unless occasioned by the ship's grounding or coming into collision, or in consequence of damage to the spars to which the sails are bent, are not charged to underwriters.

D5 Dry Dock Expenses

1. That, in practice, where repairs, for the cost of which underwriters are liable, are necessarily effected in dry dock as an immediate consequence of the casualty, or the vessel is taken out of service especially to effect such repairs in dry dock, the cost of entering and leaving the dry dock, in addition to so much of the dock dues as is necessary for the repair of the damage, shall be chargeable in full to the underwriters, notwithstanding that the shipowner may have taken advantage of the vessel being in dry dock to carry out survey for classification purposes or to effect repairs on his account which are not immediately necessary to make the vessel seaworthy.

2. (a) Where repairs on Owners' account which are immediately necessary to make the vessel seaworthy and which can only be effected in dry dock are executed concurrently with other repairs, for the cost of which underwriters are liable, and which also can only be effected in dry dock,

(b) Where the repairs, for the cost of which underwriters are liable, are deferred until a routine dry-docking and are then executed concurrently with repairs on Owners' account which require the use of the dry dock, whether or not such Owners' repairs affect the seaworthiness of the vessel,

the cost of entering and leaving the dry dock, in addition to so much of the dock dues as is common to both repairs, shall be divided equally between the shipowner and the underwriters, irrespective of the fact that the repairs for which underwriters are liable may relate to more than one voyage or accident or may be payable by more than one set of underwriters.

3. Sub-division between underwriters of the proportion of dry-docking expenses chargeable to them shall be made on the basis of voyages, and/or such other franchise units as are specified in the policies.

4. In determining whether the franchise is reached the whole cost of dry-docking necessary for the repair of the damage, less the proportion (if any) chargeable to Owners

when Section (a) of paragraph 2 applies, shall be taken into consideration, notwithstanding that there are other damages to which a portion of the cost of dry-docking has to be apportioned in ascertaining the amount actually recoverable.

D6 Tankers—Treatment of the Cost of Tank Cleaning and/or Gas-Freeing

1. That, in practice, where repairs, for the cost of which underwriters are liable, require the tanks to be rough cleaned and/or gas-freed as an immediate consequence of the casualty, or the vessel is taken out of service especially to effect such repairs, the cost of such rough cleaning and/or gas-freeing shall be chargeable in full to the underwriters, notwithstanding that the shipowner may have taken advantage of the vessel being rough cleaned and/or gas-freed to carry out survey for classification purposes or to effect repairs on his account which are not immediately necessary to make the vessel seaworthy.

2. (a) Where repairs on Owners' account which are immediately necessary to make the vessel seaworthy and which require the tanks being rough cleaned and/or gas-freed and executed concurrently with other repairs, for the cost of which underwriters are liable and which also require the tanks being rough cleaned and/or gas-freed,

   (b) Where the repairs, for the cost of which underwriters are liable, are deferred until a routine dry-docking or repair period, at which time repairs on Owners' account which also require the tanks being rough cleaned and/or gas-freed are effected, whether or not such Owners' repairs affect the seaworthiness of the vessel,

the cost of such rough cleaning and/or gas-freeing as is common to both repairs shall be divided equally between the shipowners and the underwriters, irrespective of the fact that the repairs for which underwriters are liable may relate to more than one voyage or accident or may be payable by more than one set of underwriters.

3. The cost of fine cleaning specifically for a particular repair or particular repairs shall be divided in accordance with the principles set forth above.

4. Sub-division between underwriters of the proportion of rough tank cleaning and/or gas-freeing and/or fine cleaning chargeable to them shall be made on the basis of voyages, and/or such other franchise units as are specified in the policies.

5. In determining whether the franchise is reached the whole cost of rough cleaning and/or gas-freeing and/or fine cleaning necessary for the repair of the damage, less the proportion (if any) chargeable to Owners when Section (a) of paragraph 2 applies, shall be taken into consideration, notwithstanding that there are other damages to which a portion of the cost of rough tank cleaning and/or gas-freeing and/or fine cleaning has to be apportioned in ascertaining the amount actually recoverable.

D7 Particular Average on Ship: Deduction of One-Third

The deduction for new work in place of old is fixed by custom at one-third, with the following exceptions:

Anchors are allowed in full. Chain cables are subject to one-sixth only. Metal sheathing is dealt with, by allowing in full the cost of a weight equal to the gross weight of metal sheathing stripped off minus the proceeds of the old metal. Nails, felt, and labour metalling are subject to one-third.

The rule applies to iron as well as to wooden ships, and to labour as well as material. It does not apply to the expense of straightening bent ironwork, and to the labour of taking out and replacing it.

It does not apply to graving dock expenses and removals, cartages, use of shears, stages, and graving dock materials.

It does not apply to a ship's first voyage.

D8 Scraping and Painting

Where the Policy includes a Clause to the effect that:
"No claim shall in any case be allowed in respect of scraping or painting the vessel's bottom".
  (a) Gritblasting and/or other surface preparation of new bottom plates ashore and supplying and applying any "shop" primer thereto
  (b) Gritblasting and/or other surface preparation of:
      (i) the butts or area of plating immediately adjacent to any renewed or refitted plating damaged during the course of welding and/or repairs
      (ii) areas of plating damaged during the course of fairing, either in place or ashore
  (c) Supplying and applying the first coat of primer/anticorrosive to those particular areas mentioned in (a) and (b) above
shall be allowed as part of the reasonable cost of repairs in respect of bottom plating damaged by an insured peril and shall be deemed not to be excluded by the wording of this Clause. The gritblasting and/or other surface preparation and the painting of all other areas of the bottom is excluded by the Clause.

Section E—Particular Average on Goods

E1 Adjustment on Bonded Prices

In the following cases it is customary to adjust particular average on a comparison of bonded, instead of duty-paid prices:
   In claims for damage to tea, tobacco, coffee, wine, and spirits imported into this country.

E2 Adjustment of Average on Goods Sold in Bond

That in consequence of the facilities generally offered to bond goods at their destination, at which terms they are often sold, the term "Gross Proceeds" shall, for the purpose of adjustment, be taken to mean the price at which the goods are sold to the consumer, after payment of freight and landing charges, but exclusive of Customs duty, in cases where it is the custom of the port to sell or deal with the goods in bond.

E3 Apportionment of Insured Value of Goods

That where different qualities or descriptions of cargo are valued in the policy at a lump sum, such sum shall, for the purpose of adjusting claims, be apportioned on the invoice values where the invoice distinguishes the separate values of the said different qualities or descriptions; and over the net arrived sound values in all other cases.

E4 Allowance for Water and/or Impurities in Picked Cotton

When bales of cotton are picked, and the pickings are sold wet, the allowance for water in the pickings (where there are no means of ascertaining it) is by custom fixed at one-third.
   There is a similar custom to deduct one-sixth from the gross weight of pickings of country damaged cotton to take account of dirt, moisture and other impurities.

E5 Allowance for Water in Cut Tobacco

When damaged tobacco is cut off, the allowance for water in the cuttings is one-fourth if the actual increase cannot be ascertained.

E6 Allowance for Water in Wool

Damaged wool from Australia, New Zealand, and the Cape is subject to a deduction of 3 per cent for wet, if the actual increase cannot be ascertained.

Section F—General Average Adjustment Under English Law and Practice

F1 Deckload Jettison

The jettison of a deckload carried according to the usage of trade and not in violation of the contracts of affreightment is general average.

There is an exception to this rule in the case of cargoes of cotton, tallow, acids and some other goods.

F2 Damage by Water Used to Extinguish Fire

That damage done by water poured down a ship's hold to extinguish a fire be treated as general average.

F3 Extinguishing Fire on Shipboard

Damage done to a ship and cargo, or either of them, by water or otherwise, including damage by beaching or scuttling a burning ship, in extinguishing a fire on board the ship, shall be made good as general average; except that no compensation shall be made for damage by smoke or heat however caused.

F4 Voluntary Stranding

When a ship is intentionally run on shore for the common safety, whether or not she might have been driven on shore, the consequent loss or damage shall be allowed as general average.

F5 Expenses Lightening a Ship when Ashore

When a ship is ashore in a position of peril and, in order to float her, cargo is put into lighters, and is then at once re-shipped, the whole cost of lightering, including lighter hire and re-shipping, is general average.

F6 Sails Set to Force a Ship off the Ground

Sails damaged by being set, or kept set, to force a ship off the ground or to drive her higher up the ground for the common safety, are general average.

F7 Stranded Vessels: Damage to Engines in Getting Off

That damage caused to machinery and boilers of a stranded vessel, in endeavouring to refloat for the common safety, when the interests are in peril, be allowed in general average.

F8 Resort to Port of Refuge for General Average Repairs: Treatment of the Charges Incurred

That when a ship puts into a port of refuge in consequence of damage which is itself the subject of general average, and sails thence with her original cargo, or a part of it, the outward as well as the inward port charges shall be treated as general average; and when cargo is discharged for the purpose of repairing such damage, the warehouse rent and reloading of the same shall, as well as the discharge, be treated as general average. (See *Atwood* v. *Sellar*.)

F9 Resort to Port of Refuge on Account of Particular Average Repairs: Treatment of the Charges Incurred

That when a ship puts into a port of refuge in consequence of damage which is itself the subject of particular average (or not of general average) and when the cargo has been discharged in consequence of such damage, the inward port charges and the cost of discharging the cargo shall be general average, the warehouse rent of cargo shall be a particular charge on cargo, and the cost of reloading and outward port charges shall be a particular charge on freight. (See *Svendsen* v. *Wallace*.)

F10 Treatment of Costs of Storage and Reloading at Port of Refuge

That when the cargo is discharged for the purpose of repairing, reconditioning, or diminishing damage to ship or cargo which is itself the subject of general average, the cost of storage on it and of reloading it shall be treated as general average, equally with the cost of discharging it.

F11 Insurance on Cargo Discharged under Average

That in practice, where the cost of insurance has been reasonably incurred by the shipowner, or his agents, on cargo discharged under average, such cost shall be treated as part of the cost of storage.

F12 Expenses at a Port of Refuge

When a ship puts into a port of refuge on account of accident and not in consequence of damage which is itself the subject of general average, then on the assumption that the ship was seaworthy at the commencement of the voyage, the Custom of Lloyd's is as follows:

(a) All cost of towage, pilotage, harbour dues, and other extraordinary expenses incurred in order to bring the ship and cargo into a place of safety, are general average. Under the term "extraordinary expenses" are not included wages or victuals of crew, coals, or engine stores, or demurrage.

(b) The cost of discharging the cargo, whether for the common safety, or to repair the ship, together with the cost of conveying it to the warehouse, is general average.

The cost of discharging the cargo on account of damage to it resulting from its own *vice propre*, is chargeable to the owners of the cargo.

(c) The warehouse rent, or other expenses which take the place of warehouse rent, of the cargo when so discharged is, except as under, a special charge on the cargo.

(d) The cost of reloading the cargo, and the outward port charges incurred through leaving the port of refuge, are, when the discharge of cargo falls in general average, a special charge on freight.

(e) The expenses referred to in clause (d) are charged to the party who runs the risk of freight—that is, wholly to the charterer—if the whole freight has been prepaid; and, if part only, then in the proportion which the part prepaid bears to the whole freight.

(f) When the cargo, instead of being sent ashore, is placed on board hulk or lighters during the ship's stay in port, the hulk-hire is divided between general average, cargo, and freight, in such proportions as may place the several contributing interests in nearly the same relative positions as if the cargo has been landed and stored.

AAA RULES OF PRACTICE

F13 Treatment of Costs of Extraordinary Discharge

That no distinction be drawn in practice between discharging cargo for the common safety of ship and cargo, and discharging it for the purpose of effecting at an intermediate port or ports of refuge repairs necessary for the prosecution of the voyage.

F14 Towage from a Port of Refuge

That if a ship be in a port of refuge at which it is practicable to repair her, and if, in order to save expense, she be towed thence to some other port, then the extra cost of such towage shall be divided in proportion to the saving of expense thereby occasioned to the several parties to the adventure.

F15 Cargo Forwarded from a Port of Refuge

That if a ship be in a port of refuge at which it is practicable to repair her so as to enable her to carry on the whole cargo, but, in order to save expense, the cargo, or a portion of it, be transhipped by another vessel, or otherwise forwarded, then the cost of such transhipment (up to the amount of expense saved) shall be divided in proportion to the saving expense thereby occasioned to the several parties to the adventure.

F16 Cargo Sold at a Port of Refuge

That if a ship be in a port of refuge at which it is practicable to repair her so as to enable her to carry on the whole cargo, or such portion of it as is fit to be carried on, but, in order to save expense, the cargo, or a portion of it, be, with the consent of the owners of such cargo, sold at the port of refuge, then the loss by sale including loss of freight on cargo so sold (up to the amount of expense saved) shall be divided in proportion to the saving of expense thereby occasioned to the several parties to the adventure; provided always that the amount so divided shall in no case exceed the cost of transhipment and/or forwarding referred to in the preceding rule of the Association.

F17 Interpretation of the Rule respecting Substituted Expenses

That for the purpose of avoiding any misinterpretation of the resolution relating to the apportionment of substituted expenses, it is declared that the saving of expense therein mentioned is limited to a saving or reduction of the actual outlay, including the crew's wages and provisions, if any, which would have been incurred at the port of refuge, if the vessel has been repaired there, and does not include supposed losses or expenses, such as interest, loss of market, demurrage, or assumed damage by discharging.

F18 Damage to Cargo, Fuel and Stores in Discharging, etc.

Damage to or loss of cargo, fuel and stores sustained in consequence of their handling, discharging, storing, reloading and stowing shall be made good as general average, when and only when the cost of those measures respectively is admitted as general average.

F19 Deductions from Cost of Repairs in Adjusting General Average

Repairs to be allowed in general average shall not be subject to deductions in respect of "new for old" where old materials or parts are replaced by new unless the ship is over fifteen years old in which case there shall be a deduction of one third. The deductions shall be regulated by the age of the ship from the 31st December of the year of completion of construction to the date of the general average act, except for insulation, life and similar boats, communications and navigational apparatus and equipment, machinery and boilers for which the deductions shall be regulated by the age of the particular parts to which they apply.

The deductions shall be made only from the cost of the new material or parts when finished and ready to be installed in the ship.

No deduction shall be made in respect of provisions, stores, anchors and chain cables.

Drydock and slipway dues and costs of shifting the ship shall be allowed in full.

The costs of cleaning, painting or coating of bottom shall not be allowed in general average unless the bottom has been painted or coated within the twelve months preceding the date of the general average act in which case one half of such costs shall be allowed.

F20 Freight Sacrificed: Amount to be Made Good in General Average

That the loss of freight to be made good in general average shall be ascertained by deducting from the amount of gross freight lost the charges which the owner thereof would have incurred to earn such freight, but has, in consequence of the sacrifice, not incurred.

F21 Basis of Contribution to General Average

When property saved by a general average act is injured or destroyed by subsequent accident, the contributing value of that property to a general average which is less than the total contributing value, shall, when it does not reach the port of destination, be its actual net proceeds; when it does it shall be its actual net value at the port of destination on its delivery there; and in all cases any values allowed in general average shall be added to and form part of the contributing value as above.

The above rule shall not apply to adjustments made before the adventure has terminated.

F22 Contributory Value of Freight

That freight at the risk of the shipowner shall contribute to general average upon its gross amount, deducting such charges and crew's wages as would not have been incurred in earning the freight had the ship and cargo been totally lost at the date of the general average act and have not been allowed as general average.

Uniformity Resolutions

York-Antwerp Rules 1924: Application of Rule XIV

That, in practice, in applying Rule XIV of the York-Antwerp Rules, 1924, the cost of the temporary repair of the accidental damage there referred to shall be allowed in general average up to the saving to the general average by effecting such temporary repair, without regard to the saving (if any) to other interests.

York-Antwerp Rules 1974: Application of Rule XIV

That, in practice, in considering the saving in expense referred to in the second paragraph of Rule XIV of York-Antwerp Rules 1974, the determination as to whether permanent repairs would have been necessary for the safe prosecution of the voyage shall not be affected by the fact that temporary repairs were practicable.

APPENDIX 4

INSTITUTE CLAUSES*

INSTITUTE TIME CLAUSES—HULLS
(CL.280—Institute of London Underwriters and Witherby & Co Ltd)

1/11/95 (FOR USE ONLY WITH THE CURRENT MAR POLICY FORM)

"These clauses are purely illustrative. Different policy conditions may be agreed. The specimen clauses are available to any interested person upon request. In particular:
  (a) in relation to any clause which excludes losses from the cover, insurers may agree a separate insurance policy covering such losses or may extend the clause to cover such events;
  (b) in relation to clauses making cover of certain risks subject to specific conditions each insurer may alter the said conditions".

This insurance is subject to English law and practice

1 Navigation

1.1 The Vessel is covered subject to the provisions of this insurance at all times and has leave to sail or navigate with or without pilots, to go on trial trips and to assist and tow vessels or craft in distress, but it is warranted that the Vessel shall not be towed, except as is customary or to the first safe port or place when in need of assistance, or undertake towage or salvage services under a contract previously arranged by the Assured and/or Owners and/or Managers and/or Charterers. This Clause 1.1 shall not exclude customary towage in connection with loading and discharging.
1.2 This insurance shall not be prejudiced by reason of the Assured entering into any contract with pilots or for customary towage which limits or exempts the liability of the pilots and/or tugs and/or towboats and/or their owners when the Assured or their agents accept or are compelled to accept such contracts in accordance with established local law or practice.
1.3 The practice of engaging helicopters for the transportation of personnel, supplies and equipment to and/or from the Vessel shall not prejudice this insurance.
1.4 In the event of the Vessel being employed in trading operations which entail cargo loading or discharging at sea from or into another vessel (not being a harbour or inshore craft) no claim shall be recoverable under this insurance for loss of or damage to the Vessel or liability to any other vessel arising from such loading or discharging operations, including whilst approaching, lying alongside and leaving, unless previous notice that the Vessel is to be employed in such operations has been given to the Underwriters and any amended terms of cover and any additional premium required by them have been agreed.
1.5 In the event of the Vessel sailing (with or without cargo) with an intention of being (a) broken up, or (b) sold for breaking up, any claim for loss of or damage to the

---

* The Institute clauses are reproduced with the kind permission of The Institute of London Underwriters and Witherby & Co Ltd.

Vessel occurring subsequent to such sailing shall be limited to the market value of the Vessel as scrap at the time when the loss or damage is sustained, unless previous notice has been given to the Underwriters and any amendments to the terms of cover, insured value and premium required by them have been agreed. Nothing in this Clause 1.5 shall affect claims under Clauses 8 and/or 10.

2 Continuation

Should the Vessel at the expiration of this insurance be at sea and in distress or missing, she shall, provided notice be given to the Underwriters prior to the expiration of this insurance, be held covered until arrival at the next port in good safety, or if in port and in distress until the Vessel is made safe, at a pro rata monthly premium.

3 Breach of warranty

Held covered in case of any breach of warranty as to cargo, trade, locality, towage, salvage services or date of sailing, provided notice be given to the Underwriters immediately after receipt of advices and any amended terms of cover and any additional premium required by them be agreed.

4 Classification

4.1 It is the duty of the Assured, Owners and Managers at the inception of and throughout the period of this insurance to ensure that
4.1.1 the Vessel is classed with a Classification Society agreed by the Underwriters and that her class within that Society is maintained,
4.1.2 any recommendations requirements or restrictions imposed by the Vessel's Classification Society which relate to the Vessel's seaworthiness or to her maintenance in a seaworthy condition are complied with by the dates required by that Society.
4.2 In the event of any breach of the duties set out in Clause 4.1 above, unless the Underwriters agree to the contrary in writing, they will be discharged from liability under this insurance as from the date of the breach provided that if the Vessel is at sea at such date the Underwriters' discharge from liability is deferred until arrival at her next port.
4.3 Any incident condition or damage in respect of which the Vessel's Classification Society might make recommendations as to repairs or other action to be taken by the Assured, Owners or Managers must be promptly reported to the Classification Society.
4.4 Should the Underwriters wish to approach the Classification Society directly for information and/or documents, the Assured will provide the necessary authorisation.

5 Termination

This Clause 5 shall prevail notwithstanding any provision whether written typed or printed in this insurance inconsistent therewith.

Unless the Underwriters agree to the contrary in writing, this insurance shall terminate automatically at the time of
5.1 change of the Classification Society of the Vessel, or change, suspension, discontinuance, withdrawal or expiry of her Class therein, or any of the Classification Society's periodic sureys becoming overdue unless an extension of time for such survey be agreed by the Classification Society, provided that if the Vessel is at sea such automatic termination shall be deferred until arrival at her next port.

However where such change, suspension, discontinuance or withdrawal of her Class or where a periodic survey becoming overdue has resulted from loss of damage covered by Clause 6 of this insurance or which would be covered by an insurance of the Vessel subject to current Institute War and Strikes Clauses Hulls—Time such automatic termination shall only operate should the Vessel sail from her next port without the prior approval of the Classification Society or in the case of a periodic survey becoming overdue without the Classification Society having agreed an extension of time for such survey,

5.2 any change, voluntary or otherwise, in the ownership or flag, transfer to new management, or charter on a bareboat basis, or requisition for title or use of the Vessel, provided that if the Vessel has cargo on board and has already sailed from her loading port or is at sea in ballast, such automatic termination shall if required be deferred, whilst the Vessel continues her planned voyage, until arrival at final port of discharge if with cargo or at port of destination if in ballast. However, in the event of requisition for title or use without the prior execution of a written agreement by the Assured, such automatic termination shall occur fifteen days after such requisition whether the Vessel is at sea or in port.

A pro rata daily net return of premium shall be made provided that a total loss of the Vessel, whether by insured perils or otherwise, has not occurred during the period covered by this insurance or any extension thereof.

6 Perils

6.1 This insurance covers loss of or damage to the subject-matter insured caused by
6.1.1 perils of the seas rivers lakes or other navigable waters
6.1.2 fire, explosion
6.1.3 violent theft by persons from outside the Vessel
6.1.4 jettison
6.1.5 piracy
6.1.6 contact with land conveyance, dock or harbour equipment or installation
6.1.7 earthquake volcanic eruption or lightning
6.1.8 accidents in loading discharging or shifting cargo or fuel.
6.2 This insurance covers loss of or damage to the subject-matter insured caused by
6.2.1 bursting of boilers breakage of shafts or any latent defect in the machinery or hull
6.2.2 negligence of Master Officers Crew or Pilots
6.2.3 negligence of repairers or charterers provided such repairers or charterers are not an Assured hereunder
6.2.4 barratry of Master Officers or Crew
6.2.5 contact with aircraft, helicopters or similar objects, or objects falling therefrom provided that such loss or damage has not resulted from want of due diligence by the Assured, Owners, Managers or Superintendents or any of their onshore management.
6.3 Masters Officers Crew or Pilots not to be considered Owners within the meaning of this Clause 6 should they hold shares in the Vessel.

7 Pollution hazard

This insurance covers loss of or damage to the Vessel caused by any governmental authority acting under the powers vested in it to prevent or mitigate a pollution hazard or damage to the environment, or threat thereof, resulting directly from damage to the Vessel for which the Underwriters are liable under this insurance, provided that such act of governmental authority has not resulted from want of due diligence by the Assured, Owners or Managers to prevent or mitigate such hazard or damage, or threat thereof. Master Officers Crew or Pilots not to be considered Owners within the meaning of this Clause 7 should they hold shares in the Vessel.

8 3/4ths collision liability

8.1 The Underwriters agree to indemnify the Assured for three-fourths of any sum or sums paid by the Assured to any other person or persons by reason of the Assured becoming legally liable by way of damages for

8.1.1 loss of or damage to any other vessel or property on any other vessel

8.1.2 delay to or loss of use of any such other vessel or property thereon

8.1.3 general average of, salvage of, or salvage under contract of, any such other vessel or property thereon,

where such payment by the Assured is in consequence of the Vessel hereby insured coming into collision with any other vessel.

8.2 The indemnity provided by this Clause 8 shall be in addition to the indemnity provided by the other terms and conditions of this insurance and shall be subject to the following provisions:

8.2.1 where the insured Vessel is in collision with another vessel and both vessels are to blame then, unless the liability of one or both vessels becomes limited by law, the indemnity under this Clause 8 shall be calculated on the principle of cross-liabilities as if the respective Owners had been compelled to pay to each other such proportion of each other's damages as may have been properly allowed in ascertaining the balance or sum payable by or to the Assured in consequence of the collision,

8.2.2 in no case shall the Underwriters' total liability under Clauses 8.1 and 8.2 exceed their proportionate part of three-fourths of the insured value of the Vessel hereby insured in respect of any one collision.

8.3 The Underwriters will also pay three-fourths of the legal costs incurred by the Assured or which the Assured may be compelled to pay in contesting liability or taking proceedings to limit liability, with the prior written consent of the Underwriters.

EXCLUSIONS

8.4 Provided always that this Clause 8 shall in no case extend to any sum which the Assured shall pay for or in respect of

8.4.1 removal or disposal of obstructions, cargoes or any other thing whatsoever

8.4.2 any real or personal property or thing whatsoever except other vessels or property on other vessels

8.4.3 the cargo or other property on, or the engagements of, the insured Vessel

8.4.4 loss of life, personal injury or illness

8.4.5 pollution or contamination, or threat thereof, of any real or personal property or thing whatsoever (except other vessels with which the insured Vessel is in collision or property on such other vessels) or damage to the environment, or threat thereof, save that this exclusion shall not extend to any sum which the Assured shall pay for or in respect of salvage remuneration in which the skill and efforts of the salvors in preventing or minimising damage to the environment as is referred to in Article 13 paragraph 1(b) of the International Convention on Salvage, 1989 have been taken into account.

9 Sistership

Should the Vessel hereby insured come into collision with or receive salvage services from another vessel belonging wholly or in part to the same Owners or under the same management, the Assured shall have the same rights under this insurance as they would have were the other vessel entirely the property of Owners not interested in the Vessel hereby insured; but in such cases the liability for the collision or the amount payable for the services rendered shall be referred to a sole arbitrator to be agreed upon between the Underwriters and the Assured.

10 General average and salvage

10.1 This insurance covers the Vessel's proportion of salvage, salvage charges and/or general average, reduced in respect of any under-insurance, but in case a general average sacrifice of the Vessel the Assured may recover in respect of the whole loss without first enforcing their right of contribution from other parties.

10.2 Adjustment to be according to the law and practice obtaining at the place where the adventure ends, as if the contract of affreightment contained no special terms upon the subject; but where the contract of affreightment so provides the adjustment shall be according to the York-Antwerp Rules.

10.3 When the Vessel sails in ballast, not under charter, the provisions of the York-Antwerp Rules, 1994 (excluding Rules XI(d), XX and XXI) shall be applicable, and the voyage for this purpose shall be deemed to continue from the port or place of departure until the arrival of the Vessel at the first port or place thereafter other than a port or place of refuge or a port or place of call for bunkering only. If at any such intermediate port or place there is an abandonment of the adventure originally contemplated the voyage shall thereupon be deemed to be terminated.

10.4 No claim under this Clause 10 shall in any case be allowed where the loss was not incurred to avoid or in connection with the avoidance of a peril insured against.

10.5 No claim under this Clause 10 shall in any case be allowed for or in respect of

10.5.1 special compensation payable to a salvor under Article 14 of the International Convention on Salvage, 1989 or under any other provision in any statute rule law or contract which is similar in substance

10.5.2 expenses or liabilities incurred in respect of damage to the environment, or the threat of such damage, or as a consequence of the escape or release of pollutant substances from the Vessel, or the threat of such escape or release.

10.6 Clause 10.5 shall not however exclude any sum which the Assured shall pay to salvors for or in respect of salvage remuneration in which the skill and efforts of the salvors in preventing or minimising damage to the environment as is referred to in Article 13 paragraph 1(b) of the International Convention on Salvage, 1989 have been taken into account.

11 Duty of assured (Sue and Labour)

11.1 In case of any loss or misfortune it is the duty of the Assured and their servants and agents to take such measures as may be reasonable for the purpose of averting or minimising a loss which would be recoverable under this insurance.

11.2 Subject to the provisions below and to Clause 12 the Underwriters will contribute to charges properly and reasonably incurred by the Assured their servants or agents for such measures. General average, salvage charges (except as provided for in Clause 11.5), special compensation and expenses as referred to in Clause 10.5 and collision defence or attack costs are not recoverable under this Clause 11.

11.3 Measures taken by the Assured or the Underwriters with the object of saving, protecting or recovering the subject-matter insured shall not be considered as a waiver or acceptance of abandonment or otherwise prejudice the rights of either party.

11.4 When expenses are incurred pursuant to this Clause 11 the liability under this insurance shall not exceed the proportion of such expenses that the amount insured hereunder bears to the value of the Vessel as stated herein, or to the sound value of the Vessel at the time of the occurrence giving rise to the expenditure if the sound value exceeds that value. Where the Underwriters have admitted a claim for total loss and property insured by this insurance is saved, the foregoing provisions shall not apply unless the expenses of suing and labouring exceed the value of such property saved and then shall apply only to the amount of the expenses which is in excess of such value.

11.5 When a claim for total loss of the Vessel is admitted under this insurance and expenses have been reasonably incurred in saving or attempting to save the Vessel and other property and there are no proceeds, or the expenses exceed the proceeds, then this insurance shall bear its pro rata share of such proportion of the expenses, or of the expenses in excess of the proceeds, as the case may be, as may reasonably be regarded as having been incurred in respect of the Vessel, excluding all special compensation and expenses as referred to in Clause 10.5; but if the Vessel be insured for less than its sound value at the time of the occurrence giving rise to the expenditure, the amount recoverable under this clause shall be reduced in proportion to the under insurance.

11.6 The sum recoverable under this Clause 11 shall be in addition to the loss otherwise recoverable under this insurance but shall in no circumstances exceed the amount insured under this insurance in respect of the Vessel.

12 Deductible

12.1 No claim arising from peril insured against shall be payable under this insurance unless the aggregate of all such claims arising out of each separate accident or occurrence (including claims under Clauses 8, 10 and 11) exceeds the deductible amount agreed in which case this sum shall be deducted. Nevertheless the expense of sighting the bottom after stranding, if reasonably incurred specially for that purpose, shall be paid even if no damage be found. This Clause 12.1 shall not apply to a claim for total or constructive total loss of the Vessel or, in the event of such a claim, to any associated claim under Clause 11 arising from the same accident or occurrence.

12.2 Claims for damage by heavy weather occurring during a single sea passage between two successive ports shall be treated as being due to one accident. In the case of such heavy weather extending over a period not wholly covered by this insurance the deductible to be applied to the claim recoverable hereunder shall be the proportion of the above deductible that the number of days of such heavy weather falling within the period of this insurance bears to the number of days of heavy weather during the single sea passage. The expression "heavy weather" in this Clause 12.2 shall be deemed to include contact with floating ice.

12.3 Excluding any interest comprised therein, recoveries against any claim which is subject to the above deductible shall be credited to the Underwriters in full to the extent of the sum by which the aggregate of the claim unreduced by any recoveries exceed them above deductible.

12.4 Interest comprised in recoveries shall be apportioned between the Assured and the Underwriters, taking into account the sums paid to the Underwriters and the dates when such payments were made, notwithstanding that by the addition of interest the Underwriters may receive a larger sum than they have paid.

13 Notice of claim and tenders

13.1 In the event of accident whereby loss or damage may result in a claim under this insurance, notice must be given to the Underwriters promptly after the date on which the Assured, Owners or Managers become or should have become aware of the loss or damage and prior to survey so that a surveyor may be appointed if the Underwriters so desire.

If notice is not given to the Underwriters within twelve months of that date unless the Underwriters agree to the contrary in writing, the Underwriters will be automatically discharged from liability for any claim under this insurance in respect of or arising out of such accident or the loss or damage.

13.2 The Underwriters shall be entitled to decide the port to which the Vessel shall proceed for docking or repair (the actual additional expense of the voyage arising from compliance with the Underwriters' requirements being refunded to the Assured) and shall have a right of veto concerning a place of repair or a repairing firm.

13.3 The Underwriters may also take tenders or may require further tenders to be taken for the repair of the Vessel. Where such a tender has been taken and a tender is accepted with the approval of the Underwriters, an allowance shall be made at the rate of 30% per annum on the insured value for time lost between the despatch of the invitations to tender required by the Underwriters and the acceptance of a tender to the extent that such time is lost solely as the result of tenders having been taken and provided that the tender is accepted without delay after receipt of the Underwriters' approval.

Due credit shall be given against the allowance as above for any amounts recovered in respect of fuel and stores and wages and maintenance of the Master Officers and Crew or any member thereof, including amounts allowed in general average, and for any amounts recovered from third parties in respect of damages for detention and/or loss of profit and/or running expenses, for the period covered by the tender allowance or any part thereof.

Where a part of the cost of the repair of damage other than a fixed deductible is not recoverable from the Underwriters the allowance shall be reduced by a similar proportion.

13.4 In the event of failure by the Assured to comply with the conditions of Clauses 13.2 and/or 13.3 a deduction of 15% shall be made from the amount of the determined claim.

14 New for old

Claims payable without deduction new for old.

15 Bottom treatment

In no case shall a claim be allowed in respect of scraping gritblasting and/or other surface preparation or painting of the Vessel's bottom except that

15.1 gritblasting and/or other surface preparation of new bottom plates ashore and supplying and applying any "shop" primer thereto,

15.2 gritblasting and/or other surface preparation of:
the butts or area of plating immediately adjacent to any renewed or refitted plating damaged during the course of welding and/or repairs,
areas of plating damaged during the course of fairing, either in place or ashore,

15.3 supplying and applying the first coat of primer/anti-corrosive to those particular areas mentioned in 15.1 and 15.2 above,

shall be allowed as part of the reasonable cost of repairs in respect of bottom plating damaged by an insured peril.

16 Wages and maintenance

No claim shall be allowed, other than in general average, for wages and maintenance of the Master Officers and Crew or any member thereof, except when incurred solely for the necessary removal of the Vessel from one port to another for the repair of damage covered by the Underwriters, or for trial trips for such repairs, and then only for such wages and maintenance as are incurred whilst the Vessel is under way.

17 Agency commission

In no case shall any sum be allowed under this insurance either by way of remuneration of the Assured for time and trouble taken to obtain and supply information or documents or in respect of the commission or charges of any manager, agent, managing or agency company or the like, appointed by or on behalf of the Assured to perform such services.

18 Unrepaired damage

18.1 The measure of indemnity in respect of claims for unrepaired damage shall be the reasonable depreciation in the market value of the Vessel at the time the insurance terminates arising from such unrepaired damage, but not exceeding the reasonable cost of repairs.

18.2 In no case shall the Underwriters be liable for unrepaired damage in the event of a subsequent total loss (whether or not covered under this insurance) sustained during the period covered by this insurance or any extension thereof.

18.3 The Underwriters shall not be liable in respect of unrepaired damage for more than the insured value at the time this insurance terminates.

19 Constructive total loss

19.1 In ascertaining whether the Vessel is a constructive total loss, the insured value shall be taken as the repaired value and nothing in respect of the damaged or break-up value of the Vessel or wreck shall be taken into account.

19.2 No claim for constructive total loss based upon the cost of recovery and/or repair of the Vessel shall be recoverable hereunder unless such cost would exceed the insured value. In making this determination, only the cost relating to a single accident or sequence of damages arising from the same accident shall be taken into account.

20 Freight waiver

In the event of total or constructive total loss no claim to be made by the Underwriters for freight whether notice of abandonment has been given or not.

21 Assignment

No assignment of or interest in this insurance or in any moneys which may be or become payable thereunder is to be binding on or recognised by the Underwriters unless a dated notice of such assignment or interest signed by the Assured, and by the assignor in the case of subsequent assignment, is endorsed on the Policy and the Policy with such endorsement is produced before payment of any claim or return of premium thereunder.

22 Disbursements warranty

22.1 Additional insurances as follows are permitted:

22.1.1 *Disbursements, Managers' Commissions, Profits or Excess or Increased Value of Hull and Machinery.* A sum not exceeing 25% of the value stated herein.

22.1.2 *Freight, Chartered Freight or Anticipated Freight, insured for time.* A sum not exceeding 25% of the value as stated herein less any sum insured, however described, under 22.1.1.

22.1.3 *Freight or Hire, under contracts for voyage.* A sum not exceeding the gross freight or hire for the current cargo passage and next succeeding cargo passage (such

INSTITUTE TIME CLAUSES—HULLS

insurance to include, if required, a preliminary and an intermediate ballast passage) plus the charges of insurance. In the case of a voyage charter where payment is made on a time basis, the sum permitted for insurance shall be calculated on the estimated duration of the voyage, subject to the limitation of two cargo passages as laid down herein. Any sum insured under 22.1.2 to be taken ito account and only the excess thereof may be insured, which excess shall be reduced as the freight or hire is advanced or earned by the gross amount so advanced or earned.

22.1.4 *Anticipated Freight if the Vessel sails in ballast and not under Charter.* A sum not exceeding the anticipated gross freight on next cargo passage, such sum to be reasonably estimated on the basis of the current rate of freight at time of insurance plus the charges of insurance. Any sum insured under 22.1.2 to be taken into account and only the excess thereof may be insured.

22.1.5 *Time Charter Hire or Charter Hire for Series of Voyages.* A sum not exceeding 50% of the gross hire which is to be earned under the charter in a period not exceeding 18 months. Any sum insured under 22.1.2 to be taken into account and only the excess thereof may be insured, which excess shall be reduced as the hire is advanced or earned under the charter by 50% of the gross amount so advanced or earned but the sum insured need not be reduced while the total of the sums insured under 22.1.2 and 22.1.5 does not exceed 50% of the gross hire still to be earned under the charter. An insurance under this Section may begin on the signing of the charter.

22.1.6 *Premiums.* A sum not exceeding the actual premiums of all interests insured for a period not exceeding 12 months (excluding premiums insured under the foregoing sections but including, if required, the premium or estimated calls on any Club or War etc. Risk insurance) reducing pro rata monthly.

22.1.7 *Returns of Premium.* A sum not exceeding the actual returns which are allowable under any insurance but which would not be recoverable thereunder in the event of a total loss of the Vessel whether by insured perils or otherwise.

22.1.8 *Insurance irrespective of amount against:*
Any risks excluded by Clauses 24, 25, 26 and 27 below.

22.2 Warranted that no insurance on any interests enumerated in the foregoing 22.1.1 to 22.1.7 in excess of the amounts permitted therein and no other insurance which includes total loss of the Vessel P.P.I., F.I.A., or subject to any other like term, is or shall be effected to operate during the currency of this insurance by or for account of the Assured, Owners, Managers or Mortgagees. Provided always that a breach of this warranty shall not afford the Underwriters any defence to a claim by a Mortgagee who has accepted this insurance without knowledge of such breach.

23 Returns for lay-up and cancellation

23.1 To return as follows:

23.1.1 pro rata monthly net for each uncommenced month if this insurance be cancelled by agreement,

23.1.2 for each period of 30 consecutive days the Vessel may be laid up in a port or in a lay-up area provided such port or lay-up area is approved by the Underwriters
(a)................................per cent net not under repair
(b)................................per cent net under repair.

23.1.3 The Vessel shall not be considered to be under repair when work is undertaken in respect of ordinary wear and tear of the Vessel and/or following recommendations in the Vessel's Classification Society survey, but any repairs following loss of or damage to the Vessel or involving structural alterations, whether covered by this insurance or otherwise shall be considered as under repair.

23.1.4 If the Vessel is under repair during part only of a period on which a return is claimable, the return shall be calculated pro rata to the number of days under 23.1.2(a) and (b) respectively.

23.2 PROVIDED ALWAYS THAT

23.2.1 a total loss of the Vessel whether by insured perils or otherwise, has not occurred during the period covered by this insurance or any extension thereof

23.2.2 in no case shall a return be allowed when the Vesssel is lying in exposed or unprotected waters, or in a port or lay-up area not approved by the Underwriters

23.2.3 loading or discharging operations or the presence of cargo on board shall not debar returns but no return shall be allowed for any period during which the Vessel is being used for the storage of cargo or for lightering purposes

23.2.4 in the event of any amendment of the annual rate, the above rates of return shall be adjusted accordingly.

23.2.5 in the event of any return recoverable under this Clause 23 being based on 30 consecutive days which fall on successive insurances effected for the same Assured, this insurance shall only be liable for an amount calculated at pro rata of the period rates 23.1.2(a) and/or (b) above for the number of days which come within the period of this insurance and to which a return is actually applicable. Such overlapping period shall run, at the option of the Assured, either from the first day on which the Vessel is laid up or the first day of a period of 30 consecutive days as provided under 23.1.2(a) or (b) above.

The following clauses shall be paramount and shall override anything contained in this insurance inconsistent therewith.

24 War exclusion

In no case shall this insurance cover loss damage liability or expense caused by

24.1 war civil war revolution rebellion insurrection, or civil strife arising therefrom, or any hostile act by or against a belligerent power

24.2 capture seizure arrest restraint or detainment (barratry and piracy excepted), and the consequences thereof or any attempt thereat

24.3 derelict mines torpedoes bombs or other derelict weapons of war.

25 Strikes exclusion

In no case shall this insurance cover loss damage liability or expense caused by

25.1 strikers, locked-out workmen, or persons taking part in labour disturbances, riots or civil commotions

25.2 any terrorist or any person acting from a political motive.

26 Malicious acts exclusion

In no case shall this insurance cover loss damage liability or expense arising from

26.1 the detonation of an explosive

26.2 any weapon of war

and caused by any person acting maliciously or from a political motive.

27 Radioactive contamination exclusion clause

In no case shall this insurance cover loss damage liability or expense directly or indirectly caused by or contributed to by or arising from

27.1 ionising radiations from or contamination by radioactivity from any nuclear fuel or from any nuclear waste or from the combustion of nuclear fuel

27.2 the radioactive, toxic, explosive or other hazardous or contaminating properties of any nuclear installation, reactor or other nuclear assembly or nuclear component thereof

27.3 any weapon of war employing atomic or nuclear fission and/or fusion or other like reaction or radioactive force or matter.

INSTITUTE VOYAGE CLAUSES—HULLS
(CL.285—Institute of London Underwriters and Witherby & Co Ltd)

1/11/95 (FOR USE ONLY WITH THE NEW MARINE POLICY FORM)

This insurance is subject to English law and practice

1 Navigation

1.1 The Vessel is covered subject to the provisions of this insurance at all times and has leave to sail or navigate with or without pilots, to go on trial trips and to assist and tow vessels or craft in distress, but it is warranted that the Vessel shall not be towed, except as is customary or to the first safe port or place when in need of assistance, or undertake towage or salvage services under a contract previously arranged by the Assured and/or Owners and/or Managers and/or Charterers. This Clause 1.1 shall not exclude customary towage in connection with loading and discharging.

1.2 This insurance shall not be prejudiced by reason of the Assured entering into any contract with pilots or for customary towage which limits or exempts the liability of the pilots and/or tugs and/or towboats and/or their owners when the Assured or their agents accept or are compelled to accept such contracts in accordance with established local law or practice.

1.3 The practice of engaging helicopters for the transportation of personnel, supplies and equipment to and/or from the Vessel shall not prejudice this insurance.

1.4 In the event of the Vessel being employed in trading operations which entail cargo loading or discharging at sea from or into another vessel (not being a harbour or inshore craft) no claim shall be recoverable under this insurance for loss of or damage to the Vessel or liability to any other vessel arising from such loading or discharging operations, including whilst approaching, lying alongside and leaving, unless previous notice that the Vessel is to be employed in such operations has been given to the Underwriters and any amended terms of cover and any additional premium required by them have been agreed.

2 Change of voyage

Held covered in case of deviation or change of voyage or any breach of warranty as to towage or salvage services, provided notice be given to the Underwriters immediately after receipt of advices and any amended terms of cover and any additional premium required by them be agreed.

3 Classification

3.1 It is the duty of the Assured, Owners and Managers at the inception of and throughout the period of this insurance to ensure that

3.1.1 the Vessel is classed with a Classification Society agreed by the Underwriters and that her class within that Society is maintained.

3.1.2 any recommendations requirements or restrictions imposed by the Vessel's Classification Society which relate to the Vessel's seaworthiness or to her maintenance in a seaworthy condition are complied with by the dates required by that Society.

3.2 In the event of any breach of the duties set out in Clause 3.1 above, unless Underwriters agree to the contrary in writing, they will be discharged from liability under this insurance as from the date of the breach provided that if the Vessel is at sea at such date Underwriters' discharge from liability is deferred until arrival at her next port.

INSTITUTE VOYAGE CLAUSES—HULLS

3.3 Any incident condition or damage in respect of which the Vessel's Classification Society might make recommendations as to repairs or other action to be taken by the Assured, Owners or Managers must be promptly reported to the Classification Society.

3.4 Should the Underwriters wish to approach the Classification Society directly for information and/or documents, the Assured will provide the necessary authorization.

4 Perils

4.1 This insurance covers total loss (actual or constructive) of the subject-matter insured caused by

4.1.1 perils of the seas rivers lakes or other navigable waters

4.1.2 fire, explosion

4.1.3 violent theft by persons from outside the Vessel

4.1.4 jettison

4.1.5 piracy

4.1.6 contact with land conveyance, dock or harbour equipment or installation

4.1.7 earthquake volcanic eruption or lightning.

4.1.8 accidents in loading discharging or shifting cargo or fuel

4.2 This insurance covers total loss (actual or constructive) of the subject-matter insured caused by

4.2.1 bursting of boilers breakage of shafts or any latent defect in the machinery or hull

4.2.2 negligence of Master Officers Crew or Pilots

4.2.3 negligence of repairers or charterers provided such repairers or charterers are not an Assured hereunder

4.2.4 barratry of Master Officers or Crew,
provided such loss or damage has not resulted from want of due diligence by the Assured, Owners or Managers.

4.2.5 contact with aircraft helicopters or similar objects, or objects falling therefrom.

4.3 Master Officers Crew or Pilots not to be considered Owners within the meaning of this Clause 4 should they hold shares in the Vessel.

5 Pollution hazard

This insurance covers total loss (actual or constructive) of the Vessel caused by any governmental authority acting under the powers vested in it to prevent or mitigate a pollution hazard or damage to the environment, or threat thereof, resulting directly from damage to the Vessel for which the Underwriters are liable under this insurance, provided that such act of governmental authority has not resulted from want of due diligence by the Assured, Owners or Managers to prevent or mitigate such hazard or damage, or threat thereof. Master Officers Crew or Pilots not to be considered Owners within the meaning of this Clause 5 should they hold shares in the Vessel.

6 3/4ths collision liability

6.1 The Underwriters agree to indemnify the Assured for three-fourths of any sum or sums paid by the Assured to any other person or persons by reason of the Assured becoming legally liable by way of damages for

6.1.1 loss of or damage to any other vessel or property on any other vessel

6.1.2 delay to or loss of use of any such other vessel or property thereon

6.1.3 general average of, salvage of, or salvage under contract of, any such other vessel or property thereon,
where such payment by the Assured is in consequence of the Vessel hereby insured coming into collision with any other vessel.

6.2 The indemnity provided by this Clause 6 shall be in addition to the indemnity provided by the other terms and conditions of this insurance and shall be subject to the following provisions:

6.2.1 Where the insured Vessel is in collision with another vessel and both vessels are to blame then, unless the liability of one or both vessels becomes limited by law, the indemnity under this Clause 6 shall be calculated on the principle of cross-liabilities as if the respective Owners had been compelled to pay to each other such proportion of each other's damages as may have been properly allowed in ascertaining the balance or sum payable by or to the Assured in consequence of the collision.

6.2.2 In no case shall the Underwriters' total liability under Clauses 6.1 and 6.2 exceed their proportionate part of three-fourths of the insured value of the Vessel hereby insured in respect of any one collision.

6.3 The Underwriters will also pay three-fourths of the legal costs incurred by the Assured or which the Assured may be compelled to pay in contesting liability or taking proceedings to limit liability, with the prior written consent of the Underwriters.

EXCLUSIONS

6.4 Provided always that this Clause 6 shall in no case extend to any sum which the Assured shall pay for or in respect of

6.4.1 removal or disposal of obstructions, wrecks, cargoes or any other thing whatsoever

6.4.2 any real or personal property or thing whatsoever except other vessels or property on other vessels

6.4.3 the cargo or other property on, or the engagements of, the insured Vessel

6.4.4 loss of life, personal injury or illness

6.4.5 pollution or contamination, or threat thereof, of any real or personal property or thing whatsoever (except other vessels with which the insured Vessel is in collision or property on such other vessels) or damage to the environment, or threat thereof, save that this exclusion shall not extend to any sum which the Assured shall pay for in respect of salvage remuneration in which the skill and efforts of the salvors in preventing or minimising damage to the environment as is referred to in Article 13 paragraph 1(b) of the International Convention on Salvage, 1989 have been taken into account.

7 Sistership

Should the Vessel hereby insured come into collision with or receive salvage services from another vessel belonging wholly or in part to the same Owners or under the same management, the Assured shall have the same rights under this insurance as they would have were the other vessel entirely the property of Owners not interested in the Vessel hereby insured; but in such cases the liability for the collision or the amount payable for the services rendered shall be referred to a sole arbitrator to be agreed upon between the Underwriters and the Assured.

8 General average and salvage

8.1 This insurance covers the Vessel's proportion of salvage, salvage charges and/or general average, reduced in respect of any under-insurance.

8.2 This insurance does not cover partial loss of and/or damage to the Vessel except for any proportion of general average loss or damage which may be recoverable under Clause 8.1 above.

8.3 Adjustment to be according to the law and practice obtaining at the place where the adventure ends, as if the contract of affreightment contained no special terms upon the subject; but where the contract of affreightment so provides the adjustment shall be according to the York-Antwerp Rules.

8.4 When the Vessel sails in ballast, not under charter, the provisions of the York-Antwerp Rules, 1994 (excluding rules XI(d), XX and XXI) shall be applicable, and the voyage for this purpose shall be deemed to continue from the port or place of departure until the arrival of the Vessel at the first port or place thereafter other than a port or place of refuge or a port or place of call for bunkering only. If at any such intermediate port or place there is an abandonment of the adventure originally contemplated the voyage shall thereupon be deemed to be terminated.

8.5 No claim under this Clause 8 shall in any case be allowed where the loss was not incurred to avoid or in connection with the avoidance of a peril insured against.

8.6 No claim under this Clause 8 shall in any case be allowed for in respect of

8.6.1 special compensation payable to a salvor under article 14 of the International Convention on Salvage, 1989 or under any other provision in any statute, rule, law or contract which is similar in substance

8.6.2 expenses or liabilities incurred in respect of damage to the environment, or the threat of such damage, or as a consequence of the escape or release of pollutant substances from the Vessel, or the threat of such escape or release.

8.7 Clause 8.6 shall not however exclude any sum which the Assured shall pay to salvors for or in respect of salvage remuneration in which the skill and efforts of the salvors in preventing or minimising damage to the environment as is referred to in Article 13 paragraph 1(b) of the International Convention on Salvage, 1989 have been taken into account.

9 Duty of assured (sue and labour)

9.1 In case of any loss or misfortune it is the duty of the Assured and their servants and agents to take such measures as may be reasonable for the purpose of averting or minimising a loss which would be recoverable under this insurance.

9.2 Subject to the provisions below and to Clause 10 the Underwriters will contribute to charges properly and reasonably incurred by the Assured their servants or agents for such measures. General average, salvage charges (except as provided for in Clause 9.5), special compensation and expenses as referred to in Clause 8.6 and collision defence or attack costs are not recoverable under this Clause 9.

9.3 Measures taken by the Assured or the Underwriters with the object of saving, protecting or recovering the subject-matter insured shall not be considered as a waiver or acceptance of abandonment or otherwise prejudice the rights of either party.

9.4 When expenses are incurred pursuant to this Clause 9 the liability under this insurance shall not exceed the proportion of such expenses that the amount insured hereunder bears to the value of the Vessel as stated herin, or to the sound value of the Vessel at the time of the occurrence giving rise to the expenditure if the sound value exceeds that value. Where the Underwriters have admitted a claim for total loss and property insured by this insurance is saved, the foregoing provisions shall not apply unless the expenses of suing and labouring exceed the value of such property saved and then shall apply only to the amount of the expenses which is in excess of such value.

9.5 When a claim for total loss of the Vessel is admitted under this insurance and expenses have been reasonably incurred in saving or attempting to save the Vessel and other property and there are no proceeds, or the expenses exceed the proceeds, then this insurance shall bear its pro rata share of such proportion of the expenses, or of the expenses in excess of the proceeds, as the case may be, as may reasonably be regarded as having been incurred in respect of the Vessel, excluding all special compensation and expenses as referred to in Clause 8.6; but if the Vessel be insured for less than its sound value at the time of the occurrence giving rise to the expenditure, the amount recoverable under this clause shall be reduced in proportion to the under-insurance.

9.6 The sum recoverable under this Clause 9 shall be in addition to the loss otherwise recoverable under this insurance but shall in no circumstances exceed the amount insured under this insurance in respect of the Vessel.

10 Deductible

10.1 No claim arising from a peril insured against shall be payable under this insurance unless the aggregate of all such claims arising out of each separate accident or occurrence (including claims under Clauses 6, 8, and 9) exceeds the deductible amount agreed in which case this sum shall be deducted. This Clause 10.1 shall not apply to a claim for total or constructive total loss of the Vessel, or in the event of such a claim, to any associated claim under Clause 9 arising from the same accident or occurrence.

10.2 Excluding any interest comprised therein, recoveries against any claim which is subject to the above deductible shall be credited to the Underwriters in full to the extent of the sum by which the aggregate of the claim unreduced by any recoveries exceeds the above deductible.

10.3 Interest comprised in recoveries shall be apportioned between the Assured and the Underwriters, taking into account the sums paid by the Underwriters and the dates when such payments were made, notwithstanding that by the addition of interest the Underwriters may receive a larger sum than they have paid.

11 Notice of claim

In the event of accident whereby loss or damage may result in a claim under this insurance, notice must be given to the Underwriters promptly after the date on which the Assured, Owners or Managers become or should have become aware of the loss or damage and prior to survey so that a surveyor may be appointed if the Underwriters so desire.

If notice is not given to the Underwriters within twelve months of that date unless the Underwriters agree to the contrary in writing, the Underwriters will be automatically discharged from liability for any claim under this insurance in respect of or arising out of such accident or the loss or damage.

12 New for old

Claims payable without deduction new for old.

13 Agency commission

In no case shall any sum be allowed under this insurance either by way of remuneration of the Assured for time and trouble taken to obtain and supply information or documents or in respect of the commission or charges of any manager, agent, managing or agency company or the like, appointed by or on behalf of the Assured to perform such services.

14 Constructive total loss

14.1 In ascertaining whether the Vessel is a constructive total loss, the insured value shall be taken as the repaired value and nothing in respect of the damaged or break-up value of the Vessel or wreck shall be taken into account.

14.2 No claim for constructive total loss based upon the cost of recovery and/or repair of the Vessel shall be recoverable hereunder unless such cost would exceed the insured value. In making this determination, only the cost relating to a single accident or sequence of damages arising from the same accident shall be taken into account.

15 Freight waiver

In the event of total or constructive total loss no claim to be made by the Underwriters for freight whether notice of abandonment has been given or not.

16 Assignment

No assignment of or interest in this insurance or in any moneys which may be or become payable thereunder is to be binding on or recognised by the Underwriters unless a dated notice of such assignment or interest signed by the Assured, and by the assignor in the case of subsequent assignment, is endorsed on the Policy and the Policy with such endorsement is produced before payment of any claim or return of premium thereunder.

17 Disbursements warranty

17.1 Additional insurances as follows are permitted:

17.1.1 *Disbursements, Managers' Commissions, Profits or Excess or Increased Value of Hull and Machinery.* A sum not exceeding 25% of the value stated herein.

17.1.2 *Freight, Chartered Freight or Anticipated Freight, insured for time.* A sum not exceeding 25% of the value as stated herein less any sum insured, however described, under 17.1.1.

17.1.3 *Freight or Hire, under contracts for voyage.* A sum not exceeding the gross freight or hire for the current cargo passage and next succeeding cargo passage (such insurance to include, if required, a preliminary and an intermediate ballast passage) plus the charges of insurance. In the case of a voyage charter where payment is made on a time basis, the sum permitted for insurance shall be calculated on the estimated duration of the voyage, subject to the limitation of two cargo passages as laid down herein. Any sum insured under 17.1.2 to be taken into account and only the excess thereof may be insured, which excess shall be reduced as the freight or hire is advanced or earned by the gross amount so advanced or earned.

17.1.4 *Anticipated Freight if the Vessel sails in ballast and not under Charter.* A sum not exceeding the anticipated gross freight on next cargo passage, such sum to be reasonably estimated on the basis of the current rate of freight at time of insurance plus the charges of insurance. Any sum insured under 17.1.2 to be taken into account and only the excess thereof may be insured.

17.1.5 *Time Charter Hire or Charter Hire for Series of Voyages.* A sum not exceeding 50% of the gross hire which is to be earned under the charter in a period not exceeding

18 months. Any sum insured under 17.1.2 to be taken into account and only the excess thereof may be insured, which excess shall be reduced as the hire is advanced or earned under the charter by 50% of the gross amount so advanced or earned but the sum insured need not be reduced while the total of the sums insured under 17.1.2 and 17.1.5 does not exceed 50% of the gross hire still to be earned under the charter. An insurance under this Section may begin on the signing of the charter.

17.1.6 *Premiums.* A sum not exceeding the actual premiums of all interests insured for a period not exceeding 12 months (excluding premiums insured under the foregoing sections but including, if required, the premium or estimated calls on any Club or War etc. Risk insurance) reducing pro rata monthly.

17.1.7 *Returns of Premium.* A sum not exceeding the actual returns which are allowable under any insurance but which would not be recoverable thereunder in the event of a total loss of the Vessel whether by insured perils or otherwise.

17.1.8 *Insurance irrespective of amount against*:
Any risks excluded by Clauses 18, 19, 20 and 21 below.

17.2 Warranted that no insurance on any interests enumerated in the foregoing 17.1.1 to 17.1.7 in excess of the amounts permitted therein and no other insurance which includes total loss of the Vessel P.P.I., F.I.A., or subject to any other like term, is or shall be effected to operate during the currency of this insurance by or for account of the Assured, Owners, Managers or Mortgagees. Provided always that a breach of this warranty shall not afford the Underwriters any defence to a claim by a Mortgagee who has accepted this insurance without knowledge of such breach.

The following clauses shall be paramount and shall override anything contained in this insurance inconsistent therewith.

18 War exclusion

In no case shall this insurance cover loss damage liability or expense caused by

18.1 war civil war revolution rebellion insurrection, or civil strife arising therefrom, or any hostile act by or against a belligerent power

18.2 capture seizure arrest restraint or detainment (barratry and piracy excepted), and the consequences thereof or any attempt thereat

18.3 derelict mines torpedoes bombs or other derelict weapons of war.

19 Strikes exclusion

In no case shall this insurance cover loss damage liability or expense caused by

19.1 strikers, locked-out workmen, or persons taking part in labour disturbances, riots or civil commotions

19.2 any terrorist or any person acting from a political motive.

20 Malicious acts exclusion

In no case shall this insurance cover loss damage liability or expense arising from

20.1 the detonation of an explosive

20.2 any weapon of war

and caused by any person acting maliciously or from a political motive.

21 Radioactive contamination exclusion clause

In no case shall this insurance cover loss damage liability or expense directly or indirectly caused by or contributed to by or arising from

21.1 ionising radiations from or contamination by radioactivity from any nuclear fuel or from any nuclear waste or from the combustion of nuclear fuel

21.2 the radioactive, toxic, explosive or other hazardous or contaminating properties of any nuclear installation, reactor or other nuclear assembly or nuclear component thereof

21.3 any weapon of war employing atomic or nuclear fission and/or fusion or other like reaction or radioactive force or matter.

INSTITUTE TIME CLAUSES—FREIGHT
(CL.287—Institute of London Underwriters and Witherby & Co Ltd)

1/11/95 (FOR USE ONLY WITH THE CURRENT MAR POLICY FORM)

This insurance is subject to English law and practice

1 Navigation

1.1 The Vessel has leave to dock and undock, to go into graving dock, to sail or navigate with or without pilots, to go on trial trips and to assist and tow vessels or craft in distress, but it is warranted that the Vessel shall not be towed, except as is customary or to the first safe port or place when in need of assistance, or undertake towage or salvage services under a contract previously arranged by the Assured and/or Owners and/or Managers and/or Charterers. This Clause 1 shall not exclude customary towage in connection with loading and discharging.

1.2 This insurance shall not be prejudiced by reason of the Assured entering into any contract with pilots or for customary towage which limits or exempts the liability of the pilots and/or tugs and/or towboats and/or their owners when the Assured or their agents accept or are compelled to accept such contracts in accordance with established local law or practice.

1.3 The practice of engaging helicopters for the transportation of personnel, supplies and equipment to and/or from the Vessel shall not prejudice this insurance.

2 Craft risk

Including risk of craft and/or lighter to and from the Vessel.

3 Continuation

Should the Vessel at the expiration of this insurance be at sea and in distress or missing, the subject-matter insured shall, provided notice be given to the Underwriters prior to the expiration of this insurance, be held covered until arrival of the Vessel at the next port in good safety, or if in port and in distress until the Vessel is made safe, at a pro rata monthly premium.

4 Breach of warranty

Held covered in case of any breach of warranty as to cargo, trade, locality, towage, salvage services or date of sailing, provided notice be given to the Underwriters immediately after receipt of advices and any amended terms of cover and any additional premium required by them be agreed.

5 Classification

5.1 It is the duty of the Assured, Owners and Managers at the inception of and throughout the period of this insurance to ensure that
5.1.1 the Vessel is classed with a Classification Society agreed by the Underwriters and that her class within that Society is maintained
5.1.2 any recommendations requirements or restrictions imposed by the Vessel's Classification Society which relate to the Vessel's seaworthiness or to her maintenance in a seaworthy condition are complied with by the date required by that Society.

5.2 In the event of any breach of the duties set out in Clause 5.1 above, unless the Underwriters agree to the contrary in writing, they will be discharged from liability under this insurance as from the date of the breach, provided that if the Vessel is at sea at such date the Underwriters' discharge from liability is deferred until arrival at her next port.

5.3 Any incident condition or damage in respect of which the Vessel's Classification Society might make recommendations as to repairs or other action to be taken by the Assured, Owners or Managers must be promptly reported to the Classification Society.

5.4 Should the Underwriters wish to approach the Classification Society directly for information and/or documents, the Assured will provide the necessary authorisation.

6 Termination

The Clause 6 shall prevail notwithstanding any provision whether written typed or printed in this insurance inconsistent therewith.

Unless the Underwriters agree to the contrary in writing, this insurance shall terminate automatically at the time of

6.1 change of the Classification Society of the Vessel, or change, suspension, discontinuance, withdrawal or expiry of her Class therein, or any of the Classification Society's periodic surveys becoming overdue unless an extension of time for such survey be agreed by the Classification Society, provided that if the Vessel is at sea such automatic termination shall be deferred until arrival at her next port. However where such change, suspension, discontinuance or withdrawal of her Class or where a periodic survey becoming overdue has resulted from loss or damage covered by Clause 7 of this insurance or which would be covered by an insurance of the Vessel subject to current Institute Time Clauses Hulls or Institute War and Strikes Clauses Hulls—Time such automatic termination shall only operate should the Vessel sail from her next port without the prior approval of the Classification Society or in the case of a periodic survey becoming overdue without the Classification Society having agreed an extension of time for such survey,

6.2 any change, voluntary or otherwise, in the ownership or flag, transfer to new management, or charter on a bareboat basis, or requisition for title or use of the Vessel, provided that, if the Vessel has cargo on board and has already sailed from her loading port or is at sea in ballast, such automatic termination shall if required by deferred, whilst the Vessel continues her planned voyage, until arrival at final port of discharge if with cargo or at a port of destination if in ballast. However, in the event of requisition for title or use without the prior execution of a written agreement by the Assured, such automatic termination shall occur fifteen days after such requisition whether the Vessel is at sea or in port.

A pro rata daily net return of premium shall be made provided that a total loss of the Vessel, whether by insured perils or otherwise, has not occurred during the period covered by this insurance or any extension thereof.

7 Perils

7.1 This insurance covers loss of the subject-matter insured caused by
7.1.1 perils of the seas rivers lakes or other navigable waters
7.1.2 fire, explosion
7.1.3 violent theft by persons from outside the Vessel
7.1.4 jettison
7.1.5 piracy
7.1.6 contact with land conveyance, dock or harbour equipment or installation

INSTITUTE TIME CLAUSES—FREIGHT

7.1.7 earthquake volcanic eruption or lightning
7.1.8 accidents in loading, discharging or shifting cargo or fuel.
7.2 This insurance covers loss of the subject-matter insured caused by
7.2.1 bursting of boilers breakage of shafts or any latent defect in the machinery or hull
7.2.2 negligence of Master Officers Crew or Pilots
7.2.3 negligence of repairers or charterers provided such repairers or charterers are not an Assured hereunder
7.2.4 barratry of Master Officers or Crew
7.2.5 contact with aircraft, helicopters or similar objects or objects falling therefrom provided that such loss has not resulted from want of due diligence by the Assured, Owners, Managers, or Superintendents or any of their onshore management.
7.3 Masters Officers Crew or Pilots not to be considered Owners within the meaning of this Clause 7 should they hold shares in the Vessel.

8 Pollution hazard

This insurance covers loss of the subject matter insured caused by any governmental authority acting under the powers vested in it to prevent or mitigate a pollution hazard or damage to the environment, or threat thereof, resulting directly from a peril covered by this insurance, provided that such act of governmental authority has not resulted from want of due diligence by the Assured, Owners or Managers to prevent or mitigate such hazard or damage, or threat thereof. Masters Officers Crew or Pilots not to be considered Owners within the meaning of this Clause 8 should they hold shares in the Vessel.

9 Freight collision

9.1 It is further agreed that if the Vessel shall come into collision with any other vessel and the Assured shall in consequence thereof become liable to pay and shall pay by way of damages to any other person or persons any sum or sums in respect of the amount of freight taken into account in calculating the measure of the liability of the Assured for
9.1.1 loss of or damage to any other vessel or property on any other vessel
9.1.2 delay to or loss of use of any such other vessel or property thereon
9.1.3 general average of, salvage of, or salvage under contract of, any such other vessel or property thereon,
the Underwriters will pay the Assured such proportion of three-fourths of such sum or sums so paid applying to freight as their respective subscriptions hereto bear to the total amount insured on freight, or to the gross freight earned on the voyage during which the collision occurred if this be greater.
9.2 Provided always that:
9.2.1 liability of the Underwriters in respect of any one such collision shall not exceed their proportionate part of three-fourths of the total amount insured hereon on freight, and in cases in which, with the prior consent in writing of the Underwriters, the liability of the vessel has been contested or proceedings have been taken to limit liability, they will also pay a like proportion of three-fourths of the costs, appertaining proportionately to the freight portion of damages, which the Assured shall thereby incur or be compelled to pay;
9.2.2 no claim shall attach to this insurance:
9.2.2.1 which attaches to any other insurances covering collision liabilities
9.2.2.2 which is, or would be, recoverable in the terms of the Institute 3/4ths Collision Liability Clause if the Vessel were insured in the terms of such Institute 3/4ths Collision Liability Clause for a value not less than the equivalent in pounds sterling, at the time of commencement of this insurance, of the Vessel's limit of liability calculated in accordance with Article 6.1(b) of the 1976 Limitation Convention.

- 9.2.3 this Clause 9 shall in no case extend or be deemed to extend to any sum which the Assured may become liable to pay or shall pay for or in respect of:
- 9.2.3.1 removal or disposal, under statutory powers or otherwise, of obstructions, wrecks, cargoes or any other thing whatsoever
- 9.2.3.2 any real or personal property or thing whatsoever except other vessels or property on other vessels
- 9.2.3.3 pollution or contamination, or threat thereof, of any real or personal property or thing whatsoever (except other vessels with which the insured Vessel is in collision or property on such other vessels) or damage to the environment or threat thereof, save that this exclusion shall not extend to any sum which the insured shall pay for or in respect of salvage remuneration in which the skill and efforts of the salvors in preventing or minimising damage to the environment as is referred to in Article 13 paragraph 1(b) of the International Convention on Salvage, 1989 have been taken into account
- 9.2.3.4 the cargo or other property in or the engagements of the Vessel
- 9.2.3.5 loss of life, personal injury or illness.

10 Sistership

Should the Vessel named herein come into collision with or receive salvage services from another vessel belonging wholly or in part to the same Owners, or under the same management, the Assured shall have the same rights under this insurance as they would have were the other vessel entirely the property of Owners not interested in the Vessel named herein; but in such cases the liability for the collision or the amount payable for the services rendered shall be referred to a sole arbitrator to be agreed upon between the Underwriters and the Assured.

11 General average and salvage

- 11.1 This insurance covers the proportion of general average, salvage and/or salvage charges attaching to freight at risk of the Assured, reduced in respect of any under-insurance.
- 11.2 Adjustment to be according to the law and practice obtaining at the place where the adventure ends, as if the contract of affreightment contained no special terms upon the subject; but where the contract of affreightment so provides the adjustment shall be according to the York-Antwerp Rules.
- 11.3 No claim under this Clause 11 shall in any case be allowed where the loss was not incurred to avoid or in connection with the avoidance of a peril insured against.
- 11.4 No claim under this Clause 11 shall in any case be allowed for or in respect of
- 11.4.1 special compensation payable to a salvor under Article 14 of the International Convention on Salvage, 1989 or under any other provision in any statute, rule, law or contract which is similar in substance
- 11.4.2 expenses or liabilities incurred in respect of damage to the environment, or the threat of such damage, or as a consequence of the escape or release of pollutant substances from the Vessel, or the threat of such escape or release.
- 11.5 Clause 11.4 shall not however exclude any sum which the Assured shall pay to salvors for or in respect of salvage remuneration in which the skill and efforts of the salvors in preventing or minimising damage to the environment as is referred to in Article 13 paragraph 1(b) of the International Convention on Salvage, 1989 have been taken into account.

INSTITUTE TIME CLAUSES—FREIGHT

12 Franchise

This insurance does not cover partial loss, other than general average loss, under 3% unless caused by fire, sinking, stranding or collision with another vessel. Each craft and/or lighter to be deemed a separate insurance if required by the Assured.

13 Assignment

No assignment of or interest in this insurance or in any moneys which may be or become payable thereunder is to be binding on or recognised by the Underwriters unless a dated notice of such assignment or interest signed by the Assured, and by the assignor in the case of subsequent assignment, is endorsed on the Policy and the Policy with such endorsement is produced before payment of any claim or return of premium thereunder.

14 Measure of indemnity

14.1 The amount recoverable under this insurance for any claim for loss of freight shall not exceed the gross freight actually lost.
14.2 Where insurances on freight other than this insurance are current at the time of the loss, all such insurances shall be taken into consideration in calculating the liability under this insurance and the amount recoverable hereunder shall not exceed the rateable proportion of the gross freight lost, notwithstanding any valuation in this or any other insurance.
14.3 In calculating the liability under Clause 11 all insurances on freight shall likewise be taken into consideration.
14.4 Nothing in this Clause 14 shall apply to any claim arising under Clause 16.

15 Loss of time

This insurance does not cover any claims consequent on loss of time whether arising from a peril of the sea or otherwise.

16 Total loss

16.1 In the event of the total loss (actual or constructive) of the Vessel named herein the amount insured shall be paid in full, whether the Vessel be fully or partly loaded or in ballast, chartered or unchartered.
16.2 In ascertaining whether the Vessel is a constructive total loss, the insured value in the insurances on hull and machinery shall be taken as the repaired value and nothing in respect of the damaged or break-up value of the Vessel or wreck shall be taken into account.
16.3 Should the Vessel be a constructive total loss but the claim on the insurances on hull and machinery be settled as a claim for partial loss, no payment shall be due under this Clause 16.

17 Returns for lay-up and cancellation

17.1 To return as follows:
17.1.1 pro rata monthly net for each uncommenced month if this insurance be cancelled by agreement,
17.1.2 for each period of 30 consecutive days the Vessel may be laid up in a port or in a lay-up area provided such port or lay-up area is approved by the Underwriters
    (a) ... per cent net not under repair
    (b) ... per cent net under repair.
17.1.3 The Vessel shall not be considered to be under repair when work is undertaken in respect of ordinary wear and tear of the Vessel and/or following recommenda-

tions in the Vessel's Classification Society survey, but any repairs following loss of or damage to the Vessel or involving structural alterations, whether covered by this insurance or otherwise shall be considered as under repair.

17.1.4 If the Vessel is under repair during part only of a period for which a return is claimable, the return shall be calculated pro rata to the number of days under 17.1.2(a) and (b) respectively.

17.2 PROVIDED ALWAYS THAT

17.2.1 a total loss of the Vessel, whether by insured perils or otherwise, has not occurred during the period covered by this insurance or any extension therein.

17.2.2 in no case shall a return be allowed when the vessel is lying in exposed or unprotected waters, or in a port or lay-up area not approved by the Underwriters

17.2.3 loading or discharging operations or the presence of cargo on board shall not debar returns but no return shall be allowed for any period during which the Vessel is being used for the storage of cargo or for lightering purposes

17.2.4 in the event of any amendment of the annual rate, the above rates of return shall be adjusted accordingly

17.2.5 in the event of any return recoverable under this Clause 17 being based on 30 consecutive days which fall on successive insurances effected for the same Assured, this insurance shall only be liable for an amount calculated at pro rata of the period rates 17.1.2(a) and/or (b) above for the number of days which come within the period of this insurance and to which a return is actually applicable. Such overlapping period shall run, at the option of the Assured, either from the first day on which the Vessel is laid up or for the first day of a period of 30 consecutive days as provided under 17.1.2(a) or (b) above.

INSTITUTE VOYAGE CLAUSES—FREIGHT
(CL.288—Institute of London Underwriters and Witherby & Co Ltd)

1/11/95 (FOR USE ONLY WITH THE CURRENT MAR POLICY FORM)

This insurance is subject to English law and practice

1 Navigation

1.1 The Vessel has leave to dock and undock, to go into graving dock, to sail or navigate with or without pilots, to go on trial trips and to assist and tow vessels or craft in distress, but it is warranted that the Vessel shall not be towed, except as is customary or to the first safe port or place when in need of assistance, or undertake towage or salvage services under a contract previously arranged by the Assured and/or Owners and/or Managers and/or Charterers. This Clause 1 shall not exclude customary towage in connection with loading and discharging.
1.2 This insurance shall not be prejudiced by reason of the Assured entering into any contract with pilots or for customary towage which limits or exempts the liability of the pilots and/or tugs and/or towboats and/or their owners when the Assured or their agents accept or are compelled to accept such contracts in accordance with established local law or practice.
1.3 The practice of engaging helicopters for the transportation of personnel, supplies and equipment to and/or from the Vessel shall not prejudice this insurance.

2 Craft risk

Including risk of craft and/or lighter to and from the Vessel.

3 Change of voyage

Held covered in case of deviation or change of voyage or any breach of warranty as to towage or salvage services, provided notice be given to the Underwriters immediately after receipt of advices and any amended terms of cover and any additional premium required by them be agreed.

4 Perils

4.1 This insurance covers loss of the subject-matter insured caused by
4.1.1 perils of the seas rivers lakes or other navigable waters
4.1.2 fire, explosion
4.1.3 violent theft by persons from outside the Vessel
4.1.4 jettison
4.1.5 piracy
4.1.6 contact with land conveyance, dock or harbour equipment or installation
4.1.7 earthquake volcanic eruption or lightning
4.1.8 accidents in loading discharging or shifting cargo or fuel
4.2 This insurance covers loss of the subject-matter insured caused by
4.2.1 bursting of boilers breakage of shafts or any latent defect in the machinery or hull
4.2.2 negligence of Master Officers Crew or Pilots
4.2.3 negligence of repairers or charterers provided such repairers or charterers are not an Assured hereunder
4.2.4 barratry of Master Officers or Crew

4.2.5 contact with aircraft, helicopters or similar objects, or objects falling therefrom provided that such loss has not resulted from want of due diligence by the Assured, Owners, Managers or Superintendents or any of their onshore management.

4.3 Masters Officers Crew or Pilots not to be considered Owners within the meaning of this Clause 4 should they hold shares in the Vessel.

5 Pollution hazard

This insurance covers loss of the subject matter insured caused by any governmental authority acting under the powers vested in it to prevent or mitigate a pollution hazard or damage to the environment, or threat thereof, resulting directly from a peril covered by this insurance, provided that such act of governmental authority has not resulted from want of due diligence by the Assured, Owners and Managers to prevent or mitigate such hazard or damage, or threat thereof. Masters Officers Crew or Pilots not to be considered Owners within the meaning of this Clause 5 should they hold shares in the Vessel.

6 Freight collision

6.1 It is further agreed that if the Vessel shall come into collision with any other vessel and the Assured shall in consequence thereof become liable to pay and shall pay by way of damages to any other person or persons any sum or sums in respect of the amount of freight taken into account in calculating the measure of the liability of the Assured for

6.1.1 loss of or damage to any other vessel or property of any other vessel

6.1.2 delay to or loss of use of any such other vessel or property thereon

6.1.3 general average of, salvage of, or salvage under contract of, any such other vessel or property thereon,

the Underwriters will pay the Assured such proportion of three-fourths of such sum or sums so paid applying to freight as their respective subscriptions hereto bear to the total amount insured on freight, or to the gross freight earned on the voyage during which the collision occurred if this be greater.

6.2 Provided always that:

6.2.1 liability of the Underwriters in respect of any one such collision shall not exceed their proportionate part of three-fourths of the total amount insured hereon on freight, and in cases in which, with the prior consent in writing of the Underwriters, the liability of the Vessel has been contested or proceedings have been taken to limit liability, they will also pay a like proportion of three-fourths of the costs, appertaining proportionately to the freight portion of damages, which the Assured shall thereby incur or be compelled to pay:

6.2.2 no claim shall attach to this insurance:

6.2.2.1 which attaches to any other insurances covering collision liabilities

6.2.2.2 which is, or would be, recoverable in the terms of the Institute 3/4ths Collision Liability Clause if the Vessel were insured in the terms of such Institute 3/4ths Collision Liability Clause for a value not less than the equivalent in pounds sterling, at the time of commencement of this insurance, of the Vessel's limit of liability calculated in accordance with Article 6.1(b) of the 1976 Limitation Convention,

6.2.3 this Clause 6 shall in no case extend or be deemed to extend to any sum which the Assured may become liable to pay or shall pay for in respect of:

6.2.3.1 removal or disposal, under statutory powers or otherwise, of obstructions, wrecks, cargoes or any other thing whatsoever

6.2.3.2 any real or personal property or thing whatsoever except other vessels or property on other vessels

6.2.3.3 pollution or contamination, or threat thereof, of any real or personal property or thing whatsoever (except other vessels with which the insured Vessel is in collision or property on such other vessels) or damage to the environment, or threat thereof, save that this exclusion shall not extend to any sum which the Assured shall pay for or in respect of salvage remuneration in which the skill and efforts of the salvors in preventing or minimising damage to the environment as is referred to in Article 13 paragraph 1(b) of the International Convention on Salvage, 1989 have been taken into account

6.2.3.4 the cargo or other property on or the engagements of the Vessel

6.2.3.5 loss of life, personal injury or illness.

7 Sistership

Should the Vessel named herein come into collision with or receive salvage services from another vessel belonging wholly or in part to the same Owners or under the same management, the Assured shall have the same rights under this insurance as they would have were the other vessel entirely the property of Owners not interested in the Vessel named herein; but in such cases the liability for the collision or the amount payable for the services rendered shall be referred to a sole arbitrator to be agreed upon between the Underwriters and the Assured.

8 General average and salvage

8.1 This insurance covers the proportion of general average, salvage and/or salvage charges attaching to freight at risk of the Assured, reduced in respect of any under-insurance.

8.2 Adjustment to be according to the law and practice obtaining at the place where the adventure ends, as if the contract of affreightment contains no special terms upon the subject; but where the contract so provides the adjustment shall be according to the York-Antwerp Rules.

8.3 No claim under this Clause 8 shall in any case be allowed where the loss was not incurred to avoid or in connection with the avoidance of a peril insured against.

8.4 No claim under this Clause 8 shall be in any case allowed for or in respect of

8.4.1 special compensation payable to a salvor under Article 14 of the International Convention on Salvage, 1989 or under any other provision in any statute, rule, law or contract which is similar in substance;

8.4.2 expenses or liabilities incurred in respect of damage to the environment, or the threat of such damage, or as a consequence of the escape or release of pollutant substances from the Vessel, or the threat of such escape or release.

8.5 Clause 8.4 shall not however exclude any sum which the Assured shall pay to salvors for or in respect of salvage remuneration in which the skill and efforts of the salvors in preventing or minimising damage to the environment as is referred to in Article 13 paragraph 1(b) of the International Convention on Salvage, 1989 have been taken into account.

9 Franchise

This insurance does not cover partial loss, other than general average loss, under 3% unless caused by fire, sinking, stranding or collision with another vessel. Each craft and/or lighter to be deemed a separate insurance if required by the Assured.

10 Measure of indemnity

10.1 The amount recoverable under this insurance for any claim for loss of freight shall not exceed the gross freight actually lost.

10.2 Where insurances on freight other than this insurance are current at the time of the loss, all such insurances shall be taken into consideration in calculating the liability under this insurance and the amount recoverable hereunder shall not exceed the rateable proportion of the gross freight lost, notwithstanding any valuation in this or any other insurance.

10.3 In calculating the liability under Clause 8 all insurances on freight shall likewise be taken into consideration.

10.4 Nothing in this Clause 10 shall apply to any claim arising under Clause 12.

11 Loss of time

This insurance does not cover any claim consequent on loss of time whether arising from a peril of the sea or otherwise.

12 Total loss

12.1 In the event of the total loss (actual or constructive) of the Vessel named herein the amount insured shall be paid in full, whether the Vessel be fully or partly loaded or in ballast, chartered or unchartered.

12.2 In ascertaining whether the Vessel is a constructive total loss, the insured value in the insurances on hull and machinery shall be taken as the repaired value and nothing in respect of the damaged or break-up value of the Vessel or wreck shall be taken into account.

12.3 Should the Vessel be a constructive total loss but the claim on the insurances on hull and machinery be settled as a claim for partial loss, no payment shall be due under this Clause 12.

13 Assignment

No assignment of or interest in this insurance or in any moneys which may be or become payable thereunder is to be binding on or recognised by the Underwriters unless a dated notice of such assignment or interest signed by the Assured, and by the assignor in the case of subsequent assignment, is endorsed on the Policy and the Policy with such endorsement is produced before payment of any claim or return of premium thereunder.

The following clauses shall be paramount and shall override anything contained in this insurance inconsistent therewith.

14 War exclusion

In no case shall this insurance cover loss damage liability or expense caused by

14.1 war civil war revolution rebellion insurrection, or civil strife arising therefrom, or any hostile act by or against a belligerent power

14.2 capture seizure arrest restraint or detainment (barratry and piracy excepted), and the consequences thereof or any attempt thereat

14.3 derelict mines torpedoes bombs or other derelict weapons of war.

15 Strikes exclusion

In no case shall this insurance cover loss damage liability or expense caused by

15.1 strikers, locked-out workmen, or persons taking part in labour disturbances, riots or civil commotions

15.2 any terrorist or any person acting from a political motive.

16 Malicious acts exclusion

In no case shall this insurance cover loss damage liability or expense arising from

16.1 the detonation of an explosive

16.2 any weapon of war

and caused by any person acting maliciously or from a political motive.

17 Radioactive contamination exclusion clause

In no case shall this insurance cover loss damage liability or expense directly or indirectly caused by or contributed to by or arising from

- **17.1** ionising radiations from or contamination by radioactivity from any nuclear fuel or from any nuclear waste or from the combustion of nuclear fuel
- **17.2** the radioactive, toxic, explosive or other hazardous or contaminating properties of any nuclear installation, reactor or other nuclear assembly or nuclear component thereof
- **17.3** any weapon of war employing atomic or nuclear fission and/or fusion or other like reaction or radioactive force or matter.

INSTITUTE CARGO CLAUSES (A)
(CL.252—Institute of London Underwriters and Witherby & Co Ltd)

1/1/82

Risks covered

1 Risks clause

This insurance covers all risks of loss of or damage to the subject-matter insured except as provided in Clauses 4, 5, 6 and 7 below.

2 General average clause

This insurance covers general average and salvage charges, adjusted or determined according to the contract of affreightment and/or the governing law and practice, incurred to avoid or in connection with the avoidance of loss from any cause except those excluded in Clauses 4, 5, 6 and 7 or elsewhere in this insurance.

3 "Both to Blame Collision" clause

This insurance is extended to indemnify the Assured against such proportion of liability under the contract of affreightment "Both to Blame Collision" Clause as is in respect of a loss recoverable hereunder. In the event of any claim by shipowners under the said Clause the Assured agree to notify the Underwriters who shall have the right, at their own cost and expense, to defend the Assured against such claim.

Exclusions

4 General exclusions clause

In no case shall this insurance cover
4.1 loss damage or expense attributable to wilful misconduct of the Assured
4.2 ordinary leakage, ordinary loss in weight or volume, or ordinary wear and tear of the subject-matter insured
4.3 loss damage or expense caused by insufficiency or unsuitability of packing or preparation of the subject-matter insured (for the purpose of this Clause 4.3 "packing" shall be deemed to include stowage in a container or liftvan but only when such stowage is carried out prior to attachment of this insurance or by the Assured or their servants)
4.4 loss damage or expense caused by inherent vice or nature of the subject-matter insured
4.5 loss damage or expense proximately caused by delay, even though the delay be caused by a risk insured against (except expenses payable under Clause 2 above)
4.6 loss damage or expense arising from insolvency or financial default of the owners managers charterers or operators of the vessel
4.7 loss damage or expense arising from the use of any weapon of war employing atomic or nuclear fission and/or fusion or other like reaction or radioactive force or matter

5 Unseaworthiness and unfitness exclusion clause

5.1 In no case shall this insurance cover loss damage or expense arising from unseaworthiness of vessel or craft,

unfitness of vessel craft conveyance container or liftvan for the safe carriage of the subect-matter insured,
where the Assured or their servants are privy to such unseaworthiness or unfitness, at the time the subject-matter insured is loaded therein.
5.2 The Underwriters waive any breach of the implied warranties of seaworthiness of the ship and fitness of the ship to carry the subject-matter insured to destination, unless the Assured or their servants are privy to such unseaworthiness or unfitness.

6 War exclusion clause

In no case shall this insurance cover loss damage or expense caused by
6.1 war civil war revolution rebellion insurrection, or civil strife arising therefrom, or any hostile act by or against a belligerent power
6.2 capture seizure arrest restraint or detainment (piracy excepted), and the consequences thereof or any attempt thereat
6.3 derelict mines torpedoes bombs or other derelict weapons of war.

7 Strikes exclusion clause

In no case shall this insurance cover loss damage or expense
7.1 caused by strikers, locked-out workmen, or persons taking part in labour disturbances, riots or civil commotions
7.2 resulting from strikes, lock-outs, labour disturbances, riots or civil commotions
7.3 caused by any terrorist or any person acting from a political motive.

Duration

8 Transit clause

8.1 This insurance attaches from the time the goods leave the warehouse or place of storage at the place named herein for the commencement of the transit, continues during the ordinary course of transit and terminates either
8.1.1 on delivery to the Consignees' or other final warehouse or place of storage at the destination named herein,
8.1.2 on delivery to any other warehouse or place of storage, whether prior to or at the destination named herein, which the Assured elect to use either
8.1.2.1 for storage other than in the ordinary course of transit or
8.1.2.2 for allocation or distribution, or
8.1.3 on the expiry of 60 days after completion of discharge overside of the goods hereby insured from the overseas vessel at the final port of discharge, whichever shall first occur.
8.2 If, after discharge overside from the overseas vessel at the final port of discharge, but prior to termination of this insurance, the goods are to be forwarded to a destination other than that to which they are insured hereunder, this insurance, whilst remaining subject to termination as provided for above, shall not extend beyond the commencement of transit to such other destination.
8.3 This insurance shall remain in force (subject to termination as provided for above and to the provisions of Clause 9 below) during delay beyond the control of the Assured, any deviation, forced discharge, reshipment or transhipment and during any variation of the adventure arising from the exercise of a liberty granted to shipowners or charterers under the contract of affreightment.

9 Termination of contract of carriage clause

If owing to circumstances beyond the control of the Assured either the contract of carriage is terminated at a port or place other than the destination named therein or the transit is otherwise terminated before delivery of the goods as provided for in Clause 8 above, then this insurance shall also terminate *unless prompt notice is given to the Underwriters and continuation of cover is requested when the insurance shall remain in force, subject to an additional premium if required by the Underwriters,* either

9.1 until the goods are sold and delivered at such port or place, or, unless otherwise specially agreed, until the expiry of 60 days after arrival of the goods hereby insured at such port or place, whichever shall first occur, or

9.2 if the goods are forwarded within the said period of 60 days (or any agreed extension thereof) to the destination named herein or to any other destination, until terminated in accordance with the provisions of Clause 8 above.

10 Change of voyage clause

Where, after attachment of this insurance, the destination is changed by the Assured, *held covered at a premium and on conditions to be arranged subject to prompt notice being given to the Underwriters.*

Claims

11 Insurable interest clause

11.1 In order to recover under this insurance the Assured must have an insurable interest in the subject-matter insured at the time of the loss.

11.2 Suject to 11.1 above, the Assured shall be entitled to recover for insured loss occurring during the period covered by this insurance, notwithstanding that the loss occurred before the contract of insurance was concluded, unless the Assured were aware of the loss and the Underwriters were not.

12 Forwarding charges clause

Where, as a result of the operation a risk covered by this insurance, the insured transit is terminated at a port or place other than that to which the subject-matter is covered under this insurance, the Underwriters will reimburse the Assured for any extra charges properly and reasonably incurred in unloading storing and forwarding the subject-matter to the destination to which it is insured hereunder. This Clause 12, which does not apply to general average or salvage charges, shall be subject to the exclusions contained in Clauses 4, 5, 6 and 7 above, and shall not include charges arising from the fault negligence insolvency or financial default of the Assured or their servants.

13 Constructive total loss clause

No claim for Constructive Total Loss shall be recoverable hereunder unless the subject-matter insured is reasonably abandoned either on account of its actual total loss appearing to be unavoidable or because the cost of recovering, reconditioning and forwarding the subject-matter to the destination to which it is insured would exceed its value on arrival.

14 Increased value clause

14.1 If any Increased Value insurance is effected by the Assured on the cargo insured herein the agreed value of the cargo shall be deemed to be increased to the total amount insured under this insurance and all Increased Value insurances covering the loss, and liability under this insurance shall be in such proportion as the sum insured herein bears to such total amount insured.

INSTITUTE CARGO CLAUSES (A) 205

In the event of claim the Assured shall provide the Underwriters with evidence of the amounts insured under all other insurances.

14.2 Where this insurance is on Increased Value the following clause shall apply:
The agreed value of the cargo shall be deemed to be equal to the total amount insured under the primary insurance and all Increased Value insurances covering the loss and effected on the cargo by the Assured, and liability under this insurance shall be in such proportion as the sum insured herein bears to such total amount insured.

In the event of claim the Assured shall provide the Underwriters with evidence of the amounts insured under all other insurances.

Benefit of insurance

15 Not to inure clause

This insurance shall not inure to the benefit of the carrier or other bailee.

Minimising losses

16 Duty of assured clause

It is the duty of the Assured and their servants and agents in respect of loss recoverable hereunder
- **16.1** to take such measures as may be reasonable for the purpose of averting or minimising such loss, and
- **16.2** to ensure that all rights against carriers, bailees or other third parties are properly preserved and exercised

and the Underwriters will, in addition to any loss recoverable hereunder, reimburse the Assured for any charges properly and reasonably incurred in pursuance of these duties.

17 Waiver clause

Measures taken by the Assured or the Underwriters with the object of saving, protecting or recovering the subject-matter insured shall not be considered as a waiver or acceptance of abandonment or otherwise prejudice the rights of either party.

Avoidance of delay

18 Reasonable despatch clause

It is a condition of this insurance that the Assured shall act with reasonable despatch in all circumstances within their control.

Law and practice

19 English law and practice clause

This insurance is subject to English law and practice.

NOTE:
—It is necessary for the Assured when they become aware of an event which is "held covered" under this insurance to give prompt notice to the Underwriters and the right to such cover is dependent upon compliance with this obligation.

INSTITUTE CARGO CLAUSES (B)
(CL.253—Institute of London Underwriters and Witherby & Co Ltd)

1/1/82 (FOR USE ONLY WITH THE NEW MARINE POLICY FORM)

Risks covered

1 Risks clause

This insurance covers, except as provided in Clauses 4, 5, 6 and 7 below,
1.1 loss of or damage to the subject-matter insured reasonably attributable to
1.1.1 fire or explosion
1.1.2 vessel or craft being stranded grounded sunk or capsized
1.1.3 overturning or derailment of land conveyance
1.1.4 collision or contact of vessel craft or conveyance with any external object other than water
1.1.5 discharge of cargo at a port of distress
1.1.6 earthquake volcanic eruption or lightning.
1.2 loss of or damage to the subject-matter insured caused by
1.2.1 general average sacrifice
1.2.2 jettison or washing overboard
1.2.3 entry of sea lake or river water into vessel craft hold conveyance container liftvan or place of storage,
1.3 total loss of any package lost overboard or dropped whilst loading on to, or unloading from, vessel or craft.

2 General average clause

This insurance covers general average and salvage charges, adjusted or determined according to the contract of affreightment and/or governing law and practice, incurred to avoid or in connection with the avoidance of loss from any cause except those excluded in Clauses 4, 5, 6 and 7 or elsewhere in this insurance.

3 "Both to Blame Collision" clause

This insurance is extended to indemnify the Assured against such proportion of liability under the contract of affreightment "Both to Blame Collision" Clause as is in respect of a loss recoverable hereunder. In the event of any claim by shipowners under the said Clause the Assured agree to notify the Underwriters who shall have the right, at their own cost and expense, to defend the Assured against such claim.

Exclusions

4 General exclusions clause

In no case shall this insurance cover
4.1 loss damage or expense attributable to wilful misconduct of the Assured
4.2 ordinary leakage, ordinary loss in weight or volume, or ordinary wear and tear of the subject-matter insured
4.3 loss damage or expense caused by insufficiency or unsuitability of packing or preparation of the subject-matter insured (for the purpose of this Clause 4.3

INSTITUTE CARGO CLAUSES (B)

"packing" shall be deemed to include stowage in a container or liftvan but only when such stowage is carried out prior to attachment of this insurance or by the Assured or their servants)

4.4 loss damage or expense caused by inherent vice or nature of the subject-matter insured

4.5 loss damage or expense proximately caused by delay, even though the delay be caused by a risk insured against (except expenses payable under Clause 2 above)

4.6 loss damage or expense arising from insolvency or financial default of the owners managers charterers or operators of the vessel

4.7 deliberate damage to or deliberate destruction of the subject-matter insured or any part thereof by the wrongful act of any person or persons

4.8 loss damage or expense arising from the use of any weapon of war employing atomic or nuclear fission and/or fusion or other like reaction or radioactive force or matter

5 Unseaworthiness and unfitness exclusion clause

5.1 In no case shall this insurance cover loss damage or expense arising from
unseaworthiness of vessel or craft,
unfitness of vessel craft conveyance container or liftvan for the safe carriage of the subject-matter insured,
where the Assured or their servants are privy to such unseaworthiness or unfitness, at the time the subject-matter insured is loaded therein.

5.2 The Underwriters waive any breach of the implied warranties of seaworthiness of the ship and fitness of the ship to carry the subject-matter insured to destination, unless the Assured or their servants are prviy to such unseaworthiness or unfitness.

6 War exclusion clause

In no case shall this insurance cover loss damage or expenses caused by

6.1 war civil war revolution rebellion insurrection, or civil strife arising therefrom, or any hostile act by or against a belligerent power

6.2 capture seizure arrest restraint or detainment, and the consequences thereof or any attempt thereat

6.3 derelict mines torpedoes bombs or other derelict weapons of war.

7 Strikes exclusion clause

In no case shall this insurance cover loss damage or expense

7.1 caused by strikers, locked-out workmen, or persons taking part in labour disturbances, riots or civil commotions

7.2 resulting from strikes, lock-outs, labour disturbances, riots or civil commotions

7.3 caused by any terrorist or any person acting from a political motive.

Duration

8 Transit clause

8.1 This insurance attaches from the time the goods leave the warehouse or place of storage at the place named herein for the commencement of the transit, continues during the ordinary course of transit and terminates either

8.1.1 on delivery to the Consignees' or other final warehouse or place of storage at the destination and named herein,

8.1.2 on delivery to any other warehouse or place of storage, whether prior to or at the destination named herein, which the Assured elect to use either

8.1.2.1 for storage other than in the ordinary course of transit or

8.1.2.2 for allocation or distribution,
or
8.1.3 on the expiry of 60 days after completion of discharge overside of the goods hereby insured from the overseas vessel at the final port of discharge,

whichever shall first occur.

8.2 If, after discharge overside from the oversea vessel at the final port of discharge, but prior to termination of this insurance, the goods are to be fowarded to a destination other than that to which they are insured hereunder, this insurance, whilst remaining subject to termination as provided for above, shall not extend beyond the commencement of transit to such other destination.

8.3 This insurance shall remain in force (subject to termination as provided for above and to the provisions of Clause 9 below) during delay beyond the control of the Assured, any deviation, forced discharge, reshipment or transhipment and during any variation of the adventure arising from the exercise of a liberty granted to shipowners or charterers under the contract of affreightment.

9 Termination of contract of carriage clause

If owing to circumstances beyond the control of the Assured either the contract of carriage is terminated at a port or place other than the destination named therein or the transit is otherwise terminated before delivery of the goods as provided for in Clause 8 above, then this insurance shall also terminate *unless prompt notice is given to the Underwriters and continuation of cover is requested when the insurance shall remain in force, subject to an additional premium if required by the Underwriters,* either

9.1 until the goods are sold and delivered at such port or place, or, unless otherwise specially agreed, until the expiry of 60 days after arrival of the goods hereby insured at such port or place, whichever shall first occur, or

9.2 if the goods are forwarded within the said period of 60 days (or any agreed extension thereof) to the destination named herein or to any other destination, until terminated in accordance with the provisions of Clause 8 above.

10 Change of voyage clause

Where, after attachment of this insurance, the destination is changed by the Assured, *held covered at a premium and on conditions to be aranged subject to prompt notice being given to the Underwriters.*

Claims

11 Insurable interest clause

11.1 In order to recover under this insurance the Assured must have an insurable interest in the subject-matter insured at the time of the loss.

11.2 Subject to 11.1 above, the Assured shall be entitled to recover for insured loss occurring during the period covered by this insurance, notwithstanding that the loss occurred before the contract of insurance was concluded, unless the Assured were aware of the loss and the Underwriters were not.

12 Forwarding charges clause

Where, as a result of the operation a risk covered by this insurance, the insured transit is terminated at a port or place other than that to which the subject-matter is covered under this insurance, the Underwriters will reimburse the Assured for any extra charges properly and reasonably incurred in unloading storing and forwarding the subject-matter to the destination to which it is insured hereunder. This Clause 12, which does not apply to general average or salvage charges, shall be subject to the exclusions contained in Clauses 4, 5, 6 and 7 above, and shall not include charges arising from the fault negligence insolvency or financial default of the Assured or their servants.

13 Constructive total loss clause

No claim for Constructive Total Loss shall be recoverable hereunder unless the subject-matter insured is reasonably abandoned either on account of its actual total loss appearing to be unavoidable or because the cost of recovering, reconditioning and forwarding the subject-matter to the destination to which it is insured would exceed its value on arrival.

14 Increased value clause

14.1 If any Increased Value insurance is effected by the Assured on the cargo insured herein the agreed value of the cargo shall be deemed to be increased to the total amount insured under this insurance and all Increased Value insurances covering the loss, and liability under this insurance shall be in such proportion as the sum insured herein bears to such total amount insured.
In the event of claim the Assured shall provide the Underwriters with evidence of the amounts insured under all other insurances.

14.2 Where this insurance is on Increased Value the following clause shall apply:
The agreed value of the cargo shall be deemed to be equal to the total amount insured under the primary insurance and all Increased Value insurances covering the loss and effected on the cargo by the Assured, and liability under this insurance shall be in such proportion as the sum insured herein bears to such total amount insured.
In the event of claim the Assured shall provide the Underwriters with evidence of the amounts insured under all other insurances.

Benefit of insurance

15 Not to inure clause

This insurance shall not inure to the benefit of the carrier or other bailee.

Minimising losses

16 Duty of assured clause

It is the duty of the Assured and their servants and agents in respect of loss recoverable hereunder
16.1 to take such measures as may be reasonable for the purpose of averting or minimising such loss, and
16.2 to ensure that all rights against carriers, bailees or other third parties are properly preserved and exercised
and the Underwriters will, in addition to any loss recoverable hereunder, reimburse the Assured for any charges properly and reasonably incurred in pursuance of these duties.

17 Waiver clause

Measures taken by the Assured or the Underwriters with the object of saving, protecting or recovering the subject-matter insured shall not be considered as a waiver of acceptance of abandonment or otherwise prejudice the rights of either party.

Avoidance of delay

18 Reasonable despatch clause

It is a condition of this insurance that the Assured shall act with reasonable despatch in all circumstances within their control.

Law and practice

19 English law and practice clause

This insurance is subject to English law and practice.

NOTE:
—*It is necessary for the Assured when they become aware of an event which "held covered" under this insurance to give prompt notice to the Underwriters and the right to such cover is dependent upon compliance with this obligation.*

INSTITUTE CARGO CLAUSES (C)

(CL.255—Institute of London Underwriters and Witherby & Co Ltd)

1/1/82

Risks covered

1 Risks clause

This insurance covers, except as provided in Clauses 4, 5, 6 and 7 below,
1.1 loss of or damage to the subject-matter insured reasonably attributable to
1.1.1 fire or explosion
1.1.2 vessel or craft being stranded grounded sunk or capsized
1.1.3 overturning or derailment of land conveyance
1.1.4 collision or contact of vessel craft or conveyance with any external object other than water
1.1.5 discharge of cargo at a port of distress,
1.2 loss of or damage to the subject-matter insured caused by
1.2.1 general average sacrifice
1.2.2 jettison.

2 General average clause

This insurance covers general average and salvage charges, adjusted or determined according to the contract of affreightment and/or the governing law and practice, incurred to avoid or in connection with the avoidance of loss from any cause except those excluded in Clauses 4, 5, 6 and 7 or elsewhere in this insurance.

3 "Both to Blame Collision" clause

This insurance is extended to indemnify the Assured against such proportion of liability under the contract of affreightment "Both to Blame Collision" Clause as is in respect of a loss recoverable hereunder. In the event of any claim by shipowners under the said Clause the Assured agree to notify the Underwriters who shall have the right, at their own cost and expense, to defend the Assured against such claim.

Exclusions

4 General exclusions clause

In no case shall this insurance cover
4.1 loss damage or expense attributable to wilful misconduct of the Assured
4.2 ordinary leakage, ordinary loss in weight or volume, or ordinary wear and tear of the subject-matter insured
4.3 loss damage or expense caused by insufficiency or unsuitability of packing or preparation of the subject-matter insured (for the purpose of this Clause 4.3 "packing" shall be deemed to include stowage in a container or liftvan but only when such stowage is carried out prior to attachment of this insurance or by the Assured or their servants)
4.4 loss damage or expense caused by inherent vice or nature of the subject-matter insured

- 4.5 loss damage or expense proximately caused by delay, even though the delay be caused by a risk insured against (except expenses payable under Clause 2 above)
- 4.6 loss damage or expense arising from insolvency or financial default of the owners managers charterers or operators of the vessel
- 4.7 deliberate damage to or deliberate destruction of the subject-matter insured or any part thereof by the wrongful act of any person or persons
- 4.8 loss damage or expense arising from the use of any weapon of war employing atomic or nuclear fission and/or fusion or other like reaction or radioactive force or matter

5 Unseaworthiness and unfitness exclusion clause

- 5.1 In no case shall this insurance cover loss damage or expense arising from
    unseaworthiness of vessel or craft,
    unfitness of vessel craft conveyance container or liftvan for the safe carriage of the subject-matter insured,
  where the Assured or their servants are privy to such unseaworthiness or unfitness, at the time the subject-matter insured is loaded therein.
- 5.2 The Underwriters waive any breach of the implied warranties of seaworthiness of the ship and fitness of the ship to carry the subject-matter insured to destination, unless the Assured or their servants are privy to such unseaworthiness or unfitness.

6 War exclusion clause

In no case shall this insurance cover loss damage or expense caused by
- 6.1 war civil war revolution rebellion insurrection, or civil strife arising therefrom, or any hostile act by or against a belligerent power
- 6.2 capture seizure arrest restraint or detainment, and the consequences thereof or any attempt thereat
- 6.3 derelict mines torpedoes bombs or other derelict weapons of war.

7 Strikes exclusion clause

In no case shall this insurance cover loss damage or expense
- 7.1 caused by strikers, locked-out workmen, or persons taking part in labour disturbances, riots or civil commotions
- 7.2 resulting from strikes, lock-outs, labour disturbances, riots or civil commotions
- 7.3 caused by any terrorist or any person acting from a political motive.

Duration

8 Transit clause

- 8.1 This insurance attaches from the time the goods leave the warehouse or place of storage at the place named herein for the commencement of the transit, continues during the ordinary course of transit and terminates either
- 8.1.1 on delivery to the Consignees' or other final warehouse or place of storage at the destination named herein,
- 8.1.2 on delivery to any other warehouse or place of storage, whether prior to or at the destination named herein, which the Assured elect to use either
- 8.1.2.1 for storage other than in the ordinary course of transit or
- 8.1.2.2 for allocation or distribution,
    or
- 8.1.3 on the expiry of 60 days after completion of discharge overside of the goods hereby insured from the overseas vessel at the final port of discharge,
    whichever shall first occur.

8.2 If, after discharge overside from the oversea vessel at the final port of discharge, but prior to termination of this insurance, the goods are to be forwarded to a destination other than that to which they are insured hereunder, this insurance, whilst remaining subject to termination as provided for above, shall not extend beyond the commencement of transit to such other destination.

8.3 This insurance shall remain in force (subject to termination as provided for above and to the provisions of Clause 9 below) during delay beyond the control of the Assured, any deviation, forced discharge, reshipment or transhipment and during any variation of the adventure arising from the exercise of a liberty granted to shipowners or charterers under the contract of affreightment.

9 Termination of contract of carriage clause

If owing to circumstances beyond the control of the Assured either the contract of carriage is terminated at a port or place other than the destination named therein or the transit is otherwise terminated before delivery of the goods as provided for in Clause 8 above, then this insurance shall also terminate *unless prompt notice is given to the Underwriters and continuation of cover is requested when the insurance shall remain in force, subject to an additional premium if required by the Underwriters,* either

9.1 until the goods are sold and delivered at such port or place, or, unless otherwise specially agreed, until the expiry of 60 days after arrival of the goods hereby insured at such port or place, whichever shall first occur,

or

9.2 if the goods are forwarded within the said period of 60 days (or any agreed extension thereof) to the destination named herein or to any other destination, until terminated in accordance with the provisions of Clause 8 above.

10 Change of voyage clause

Where, after attachment of this insurance, the destination is changed by the Assured, *held covered at a premium and on conditions to be arranged subject to prompt notice being given to the Underwriters.*

Claims

11 Insurable interest clause

11.1 In order to recover under this insurance the Assured must have an insurable interest in the subject-matter insured at the time of the loss.

11.2 Subject to 11.1 above, the Assured shall be entitled to recover for insured loss occurring during the period covered by this insurance, notwithstanding that the loss occurred before the contract of insurance was concluded, unless the Assured were aware of the loss and the Underwriters were not.

12 Forwarding charges clause

Where, as a result of the operation a risk covered by this insurance, the insured transit is terminated at a port or place other than that to which the subject-matter is covered under this insurance, the Underwriters will reimburse the Assured for any extra charges properly and reasonably incurred in unloading storing and forwarding the subject-matter to the destination to which it is insured hereunder. This Clause 12, which does not apply to general average or salvage charges, shall be subject to the exclusions contained in Clauses 4, 5, 6 and 7 above, and shall not include charges arising from the fault negligence insolvency or financial default of the Assured or their servants.

13 Constructive total loss clause

No claim for Constructive Total Loss shall be recoverable hereunder unless the subject-matter insured is reasonably abandoned either on account of its actual total loss appearing to be unavoidable or because the cost of recovering, reconditioning and forwarding the subject-matter to the destination to which it is insured would exceed its value on arrival.

14 Increased value clause

14.1 If any Increased Value insurance is effected by the Assured on the cargo insured herein the agreed value of the cargo shall be deemed to be increased to the total amount insured under this insurance and all Increased Value insurances covering the loss, and liability under this insurance shall be in such proportion as the sum insured herein bears to such total amount insured.
In the event of claim the Assured shall provide the Underwriters with evidence of the amounts insured under all other insurances.

14.2 Where this insurance is on Increased Value the following clause shall apply:
The agreed value of the cargo shall be deemed to be equal to the total amount insured under the primary insurance and all Increased Value insurances covering the loss and effected on the cargo by the Assured, and liability under this insurance shall be in such proportion as the sum insured herein bears to such total amount insured.
In the event of claim the Assured shall provide the Underwriters with evidence of the amounts insured under all other insurances.

Benefit of insurance

15 Not to inure clause

This insurance shall not inure to the benefit of the carrier or other bailee.

Minimising losses

16 Duty of assured clause

It is the duty of the Assured and their sevants and agents in respect of loss recoverable hereunder
16.1 to take such measures as may be reasonable for the purpose of averting or minimising such loss, and
16.2 to ensure that all rights against carriers, bailees or other third parties are properly preserved and exercised
and the Underwriters will, in addition to any loss recoverable hereunder, reimburse the Assured for any charges properly and reasonably incurred in pursuance of these duties.

17 Waiver clause

Measures taken by the Assured or the Underwriters with the object of saving, protecting or recovering the subject-matter insured shall not be considered as a waiver of acceptance of abandonment or otherwise prejudice the rights of either party.

Avoidance of delay

18 Reasonable despatch clause

It is a condition of this insurance that the Assured shall act with reasonable despatch in all circumstances within their control.

Law and practice

19 English law and practice clause

This insurance is subject to English law and practice.

NOTE:
—*It is necessary for the Assured when they become aware of an event which is "held covered" under this insurance to give prompt notice to the Underwriters and the right to such cover is dependent upon compliance with this obligation.*

INSTITUTE TIME CLAUSES—HULLS: EXCESS LIABILITIES
(CL.291—Institute of London Underwriters and Witherby & Co Ltd)

1/11/95

This insurance is subject to English law and practice

1 1.1 This insurance covers only:
1.1.1 **General Average, Salvage and Salvage Charges** recoverable under the insurances on hull and machinery but not recoverable in full by reason of the difference between the insured value of the Vessel as stated therein (or any reduced value arising from the deduction therefrom in process of adjustment of any claim which law or practice or the terms of the insurances covering hull and machinery may have required) and the value of the Vessel adopted for the purpose of contribution to general average, salvage or salvage charges, the liability under this insurance being for such proportion of the amount not recoverable as the amount insured hereunder bears to the said difference or to the total sum insured against excess liabilities if it exceed such difference.
1.1.2 **Sue and Labour Charges** recoverable under the insurances on hull and machinery but not recoverable in full by reason of the difference between the insured value of the Vessel as stated therein and the value of the Vessel adopted for the purpose of ascertaining the amount recoverable under the insurances on hull and machinery, the liability under this insurance being for such proportion of the amount not recoverable as the amount insured hereunder bears to the said difference or to the total sum insured against excess liabilities if it exceed such difference.
1.1.3 **Collision Liability (three-fourths)** recoverable under the Institute 3/4ths Collision Liability and Sistership Clauses in the insurances on hull and machinery but not recoverable in full by reason of such three-fourths liability exceeding three-fourths of the insured value of the Vessel as stated therein, in which case the amount recoverable under this insurance shall be such proportion of the difference so arising as the amount insured hereunder bears to the total sum insured against excess liabilities.
1.2 The Underwriters' liability under 1.1.1, 1.1.2 and 1.1.3 separately, in respect of any one claim, shall not exceed the amount insured hereunder.

2 Returns

To return pro rata monthly net for each uncommenced month if this insurance be cancelled by agreement.

The following clauses shall be paramount and shall override anything contained in this insurance inconsistent therewith.

3 War exclusion

In no case shall this insurance cover loss damage liability or expense caused by
3.1 war civil war revolution rebellion insurrection, or civil strife arising therefrom, or any hostile act by or against a belligerent power
3.2 capture seizure arrest restraint or detainment (barratry and piracy excepted), and the consequences thereof or any attempt thereat
3.3 derelict mines torpedoes bombs or other derelict weapons of war.

4 Strikes exclusion

In no case shall this insurance cover loss damage liability or expense caused by
- 4.1 strikers, locked-out workmen, or persons taking part in labour disturbances, riots or civil commotions
- 4.2 any terrorist or any person acting from a political motive.

5 Malicious acts exclusion

In no case shall this insurance cover loss damage liability or expense arising from
- 5.1 the detonation of an explosive
- 5.2 any weapon of war

and caused by any person acting maliciously or from a political motive.

6 Radioactive contamination exclusion clause

In no case shall this insurance cover loss damage liability or expense directly or indirectly caused by or contributed to by or arising from
- 6.1 ionising radiations from or contamination by radioactivity from any nuclear fuel or from any nuclear waste or from the combustion of nuclear fuel
- 6.2 the radioactive, toxic, explosive or other hazardous or contaminating properties of any nuclear installation, reactor or other nuclear assembly or nuclear component thereof
- 6.3 any weapon of war employing atomic or nuclear fission and/or fusion or other like reaction or radioactive force of matter.

INSTITUTE TIME CLAUSES—HULLS: DISBURSEMENTS AND INCREASED VALUE (TOTAL LOSS ONLY, INCLUDING EXCESS LIABILITIES)

(CL.290—Institute of London Underwriters and Witherby & Co Ltd)

1/11/95

This insurance is subject to English law and practice

1 Navigation

1.1 The subject-matter insured is covered subject to the provisions of this insurance at all times and the Vessel has leave to sail or navigate with or without pilots, to go on trial trips and to assist and tow vessels or craft in distress, but it is warranted that the Vessel shall not be towed, except as is customary or to the first safe port or place when in need of assistance, or undertake towage or salvage services under a contract previously arranged by the Assured and/or Owners and/or Managers and/or Charterers. This Clause 1.1 shall not exclude customary towage in connection with loading and discharging.

1.2 This insurance shall not be prejudiced by reason of the Assured entering into any contract with pilots or for customary towage which limits or exempts the liability of the pilots and/or tugs and/or towboats and/or their owners when the Assured or their agents accept or are compelled to accept such contracts in accordance with established local law or practice.

1.3 The practice of engaging helicopters for the transportation of personnel, supplies and equipment to and/or from the Vessel shall not prejudice this insurance.

1.4 In the event of the Vessel being employed in trading operations which entail cargo loading or discharging at sea from or into another vessel (not being a harbour or inshore craft) no claim shall be recoverable under this insurance in respect of loss of or damage to the subject-matter insured or for liability to any other vessel arising from such loading or discharging operations, including whilst approaching, lying alongside and leaving, unless previous notice that the Vessel is to be employed in such operations has been given to the Underwriters and any amended terms of cover and any additional premium required by them have been agreed.

1.5 In the event of the Vessel sailing (with or without cargo) with an intention of being (a) broken up, or (b) sold for breaking up, no claim shall be recoverable under this insurance in respect of loss or damage to the Vessel occurring subsequent to such sailing unless previous notice has been given to the Underwriters and any amendments to the terms of cover, amount insured and premium required by them have been agreed.

2 Continuation

Should the Vessel at the expiration of this insurance be at sea and in distress or missing, she shall, provided notice be given to the Underwriters prior to the expiration of this insurance, be held covered until arrival at the next port in good safety, or if in port and in distress until the Vessel is made safe, at a pro rata monthly premium.

3 Breach of warranty

Held covered in case of any breach of warranty as to cargo, locality, trade, towage, salvage services or date of sailing, provided notice be given to the Underwriters immediately after receipt of advices and any amended terms of cover and any additional premium required by them be agreed.

4 Classification

4.1 It is the duty of the Assured, Owners and Managers at the inception of and throughout the period of this insurance to ensure that
4.1.1 the Vessel is classed with a Classification Society agreed by the Underwriters and that her class within that Society is maintained,
4.1.2 any recommendations requirements or restrictions imposed by the Vessel's Classification Society which relate to the Vessel's seaworthiness or to her maintenance in a seaworthy condition are complied with by the dates required by that Society.
4.2 In the event of any breach of the duties set out in Clause 4.1 above, unless the Underwriters agree to the contrary in writing, they will be discharged from liability under this insurance as from the date of the breach provided that if the Vessel is at sea at such date the Underwriters discharge from liability is deferred until arrival at her next port.
4.3 Any incident condition or damage in respect of which the Vessel's Classification Society might make recommendations as to repairs or other action to be taken by the Assured, Owners or Managers must be promptly reported to the Classification Society.
4.4 Should the Underwriters wish to approach the Classification Society directly for information and/or documents, the Assured will provide the necessary authorisation.

5 Termination

This Clause 5 shall prevail notwithstanding any provision whether written typed or printed in this insurance inconsistent therewith.

Unless the Underwriters agree to the contrary in writing, this insurance shall terminate automatically at the time of
5.1 change of the Classification Society of the Vessel, or change, suspension, discontinuance, withdrawal or expiry of her Class therein, or any of the Classification Society's periodic surveys becoming overdue unless an extension of time for such survey be agreed by the Classification Society, provided that if the Vessel is at sea such automatic termination shall be deferred until arrival at her next port. However where such change, suspension, discontinuance or withddrawal of her Class or where a periodic survey becoming overdue has resulted from loss or damage covered by Clause 6 of this insurancr or which would be covered by an insurance of the Vessel subject to current Institute Time Clauses—Hulls or Institute War and Strikes Clauses Hulls—Time such automatic termination shall only operate should the Vessel sail from her next port without the prior approval of the Classification Society or in the case of a periodic survey becoming overdue without the Classification Society having agreed an extension of time for such survey.
5.2 any change, voluntary or otherwise, in the ownership or flag, transfer to new management, or charter on a bareboat basis, or requisition for title or use of the Vessel, provided that, if the Vessel has cargo on board and has already sailed from her loading port or is at sea in ballast, such automatic termination shall if required be deferred, whilst the Vessel continues her planned voyage, until arrival at final port of discharge if with cargo or at port of destination if in ballast. However, in the event of requisition for title or use without the prior execution of a written agreement by the

Assured, such automatic termination shall occur fifteen days after such requisition whether the Vessel is at sea or in port.

A pro rata daily net return of premium shall be made provided that a total loss of the Vessel, whether by insured perils or otherwise, has not occurred during the period covered by this insurance or any extension thereof.

6 Perils

6.1 This insurance covers total loss (actual or constructive) of the subject-matter insured caused by

6.1.1 perils of the seas rivers lakes or other navigable waters

6.1.2 fire, explosion

6.1.3 violent theft by persons from outside the Vessel

6.1.4 jettison

6.1.5 piracy

6.1.6 contact with land conveyance, dock or harbour equipment or installation

6.1.7 earthquake volcanic eruption or lightning

6.1.8 accidents in loading discharging or shifting cargo or fuel.

6.2 This insurance covers total loss (actual or constructive) of the subject-matter insured caused by

6.2.1 bursting of boilers breakage of shafts or any latent defect in the machinery or hull

6.2.2 negligence of Master Officers Crew or Pilots

6.2.3 negligence of repairers or charterers provided such repairers or charterers are not an Assured hereunder

6.2.4 barratry of Master Officers or Crew

6.2.5 contact with aircraft, helicopters or similar objects, or objects falling therefrom provided that such loss has not resulted from want of due diligence by the Assured, Owners, Managers or Superintendents or any of their onshore management.

6.3 Masters Officers Crew or Pilots not to be considered Owners within the meaning of this Clause 6 should they hold shares in the Vessel.

6.4 This insurance covers:

6.4.1 General Average, Salvage and Salvage Charges recoverable under the insurances on hull and machinery but not recoverable in full by reason of the difference between the insured value of the Vessel as stated therein (or any reduced value arising from the deduction therefrom in process of adjustment of any claim which law or practice of the terms of the insurances covering hull and machinery may have required) and the value of the Vessel adopted for the purpose of contribution to general average, salvage or salvage charges, the liability under this insurance being for such proportion of the amount not recoverable as the amount insured hereunder bears to the said difference or to the total sum insured against excess liabilities if it exceed such difference.

6.4.2 Sue and Labour Charges recoverable under the insurances on hull and machinery but not recoverable in full by reason of the difference between the insured value of the Vessel as stated therein and the value of the Vessel adopted for the purpose of ascertaining the amount recoverable under the insurances on hull and machinery, the liability under this insurance being for such proportion of the amount not recoverable as the amount insured hereunder bears to the said difference or to the total sum insured against excess liabilities if it exceed such difference.

6.4.3 Collision Liability (three-fourths) recoverable under the Institute 3/4ths Collision Liability and Sistership Clauses in the insurances on hull and machinery but not recoverable in full by reason of such three-fourths liability exceeding three-fourths of the insured value of the Vessel as stated therein, in which case the amount recoverable under this insurance shall be such proportion of the difference so arising as the amount insured hereunder bears to the total sum insured against excess liabilities.

6.5 The Underwriters' liability under 6.4.1, 6.4.2 and 6.4.3 separately, in respect of any one claim, shall not exceed the amount insured hereunder.

7 Pollution hazard

This insurance covers total loss (actual or constructive) of the Vessel caused by any governmental authority acting under the powers vested in it to prevent or mitigate a pollution hazard or damage to the environment, or threat thereof, resulting directly from damage to the Vessel caused by a peril covered by this insurance, provided that such act of governmental authority has not resulted from want of due diligence by the Assured, Owners or Managers to prevent or mitigate such hazard or damage, or threat thereof. Master Officers Crew or Pilots not to be considered Owners within the meaning of this Clause 7 should they hold shares in the Vessel.

8 Notice of claim

In the event of accident whereby loss or damage may result in a claim under this insurance, notice must be given to the Underwriters promptly after the date on which the Assured, Owners or Managers become or should have become aware of the loss or damage and prior to survey so that a surveyor may be appointed if the Underwriters so desire.

If notice is not given to the Underwriters within twelve months of that date unless the Underwriters agree to the contrary in writing, the Underwriters will be automatically discharged from liability for any claim under this insurance in respect of or arising out of such loss or damage.

9 Constructive total loss

9.1 In ascertaining whether the Vessel is a constructive total loss, the insured value in the insurances on hull and machinery shall be taken as the repaired value and nothing in respect of the damaged or break-up value of the Vessel or wreck shall be taken into account.

9.2 No claim for constructive total loss based upon the cost of recovery and/or repair of the Vessel shall be recoverable hereunder unless such cost would exceed the insured value in the insurances on hull and machinery. In making this determination, only the cost relating to a single accident or sequence of damages arising from the same accident shall be taken into account.

9.3 Provided that the Constructive Total Loss Clause in the current Institute Time Clauses Hulls or a clause having a similar effect is contained in the insurances on hull and machinery, the settlement of a claim for constructive total loss thereunder shall be accepted as proof of the constructive total loss of the Vessel.

9.4 Should the Vessel be a constructive total loss but the claim on the insurances on hull and machinery be settled as a claim for partial loss, no payment shall be due under Clause 9.

10 Compromised total loss

In the event of a claim for total loss or constructive total loss being settled on the insurances on hull and machinery as a compromised total loss the amount payable hereunder shall be the same percentage of the amount insured as is paid on the said insurances.

11 Assignment

No assignment of or interest in this insurance or in any moneys which may be or become payable thereunder is to be binding on or recognised by the Underwriters unless a dated notice of such assignment or interest signed by the Assured and by the assignor in the case of subsequent assignment, is endorsed on the Policy and the Policy with such endorsement is produced before payment of any claim or return of premium thereunder.

12 Returns for lay-up and cancellation

12.1 To return as follows:

12.1.1 pro rata monthly net for each uncommenced month if this insurance be cancelled by agreement,

12.1.2 for each period of 30 consecutive days the Vessel may be laid up in a port or in a lay-up area provided such port or lay-up area is approved by the Underwriters

    (a) ... per cent net not under repair

    (b) ... per cent net under repair.

12.1.3 The Vessel shall not be considered to be under repair when work is undertaken in respect of ordinary wear and tear of the Vessel and/or following recommendations in the Vessel's Classification Society survey, but any repairs following loss of or damage to the Vessel or involving structural alterations, whether covered by this insurance or otherwise shall be considered as under repair.

12.1.4 If the Vessel is under repair during part only of a period for which a return is claimable, the return shall be calculated pro rata to the number of days under 12.1.2(a) and (b) respectively.

12.2 PROVIDED ALWAYS THAT

12.2.1 a total loss of the Vessel, whether by insured perils or otherwise, has not occurred during the period covered by this insurance or any extension thereof

12.2.2 in no case shall a return be allowed when the Vessel is lying in exposed or unprotected waters, or in a port or lay-up area not approved by the Underwriters

12.2.3 loading or discharging operations or the presence of cargo on board shall not debar returns but no return shall be allowed for any period during which the Vessel is being used for the storage of cargo or for lightering purposes

12.2.4 in the event of any amendment of the annual rate, the above rates of return shall be adjusted accordingly

12.2.5 in the event of any return recoverable under this Clause 12 being based on 30 consecutive days which fall on successive insurances effected for the same Assured, this insurance shall only be liable for an amount calculated at pro rata of the period rates 12.1.2(a) and/or (b) above for the number of days which come within the period of this insurance and to which a return is actually applicable. Such overlapping period shall run, at the option of the Assured, either from the first day on which the Vessel is laid up or the first day of a period of 30 consecutive days as provided under 12.1.2(a) or (b) above.

The following clauses shall be paramount and shall override anything contained in this insurance inconsistent therewith.

13 War exclusion

In no case shall this insurance cover loss damage liability or expense caused by

13.1 war civil war revolution rebellion insurrection, or civil strife arising therefrom, or any hostile act by or against a belligerent power

13.2 capture seizure arrest restraint or detainment (barratry and piracy excepted), and the consequences thereof or any attempt thereat

13.3 derelict mines torpedoes bombs or other derelict weapons of war.

14 Strikes exclusion

In no case shall this insurance cover loss damage liability or expense caused by
- 14.1 strikers, locked-out workmen, or persons taking part in labour disturbances, riots or civil commotions
- 14.2 any terrorist or any person acting from a political motive.

15 Malicious acts exclusion

In no case shall this insurance cover loss damage liability or expense arising from
- 15.1 the detonation of an explosive
- 15.2 any weapon of war

and caused by any person acting maliciously or from a political motive.

16 Radioactive contamination exclusion clause

In no case shall this insurance cover loss damage liability or expense directly or indirectly caused by or contributed to by or arising from
- 16.1 ionising radiations from or contaminations by radioactivity from any nuclear fuel or from any nuclear waste or from the combustion of nuclear fuel
- 16.2 the radioactive, toxic, explosive or other hazardous or contaminating properties of any nuclear installation, reactor or other nuclear assembly or nuclear component thereof
- 16.3 any weapon of war employing atomic or nuclear fission and/fusion or other like reaction or radioactive force or matter.

AVERAGE DISBURSEMENTS CLAUSES (A)

(CL.342—Institute of London Underwriters and Witherby & Co Ltd)
Agreed by the Association of Average Adjusters
and the Institute of London Underwriters

14/5/87 (FOR USE ONLY WITH THE NEW MARINE POLICY FORM)

1 Assured

This insurance is effected for account of all parties concerned in the property and freight at risk as interest may appear.

2 Duration

2.1 This insurance shall attach as the disbursements costs and charges specified in Clause 4 are incurred or as liability for advancing such disbursements costs and charges is incurred.
Provided that no risk shall attach in respect of loss of or damage to the property and freight at risk occurring prior to the agreed time of attachment as stated herein.
2.2 This insurance shall continue until termination of the common maritime adventure in accordance with the provisions for General Average in the contract of affreightment or in the absence of such provisions in accordance with the governing law and practice.
Provided that in the event of discharge, reshipment, transhipment, delay or forwarding by any other vessel, craft or conveyance, prompt notice shall be given to the Underwriters and an additional premium agreed if required.

3 Deviation or change of voyage

3.1 The vessel or forwarding vessel or craft has leave to call at any ports or places in any order for any purpose whatsoever and to dry dock with or without cargo on board.
3.2 Held covered subject to prompt notice and to a reasonable additional premium if required in the event of a change of voyage.

4 Subject-matter insured

This insurance is in respect of general average disbursements and salvage and salvage charges inclusive of costs.

5 Amount insured

5.1 The insurable value of the subject-matter shall be the amount finally ascertained in respect of the disbursements costs and charges described in Clause 4 plus the charges of insurance thereon.
5.2 The insurance shall be opened for the estimated amount of such disbursements costs and charges at the inception of the risk. If found to be deficient this may be increased by not more than 25% subject to a pro rata additional premium.
5.3 If the amount provisionally insured in accordance with Clause 5.2 exceeds the insurable value as defined in Clause 5.1 a pro rata return of premium shall be allowed.

6 Cover

6.1 Except as provided in Clause 11 and subject to the provisions of Clause 7 this insurance covers extinction or reduction of the contributory value of the property and freight at risk arising from
6.1.1 the risks of loss of or damage to such property or freight
6.1.2 special charges or other expense incurred to avert or minimise such loss or damage
6.1.3 contributions to any subsequent General Average
6.1.4 damage or injury to third parties during the period of this insurance.
6.2 Contributory values to be calculated in accordance with the provisions for General Average in the contract of affreightment or in the absence of such provisions in accordance with the governing law and practice.

7 Measure of indemnity

In the event of loss covered by this insurance the measure of indemnity shall be
7.1 Where there are no contributory values,
the amount insured.
7.2 Where the contributory values calculated in accordance with Clause 6.2 have been reduced,
such proportion of the insurable value as the reduction bears to such contributory values as they would have been but for the loss.
If the total of the disbursements costs and charges is not fully insured hereunder the amount payable shall be reduced in proportion to the under-insurance.

8 Seaworthiness

Seaworthiness and fitness of vessel, containers, craft and conveyances for the safe carriage of the cargo is admitted.

9 Benefit of insurance

This insurance is without benefit of any other insurance.

10 Law and practice

This insurance is subject to English law and practice.

The following clause shall be Paramount and shall override anything in this insurance inconsistent therewith.

11 Exclusions

This insurance excludes any claim arising from
11.1 wilful misconduct of the Assured but this exclusion shall not defeat a claim hereunder by an innocent Assured
11.2 the risks excluded by Clause 6 of the Institute Cargo Clauses (A) 1/1/82, except to the extent that such risks are covered by the Institute War Clauses (Cargo) 1/1/82.

AVERAGE DISBURSEMENTS CLAUSES (B)
(CL.343—Institute of London Underwriters and Witherby & Co Ltd)
Agreed by the Association of Average Adjusters
and the Institute of London Underwriters

14/5/87   (FOR USE ONLY WITH THE NEW MARINE POLICY FORM)

1 Assured

This insurance is effected for account of all parties concerned in the property and freight at risk as interest may appear.

2 Duration

2.1 This insurance shall attach as the disbursements costs and charges specified in Clause 4 are incurred or as liability for advancing such disbursements costs and charges is incurred.
Provided that no risk shall attach in respect of loss of or damage to the property and freight at risk occurring prior to the agreed time of attachment as stated herein.

2.2 This insurance shall continue until termination of the common maritime adventure in accordance with the provisions for General Average in the contract of affreightment or in the absence of such provisions in accordance with the governing law and practice.
Provided that in the event of discharge, reshipment, transhipment, delay or forwarding by any other vessel, craft or conveyance, prompt notice shall be given to the Underwriters and an additional premium agreed if required.

3 Deviation or change of voyage

3.1 The vessel or forwarding vessel or craft has leave to call at any ports or places in any order for any purpose whatsoever and to dry dock with or without cargo on board.

3.2 Held covered subject to prompt notice and to a reasonable additional premium if required in the event of a change of voyage.

4 Subject-matter insured

This insurance is in respect of general average disbursements and salvage and salvage charges inclusive of costs.

5 Amount insured

5.1 The insurable value of the subject-matter shall be the amount finally ascertained in respect of the disbursements costs and charges described in Clause 4 plus the charges of insurance thereon.

5.2 The insurance shall be opened for the estimated amount of such disbursement costs and charges at the inception of the risk. If found to be deficient this may be increased by not more than 25% subject to a pro rata additional premium.

5.3 If the amount provisionally insured in accordance with Clause 5.2 exceeds the insurable value as defined in Clause 5.1 a pro rata return of premium shall be allowed.

6 Cover

6.1 Except as provided in Clause 11 and subject to the provisions of Clause 7 this insurance covers extinction or reduction of the contributory value of the property and freight at risk arising from
6.1.1 the risks of loss of or damage to such property or freight
6.1.2 special charges or other expense incurred to avert or minimise such loss or damage
6.1.3 contribution to any subsequent General Average
6.1.4 damage or injury to third parties during the period of this insurance.
6.2 Contributory values to be calculated in accordance with the provisions for General Average in the contract of affreightment or in the absence of such provisions in accordance with the governing law and practice.

7 Measure of indemnity

In the event of loss covered by this insurance the measure of indemnity shall be
7.1 Where there are no contributory values,
the amount insured.
7.2 Where the contributory values calculated in accordance with Clause 6.2 are less than the total of the disbursements costs and charges described in Clause 4,
such proportion of the insurable value as the deficiency bears to the total of the disbursements costs and charges.
If the total of the disbursements costs and charges is not fully insured hereunder the amount payable shall be reduced in proportion to the under-insurance.

8 Seaworthiness

Seaworthiness and fitness of vessel, containers, craft and conveyances for the safe carriage of the cargo is admitted.

9 Benefit of insurance

This insurance is without benefit of any other insurance.

10 Law and practice

This insurance is subject to English law and practice.

The following clause shall be Paramount and shall override anything in this insurance inconsistent therewith.

11 Exclusions

This insurance excludes any claim arising from
11.1 wilful misconduct of the Assured but this exclusion shall not defeat a claim hereunder by an innocent Assured
11.2 the risks excluded by Clause 6 of the Institute Cargo Clauses (A) 1/1/82, except to the extent that such risks are covered by the Institute War Clauses (Cargo) 1/1/82.

APPENDIX 5

LLOYD'S STANDARD FORMS*

LLOYD'S AVERAGE BOND

LAB 77

To ....
Owner(s) of the ....
Voyage and date ....
      Port of shipment ....
      Port of destination/discharge ....
      Bill of lading or waybill number(s) ....

Quantity and description of goods

In consideration of the delivery to us or to our order, on payment of the freight due, of the goods noted above we agree to pay the proper proportion of any salvage and/or general average and/or special charges which may hereafter be ascertained to be due from the goods or the shippers or owners thereof under an adjustment prepared in accordance with the provisions of the contract of affreightment governing the carriage of the goods or, failing such provision, in accordance with the law and practice of the place where the common maritime adventure ended and which is payable in respect of the goods by the shippers or owners thereof.

    We also agree to:
(i) *furnish particulars of the value of the goods, supported by a copy of the commercial invoice rendered to us, or, if there is no such invoice, details of the shipped value and*
(ii) *make a payment on account of such sum as is duly certified by the average adjusters to be due from the goods and which is payable in respect of the goods by the shippers or owners thereof.*

Date .... Signature of receiver of goods ....
Full name and address ....
....
....

* Reproduced with the kind permission of the Committee of Lloyd's.

GUARANTEE BY CORPORATION OF LLOYD'S TO THE SHIPOWNERS

IN consideration of the immediate delivery to the consignees thereof of the merchandise specified below, the Corporation of Lloyd's hereby guarantees the due payment to the Shipowners of any contribution for General Average and/or Salvage and/or other Charges which may be properly chargeable against the said merchandise.

Vessel
Voyage and Date
Description of Goods

For the Corporation of Lloyd's

Dated, LLOYD'S,

LLOYD'S GENERAL AVERAGE BOND AND GUARANTEE
Form Y

Settlement of Claims Abroad

AN AGREEMENT made this   day of   19
BETWEEN the Corporation of Lloyd's (hereinafter called "Lloyd's") of the first part Messrs.   (hereinafter called "the Shipowner") of the second part and the other several Persons whose names or firms are subscribed hereto (hereinafter called "the Consignees") of the third part
WHEREAS the ship or vessel   lately arrived at the port of   on a voyage from   and it is alleged that during such voyage the vessel met with a casualty and sustained damage and loss and that sacrifices were made and expenditure incurred which may form a charge on the cargo or some part thereof or be the subject of a Salvage and/or a General Average Contribution but the same cannot be immediately ascertained and in the meantime it is desirable that the cargo shall be delivered NOW THEREFORE THESE PRESENT WITNESS and the Parties hereto severally agree as follows:

1. The Shipowner agrees with the Consignees that he will deliver to them respectively or to their order respectively their respective consignments particulars whereof are contained in the Schedule hereto on payment of the freight payable on delivery if any and the Consignees in consideration of such delivery agree for themselves severally and respectively that they will pay as herein provided the proper and respective proportion of any Salvage and/or General Average and/or Particular and/or other Charges which may be chargeable upon their respective consignments particulars whereof are contained in the Schedule hereto or to which the Shippers or Owners of such consignments may be liable to contribute in respect of such damage loss sacrifice or expenditure. And the consignees further promise and agree forthwith to furnish to the Shipowner a correct account and particulars of the amount and value of the cargo delivered to them respectively in order that any such Salvage and/or General Average and/or Particular and/or other Charges may be ascertained and adjusted in the usual manner.

2. In consideration of the delivery as aforesaid by the Shipowner of the said merchandise to the Consignees respectively without the requirement of any cash deposit Lloyd's hereby guarantees to the Shipowner the due payment by the Consignees and/or their Underwriters of the whole of the said Salvage and/or General Average and/or Particular and/or other Charges which may be properly chargeable against the said merchandise.

3. Lloyd's further agrees with the Shipowner that Lloyd's will pending the preparation of the usual Average Statement make interim payment or payments to the Shipowner in respect of the amounts which may ultimately be found due to him from the Consignees respectively in respect of the matters aforesaid. Provided always that Lloyd's shall only be liable to make any such payment upon the receipt of and to the amount shown by a Certificate in writing stating the proper amount of any such payment; such Certificate to be signed by the Adjuster or firm of Adjusters who may be employed in the preparation of the said Average Statement.

4. In consideration of these presents the Shipowner hereby assigns to Lloyd's all the sums which may be due and payable by the Consignees respectively to the Shipowner in respect of the aforesaid Salvage and/or General Average and/or Particular and/or other Charges and all his right and title to recover the same from the Consignees respectively whether under the Contract of Affreightment or under this Agreement or otherwise howsoever. And the Consignees hereby take cognizance of and admit the receipt of notice of the assignment herein contained.

5. The Consignees in consideration of these presents hereby severally certify and warrant to Lloyd's (i) that the merchandise specified in the first column of the Schedule hereto is respectively insured by the Policy or Policies specified in the second column; (ii) that such Policy or Policies have been fully subscribed for the amount appearing in the third column. The Consignees hereby severally assign to Lloyd's all their respective rights under such Policy or Policies in respect of the recovery thereunder of the sums which may be due and payable by them respectively to the Shipowner in respect of the aforesaid Salvage and/or General Average and/or Particular and/or other Charges and severally to undertake to do all things necessary to make such assignment valid and effectual. Provided always and it is hereby declared that nothing herein contained shall in any way relieve the Consignees from their personal liability in respect of the whole or any part of the aforesaid sums which Lloyd's may not be able for any reason whatever to recover under the aforesaid Policy or Policies.

For the Corporation of Lloyd's
By Special Authority

....

Lloyd's Agents at ....

....

SCHEDULE

Description and Quantity of Cargo	Number of Policy and Insurance Certificate, if any	Amount Insured	Signature of Consignees

GENERAL AVERAGE DEPOSIT RECEIPT

NOTE FOR DEPOSITORS: IF INSURED you may wish to send this receipt together with the original policy or certificate of insurance to your insurers who, subject to the policy conditions, may be prepared to refund this deposit.
IF NOT INSURED you should notify the Average Adjusters direct of your interest and retain this receipt until the adjustment is issued when any credit balance can be claimed.

NOTE FOR INSURERS: When a repayment of this deposit has been made, advise the Average Adjusters and thus assist in final settlement.

NO DUPLICATE OF THIS RECEIPT CAN BE ISSUED

No. .....

General Average Deposit Receipt

LLOYD'S FORM

Dated at ....
          19 ....
Vessel ....
Depositors, Messrs. ....
....
Contributory Value ....
   (provisional)
B/L or Waybill No. ....
Amount of Deposit ....
Description of Goods:

No. .....

GENERAL AVERAGE DEPOSIT RECEIPT

LLOYD'S FORM

Dated at .... 19 ......
Vessel .... from .... to ....
Nature and date of Accident ....
RECEIVED from Messrs. ....
the sum of ....
deposit on account of General Average and or Salvage and or Charges, being .... per cent on .... provisionally adopted as the contributory value of the following goods, viz.:
....
....
(Marks and Nos. and Description of Interest to be Inserted here.)
B/L or Waybill No. ...
£
——————— ....
                for and on behalf of the Trustee(s) or nominated representative(s).
N.B.—The refund, if any, will be made only to the bearer of, and in exchange for, this Receipt, and will be the whole balance of the deposit after satisfying the General Average and or Salvage and or Charges, without deduction or set off of any other claims of the Shipowner against the Shipper or Consignee.
The General Average will be adjusted in .... and the Shipowners have given the necessary instructions to Messrs. .... Average Adjusters.

VALUATION FORM

To ....
Owner(s) of the ....
Voyage and date ....
    Port of shipment ....
    Port of destination/discharge ....
    Bill of lading or waybill number(s) ....

Quantity and description of goods	Particulars of value	
	A Invoice value	B Shipped value
	(specify currency)	
Currency		

1. If the goods are insured please state the following details (if known):—
   Name and address of insurers or brokers ....
   Policy or certificate number and date .... Insured value ....
2. If the goods arrived subject to loss or damage, please state nature and extent thereof
   ....
   ....
   and ensure that copies of supporting documents are forwarded either direct or through the insurers to the average adjusters named below.
3. If a general average deposit has been paid, please state:—
     (a) Amount of the deposit .... (b) Deposit receipt number ......
     (c) Whether you have made any claim on your
       insurers for reimbursement ....

Date .... Signature ....
Full name and address ....
....
....

NOTES

1. If the goods form the subject of a commercial transaction, fill in column A with the amount of the commercial invoice rendered to you, **and attach a copy of this invoice hereto**.
2. If there is no commercial invoice covering the goods, state the shipped value, if known to you, in column B.
3. In either case, state the currency involved.
4. The shipowners have appointed as average adjusters ....
   to whom this form should be sent duly completed together with a copy of the commercial invoice.

LLOYD'S STANDARD FORM OF SALVAGE AGREEMENT— LOF 1995

LOF 1995

LLOYD'S

NOTES

1. Insert name of person signing on behalf of Owners of property to be salved. The Master should sign wherever possible.

2. The Contractor's name should always be inserted in line 4 and whenever the Agreement is signed by the Master of the Salving vessel or other person on behalf of the Contractor the name of the Master or other person must also be inserted in line 4 before the words "for and on behalf of". The words "for and on behalf of" should be deleted where a Contractor signs personally.

3. Insert place if agreed in clause 1(a)(i) and currency if agreed in clause 1(e).

STANDARD FORM OF

SALVAGE AGREEMENT

(APPROVED AND PUBLISHED BY THE COUNCIL OF LLOYD'S)

NO CURE - NO PAY

On board the..

Dated..................................

+ See Note 1 above

IT IS HEREBY AGREED between Captain +..
for and on behalf of the Owners of the ".." her
cargo freight bunkers stores and any other property thereon (hereinafter collectively called "the Owners")

* See Note 2 above

and..for and on behalf of ....
....(hereinafter called "the Contractor"*) that:-

1. (a) The Contractor shall use his best endeavours:-

    # See Note 3 above

    (i) to salve the ".."and/or her cargo freight bunkers
    stores and any other property thereon and take them to #.. or
    to such other place as may hereafter be agreed either place to be deemed a place of safety or if no such
    place is named or agreed to a place of safety and
    (ii) while performing the salvage services to prevent or minimize damage to the environment.

    (b) Subject to the statutory provisions relating to special compensation the services shall be rendered and accepted as salvage services upon the principle of "no cure - no pay."

    (c) The Contractor's remuneration shall be fixed by Arbitration in London in the manner hereinafter prescribed and any other difference arising out of this Agreement or the operations thereunder shall be referred to Arbitration in the same way.

    (d) In the event of the services referred to in this Agreement or any part of such services having been already rendered at the date of this Agreement by the Contractor to the said vessel and/or her cargo freight bunkers stores and any other property thereon the provisions of this Agreement shall apply to such services.

    # See Note 3 above

    (e) The security to be provided to the Council of Lloyd's (hereinafter called "the Council") the Salved Value(s) the Award and/or any Interim Award(s) and/or any Award on Appeal shall be in #.. currency.

    (f) If clause 1(e) is not completed then the security to be provided and the Salved Value(s) the Award and/or Interim Award(s) and/or Award on Appeal shall be in Pounds Sterling.

    (g) This Agreement and Arbitration thereunder shall except as otherwise expressly provided be governed by the law of England, including the English law of salvage.

15.1.08
3.12.24
13.10.26
12.4.50
10.6.53
20.12.67
23.2.72
21.5.80
5.9.90
1.1.95

LOF 1995

PROVISIONS AS TO THE SERVICES

2. *Definitions*: In this Agreement any reference to "Convention" is a reference to the International Convention on Salvage 1989 as incorporated in the Merchant Shipping (Salvage and Pollution) Act 1994 (and any amendment thereto). The terms "Contractor" and "services"/"salvage services" in this Agreement shall have the same meanings as the terms "salvor(s)" and "salvage operation(s)" in the Convention.

3. *Owners Cooperation*: The Owners their Servants and Agents shall co-operate fully with the Contractor in and about the salvage including obtaining entry to the place named or the place of safety as defined in clause 1. The Contractor may make reasonable use of the vessel's machinery gear equipment anchors chains stores and other appurtenances during and for the purpose of the salvage services free of expense but shall not unnecessarily damage abandon or sacrifice the same or any property the subject of this Agreement.

4. *Vessel Owners Right to Terminate*: When there is no longer any reasonable prospect of a useful result leading to a salvage reward in accordance with Convention Article 13 the owners of the vessel shall be entitled to terminate the services of the Contractor by giving reasonable notice to the Contractor in writing.

PROVISIONS AS TO SECURITY

5. (a) The Contractor shall immediately after the termination of the services or sooner notify the Council and where practicable the Owners of the amount for which he demands salvage security (inclusive of costs expenses and interest) from each of the respective Owners.

(b) Where a claim is made or may be made for special compensation, the owners of the vessel shall on the demand of the Contractor whenever made provide security for the Contractor's claim for special compensation provided always that such demand is made within two years of the date of termination of the services.

(c) The amount of any such security shall be reasonable in the light of the knowledge available to the Contractor at the time when the demand is made. Unless otherwise agreed such security shall be provided (i) to the Council (ii) in a form approved by the Council and (iii) by persons firms or corporations either acceptable to the Contractor or resident in the United Kingdom and acceptable to the Council. The Council shall not be responsible for the sufficiency (whether in amount or otherwise) of any security which shall be provided nor the default or insolvency of any person firm or corporation providing the same.

(d) The owners of the vessel their Servants and Agents shall use their best endeavours to ensure that the cargo owners provide their proportion of salvage security before the cargo is released.

6. (a) Until security has been provided as aforesaid the Contractor shall have a maritime lien on the property salved for his remuneration.

(b) The property salved shall not without the consent in writing of the Contractor (which shall not be unreasonably withheld) be removed from the place to which it has been taken by the Contractor under clause 1(a). Where such consent is given by the Contractor on condition that the Contractor is provided with temporary security pending completion of the voyage the Contractor's maritime lien on the property salved shall remain in force to the extent necessary to enable the Contractor to compel the provision of security in accordance with clause 5(c).

(c) The Contractor shall not arrest or detain the property salved unless:-

   (i) security is not provided within 14 days (exclusive of Saturdays and Sundays or other days observed as general holidays at Lloyd's) after the date of the termination of the services or
   (ii) he has reason to believe that the removal of the property salved is contemplated contrary to clause 6(b) or
   (iii) any attempt is made to remove the property salved contrary to clause 6(b).

(d) The Arbitrator appointed under clause 7 or the Appeal Arbitrator(s) appointed under clause 13(d) shall have power in their absolute discretion to include in the amount awarded to the Contractor the whole or part of any expenses reasonably incurred by the Contractor in:-

   (i) ascertaining demanding and obtaining the amount of security reasonably required in accordance with clause 5.
   (ii) enforcing and/or protecting by insurance or otherwise or taking reasonable steps to enforce and/or protect his lien.

PROVISIONS AS TO ARBITRATION

7. (a) Whether security has been provided or not the Council shall appoint an Arbitrator upon receipt of a written request made by letter telex facsimile or in any other permanent form provided that any party requesting such appointment shall if required by the Council undertake to pay the reasonable fees and expenses of the Council and/or any Arbitrator or Appeal Arbitrator(s).

(b) Where an Arbitrator has been appointed and the parties do not proceed to arbitration the Council may recover any fees costs and/or expenses which are outstanding.

8. The Contractor's remuneration and/or special compensation shall be fixed by the Arbitrator appointed under clause 7. Such remuneration shall not be diminished by reason of the exception to the principle of "no cure - no pay" in the form of special compensation.

REPRESENTATION

9. Any party to this Agreement who wishes to be heard or to adduce evidence shall nominate a person in the United Kingdom to represent him failing which the Arbitrator or Appeal Arbitrator(s) may proceed as if such party had renounced his right to be heard or adduce evidence.

CONDUCT OF THE ARBITRATION

10. (a) The Arbitrator shall have power to:-

   (i) admit such oral or documentary evidence or information as he may think fit
   (ii) conduct the Arbitration in such manner in all respects as he may think fit subject to such procedural rules as the Council may approve
   (iii) order the Contractor in his absolute discretion to pay the whole or part of the expense of providing excessive security or security which has been unreasonably demanded under Clause 5(b) and to deduct such sum from the remuneration and/or special compensation
   (iv) make Interim Award(s) including payment(s) on account on such terms as may be fair and just
   (v) make such orders as to costs fees and expenses including those of the Council charged under clauses 10(b) and 14(b) as may be fair and just.

(b) The Arbitrator and the Council may charge reasonable fees and expenses for their services whether the Arbitration proceeds to a hearing or not and all such fees and expenses shall be treated as part of the costs of the Arbitration.

(c) Any Award shall (subject to Appeal as provided in this Agreement) be final and binding on all the parties concerned whether they were represented at the Arbitration or not.

INTEREST & RATES OF EXCHANGE

11. *Interest*: Interest at rates per annum to be fixed by the Arbitrator shall (subject to Appeal as provided in this Agreement) be payable on any sum awarded taking into account any sums already paid:-

   (i) from the date of termination of the services unless the Arbitrator shall in his absolute discretion otherwise decide until the date of publication by the Council of the Award and/or Interim Award(s) and
   (ii) from the expiration of 21 days (exclusive of Saturdays and Sundays or other days observed as general holidays at Lloyd's) after the date of publication by the Council of the Award and/or Interim Award(s) until the date payment is received by the Contractor or the Council both dates inclusive.

For the purpose of sub-clause (ii) the expression "sum awarded" shall include the fees and expenses referred to in clause 10(b).

12. *Currency Correction*: In considering what sums of money have been expended by the Contractor in rendering the services and/or in fixing the amount of the Award and/or Interim Award(s) and/or Award on Appeal the Arbitrator or Appeal Arbitrator(s) shall to such an extent and in so far as it may be fair and just in all the circumstances give effect to the consequences of any change or changes in the relevant rates of exchange which may have occurred between the date of termination of the services and the date on which the Award and/or Interim Award(s) and/or Award on Appeal is made.

PROVISIONS AS TO APPEAL

13. (a) Notice of Appeal if any shall be given to the Council within 14 days (exclusive of Saturdays and Sundays or other days observed as general holidays at Lloyd's) after the date of the publication by the Council of the Award and/or Interim Award(s).

LOF 1995

(b) Notice of Cross-Appeal if any shall be given to the Council within 14 days (exclusive of Saturdays and Sundays or other days observed as general holidays at Lloyd's) after notification by the Council to the parties of any Notice of Appeal. Such notification if sent by post shall be deemed received on the working day following the day of posting.

(c) Notice of Appeal or Cross-Appeal shall be given to the Council by letter telex facsimile or in any other permanent form.

(d) Upon receipt of Notice of Appeal the Council shall refer the Appeal to the hearing and determination of the Appeal Arbitrator(s) selected by it.

(e) If any Notice of Appeal or Cross-Appeal is withdrawn the Appeal hearing shall nevertheless proceed in respect of such Notice of Appeal or Cross-Appeal as may remain.

(f) Any Award on Appeal shall be final and binding on all the parties to that Appeal Arbitration whether they were represented either at the Arbitration or at the Appeal Arbitration or not.

CONDUCT OF THE APPEAL

14. (a) The Appeal Arbitrator(s) in addition to the powers of the Arbitrator under clauses 10(a) and 11 shall have power to:-

    (i) admit the evidence which was before the Arbitrator together with the Arbitrator's notes and reasons for his Award and/or Interim Award(s) and any transcript of evidence and such additional evidence as he or they may think fit.

    (ii) confirm increase or reduce the sum awarded by the Arbitrator and to make such order as to the payment of interest on such sum as he or they may think fit.

    (iii) confirm revoke or vary any order and/or Declaratory Award made by the Arbitrator.

    (iv) award interest on any fees and expenses charged under paragraph (b) of this clause from the expiration of 21 days (exclusive of Saturdays and Sundays or other days observed as general holidays at Lloyd's) after the date of publication by the Council of the Award on Appeal and/or Interim Award(s) on Appeal until the date payment is received by the Council both dates inclusive.

(b) The Appeal Arbitrator(s) and the Council may charge reasonable fees and expenses for their services in connection with the Appeal Arbitration whether it proceeds to a hearing or not and all such fees and expenses shall be treated as part of the costs of the Appeal Arbitration.

PROVISIONS AS TO PAYMENT

15. (a) In case of Arbitration if no Notice of Appeal be received by the Council in accordance with clause 13(a) the Council shall call upon the party or parties concerned to pay the amount awarded and in the event of non-payment shall subject to the Contractor first providing to the Council a satisfactory Undertaking to pay all the costs thereof realize or enforce the security and pay therefrom to the Contractor (whose receipt shall be a good discharge to it) the amount awarded to him together with interest if any. The Contractor shall reimburse the parties concerned to such extent as the Award is less than any sums paid on account or in respect of Interim Award(s).

(b) If Notice of Appeal be received by the Council in accordance with clause 13 it shall as soon as the Award on Appeal has been published by it call upon the party or parties concerned to pay the amount awarded and in the event of non-payment shall subject to the Contractor first providing to the Council a satisfactory Undertaking to pay all the costs thereof realize or enforce the security and pay therefrom to the Contractor (whose receipt shall be a good discharge to it) the amount awarded to him together with interest if any. The Contractor shall reimburse the parties concerned to such extent as the Award on Appeal is less than any sums paid on account or in respect of the Award or Interim Award(s).

(c) If any sum shall become payable to the Contractor as remuneration for his services and/or interest and/or costs as the result of an agreement made between the Contractor and the Owners or any of them the Council in the event of non-payment shall subject to the Contractor first providing to the Council a satisfactory Undertaking to pay all the costs thereof realize or enforce the security and pay therefrom to the Contractor (whose receipt shall be a good discharge to it) the said sum.

(d) If the Award and/or Interim Award(s) and/or Award on Appeal provides or provide that the costs of the Arbitration and/or of the Appeal Arbitration or any part of such costs shall be borne by the Contractor such costs may be deducted from the amount awarded or agreed before payment is made to the Contractor unless satisfactory security is provided by the Contractor for the payment of such costs.

(e) Without prejudice to the provisions of clause 5(c) the liability of the Council shall be limited in any event to the amount of security provided to it.

GENERAL PROVISIONS

16. *Scope of Authority*: The Master or other person signing this Agreement on behalf of the property to be salved enters into this Agreement as agent for the vessel her cargo freight bunkers stores and any other property thereon and the respective Owners thereof and binds each (but not the one for the other or himself personally) to the due performance thereof.

17. *Notices*: Any Award notice authority order or other document signed by the Chairman of Lloyd's or any person authorised by the Council for the purpose shall be deemed to have been duly made or given by the Council and shall have the same force and effect in all respects as if it had been signed by every member of the Council.

18. *Sub-Contractor(s)*: The Contractor may claim salvage and enforce any Award or agreement made between the Contractor and the Owners against security provided under clause 5 or otherwise if any on behalf of any Sub-Contractors his or their Servants or Agents including Masters and members of the crews of vessels employed by him or by any Sub-Contractors in the services provided that he first provides a reasonably satisfactory indemnity to the Owners against all claims by or liabilities to the said persons.

19. *Inducements prohibited*: No person signing this Agreement or any party on whose behalf it is signed shall at any time or in any manner whatsoever offer provide make give or promise to provide demand or take any form of inducement for entering into this Agreement.

For and on behalf of the Contractor	For and on behalf of the Owners of property to be salved.
....	....
(To be signed by the Contractor personally or by the Master of the salving vessel or other person whose name is inserted in line 4 of this Agreement)	(To be signed by the Master or other person whose name is inserted in line 1 of this Agreement)

INTERNATIONAL CONVENTION ON SALVAGE 1989

The following provisions of the Convention are set out below for information only.

Article 1

Definitions

    (a) *Salvage operation* means any act or activity undertaken to assist a vessel or any other property in danger in navigable waters or in any other waters whatsoever

    (b) *Vessel* means any ship or craft, or any structure capable of navigation

    (c) *Property* means any property not permanently and intentionally attached to the shoreline and includes freight at risk

    (d) *Damage to the environment* means substantial physical damage to human health or to marine life or resources in coastal or inland waters or areas adjacent thereto, caused by pollution, contamination, fire, explosion or similar major incidents

    (e) *Payment* means any reward, remuneration or compensation due under this Convention

Article 6

Salvage Contracts

1. This Convention shall apply to any salvage operations save to the extent that a contract otherwise provides expressly or by implication

2. The master shall have the authority to conclude contracts for salvage operations on behalf of the owner of the vessel. The master or the owner of the vessel shall have the authority to conclude such contracts on behalf of the owner of the property on board the vessel

Article 8

Duties of the Salvor and of the Owner and Master

1. The salvor shall owe a duty to the owner of the vessel or other property in danger:

    (a) to carry out the salvage operations with due care;
    (b) in performing the duty specified in subparagraph (a), to exercise due care to prevent or minimize damage to the environment;
    (c) whenever circumstances reasonably require, to seek assistance from other salvors; and
    (d) to accept the intervention of other salvors when reasonably requested to do so by the owner or master of the vessel or other property in danger; provided however that the amount of his reward shall not be prejudiced should it be found that such a request was unreasonable

2. The owner and master of the vessel or the owner of other property in danger shall owe a duty to the salvor:

    (a) to co-operate fully with him during the course of the salvage operations;
    (b) in so doing, to exercise due care to prevent or minimize damage to the environment; and
    (c) when the vessel or other property has been brought to a place of safety, to accept redelivery when reasonably requested by the salvor to do so

Article 13

Criteria for fixing the reward

1. The reward shall be fixed with a view to encouraging salvage operations, taking into account the following criteria without regard to the order in which they are presented below:

    (a) the salved value of the vessel and other property;
    (b) the skill and efforts of the salvors in preventing or minimizing damage to the environment;
    (c) the measure of success obtained by the salvor;
    (d) the nature and degree of the danger;
    (e) the skill and efforts of the salvors in salving the vessel, other property and life;
    (f) the time used and expenses and losses incurred by the salvors;
    (g) the risk of liability and other risks run by the salvors or their equipment;
    (h) the promptness of the services rendered;
    (i) the availability and use of vessels or other equipment intended for salvage operations;
    (j) the state of readiness and efficiency of the salvor's equipment and the value thereof

2. Payment of a reward fixed according to paragraph 1 shall be made by all of the vessel and other property interests in proportion to their respective salved values

3. The rewards, exclusive of any interest and recoverable legal costs that may be payable thereon, shall not exceed the salved value of the vessel and other property

Article 14

Special Compensation

1. If the salvor has carried out salvage operations in respect of a vessel which by itself or its cargo threatened damage to the environment and has failed to earn a reward under Article 13 at least equivalent to the special compensation assessable in accordance with this Article, he shall be entitled to special compensation from the owner of that vessel equivalent to his expenses as herein defined

2. If, in the circumstances set out in paragraph 1, the salvor by his salvage operations has prevented or minimized damage to the environment, the special compensation payable by the owner to the salvor under paragraph 1 may be increased up to a maximum of 30% of the expenses incurred by the salvor. However, the Tribunal, if it deems it fair and just to do so and bearing in mind the relevant criteria set out in Article 13, paragraph 1, may increase such special compensation further, but in no event shall the total increase be more than 100% of the expenses incurred by the salvor

3. Salvor's expenses for the purpose of paragraphs 1 and 2 means the out-of-pocket expenses reasonably incurred by the salvor in the salvage operation and a fair rate for equipment and personnel actually and reasonably used in the salvage operation, taking into consideration the criteria set out in Article 13, paragraph 1(h), (i) and (j)

4. The total special compensation under this Article shall be paid only if and to the extent that such compensation is greater than any reward recoverable by the salvor under Article 13

5. If the salvor has been negligent and has thereby failed to prevent or minimize damage to the environment, he may be deprived of the whole or part of any special compensation due under this Article

6. Nothing in this Article shall affect any right of recourse on the part of the owner of the vessel

APPENDIX 5—LLOYD'S STANDARD FORMS

LOF 1995 PROCEDURAL RULES

LLOYD'S

STANDARD FORM OF

SALVAGE AGREEMENT

PROCEDURAL RULES

made by the Council of Lloyd's

(pursuant to clause 10(a)(ii) of LOF 1995)

1. (a) The Arbitrator appointed by the Council under clause 7 of LOF 95 shall within six weeks of his appointment or so soon thereafter as is reasonable or can reasonably be arranged hold a meeting unless a consent order shall have been agreed previously between the parties and approved by him/her.

    (b) When agreed by the Arbitrator and the parties the meeting may take the form of a conference telephone call.

    (c) When such a consent order is sought the Arbitrator must be provided with a brief summary in the form of a check list of the case prepared by the Contractor, any other party providing such comments as they deem appropriate, so that the Arbitrator is placed in a position to decide whether to make the order sought.

2. Unless there are special reasons, every initial order shall include:-

    (a) a date for discovery,

    (b) a date for proof of values,

    (c) a date by which any party wishing to adduce expert evidence shall state the type of evidence deemed necessary together with briefly stated reasons, unless the Arbitrator has been informed that all represented parties are agreed,

    (d) a date by which any party applying for pleadings shall state the issue to which pleadings should be directed, unless the Arbitrator has been informed of agreement as in (c) above,

    (e) a date for a progress meeting or additional progress meetings unless all represented parties with reasonable notice agree that the same is unnecessary,

    (f) unless agreed by all represented parties to be premature, a date for the hearing and estimates for the likely time required by the Arbitrator to read in advance and for the length of the hearing,

    (g) any other matters deemed by the Arbitrator or any party to be appropriate to be included in the initial order.

[P.T.O]

3. In determining the terms of the initial order regard shall be had to:

   (a) the interests of unrepresented parties,

   (b) whether some form of shortened and/or simplified procedure is appropriate.

4. The date for the hearing shall be maintained unless application to the contrary is made to the Arbitrator within 14 days of the completion of discovery or unless the Arbitrator in the exercise of his discretion determines at a later time that an adjournment is necessary or desirable in the interests of justice or fairness.

5. In fixing or agreeing to a date for the hearing of an arbitration or arbitration on appeal, the Arbitrator or Arbitrator on Appeal shall not, unless agreed by all represented parties, fix or accept a date unless he/she can allow time to read the principal evidence in advance, hear the arbitration and produce his/her award to Lloyd's in not more than one month from the conclusion of the hearing.

6. If a hearing date cannot be agreed, fixed or maintained in accordance with Rules 4 and/or 5 due to the commitments of the Arbitrator or Arbitrator on Appeal such Arbitrator shall relinquish his/her appointment and the Council of Lloyd's shall appoint in his/her stead another Arbitrator who is able to accommodate the requirements of Rules 4 and/or 5.

7. The Arbitrator and/or Arbitrator on Appeal shall call for and/or hear such further preliminary meetings or consider such further consent orders as he/she or the parties consider necessary.

8. In case of non-compliance and/or late compliance with any such order the Arbitrator shall fix such terms as may be fair and just.

9. Nothing in the foregoing shall restrict or curtail the existing power of the Arbitrator or restrict the rights of the parties to apply to the Arbitrator for additional orders as to directions or payments on account.

10. **Appeals**

    (a) In any case in which a party giving notice of appeal intends to contend that the Arbitrator's findings on the salved value of all or any of the salved property were erroneous or that the Arbitrator has erred in any finding as to the person whose property was at risk, a statement of such grounds of appeal shall be given in or accompanying the notice of appeal.

    (b) In all cases grounds of appeal or cross-appeal will be lodged within 21 days of the notice of appeal or cross-appeal unless an extension of time is agreed.

    (c) Any Respondent to an appeal who intends to contend that the award of the original Arbitrator should be affirmed on grounds other than those relied upon by the original Arbitrator shall give notice to that effect specifying the grounds of his contention within 14 days of receipt of the grounds of appeal mentioned in (b) above unless an extension of time is agreed.

INDEX

Abandonment
  effect, 130
  Marine Insurance Act 1906, 128–131
  notice, 130
  ports of refuge expenses, 59
  voyages, 59
Actual total loss, 129
Adjustment. *See* Average adjustment
Admiralty
  average adjustment, 94
  human lives, 15
  jurisdiction, 94, 139–144
Agents, 29–30
Aircraft, 16
Association of Average Adjusters
  general average, 161–164
  marine insurance contracts, 114–115
  particular average, 168–169
  repairs, 165–168
  Rules of Practice, 160–172
  salvage, 54
  uniformity resolutions, 172
  York-Antwerp Rules, 12, 164–165
Authority
  act, to, 26–31
  agents, 29–30
  common law, 31
  contribution, 29, 30
  delegation, 28
  exclusion of liability, 30–31
  exercisable, 30
  masters, 27–29
  proper person, 26–30
  ratification, 29
  restitution, 30
  strangers, 28–30
Average. *See also* Association of Average
    Adjusters, General average, Particular
    average
  bonds, 81–84, 228–231
  contribution, 82
  guarantees, 81
  limitation periods, 84

Average—*cont.*
  loss, as meaning, 2
Average adjustment, 87–103
  average adjusters, 92–93
  Bigham Clause, 91
  cargo, 90
  charges, 88
  claims, 12
  common adventure, 88, 91
  common law, 89
  contributions, 84, 87, 88–89, 92–93
  contributory values, 88, 89–92
  costs, 48
  danger, 91
  enforcement, 91
  expenditure, 89, 91
  foreign, 116–118
  governing law, 84, 94–97
  insurance, 89
  interests of parties, 88–89
  marine insurance contracts, 114, 116–118
  jettison, 87
  jurisdiction, 93–94
  liens, 81, 90–91
  place, 84, 116–118
  ports of refuge, 90–91
  regime, 116–118
  sacrifices, 89
  time, 84
  value, 87–89, 97–103
  York-Antwerp Rules, 88, 89–92

Bigham Clause, 91
Boilers, 50, 147, 154
Bottomry, 120
Brussels Convention 1968, 93
Burden of proof, 13

Cargo
  average adjustment, 90
  condition, 69–70
  contribution, 13–14, 44
  danger, 69–70
  deck, 65–66

INDEX

Cargo—cont.
  fault, 77
  freight, 14
  personal effects, 14
  ports of refuge, 102
  sacrifice, 44, 100, 101
  sale, 101
  undeclared, 151
  valuation, 97, 100–102
  wrongly declared, 151
  York-Antwerp Rules, 14, 101, 102, 149, 151, 154, 156, 158
Causation, 47–49
Charges
  Marine Insurance Act 1906, 121
  particular, 3–4
  salvage, 3, 131, 133
Charterparties
  average adjustment, 96
  contract, 80
  freight, 107
  incorporation, 10, 96
  marine insurance contracts, 107
  valuation, 99–100
  voyage, 107
  York-Antwerp Rules, 10
Choice of law, 95
Claims procedure, 12
Collision, 142–143
Common adventure
  average adjustment, 88, 91
  common law, 37
  contracts, 80
  contribution, 38
  danger, 19–26
  duration, 19–26
  intention, 36–38
  masters, 36–38
  ports of refuge expenses, 55
  termination, 39–45
  valuation, 97
  value, 39–45
  York-Antwerp Rules, 37, 38
Common benefit, 8–9
Common law
  authority, 31
  average adjustment, 89
  common adventure, 37
  contracts, 10
  contribution, 42, 82
  expenditure, 42
  freedom, of, 10
  limitation periods, 84
  ports of refuge expenses, 55–56
  sacrifice, 42
  salvage, 9
  York-Antwerp Rules, 9
Common safety, 8–9

Compensation
  environmental pollution, 52–53, 77
  salvage, 52–53
Condemnation, 59
Constructive total loss, 129–130
Contract
  average adjustment, 94
  average bonds, 83
  cargo, 77
  common law, 10
  compensation, 77
  contribution, 72–73, 76–77, 80
  environmental pollution, 77
  exceptions to liability, 76–77
  exclusions, 72–73
  governing law, 94–95
  implied, 6–7
  incorporation, 83
  indemnity, 72
  liability, 50
  Lloyd's Standard Form, 52
  loss, 50, 76, 77
  negligence, 72
  onerous, 38
  reasonableness, 38, 50
  Rome Convention 1980, 96
  salvage, 52
  variation, 10, 73
  York-Antwerp Rules, 77, 83
Contribution, 2, 6, 79–80, 133
  authority, 29, 30
  average adjustment, 84, 87, 88, 92–93
  average bonds, 82
  cargo, 13–14, 44
  causation, 47
  charterparties, 80
  claims, 39–45
  common adventure, 38, 80
    termination of, 39–45
  common law, 42, 82–83
  contracts, 72–73, 76–77, 80
  damages, 84
  danger, 23, 43
  deck cargo, 65–66
  economic loss, 84
  enforcement, 79
  exceptions to liability, 65–78
  excluding the requirement of success, 44
  exclusion of liability, 74
  expenditure, 41–42
  failure, 45
  fault, 66–76
  illegality, 78
  Jason Clause, 75
  liens, 42
  limitation of actions, 85
  marine insurance, 42
  marine insurance contracts, 105, 106–107, 109, 111–116

INDEX

Contribution—*cont.*
  necessitous intervention, 40
  particular average, 45
  ports of refuge, 41–42, 55, 56
  preservation of ship, 43–44
  reasonableness, 38, 39
  repairs, 62
  restitution, 43
  sacrifice, 32, 41, 42, 43, 44
  salvage, 52, 53
  stranding, 44
  substituted expenses, 59, 60, 61
  unjust enrichment, 43
  value of interests, 39–45
  York-Antwerp Rules, 39–40, 42, 44, 80
Contributory values, 4–5, 88, 89–92, 97–98, 115–116, 150–151, 157–158
Costs
  average adjusters, 48
  litigation, 48
  ports of refuge expenses, 58
Crew
  ports of refuge expenses, 56, 148–149, 155–156
  wages, 56, 121, 148–149, 155–156

Damages
  contribution, 84
  economic loss, 84
  fault, 69
Danger, 17–26
  average adjustment, 91
  cargo, 69–70
  common adventure, 19–26
    duration, 20–21
  contribution, 23, 43
  different interests, 24–26
  fault, 69–70
  human lives, 23
  intended beneficiary, 25–26
  loss exceeding benefit, 25
  masters, 18–19
  perils, 18–19
  ports of refuge expenses, 21–23
  reasonableness, 39
  restitution, 25
  sacrifice, 36
  salvage, 25–26
  single interest, 19–20, 23–25
  York-Antwerp Rules, 17–19, 21, 25
Deck cargo
  contribution, 65–66
  exceptions to liability, 65–66
  jettison, 65
  stowage, 65
  York-Antwerp Rules, 65–66
Declarations, 84–85
Delay, 49, 127–128
Delegation, 28

Deposits, 81–82, 151–152, 158–159, 232
Detention, 58
Deviation, 127–128
Disbursements, 103, 224–227
Disclosure, 122–123
Double insurance, 124–125
Dry-docking, 60

Economic loss, 84
Environmental pollution
  compensation, 52–53, 77
  fault, 77
  marine insurance contracts, 113–114
  salvage, 51–54, 77, 113–114
  York-Antwerp Rules, 51, 53
Exceptions to liability
  contracts, 76–77
  contributions, 65–78
  deck cargo, 65–66
  fault of claimant, 66–76
  illegality, 78
Exclusion of liability
  authority, 30–31
  contracts, 72–73
  contribution, 74
  fault, 71, 72–74
  Hague-Visby Rules, 74
  Jason Clause, 75–76
  scope, 74–76
  seaworthiness, 74
  statutory, 73–74
Expenditures. *See also* Expenses
  average adjustment, 89, 91
  common law, 42
  contribution, 41–42
  disbursements, 103
  extraordinary, 2, 31–36
  fault, 69, 73
  marine insurance, 42
  marine insurance contracts, 105, 111–113
  repairs, 32–33
  substituted expenses, 59
  valuation, 89, 97, 103
Expenses. *See also* Substituted expenses
  causation, 47
  indemnities, 4
  ports of refuge, 21–23, 41, 55–59, 147–148, 154–155
  York-Antwerp Rules, 5, 8, 147–148, 154–156
Extraordinary expenditures, 2
Extraordinary sacrifices, 2

Fault
  actionable, 69
  cargo, 69–70
  claimants', 66–76
  contract, 72–73
  contributions, 66–76

Fault—*cont.*
  damages, 69
  danger, 69–70
  exceptions to liability, 66–76
  exclusion of liability, 72
  expenditure, 69, 73
  Hague Rules, 71
  indemnity, 72
  jettison, 76
  joint tortfeasors, 70–71
  limitation of actions, 71
  limitation of liability, 71
  negligence, 72
  sacrifice, 69
  seaworthiness, 73
  third parties, 76
  York-Antwerp Rules, 68, 70
Fire, 49, 146, 153–154
Freight
  Association of Average Adjusters, 102
  calculation, 14
  cargo, 14
  charterparties, 107
  hire, 102
  jettison, 48
  partial loss, 132
  ports of refuge expenses, 56
  pre-paid, 14
  sacrifice, 31
  valuation, 102
  York-Antwerp Rules, 15, 150, 157

Gaming, 120
General average
  acts, 2
  conditions, 13–45
  definition, 1–2
  examples, 5
  justification, 6–8
  nature, 1–12
Good faith, 122
Governing law
  average adjustment, 94–96
  charterparties, 96
  choice of law, 95
  contracts, 94–96
  incorporation, 95, 96
  proper law, 96
  Rome Convention 1980, 96
  York-Antwerp Rules, 95–96
Governing rules, 8–12
Grounding, 18
Guarantees
  average, 81–82
  liens, 12
  limitation of actions, 85
  Lloyd's, 229, 230–231
  marine insurance contracts, 110

Hague-Visby Rules, 74, 118
High seas, 17
Hire, 102
Human lives, 15–16
  Admiralty jurisdiction, 15
  danger, 23
  marine insurance, 16
  restitution, 16
  salvage, 15
  York-Antwerp Rules, 16

Illegality, 78
Incorporation
  average adjustment, 91, 95, 96
  charterparties, 10, 96
  contracts, 83
  contribution, 40
  governing law, 95
  Jason Clause, 76
  York-Antwerp Rules, 10, 40, 83, 91, 96
Indemnities
  contracts, 72
  expenses, 4
  Marine Insurance Act 1906, 131–134
  marine insurance contracts, 106, 108–115
Inland waters, 17
Institute Clauses, 108, 110, 113–114,
    117–118, 173–227
  Average Disbursements Clauses, 224–227
  Institute Cargo Clauses (A), 202–205
  Institute Cargo Clauses (B), 206–210
  Institute Cargo Clauses (C), 211–215
  Institute Time Clauses—Freight, 191–196
  Institute Time Clauses—Hulls, 173–183
    Disbursements and Increased Value,
      218–223
  Institute Time Clauses—Hulls excess
      Liabilities, 216–217
  Institute Voyage Clauses—Freight,
      197–201
  Institute Voyage Clauses—Hulls, 184–190
Insurable interest, 120–121
Insurance. *See also* Marine insurance
  general average, 7
  liability, 86
Interest, 85, 121, 158
International Convention on Salvage 1989, 53
International trade, 10

Jason Clause
  contribution, 75
  fault, 75–76
  incorporation, 76
  negligence, 75, 76
  new, 75–76
  public policy, 75
  seaworthiness, 75, 76
  United States, 75–76
Jettison, 5

INDEX

Jettison—*cont.*
  average adjustment, 87
  deck cargo, 65
  fault, 76
  freight, 48
  third parties, 76
  York-Antwerp Rules, 49, 146, 153
Joint tortfeasors, 70–71
Jurisdiction
  admiralty, 94, 139–144
  average adjustment, 93–94
  Brussels Convention 1968, 93
  Rhine Navigation, 143
Justinian, 1

Land, 16–17
Liens, 81–82
  average adjusters, 81, 90, 91
  claims, 12
  enforcement, 81
  guarantees, 12
  masters, 81
  possessory, 81, 82, 83
  release, 12
  salvage, 52
Lightening, 51–54, 147, 154
Limitation of actions, 84–85
  average bonds, 84, 85
  common law, 84
  declarations, 84–85
  fault, 71
  guarantees, 85
  York-Antwerp Rules, 85
Limitation of liability, 85
Litigation costs, 48
Lloyd's Average Bond, 83, 228–231
Lloyd's Standard Forms, 52, 228–241
LOF 95, 234–241
Loss. *See also* Partial losses, Total losses
  average, as meaning, 2
  benefit, exceeding, 25
  causation, 47–49
  contractual liability, 50, 76, 77
  danger, 25
  environment, 51–54
  expenses, 59–61
  foreseeability, 48
  general average, 2, 3
  lightening, 51–54
  Marine Insurance Act 1906, 128–131, 134
  marine insurance contracts, 105, 110, 113
  mitigation, 63
  negligence, 50–51
  particular average, 3, 131
  ports of refuge expenses, 55–59
  qualifying, 47–63
  remoteness, 47–49
  repairs, 61–63
  salvage, 51–54

Loss—*cont.*
  ships, 129
  successive, 134
  third party liability, 50–51
  transhipment, 129
  York-Antwerp Rules, 49–50

Machinery, 50, 147, 154
Marine insurance. *See also* Marine Insurance Act 1906, Marine insurance contracts
  contribution, 42
  definition, 119
  expenditure, 42
  human lives, 16
  inland waters, 17
  insurable interest, 120–121
  land, 17
  substituted expenses, 59–60
Marine Insurance Act 1906, 1
  marine insurance contracts, 108, 110, 111, 112, 115
  ships, 98
  text, 119–139
  valuation, 98
Marine insurance contracts, 105–118
  Association of Average Adjusters, 114–115
  assured with more than one interest, 106–107
  average adjustment, 114, 116–118
  contribution, 105, 106–107, 109, 111–116
  contributory value, 115–116
  environmental pollution, 113–115
  excess liabilities, 109–110
  expenditures, 105, 111–113
  guarantees, 110
  hulls clauses, 105–106
  indemnity, 106, 108–115
  Institute Clauses, 108, 110, 113–114, 117–118
  insured amount, 114–116
  insurers' liability, 107–110
  loss, 105, 110, 113
  Marine Insurance Act 1906, 108, 110, 111, 112, 115
  partial losses, 3
  particular average, 116
  perils, 107–109
  protection and indemnity insurance, 118
  sacrifices, 105, 107, 111
  salvage, 3, 4, 113–114
  subject-matter, 107–109, 113
  sue and labour, 105
  third parties, 111
  under-insurance, 109
  valuation, 110
  value insured, 109
  values, 115
  York-Antwerp Rules, 114

Maritime adventures, 16–17
Masters
    authority, 27–29
    common adventure, 36–38
    danger, 18–19
    disbursements, 103
    liens, 81
    perils, 18–19
    ports of refuge expenses, 56
    reasonableness, 38
    sacrifice, 33–34
    valuation, 103
    wages, 56, 57, 121
    York-Antwerp Rules, 19
Mitigation. *See also* Sue and labour
Mixed sea and land risks, 119
Mutual insurance, 118, 136

Necessity
    defence, 79
    intervenors, 30, 40
    salvage, 9
Negligence
    contracts, 72
    foreseeability, 51
    Jason Clause, 75, 76
    loss, 50–51
    third party liability, 50–51

P & I, 118
Partial losses, 3–5, 129, 131, 132–133
Particular average, 2
    Association of Average Adjusters, 168–169
    contribution, 45
    marine insurance contracts, 116
    ports of refuge expenses, 55
Particular charges, 3–4
Perils
    danger, 18–19
    definition, 119–120
    marine insurance contracts, 107–109
    masters, 18–19
    sacrifice, 33–34, 38
Personal effects, 14
Pollution. *See* Environmental pollution
Ports of refuge, 9
    abandonment, 59
    average adjustment, 90–91
    cargo, 102
    common adventure, 55
    common law, 55–56
    condemnation, 59
    contributions, 41–42, 55, 56
    costs, 58
    danger, 21–23
    detention, 58
    expenses, 21–23, 41–42, 55–59, 147–148, 154–156
    freight, 56

Ports of refuge—*cont.*
    losses, 55–59
    particular average, 55
    reasonableness, 38
    repairs, 57, 58, 62
    sacrifice, 55
    stowage, 59
    wages, 56, 57, 148–149, 155–156
    York-Antwerp Rules, 56–59, 147–149, 154–156
Proper law, 96
Protection and indemnity, 118
Public policy, 6, 75

Reasonableness, 38–39
    contracts, 38, 50
    contribution, 38, 39
    danger, 39
    masters, 38
    perils, 38
    ports of refuge, 38
    sacrifice, 38
    York-Antwerp Rules, 39
Reinsurance, 120
Remoteness, 47–49
Repairs
    Association of Average Adjusters, 165–168
    contribution, 62
    expenditure, 32–33
    losses, 61–63
    ports of refuge expenses, 57, 58, 62
    ships, 99–100
    spare parts, 60
    substituted expenses, 60, 62
    temporary, 61–63, 149, 157
    valuation, 99–100
    York-Antwerp Rules, 61, 63, 149, 156–157
Restitution
    authority, 30
    contribution, 43
    danger, 25
    human lives, 16
    unjust enrichment, 7, 43
Rhine Navigation, 143
Rhodian law, 1
Rome Convention 1980, 96
Rule Paramount, 152

Sacrifices
    average adjustment, 89
    cargo, 44, 100, 101
    common law, 42
    contributions, 32, 41, 42, 43
    danger, 36
    differences in kind and in degree, 34–35
    extraordinary, 2, 31–36, 42
    fault, 69
    freight, 31
    marine insurance contracts, 105, 107, 111

INDEX

Sacrifices—*cont.*
  masters, 34
  ports of refuge expenses, 55
  real, 35–36
  reasonableness, 38
  valuation, 89, 100, 101
  wrecks, 35
  York-Antwerp Rules, 33, 35, 153, 157
Salvage. *See also* Salved value
  Association of Average Adjusters, 54
  charges, 3, 4, 131, 133
  common law, 9
  compensation, 52–53
  complex, 53
  contracts, 51–52
  contribution, 52, 53
  danger, 25–26
  environmental pollution, 51–54, 113–114
  human lives, 15
  International Convention on Salvage 1989, 53
  liens, 52
  lightening, 51–54
  Lloyd's Standard Form, 52, 234–241
  Marine Insurance Act 1906, 3, 4
  marine insurance contracts, 113–114
  necessity, 9, 51
  York-Antwerp Rules, 52, 53, 54, 146–147
Salved value, 4, 154
Seaworthiness
  exclusions of liability, 74
  fault, 73
  Jason Clause, 75, 76
  warranties, 126
Security, 81–83
Ships
  condemnation, 59
  contribution, 43–44
  contributory value, 98
  floating policy, 124
  loss, 129
  missing, 129
  ports of refuge expenses, 59
  preservation, 43–44
  repairs, 99–100
  valuation, 98–100
  York-Antwerp Rules, 98–99, 100, 150–151, 158
Stowage
  deck cargo, 65
  ports of refuge expenses, 59
Stranding
  contribution, 44
  York-Antwerp Rules, 44, 50, 146, 154
Subject-matter, 13–16
  cargo, 13–14
  freight, 14–15
  human lives, 15–16

Subject-matter—*cont.*
  marine insurance contracts, 107–109
Subrogation, 134
Substituted expenses
  contribution, 59–60
  dry-docking, 60
  expenditure, 59
  losses, 59–61
  marine insurance, 59–60
  repairs, 60, 61, 62
  towage, 60
  wages, 60
  York-Antwerp Rules, 60–61
Sue and labour clauses, 4, 105, 134
Supreme Court Act 1981, 139–144

Third party
  fault, 76
  jettison, 76
  liability, 50–51
  Marine Insurance Act 1906, 133
  negligence, 50–51
Through transport, 16, 17
Time limits. *See* Limitation of actions
Total losses, 3, 129–130, 132
Towage, 60
Transhipment, 129

Under-insurance, 109, 135
Unjust enrichment, 7, 43
Utmost good faith, 122

Valuation
  apportionment, 133
  Association of Average Adjusters, 102
  average adjustment, 88–89, 97–103
  cargo, 97, 100–102
  charterparties, 99–100
  common adventure, 97
  contributory interests, 89
  contributory values, 97–98
  disbursements, 103
  expenditure, 89, 97, 103
  forms, 233
  freight, 102
  hire, 102
  Marine Insurance Act 1906, 98
  marine insurance contracts, 110
  masters, 103
  repairs, 99–100
  sacrifices, 89, 100, 101
  ships, 98–100
  York-Antwerp Rules, 97–103
Values. *See also* Valuation
  average adjustment, 87
  common adventure, 39–45
  contribution, 39–45
  contributory, 4–5, 88, 89–92, 97–98, 115–116, 150–151, 157–158

Values—*cont.*
  insurable, 121–122
  insured, 109
  marine insurance contracts, 109, 115
  salved, 4
Vessels. *See* Ships
Voyages, 16–17
  abandonment, 59
  average adjustment, 88–90
  end, 88–89, 90
  Marine Insurance Act 1906, 126–128
  ports of refuge expenses, 59

Wagering, 120
Wages
  Marine Insurance Act 1906, 121
  overtime, 60
  ports of refuge expenses, 56, 148–149, 155–156
  substituted expenses, 60
Warranties, 125–126, 133–134
Wrecks, 35, 146, 154

York-Antwerp Rules, 2, 10–12, 145–159
  Association of Average Adjusters Rules of Practice, 12, 164–165
  average adjustments, 88–92
  boilers, 50, 147, 154
  burden of proof, 13
  cargo, 14, 101, 102, 149, 151, 154, 156–158
  common adventure, 37, 38
  common law, 9
  compensation, 53
  contract, 77, 83
  contribution, 39–40, 44, 80
  contributory values, 150, 157–158

York-Antwerp Rules—*cont.*
  costs, 50
  danger, 17–19, 21, 25
  deck cargo, 65–66
  delay, 49
  deposits, 82, 151–152, 158–159
  development, 10–11
  disbursements, 103
  environmental pollution, 51, 53
  expenses, 5, 8, 147–148, 154–155
  fault, 68, 70
  fire, 49, 146, 153–154
  freight, 15, 150, 157
  grounding, 18
  hire, 102
  incorporation, 10–11, 40, 83, 91, 96
  interest, 85, 151, 158
  interpretation, 11–12, 145, 152
  jettison, 49, 146, 153
  lightening, 147, 154
  loss, 49–50, 151, 158
  machinery, 50, 147, 154
  marine insurance contracts, 114
  masters, 19
  mitigation, 63
  ports of refuge expenses, 56, 147–149, 154–156
  reasonableness, 39
  repairs, 61, 63, 149, 156–157
  Rule paramount, 152
  sacrifice, 33, 35, 101, 146, 150, 153, 157
  salvage, 52, 53, 54, 146–147, 154
  ships, 98, 150–151, 158
  stranding, 44, 50, 146, 154
  substituted expenses, 60–61
  valuation, 97–103
  wages, 148–149, 155–156
  wrecks, 146, 154